The term 'ergativity' is used to describe
the subject of an intransitive clause is trea
of a transitive clause, and differently fr .... thus
complementary to the familiar pattern of accusativity. Although there is
only one ergative language (Basque) among the familiar languages of
Europe, perhaps one-quarter of the world's languages show ergative
properties, and therefore pose considerable difficulties for many current
linguistic theories. R. M. W. Dixon here provides a full survey of
morphological ergativity splits, and investigates their semantic bases.
There is discussion of how an ergative system can change into an
accusative one, and vice versa; of the discourse basis of ergativity; and
briefly of the problems that ergative systems pose for a number of current
theoretical models.

CAMBRIDGE STUDIES IN LINGUISTICS

Ergativity

In this series

52 MICHAEL S. ROCHEMONT and PETER W. CULICOVER: *English focus constructions and the theory of grammar*
53 PHILIP CARR: *Linguistic realities: an autonomist metatheory for the generative enterprise*
54 EVE SWEETSER: *From etymology to pragmatics: metaphorical and cultural aspects of semantic structure*
55 REGINA BLASS: *Relevance relations in discourse: a study with special reference to Sissala*
56 ANDREW CHESTERMAN: *On definiteness: a study with special reference to English and Finnish*
57 ALESSANDRA GIORGI and GIUSEPPE LONGOBARDI: *The syntax of noun phrases: configuration, parameters and empty categories*
58 MONIK CHARETTE: *Conditions on phonological government*
59 M. H. KLAIMAN: *Grammatical voice*
60 SARAH M. B. FAGAN: *The syntax and semantics of middle constructions: a study with special reference to German*
61 ANJUM P. SALEEMI: *Universal Grammar and language learnability*
62 STEPHEN R. ANDERSON: *A-Morphous Morphology*
63 LESLEY STIRLING: *Switch reference and discourse representation*
64 HENK J. VERKUYL: *A theory of aspectuality: the interaction between temporal and atemporal structure*
65 EVE V. CLARK: *The lexicon in acquisition*
66 ANTHONY R. WARNER: *English auxiliaries: structure and history*
67 P. H. MATTHEWS: *Grammatical theory in the United States from Bloomfield to Chomsky*
68 LJILJANA PROGOVAC: *Negative and Positive Polarity: a Binding approach*
69 R. M. W. DIXON: *Ergativity*

Supplementary volumes

MICHEAL O SIADHAIL: *Modern Irish: grammatical structure and dialectal variation*
ANNICK DE HOUWER: *The acquisition of two languages from birth: a case study*
LILIANE HAEGEMAN: *Theory and description in generative syntax. A case study in West Flemish*

Earlier issues not listed are also available

ERGATIVITY

R. M. W. DIXON

Professor of Linguistics, Australian National University

Published by the Press Syndicate of the University of Cambridge
The Pitt Building, Trumpington Street, Cambridge, CB2 1RP
40 West 20th Street, New York, NY 10011-4211, USA
10 Stamford Road, Oakleigh, Melbourne 3166, Australia

First published 1994
Reprinted 1995, 1998

A catalogue record for this book is available from the British Library

Library of Congress cataloguing in publication data

Dixon, Robert M. W.
    Ergativity / R. M. W. Dixon.
      p.   cm. – (Cambridge studies in linguistics; 69)
    Includes bibliographical references and index.
    ISBN 0 521 44446 2. (hardback) – ISBN 0 521 44898 0 (paperback)
    1. Grammar, Comparative and general – Ergative constructions.
    I. Title. II. Series.
    P291.5.D59   1994
    415 – dc20   93-15925 CIP

ISBN 0 521 44446 2 hardback
ISBN 0 521 44898 0 paperback

Transferred to digital printing 2002

para Sasha

a única mulher ergativa

Contents

Preface   xiii
Acknowledgements   xviii
Appeal   xxi
List of abbreviations   xxii

1.   **Introduction**   1
      1.1 S, A and O: the universal syntactic-semantic
           primitives   6
      1.2 Introductory exemplification   8
      1.3 Other uses of the term 'ergative'   18

2.   **Syntactically based and semantically based marking**   23
      2.1 Syntactically based marking   25
      2.2 Semantically based marking   28
      Appendix: Both kinds of marking in one language   35

3.   **Intra-clausal or morphological ergativity**   39
      3.1 Types of marking of core syntactic relations   40
           3.1.1 Case inflections   40
           3.1.2 Particles and adpositions   41
           3.1.3 Cross-referencing   42
           3.1.4 Two cross-referencing mechanisms   45
      3.2 Intra-clausal constituent order ('word order')   49
      3.3 Semantic basis   52
      3.4 Markedness   56
           3.4.1 Absolutive unmarked, ergative marked   58
           3.4.2 Nominative unmarked, accusative marked   62
           3.4.3 Marked nominative   63
           3.4.4 Marking in cross-referencing systems   67

4. **Types of split system**   70
    4.1 Split conditioned by the semantic nature of the verb   70
        4.1.1 Split-S systems   71
        4.1.2 Fluid-S systems   78
    4.2 Split conditioned by the semantic nature of NPs   83
        4.2.1 'Bound' versus 'free' split   94
    4.3 Split conditioned by tense/aspect/mood   97
    4.4 'Main' versus 'subordinate' clause split   101
    4.5 Combinations of different kinds of split   104
    4.6 Summary   108
    Appendix: Inventory of types of split   109

5. **The category of 'subject'**   111
    5.1 Universal definition of 'subject'   113
    5.2 Keenan's discussion of 'subject'   127
    5.3 Universal syntactic phenomena dependent on
         'subject'   131
        5.3.1 Imperatives   131
        5.3.2 'Can', 'try', 'begin', 'want' and similar verbs   134
        5.3.3 Control in reflexives   138
        5.3.4 Causatives   139
        5.3.5 Summary   141

6. **Inter-clausal or syntactic ergativity**   143
    6.1 Passive and antipassive   146
    6.2 Syntactic pivots   152
        6.2.1 Basic framework for pivot investigation   157
        6.2.2 The S/O pivot in Dyirbal   160
        6.2.3 Languages with morphological ergativity and
               an S/A pivot   172
        6.2.4 Languages with mixed pivots   175
    6.3 Languages with ergative inter-clausal syntax   177
    Appendix: Chamalal   180

7. **Language change**   182
    7.1 Accusative to ergative   187
    7.2 Ergative to accusative   193
    7.3 General comments   203

8. **The rationale for ergativity**   207
8.1 The discourse basis   207
8.2 What it means for a language to be ergative   214
8.3 Summary   223
8.4 Envoi   229

Appendix: A note on theoretical models   232

References   237
Index of authors   259
Index of languages and language families   263
Subject index   269

Preface

I never intended to work on ergativity. The topic more or less crept up on me, embraced me, and has never really relaxed its hold. Not that I am complaining – working on ergativity has provided the most intense intellectual satisfaction.

When I first went out to Australia to study an indigenous language, in 1963, the word 'ergative' wasn't in my linguistic vocabulary. The Australian Institute of Aboriginal Studies suggested working in the Cairns Rain Forest region and I chose Dyirbal for my major focus of study simply because it was the language with the most speakers (perhaps 100 fluent speakers, at that time). When I returned to London and explained the structure of Dyirbal to M. A. K. Halliday he told me that these unusual-looking grammatical patterns I had uncovered were 'ergative'. It was only on a return field trip in 1967 that it was brought home to me how thoroughly ergative Dyirbal is at the syntactic level (as well as being split-ergative at the morphological level).

John Lyons, external examiner for my PhD thesis on Dyirbal (submitted in December 1967), was at that time editor of the *Journal of Linguistics* and he invited me to submit a paper on ergativity in Dyirbal. I planned to do so, ahead of publishing the full grammar, since it seemed to me that people were more likely to take note of a short article in a leading journal than of something hidden away in a long monograph. But I never did get around to this and the first statement of the ergative properties of the language was in *The Dyirbal language of North Queensland*, a revision of my PhD thesis, published by Cambridge University Press in December 1972. This immediately captured the interest of other linguists; the attention paid to Dyirbal could scarcely have been greater if I had followed my original plan and published the main points in a journal paper.

During the 1970s there was a flurry of interest in ergativity. In 1973 Michael Silverstein wrote a short paper explaining by means of a hierarchy the kinds of ergativity split that are conditioned by the semantic content of

NPs. The following year Peter Ucko, Principal of the Australian Institute of Aboriginal Studies, organised a huge international conference in Canberra, and at the linguistics section Jeffrey Heath, one of Silverstein's students, talked about Silverstein's hierarchy. Although Heath had given full credit to Silverstein, some of the conference participants began to talk about 'Heath's idea' (e.g. Sutton 1976: 270). I suggested to Silverstein that he might like to publish his paper in the proceedings of this conference – it appeared as Silverstein (1976) and has been much referred to. Silverstein greatly expanded his original draft; as editor I was able to make several suggestions which led him to revise a number of sections, making them more accessible to the reader. At about this time, Bernard Comrie wrote a number of insightful papers, culminating in a seminal study called just 'Ergativity', published in 1978. (The same year H. Wagner also published a useful survey article.)

Meanwhile, I had been doing field work on Dyirbal's northerly and southerly neighbours – Yidin\ʸ, which has more complex ergativity splits than Dyirbal (see Dixon 1977a), and Warrgamay, where one can see the start of a diachronic shift from an ergative to an accusative system (Dixon 1981a, b).

While I was on sabbatical in London in 1976, David Kilby invited me to give a lecture at the University of Essex and suggested ergativity as the topic. I was at first a bit doubtful, since I thought I'd written all that I had to say on the topic at that time. Then, one Sunday morning in September, I was sitting on Primrose Hill re-reading one of the great under-rated classics of linguistics, *Time, tense and the verb* by William E. Bull (1960). It got me thinking about ergativity splits conditioned by tense and aspect. The ideas took over, spread out, swamped all the other projects I had planned to work on. This led to the draft of a long, inclusive paper which was circulated in early 1977, revised in early 1978 and published in the March 1979 issue of *Language*.

At about the same time there appeared a most useful collection of papers, in a volume called *Ergativity* edited by Frans Plank (1979). In 1981, Comrie's *The languages of the Soviet Union* appeared, with a good deal of new information on ergative languages (including a chapter on Caucasian languages by George Hewitt, and a section on Iranian languages by John Payne). During the 1980s many important papers were published on ergativity in a wide geographical spread of languages, many of them framed in terms of the parameters in my 1979 paper. I undertook field work on Fijian (Dixon 1988a) but couldn't discover anything ergative about it. In 1985 the editors of *Lingua* invited me to edit a special issue on ergativity, which eventually became a complete journal volume (volume 71, also published as Dixon 1987). In the 'Introduction' to this volume I wrote 'no African language is known to have ergative characteristics'. This elicited an elegant paper by Torben Andersen (1988) on Päri, an African language that is most decidedly ergative.

In the 1979 paper I'd mentioned a couple of South American languages, Cashinawa and Guaraní. Papers appeared in *IJAL* in the early and mid-1980s describing ergative systems in other South American languages. Then in 1986 there appeared the first volume of the *Handbook of Amazonian languages*, edited by Desmond C. Derbyshire and Geoffrey K. Pullum, revealing further ergative grammars and including a paper by Carl Harrison that pointed out all sorts of counter-examples to my 1979 conclusions. My 1979 survey article, though still often quoted, was rapidly becoming out-of-date. It was plain that it required updating and expanding. In 1989 I wrote a draft of the present volume but knew that it was incomplete in one important way – I just didn't know enough about the languages of South America, which I now saw had more diverse kinds of ergative systems and ergative splits than those from any other part of the world.

The only way of remedying this was to learn to read Spanish and Portuguese, and make a visit to South America to talk to some of the linguists there (Amazonian languages had so gripped my fancy that I also planned to undertake field work on one or two of them). From February through April 1991 and again in June 1992 I travelled around Brazil, talking to linguists at the Federal University in Brasilia, the Goeldi Museum in Belém, the Federal University in Rio, the National Museum in Rio, the State University of Campinas, and the Federal University of Santa Catarina in Florianópolis, as well as at the SIL Centers in Brasilia, Belém and Porto Velho. On my first day in Brasilia, Helen Weir began explaining the extensive ergative properties of Nadëb and I knew then that the trip had been worthwhile; all the other linguists I met were friendly and helpful and all had the most interesting data to share.

A study such as this could not pretend to be definitive until good descriptions have been provided for a much greater proportion of the world's languages (and until I have had the chance to read them). But, hopefully, the framework presented in this volume will provide a basis in

terms of which field workers, typologists and theoreticians may work, and
which can be extended and amended as new data and new insights become
available.

I have only been able to mention a portion of the available literature. A
fair number of works on ergativity are not referred to here – because they
are not relevant to my general theme, or because they make claims that I
do not find fully authenticated or convincing,[1] or because they just provide
additional instances of some point already adequately exemplified.

The discussion in this book is in terms of the established theoretical ideas
of linguistics, as these have developed over the past two thousand and
more years – the ideas of clause and sentence, syntactic relations, relative
clauses and so on. My own theoretical basis includes taking as primitives
the universal syntactic relations S, A and O, and describing systems of
morphological marking and syntactic operations in terms of them. I have
not cast the discussion in terms of any of the more restricted theoretical
models that are now current (GB, LFG, GPSG, HPSG, RG, APG, RRG,
etc.). To have chosen any one of these would have constrained the
presentation. I consider that the facts, explanations and generalisations
given here are most usefully shown through a general typology theory.
Also, I hope that the usefulness of the framework and discussions in this
book will last beyond the lives of many of these initialled models.

In most cases I have tried to reflect the majority opinion of scholars
working on a language or language family concerning its ergative features.
In one or two cases there is disagreement, which I mention, e.g. concerning
proto-Carib and proto-Polynesian (see §7.1). In a couple of instances there
is such severe disagreement that I have preferred to keep to a minimum the
references to that language or group of languages. These include Tagalog
and other Philippine languages (see note 28 to Chapter 6); and Georgian,
which some scholars say is ergative (e.g. Hewitt 1987) while others
maintain that it is active (e.g. Harris 1990). In the latter debate, especially,
I prefer not to take sides (see Dixon 1987: 14).

I have employed the spelling of a language name used in the source book
or paper I quote from, even where the author, or some other expert, tells
me that they now prefer an alternative spelling. In the references, each

---

[1] To mention just one of many instances, Diakonoff (1988: 101) suggests that 'almost
certainly' proto-Afro-Asiatic 'originally had an ergative construction of the sentence'.
However, the evidence he presents does not seem sufficient to fully validate such a
conclusion.

author is referred to by name and initials, in the normal British manner. There is a single exception – to avoid the possibility of confusion, first names are always included for David Payne, Doris Payne, John Payne, Judith Payne and Thomas Payne.

This volume presents a survey of the types of ergativity found in languages of the world. It is essentially superficial, as all surveys must be. To illustrate a point, I generally mention just one aspect of the grammar of a language; however, its significance can only be fully appreciated in the context of the complete grammatical system. My hope is that this book will encourage readers to consult the original grammars and papers referred to, and study the full grammatical systems they describe. I hope it may also encourage some people to undertake their own field work on some previously undescribed language, always keeping an eye open for ergative properties (but not, of course, forcing an ergative interpretation on the data where this is not appropriate). Languages are becoming extinct at a faster rate than ever before; there is a great need for trained linguists to get out into the field to describe them.

Canberra
February 1993

Acknowledgements

My first debt is to those indigenous Australians who taught me their languages – which are ergative in such interesting ways – and explained their structures: Chloe Grant, George Watson, Dick Moses, Tilly Fuller, John Tooth, among many others.

Another important debt is to my students. The Australian National University is perhaps the only institution in the world where the normal expectation is that a PhD student in linguistics should undertake original field work and write a descriptive grammar of some previously undescribed language (paying particular attention to aspects of the structure that are of theoretical interest); some MA students also do this. I learnt an awful lot (about ergativity and other things) from supervising Gedda Aklif, Peter Austin, Terry Crowley, Alan Dench, Tamsin Donaldson, Bronwyn Eather, Nicholas Evans, Lys Ford, Cliff Goddard, Ian Green, Rebecca Green, Debbie Hill, Joyce Hudson, Jennifer Lee, Graham McKay, Frances Morphy, Masayuki Onishi, Midori Osumi, Elizabeth Patz, Nick Piper, Nicholas Reid, Annette Schmidt, Bronwyn Stokes and Michael Walsh.

I am most grateful to those people who sent me copies of their papers on topics related to ergativity, and/or answered my questions and discussed things with me (by correspondence or in person): Sander Adelaar, Alexandra Aikhenvald, W. S. Allen, Steve Anderson, Avery Andrews, C. E. Bazell, D. N. S. Bhat, Maria Bittner, Paul Black, Barry Blake, Robert S. Bleven, Fred and Paula Boley, Dwight Bolinger, Georg Bossong, Gavan Breen, Victoria Bricker, Les Bruce, Thea Bynon, Elizabeth Camp, Arthur Capell, Ian Catford, Ray Cattell, Wallace Chafe, Betty Shefts Chang, Kim Chang, Sandra Chung, Bernard Comrie, Ann Cooreman, Raquel Costa, Simon Crisp, Robert E. Cromack, W. D. Davies, Scott DeLancey, Des Derbyshire, Simon Dik, Mark Donohue, Matthew Dryer, Jack Du Bois, Alessandro Duranti, Mark Durie, Tom Dutton, Diana Eades, Barbara Edmonson, Munro Edmonson, Charlotte Emmerich, Nora England, Charles Fillmore, Bill Foley, Zygmunt Frajzyngier, Bruna Franchetto,

Nilson Gabas Júnior, T. Givón, Chuck Grimes, Mary Haas, William Haas, John Haiman, Ken Hale, Michael Halliday, Alice Harris, Carl Harrison, S. P. Harrison, Jeff Heath, Luise Hercus, Robert Hetzron, George Hewitt, Dee Holisky, P. E. Hook, Paul Hopper, Rodney Huddleston, Dick Hudson, Osamu Ikari, Eloise Jelinek, Cheryl Jensen, Marion Johnson, Linda Jones, Paul Kay, Ed Keenan, Ruth Kempson, Alexandr Kibrik, David Kilby, Geoff Kimball, M. H. Klaiman, Harold Koch, Sally and Ed Koehn, Terry Klokeid, O. N. Koul, Paul Kroeger, Hans Kuhn, A. H. Kuipers, Utpal Lahiri, Ron Langacker, Margaret Langdon, Gilbert Lazard, F. K. Lehman, Yonne Leite, Charles Li, Patrick McConvell, Maryalyce McDonald, Bill McGregor, Sally McLendon, Alec Marantz, Jack Martin, Colin Mayrhofer, Igor Mel'čuk, Francesca Merlan, Piotr Michalowski, George Milner, Elizabeth Minchin, Marianne Mithun, Carol Mock, Ruth Monserrat, Denny Moore, Yves-Charles Morin, Ulrike Mosel, Jean Mulder, Pamela Munro, John Myhill, David Nash, Johanna Nichols, Keigou Noda, Andrew Pawley, David Payne, Doris Payne, John Payne, Tom Payne, Frans Plank, Maria S. Polinskaja, Harold Popovich, Geoff Pullum, Clifford Pye, Gil Rappaport, Karl Rensch, Sharon Reece, Bruce Rigsby, Nicole Rivière, Aryon Rodrigues, David Rood, Malcolm Ross, Noel Rude, Alan Rumsey, Kristina Sands, Janine Scancarcelli, Paul Schachter, Bambi Schieffelin, Jonathan Seely, Lucy Seki, Tim Shopen, Michael Silverstein, Nicholas Sims-Williams, Thom Smith-Stark, Marília Facó Soares, Andrew Taylor, Claude Tchekhoff, Yakov Testelec, Sandra Thompson, Takako Toda, Larry Trask, Rudolph Troike, Tasaku Tsunoda, Greg Urban, Tine Van der Meer, Robert Van Valin, John Verhaar, Franscisco Villar, Alan Vogel, Hans Vogt, H. Wagner, Cal Watkins, Helen Weir, Anna Wierzbicka, G. D. Wijayawardana, David Wilkins, Kemp Williams, Frank Wordick, Anthony Woodbury and Stephen Wurm.

A special word of thanks is due to those scholars who read through all or part of a draft of this book (circulated in mid-1992) and provided comments, corrections, ideas and encouragement: Paul Kent Andersen, Torben Andersen, Peter Austin, Tony Backhouse, Victoria Bricker, Les Bruce, Thea Bynon, Betty Shefts Chang, Alan Dench, Des Derbyshire, Tom Dutton, Nora England, Bruna Franchetto, Nilson Gabas Júnior, Andrew Garrett, Spike Gildea, Ian Green, Ken Hale, George Hewitt, Eloise Jelinek, Cheryl Jensen, Geoff Kimball, Yonne Leite, Jack Martin, Marianne Mithun, Denny Moore, V. P. Nedjalkov, Doris Payne, Lucy Seki, Greg Urban and Helen Weir. Invaluable comments on almost every section came from the following friends: Alexandra Aikhenvald, Barry Blake, Bernard Comrie, Mark Durie, Chuck Grimes, Alexandr Kibrik, Ulrike Mosel, Alan Rumsey and Anna Wierzbicka. My deepest debt is to Barbara Edmonson and Johanna Nichols, who offered the most helpful criticisms and comments on virtually every page.

Finally, Ellalene Seymour typed and corrected the book through four or five drafts with the skill, dedication and cheerfulness that she always exhibits. My thanks are due equally to her.

Appeal

This is a long way from being the last word on ergativity. I would welcome correspondence, counter-examples, ideas and data, with a view to refining and improving the generalisations attempted here. Please send them to me at the Department of Linguistics, Arts, Australian National University, Canberra, ACT, Australia 0200.

Abbreviations

A	transitive subject function	OBL	oblique
ABS	absolutive	PL, pl.	plural
ACC	accusative	POSS	possessive
ANTIPASS	antipassive	PRES	present
CAUS	causative	PURP	purposive
DAT	dative	REFL	reflexive
DECL	declarative	REL	relative clause verbal inflection
ERG	ergative	S	intransitive subject function
EXCL	exclusive		
FEM, fem.	feminine	S_a	intransitive subject marked like transitive subject
IMP	imperative		
INCHO.PASS	inchoative passive		
INDIC	indicative	S_o	intransitive subject marked like transitive object
INST	instrumental case		
INSTV	instrumentive verbal suffix	SG, sg.	singular
LOC	locative	VOC	vocative
MASC, masc.	masculine	1	first person
NOM	nominative	2	second person
NONFUT	non-future	3	third person
NP	noun phrase		
O	transitive object function		

1 *Introduction*

The term 'ergativity' is, in its most generally accepted sense, used to describe a grammatical pattern in which the subject of an intransitive clause is treated in the same way as the object of a transitive clause, and differently from transitive subject. The term was first used to refer to the case marking on constituents of a noun phrase: 'ergative' is the case marking transitive subject, contrasting with another case – originally called 'nominative' but nowadays 'absolutive' – marking intransitive subject and transitive object.

Ergativity is thus complementary to the familiar grammatical pattern of accusativity, in which one case (nominative) marks both intransitive and transitive subject, with another case (accusative) being employed for transitive object.

Use of the terms 'ergative' and 'absolutive' has been extended to the marking of syntactic functions by particles or adpositions, by pronominal cross-referencing markers on a main or auxiliary verb, and by constituent order. The term 'ergative' has been used in a further, syntactic, sense to apply to coreferentiality constraints on the formation of complex sentences, through coordination and subordination; if these constraints treat intransitive subject and transitive object in the same way the language is said to have 'ergative syntax', and if they treat intransitive subject and transitive subject in the same way there is said to be 'accusative syntax'. Preliminary exemplification is given in §§1.1, 1.2. Some writers have used 'ergative' in further ways, that are sometimes confusing and even contradictory; these are mentioned in §1.3 below.

Chapter 2 draws a critical distinction between languages where grammatical marking *directly* reflects the meaning of a particular sentence in an instance of use (e.g. whether the action is purposeful or accidental), and languages of familiar type where grammatical marking relates to the *prototypical* meaning of the verb used (e.g. the subject of 'hit' will always be marked in the same way, irrespective of whether the hitting was done

1

accidentally or on purpose). Languages of the first type can be said to have *semantically based marking* of the arguments of a verb, and those of the second type *syntactically based marking*. Case labels – such as ergative, absolutive, nominative and accusative – are only properly applicable to languages with syntactically based marking.

Chapters 3 and 4 deal with the marking of core syntactic relations within a simple clause – what is often called 'morphological ergativity'. Many languages have a mixture of ergative and accusative systems, with these splits being conditioned by the semantic nature of any one or more of various types of obligatory sentence components – verb, noun phrases, aspect/tense/mood – or by the distinction between main and subordinate clauses.

Chapter 5 discusses the category of 'subject' and how this applies to languages of ergative character. The following chapter considers 'valency-changing' operations such as passive and antipassive, and the categorisation of a language as syntactically accusative, syntactically ergative, a combination of the two, or none of these.

Chapter 7 surveys the ways in which an accusative system can develop into an ergative one, and vice versa, paying attention to the different types of factor which condition these two directions of change.

The final chapter asks why some grammatical systems are accusative and others ergative, finding a partial basis in the organisation of discourse. After discussing ideas that have been put forward concerning the mental, social and linguistic correlates of ergativity, there is a summary of the main conclusions of this work and then a statement of the implications of this study for an integrated theory of language. A short appendix refers to the treatment of ergativity in some recent theoretical models.

The purpose of this volume is, then, to survey the different ergative properties that human languages show, describing and explaining how these interrelate, their grammatical and semantic conditioning and their role in the organisation of discourse.

Ergativity (as the term is used here) is not a phenomenon encountered in the familiar languages of Europe. It does occur in – at a rough estimate – about a quarter of the languages of the world:

Basque, the language isolate spoken in the Pyrenees, is fully ergative at the morphological level (see N'Diaye 1970; Brettschneider 1979; Bossong 1984; Ortiz de Urbina 1989; among many other sources).

Ergative characteristics have been reported for each of the three language families spoken in and around the Causasus – **North-east Caucasian** (with Nakh and Dagestanian subdivisions), **North-west Cau-**

casian, and **South Caucasian** (or Kartvelian). Note that no genetic links between these three Caucasian families are generally accepted. It seems that the first use of the term 'ergative' (based upon the Greek *ergon* 'work, deed') was by Dirr (1912) in a description, written in Russian, of the Dagestanian language Rutul. However, the term did not come into general circulation until the publication of Dirr's (1928) survey, written in German, of thirty-five Caucasian languages.[1]

Ergative characteristics are apparent in a number of languages of the ancient Near East (all were extinct well before the beginning of the Christian era) – **Sumerian** (Michalowski 1980; Thomsen 1984: 49–51; Foxvog 1975), **Hurrian** (Speiser 1941), **Urartian, Hattic** and **Elamite** (see Steiner 1979, and further references therein). (Urartian is related to Hurrian, and it has been suggested that Elamite may be related to the Dravidian family from south India (McAlpin 1974) – whose modern languages are entirely accusative – but no other genetic links involving these languages appear plausible.)

There have been various suggestions, of different kinds, that proto-Indo-European had ergative characteristics (e.g. Uhlenbeck 1901); none stands up under detailed scrutiny (see Rumsey 1987a, b). However, it does appear that various branches of the Indo-European family developed ergative features. This happened in Hittite and other languages of the **Anatolian** branch (Garrett 1990) which were spoken in the Near East during the second and first centuries BC. It seems that in this part of the world, at that time, there was a 'linguistic area', consisting of a number of language isolates and small subgroups, not known to be genetically related, all of which showed some ergative characteristics – the Anatolian subgroup of Indo-European, Sumerian, Elamite and Hurrian-Urartian, and perhaps the proto-languages for some or all of the three modern Caucasian families.

Comrie (1981a: 181) mentions that **Classical Armenian** had some ergative characteristics. And, as is well known, an ergative pattern has developed in past tense/perfective aspect for some languages from the **Iranian** subgroup (e.g. John Payne 1980), and also for some from the **Indic** subgroup (e.g. Klaiman 1987; Allen 1951).

Burushaski, a language isolate spoken in inaccessible mountain valleys of the Karakoram Range on the border between Kashmir and Tibet, also shows ergative inflection in past-based tenses (Lorimer 1935; Tiffou and Morin 1982).

[1] See Seely (1977) for an exemplary historical account of the use of 'ergative' and related labels.

It has been suggested that the Vakh dialect of **Khanty**, a Uralic language, shows a modicum of ergativity (Comrie 1981a: 130; Perrot 1986, 1989).

Many languages from the **Tibeto-Burman** family have ergative characteristics, and it is generally considered that proto-Tibeto-Burman may also have had these (DeLancey 1987, 1989; Regamey 1954).

The wide-ranging Austronesian family contains a number of pockets of ergativity. Some Polynesian languages, including **Tongan** (Churchward 1953) and **Samoan** (Mosel and Hovdhaugen 1992), show ergative marking on NPs although other Polynesian languages have an accusative system; and scholars are divided as to whether the proto-Polynesian system was accusative or ergative – see §7.1 below. Ergativity has also been reported for the **Tamanic** subgroup, on the island of Borneo (Adelaar forthcoming) and for the **South Suluwesi** subgroup (Friberg 1991; Mithun 1991b). There has been much discussion of the most appropriate grammatical characterisation of **Tagalog** and other Philippines languages, with a number of scholars arguing for an ergative interpretation (see note 28 to Chapter 6 and Cena 1977, 1979; Blake 1988; Gerdts 1988; De Guzman 1988; Kroeger 1991a, b; Mithun forthcoming).

'**Papuan**' is used as a cover term for the non-Austronesian languages spoken on New Guinea and neighbouring islands, which fall into perhaps sixty distinct language families. Superficial ergative features are found in a number of Papuan languages, including Enga (Li and Lang 1979), Hua (Haiman 1980), Yimas (Foley 1991), Yawa (Jones 1986), Koiari (Dutton, personal communication), Kaluli (Schieffelin 1979, 1985 – and see Chapter 5), Ku Wara (Merlan and Rumsey 1990) and Kanum (Boelaars 1950: 37), all from different families (see Foley 1986: 106–10).

The **Australian** language family can be divided into the Pama-Nyungan group, including almost 200 languages, and a number of smaller groups collectively known as non-Pama-Nyungan (containing perhaps sixty languages between them). The great majority of modern Pama-Nyungan languages show ergative features, which appear to have a considerable time-depth; and there are ergative features in a number of non-Pama-Nyungan languages (see Blake 1987a: 187).

There are a number of small language families and language isolates grouped together, on geographical grounds, as Paleo-Siberian. Of these **Chukotko-Kamchatkan** (which includes the Chukchee and Alutor languages) and **Yukagir** show ergative grammar (Comrie 1981a: 246–52, 261).

Ergativity occurs in only a small number of the language families of North America. The best known is **Eskimo-Aleut**, which extends from Greenland to Alaska and across the Bering Strait, where it is contiguous with Chukchee. It may be that the first informed discussion of the ergative construction was Fabricius (1801: 78–9) on Greenlandic Eskimo; he used the term 'nominativus transitivus' for what would nowadays be called 'ergative case' (see Seely 1977: 192). Ergativity is also reported for **Tsimshian** from British Columbia (Boas 1911; Rigsby 1975; Mulder 1989a, b) and **Chinook** from Oregon (Silverstein 1976). (These two languages were classed as Penutian by Sapir 1929, but it has not been possible to sustain a genetic relationship between them – Campbell and Mithun 1979.)

In Central America, languages of the **Mayan** family have strong ergative characteristics, which can also be seen in the language of Mayan hieroglyphs (Bricker 1986), and has been posited for proto-Mayan (see, for instance, Larsen and Norman 1979).

South America shares with New Guinea the distinction of having the greatest linguistic diversity, and also the largest number of languages in need of description. There are in this continent the most complexly conditioned types of ergative splits (see Chapter 4). Ergative structures have been reported for languages from at least the following families: **Jê** (e.g. Urban 1985), **Arawak** (e.g. Aikhenvald-Angenot and Angenot 1991), **Tupí-Guaraní** (e.g. Jensen 1990; Seki 1990), **Panoan** (see §§4.2, 4.3 below), **Tacanan** (Camp 1985), **Chibchan** (Constenla 1982), **Maku** (Helen Weir, personal communication) and **Carib** (Franchetto 1990; Thomas Payne 1990). There is currently debate as to whether or not proto-Carib had an ergative character – see §7.1. There are a number of further language families in Amazonia and in the southern part of the continent, for some of which little information is available, and there are a number of language isolates; of the latter, ergative features are found in **Trumai** (Guirardello, 1992) and **Jabuti** (Pires 1992), for instance.

Ergativity is remarkably rare among languages of the African continent. However, it is found in a number of **Western Nilotic** languages, from the southern Sudan, including **Päri** (Andersen 1988). A trace of ergativity has also been reported by Frajzyngier (1984a, b) for **Mandara** and other languages from the Chadic branch of the Afroasiatic family (see note 3 to Chapter 3).[2]

---

[2] There is a further very marginal example of an ergative-type pattern reported for Loma, from the Mande subgroup of Niger-Congo. Rude (1983) explains how in an earlier stage of the language there was a nasal prefix *Ň*- on each NP, and the clitic *Ň*- also served as

1.1   S, A and O: the universal syntactic–semantic primitives

All languages distinguish between clauses that involve a verb and one core noun phrase (intransitive clauses) and those that involve a verb and two or more core NPs (transitive clauses, including ditransitive as a subtype). In some languages almost every verb is strictly classified as intransitive or transitive – Latin[3] and the Australian language Dyirbal are of this type. In other languages the transitivity of verb roots is more fluid – in English, for instance, some verbs (e.g. *go, shudder*) can only be used in intransitive clauses, some (e.g. *hit, take*) only in transitive clauses, but there are many verbs that may be used either intransitively or transitively (e.g. *eat, knit, help; walk, bend, spill*). And there are languages in which almost every verb root may be used in either type of clause, although often with an appropriate morphological marking; most verbs in Fijian may be used transitively, and then take a transitive suffix e.g. *la'o-vi* 'go for', *dola-vi* 'open', or they can be used intransitively and then take no suffix, e.g. *la'o* 'go', *dola* 'be open' (Dixon 1988a: 200–19).

It is a premiss of this book that all languages work in terms of three primitive relations:[4]

S – intransitive subject

A – transitive subject

O – transitive object

In languages with a nominative–accusative grammar, S and A naturally group together. Languages of the absolutive–ergative type link S and O. Many languages have some accusative and some ergative characteristics, linking S with A for certain purposes and S with O for other purposes. For

third person object marker. Constituent order is fixed: AOV, SV. Then consonantal lenition occurred on the first syllable of a word, but this lenition was blocked by an immediately preceding *Ń-* . Then *Ń-* was dropped. What we have now is that a verb does not show initial lenition when O is unexpressed, i.e. when the verb is immediately preceded by A (this lack of lenition is a reflex of the original third person object marker *Ń-*); but the verb does show lenition when immediately preceded by S or O. The net result is that S and O are treated (in this respect) in the same way, by an accident of phonological change. As Rude says, this has no grammatical significance. One could almost say that Loma has 'phonological' (rather than morphological or syntactic) ergativity. (See also note 30 to Chapter 4.)

[3] Feltenius (1977) discusses the relatively small number of transitive verbs which developed an additional intransitive use during the history of Latin.

[4] A survey of the literature shows that the letters S, A and O (which were first used in Dixon 1968, then Dixon 1972) are the most common symbols used for the three primitives. However, some scholars use P (for patient) in place of O (e.g. Comrie 1978) while Lazard and his colleagues employ X, Y and Z for A, O and S respectively (e.g. Lazard 1986, 1991).

any discussion of universal grammar, it is most useful to take S, A and O as the basic grammatical relations, and to define 'subject' (and 'pivot' – see §6.2) in terms of them. There is further discussion of this in Chapter 5.

The single core argument of an intransitive clause will always be mapped onto the S basic relation. This applies both for verbs that involve volition (e.g. 'jump', 'speak', 'wink', 'stand') and those that do not (e.g. 'fall', 'grow', 'die'). For transitive clauses with two core arguments, one will be mapped onto the A relation and the other onto the O relation. If there are three (or more) core arguments, then two will be mapped onto A and O, with the remainder being marked in some other way (e.g. by prepositions or postpositions). There is always a semantic basis for the assignment of A and O relations, and it relates to the prototypical meaning of the verb used.

Words belonging to the verb class, in any language, refer to a wide range of actions and states. It is convenient to recognise a number of what I call 'semantic types', each being a class of verbs which has a common meaning component and shared grammatical properties. (There is a fuller introduction to, and justification of, the theory of semantic types, in Dixon 1991a; see also Dixon 1982: 9–62.)

There are a number of 'semantic roles' associated with each semantic type. Some of the semantic types of verbs which appear in all languages are (with example members from English):

SEMANTIC TYPES	Semantic Roles
AFFECT, e.g. *hit, cut, burn*	Agent, Manip (thing manipulated), Target[5]
GIVING, e.g. *give, lend, pay*	Donor, Gift, Recipient
SPEAKING, e.g. *talk, tell, order*	Speaker, Addressee, Message[6]
ATTENTION,[7] e.g. *see, hear, watch*	Perceiver, Impression

---

[5] Reasons for preferring the labels Manip and Target over, say, Instrument and Patient are given in Dixon (1991a: 102–4). As can be seen from the examples given in the next paragraph but one, either Manip or Target can be the thing most affected by the activity (and is then in O function).

[6] There is a fourth, less central, semantic role associated with the SPEAKING type: Medium, e.g. language or style used (as *French* in *He asked a question in French, They don't speak French here*). See Dixon (1991a: 140ff.).

[7] In some languages the ATTENTION type is not associated with the main grammatical class of transitive verbs but enters into a different construction type, e.g. in the Polynesian language Tongan, the Perceiver is marked as intransitive subject and the Impression with dative case (Churchward 1953) and in Dagestanian languages such as Avar the Perceiver is marked with locative and the Impression with absolutive case (Černý 1971). See the discussion in §5.1.

For transitive verbs, one semantic role is mapped onto the A syntactic relation. What has always seemed to me remarkable is that different languages, from all over the world, show a fair consistency in the way this is done. It is almost always the Agent for AFFECT verbs, the Donor for GIVING, the Speaker for SPEAKING and the Perceiver for ATTENTION that are identified as A. The underlying principle appears to be: that role which is most likely to be relevant to the success of the activity will be identified as A. This can be something inanimate (as in *The wind wrecked the house*, *The midday sun melted the butter*); most often, the role mapped onto A will be human and 'most relevant to the success of the activity' then equates with 'could initiate or control the activity'.

If a verb has just two core roles then that role which is not mapped onto A will be identified with O syntactic relation, e.g. *the nuts* in all of *John fetched the nuts*, *Mary noticed the nuts*, *The squirrel ate the nuts*. Where there are three roles there may often be two constructions available, so that either of the two non-A roles may be coded as O, according as it is most saliently affected by the activity, e.g. *John* (Agent:A) *hit the vase* (Target:O) *with a stick* (Manip) (with the vase breaking), and *John* (Agent:A) *hit the piece of chalk* (Manip:O) *against the table* (Target) (with the chalk breaking). Sometimes there are two verbs with similar meanings and the same set of semantic roles but different conventions for mapping these onto syntactic relations. *Mention* and *inform* both belong to the SPEAKING type, requiring Speaker, Addressee and Message, but *mention* has Message as O and *inform* has Addressee as O, e.g. *John mentioned the decision to Mary*, and *John informed Mary of the decision*.

It will thus be seen that there is a semantic basis to the mapping of semantic roles (for a given verb, from a particular semantic type) onto A and O syntactic relations. The basic relation S, in contrast, relates to the single core NP of any intransitive verb, whatever the meaning of the verb. In §3.3 there is discussion of ways in which S groups with A, and ways in which it groups with O; in §5.1 a definition of 'subject' is provided, that links together A and S; and in §4.1 we examine languages that distinguish two subtypes of S, one related to A and the other related to O.

1.2   Introductory exemplification

The three basic syntactic relations are grouped together in different ways for nominative–accusative and for absolutive–ergative grammatical systems:

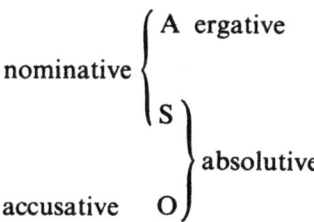

Nominative–accusative case systems can be illustrated for Latin:

(1)   *domin-us veni-t*, the master comes
(2)   *serv-us veni-t*, the slave comes
(3)   *domin-us serv-um audi-t*, the master hears the slave
(4)   *serv-us domin-um audi-t*, the slave hears the master

The same case inflection, nominative singular *-us* (for the second declension, to which the two nouns used here belong) is used for S in (1–2) and for A in (3–4), while a different inflection, accusative *-um*, is used for the O NPs in (3–4). In Latin the ending on a verb indicates tense, voice and mood (present, active, indicative in these examples) and also the person and number of the S constituent in an intransitive clause, as in (1–2), or of an A constituent in a transitive clause, as in (3–4). The verbal ending *-t* indicates third person singular S or A (for the fourth conjugation, to which the verbs 'come' and 'hear' belong). If the verb endings were changed to third person plural *-unt* (*veni-unt* and *audi-unt*) this would indicate a plural S or A, but convey no information about the O in (3–4). We would then have to mark the S or A NP with nominative plural case inflection *-ī*, e.g.

(1′)   *domin-ī veni-unt*, the masters come
(4′)   *serv-ī domin-um audi-unt*, the slaves hear the master

If the O NP is plural it must take accusative plural ending *-ōs*, e.g.

(4″)   *serv-us domin-ōs audi-t*, the slave hears the masters

We explained that a nominative–accusative system is one in which S is treated in the same way as A, and differently from O. It will be seen that Latin is nominative-accusative both in its case marking and in verb agreement.

Contrast this grammatical system with that in Dyirbal, from north-east Australia:[8]

[8] Each NP in Dyirbal generally also contains a 'noun marker' that agrees with the head noun in case, shows its noun (gender) class, and indicates whether the referent is 'here', 'there' or 'not visible'. To simplify the discussion here, noun markers – which have a

(5)   *ŋuma   banaga-nʸu*
        father + ABS   return-NONFUT
        father(S) returned

(6)   *yabu   banaga-nʸu*
        mother + ABS   return-NONFUT
        mother(S) returned

(7)   *ŋuma   yabu-ŋgu   bura-n*
        father + ABS   mother-ERG   see-NONFUT
        mother(A) saw father(O)

(8)   *yabu   ŋuma-ŋgu   bura-n*
        mother + ABS   father-ERG   see-NONFUT
        father(A) saw mother(O)

Here a noun occurs in plain form, with no affix, when it is in S function, in (5–6) and also when in O function, in (7–8). This is said to be absolutive case, which has zero realisation. Transitive subject function, A, is marked by ergative case ending, here *-ŋgu*. (Noun inflections in Dyirbal show case but, unlike Latin, they do not indicate number.) The verb inflections here indicate non-future tense, *-nʸu* for *banaga-*, which belongs to the *-y* conjugation and *-n* for *bura-*, from the *-l* conjugation; in Dyirbal the verb does not cross-reference the person or number of any of S, O or A.

Each of (1–8) was given in the normal constituent order for that language. Looking at transitive clauses, in Latin an NP in nominative case (A function) will generally precede one in accusative case (O) whereas in Dyirbal, for NPs whose heads are nouns, the absolutive (O) constituent will generally precede the ergative (A) one. However, since for both Latin and Dyirbal syntactic function is fully specified by case ending, the words from any sentence can potentially be rearranged into any order, without a change of meaning. This contrasts with English, where syntactic function is shown by constituent order (S or A before the verb, O after) and a change in constituent order does change the meaning (compare *The master hears the slave* and *The slave hears the master*).

slightly irregular paradigm – have been omitted; they do not in any way affect the grammatical points being made. The 'there' (and unmarked) forms of the masculine noun markers are ABS *bayi*, ERG *baŋgul*, DAT *bagul*; of the feminine marker, ABS *balan*, ERG *baŋgun*, DAT *bagun*. Full forms of the Dyirbal sentences are thus: (5) *bayi ŋuma banaga-nʸu*; (6) *balan yabu banaga-nʸu*; (7) *bayi ŋuma baŋgun yabu-ŋgu bura-n*; and so on. Similarly for later examples – (12) *bayi ŋuma bural-ŋa-nʸu bagun yabu-gu*; etc. An NP can consist of just a noun marker, which is then functioning like a third person pronoun.

That case which includes S function is most often the unmarked term in the system – absolutive in Dyirbal and nominative in Latin. This will be the case form used for citation,[9] and it is most likely to be the left-most NP in a clause. It may also be the pivot for various syntactic operations, such as coordination and relativisation; syntactic derivations may be applied to bring an NP into a derived function in which it is in the unmarked case, as will be illustrated below.

In any system of case inflection there is often one case that has zero realisation (as absolutive in Dyirbal) or else a zero allomorph (nominative in Latin has zero ending with some nouns, e.g. *puer* 'boy'). In an 'ergative' system the unmarked case, absolutive, almost always has zero realisation or at least a zero allomorph. Similarly, it is nominative that most frequently has zero realisation, or a zero allomorph, in an 'accusative' system. Note, though, that the parallel between absolutive and nominative is not complete here. There are a few well-attested instances where accusative has zero realisation, while nominative involves a positive affix (see §3.4.3), but none where ergative has zero form and absolutive is non-zero.

Moving on to another grammatical level, languages can be said to have 'accusative syntax' – i.e. some rules of coordination and/or subordination will treat S and A in the same way, and O rather differently – or 'ergative syntax' – where these sorts of rules treat S and O in the same way, and A differently. If a language treats S and A in the same way for rules of clause combining, it will be said to have an 'S/A pivot'; if S and O are treated in the same way, we will talk of an 'S/O pivot'. The term 'pivot' corresponds to what has been called 'surface subject' by earlier writers. In Chapters 5 and 6 I explain the difficulties associated with using traditional terms 'subject' and 'object' for ergative languages and suggest that 'subject' be employed to link together S and A relations in underlying structure, while 'pivot' be used to describe syntactic equivalence (of S and A, or of S and O) in clause-linking operations that work in terms of derived structures. The idea of pivot will be briefly illustrated here; it is discussed in more detail in Chapter 6.

English is an example of a language with accusative syntax. Any two clauses may be coordinated, and if there is a shared NP it can be replaced by a pronoun whatever the function of the common NP in each clause. But a common NP can only be omitted, from its second occurrence, if it is in S or A function in each clause. Thus from *Father*(S) *returned* and *Father*(A) *saw mother*(O) can be obtained *Father returned and saw mother* or *Father*

[9] Hence the Latin label 'nominative'.

saw mother and returned. If the common NP is in O function in one of the clauses then NP omission is not possible; from *Father*(S) *returned* and *Mother*(A) *saw father*(O) we cannot obtain **Father returned and mother saw* or **Mother saw father and returned* (with the meaning: 'father returned').

One function of passive is to put an underlying O NP into derived S function so that this coreferential omission (according to the syntactic rule of English) can take place. Instead of the active clause *Mother*(A) *saw father*(O) we may use the corresponding passive, *Father*(S) *was seen by mother.* This may now be linked with *Father*(S) *returned.* Since the common NP (*father*) is in S function in each clause it can be omitted from the second clause in a coordination, yielding *Father returned and was seen by mother* or *Father was seen by mother and returned.* We say that English operates with an S/A syntactic pivot, i.e. that it has accusative syntax.

Dyirbal, in contrast, has ergative syntax, working in terms of an S/O pivot. For this language two clauses may only be joined in a coordinate structure if they share an NP which is in S or O function in each clause. The occurrence of the common NP in the second clause is then usually omitted and the whole biclausal construction can make up one intonation group (note that there is no overt coordinating particle in Dyirbal, similar to English *and*). Thus, from (5) and (7) we can derive:

(9)   *ŋuma   banaga-nʸu   yabu-ŋgu   bura-n*
       father + ABS return-NONFUT mother-ERG see-NONFUT
       father(S) returned and mother(A) saw him(O)

There is no O NP stated for *buran* 'saw' in (9) and so – in terms of Dyirbal's S/O pivot – it is taken to be identical to the S NP of the preceding (intransitive) clause in the coordination. Similarly, (7) and (5) can be combined as:

(10)   *ŋuma   yabu-ŋgu   bura-n   banaga-nʸu*
        father + ABS mother-ERG see-NONFUT return-NONFUT
        mother(A) saw father(O) and he(S) returned

There is no S NP stated for the verb of the second clause, *banaga-nʸu* 'return' and so – in terms of the pivot – it is taken to be identical with the O NP of the first clause.

If we wish to conjoin (5) and (8), we find that the syntactic condition on coordination is not met. The NP *ŋuma* 'father' is common to the two clauses but although it is in S function in (5) it is in the non-pivot function,

A, in (8). This is similar to the English examples with *Father returned* and *Mother saw father*, where 'father' was not in pivot (here S/A) function in the second clause. This was overcome by using a passive construction, *Father was seen by mother*, where 'father' is now in a pivot function (S). In Dyirbal a transitive construction can be recast into a derived intransitive form, called 'antipassive'. Underlying A becomes S of the antipassive, underlying O goes into dative case (which is *-gu* with nouns and *-ngu* with pronouns),[10] and the verb bears an antipassive derivation suffix, *-ŋa-y*, between root and inflection:

(11) NP^1_A NP^2_O V + tense
      $\Rightarrow \text{NP}^1_\text{S}$ NP^2_DAT V + *ŋa-y* + tense

The antipassive version of (8) is:

(12)   *ŋuma*   *bural-ŋa-n^{y}u*   *yabu-gu*
      father + ABS see-ANTIPASS-NONFUT mother-DAT
      father(S) saw mother

Note that (8) and (12) have the same cognitive meaning, in the same way that an active and the corresponding passive do in English.

Now (5) and (12) have a common NP, *ŋuma* 'father', which is in S function in each clause, and they can be coordinated together in either order (see also §6.2.2):

(13)   *ŋuma*   *banaga-n^{y}u*   *bural-ŋa-n^{y}u*   *yabu-gu*
      father + ABS return-NONFUT see-ANTIPASS-NONFUT mother-DAT
      father(S) returned and he(S) saw mother

(14)   *ŋuma*   *bural-ŋa-n^{y}u*   *yabu-gu*   *banaga-n^{y}u*
      father + ABS see-ANTIPASS-NONFUT mother-DAT return-NONFUT
      father(S) saw mother and he(S) returned

Many languages which have a wholly or partly ergative morphology do not have ergative syntax; instead, syntactic rules operate on an accusative principle, treating S and A in the same way (see §6.2). Dyirbal is unusual in that all major syntactic operations – those of relativisation and complementation, as well as coordination – treat S and O in the same way.

---

[10] Instrumental (= ergative) is possible here as an infrequent alternative to dative, just on nouns. See Dixon (1972: 66, 170ff.).

I shall (in §3.3 and in Chapter 5) discuss certain universal characteristics through which S and A are linked together in some ways and S and O are linked in other ways, in all languages (whatever their grammatical orientation). Leaving these aside, there are some languages that appear to be fully accusative, in both morphological marking and syntactic constraints. However – and this is a most interesting and significant fact – no language has thus far been reported that is fully ergative, at both morphological and syntactic levels. There are languages which have an ergative pattern for marking syntactic function within a simple clause (by case inflections and/or verbal cross-referencing, etc.) but then work in terms of an S/A pivot, i.e. they have accusative syntax (see §6.2.3). Dyirbal has ergative syntax and ergative case marking on nouns (and on adjectives) but its pronouns inflect in an accusative paradigm. At the morphological level Dyirbal is like many other languages in being what is called 'split-ergative' (i.e. part-ergative and part-accusative).

The contrasting case systems for nouns and for pronouns in Dyirbal are shown in Table 1.1. (This uses plural pronouns simply because they have a more regular inflection than singular forms.)[11]

Whereas nouns use the simple root for absolutive (S and O functions) and show ergative case (A function) by *-ŋgu*, pronouns employ only the root for nominative case (S and A functions) and add an affix *-na* for accusative (O). Sentences involving pronouns are:

(15)   *ŋana   banaga-nʸu*
        we all + NOM return-NONFUT
        we(S) returned

(16)   *nʸurra   banaga-nʸu*
        you all + NOM return-NONFUT
        you all(S) returned

(17)   *nʸurra   ŋana-na   bura-n*
        you all + NOM we all-ACC   see-NONFUT
        you all(A) saw us(O)

(18)   *ŋana   nʸurra-na   bura-n*
        we all + NOM you all-ACC see-NONFUT
        we(A) saw you all(O)

---

[11] The pronoun class in Dyirbal only covers first and second persons. There are no third person singular pronouns as such, although 'noun markers' (see note 8) can have a pronominal function; these inflect on an ergative--absolutive pattern, like nouns and adjectives.

Table 1.1. *Sample case inflections of nouns and pronouns in Dyirbal*

ROOT	*yabu* 'mother'	*ŋuma* 'father'	*ŋana* 'we all'	*nʸurra* 'you all'
A function	*yabu-ŋgu*	*ŋuma-ŋgu*	*ŋana*	*nʸurra*
S function	*yabu*	*ŋuma*		
O function			*ŋana-na*	*nʸurra-na*

Note that, in unmarked constituent order, a nominative pronoun will precede one in accusative case – that is, there is a preferred order 'A before O' for pronouns, but (as mentioned above) 'O before A' for nouns (see also §3.2). Clauses, and even individual NPs, can involve any mixture of pronouns, nouns and adjectives without possibility of confusion. (Sceptical readers are invited to construct a few examples for themselves.)

It is important to distinguish morphological and syntactic ergativity/ accusativity since these are, potentially, independent parameters. As just mentioned, some languages have ergative morphology but accusative syntax. Dyirbal has a split-ergative morphology but an entirely ergative syntax. That is, two clauses in Dyirbal can only be coordinated if they involve a common NP which is in S or O function in each clause – and this applies irrespective of whether the NPs contain nouns or pronouns (or a mixture of the two). Thus (15) and (17) can be coordinated, in either order, just like (5) and (7):

(19) *ŋana   banaga-nʸu   nʸurra   bura-n*
      we all + NOM return-NONFUT you all + NOM see-NONFUT
      we(S) returned and you all(A) saw us(O)

(20) *nʸurra   ŋana-na   bura-n   banaga-nʸu*
      you all + NOM we all-ACC   see-NONFUT   return-NONFUT
      you all(A) saw us(O) and we(S) returned

The NP 'we all' occurs in S function in (15) – with form *ŋana* – and in O function in (17) – with form *ŋana-na*. The fact that it is in a pivot function in each clause permits coordination; its being in a different form in each clause is irrelevant as far as the coordination rule is concerned. The occurrence of this NP from the first coordinand is retained (this is *ŋana* in (19) and *ŋana-na* in (20)) with its occurrence from the second clause being omitted.

If we try to conjoin (15) and (18) we find that although each clause includes a pronoun, *ŋana*, it is in S function in the first instance and in A in the second. The S/O pivot condition is not met, and straightforward coordination is not possible.[12] We must follow the same plan as for coordinating (5) and (8), i.e. (18) must be put into antipassive form:

(21)   ŋana   bural-ŋa-n^{y}u   n^{y}urra-ngu
        we all + NOM see-ANTIPASS-NONFUT you all-DAT
        we(S) saw you all

'We' has the same form, *ŋana*, in both (18) and (21) but in the transitive clause (18) it is in non-pivot function, A, while in the derived intransitive (21) it is in a pivot function, S. We can now coordinate (15) and (21), in either order (see also §6.2.2):

(22)   ŋana   banaga-n^{y}u   bural-ŋa-n^{y}u   n^{y}urra-ngu
        we all + NOM return-NONFUT see-ANTIPASS-NONFUT you all-DAT
        we(S) returned and we(S) saw you all

(23)   ŋana   bural-ŋa-n^{y}u   n^{y}urra-ngu banaga-n^{y}u
        we all + NOM see-ANTIPASS-NONFUT you all-DAT return-NONFUT
        we(S) saw you all and we(S) returned

These examples demonstrate an important point – that in Dyirbal it is the function of an NP that determines its availability to grammatical operations, not its form.

In summary, the terms 'ergative' and 'ergativity' – and 'accusative' and 'accusativity' – may be used:

1. To describe the ways in which the syntactic functions of predicate arguments are marked in simple transitive and intransitive clauses, i.e. whether S is marked in the same way as O and differently from A (an ergative arrangement) or whether S is marked in the same way as A and differently from O (an accusative arrangement). This is 'morphological' or 'intra-clausal' ergativity/accusativity and it relates to the marking of syntactic relations in derived structure (not at any level of underlying structure).

2. To describe syntactic constraints that a language may place on the combining of simple clauses into complex sentences, by coordination, subordination, complementation, etc. Again, if S and O are treated as equivalent (functioning as syntactic pivot) and A is treated differently, then

[12] *ŋana banaga-n^{y}u, n^{y}urra-na bura-n* can only mean 'We returned and you all were seen (by someone other than us)'. That is, it would have to be said with sentence-final intonation on *banaga-n^{y}u*; the second sentence would then be taken to have an unspecified A NP. These four words could *not* be understood as 'We returned and we saw you all' – this has to be rendered through (22).

the language is said to be ergative, and if S and A are treated in the same way (functioning as pivot) and O is treated differently then the language can be characterised as accusative at the syntactic or inter-clausal level.

In some languages the syntactic pivot may have an additional function, relating to syntactic processes within a clause. For instance, in some Mayan languages, only an NP in pivot function (here S or O) can be questioned. An antipassive derivation may be used to bring an A NP into the pivot function, S, if it is to be questioned. See §6.3.

We have seen that a language may have syntactic derivations for putting an argument that is, in underlying structure, in a non-pivot function into a pivot function. Languages with accusative syntax often have a passive derivation, one of whose purposes is to place an underlying O NP into derived S relation, and languages with ergative syntax almost always (or always?) have an antipassive derivation which puts an underlying A argument into derived S function. There can be other syntactic operations which 'feed' a pivot constraint, e.g. in Dyirbal a transitive verb can take the derivational affix -*ma-l* and then an underlying instrumental NP is placed in O function, enabling it to enter into coordinate and subordinate constructions, all of which demand an S/O pivot (the A NP stays as it is, and underlying O is placed in dative case – see §6.2.2 below and Dixon 1972: 45–6).

There is a certain symmetry between passive in a syntactically accusative language and antipassive in an ergative language. However, these two derivations do have rather different semantic effects – see §6.1. And, in fact, both kinds of operation do occur in the same language.

A warning must be issued at this point. As illustrated in (8) and (12) above, an antipassive places an underlying A into derived S function. But this is not a 'link' between S and A that could be taken as evidence of the 'accusative' character of a language. Quite the contrary, it is generally found in syntactically ergative languages and serves to feed an S/O pivot – it is this pivot that defines the syntactic character of the language. Similarly, passive puts underlying O into derived S but this is not evidence of 'ergativity'; rather it is likely to be found in an accusative language, feeding an S/A pivot. Syntactic derivations that replace a certain syntactic function of a clausal argument by another are not to be taken as evidence for ergativity or accusativity (they would be likely to give contradictory characterisations to those obtained under 2 above). This applies both to valency-reducing operations such as passive and antipassive and also to valency-increasing operations such as causative which typically (in both ergative and accusative languages) derives, from an intransitive clause, a transitive causative construction in which S becomes O – this is most emphatically not evidence of 'ergativity'.

This section has summarised the two main uses of the term 'ergative' in current descriptive work. However, a number of scholars, mostly working within particular theoretical positions, have used 'ergative' in a quite different way (sometimes contradictory to the uses presented here). The next section briefly discusses these.

1.3   Other uses of the term 'ergative'

We mentioned that in some languages almost every verb is strictly transitive or intransitive whereas in other languages almost every verb may take either transitivity value. Fijian was given as an example of the latter type – if a verb shows a suffix then it is transitive (taking A and O arguments), and if there is no suffix it is intransitive (with just an S core argument). The interesting question here is which of the transitive arguments corresponds to the intransitive argument. I found, from a sample of 460 verbs, that 53 per cent were of type S = A (e.g. *la'o* 'go', *la'o-vi* 'go for') and 47 per cent of type S = O (e.g. *dola* 'be open', *dola-vi* 'open'); see Dixon 1988a: 200ff. This is entirely a matter of lexical semantics, and does not relate to the grammatical characterisation of a language as ergative or accusative.[13]

English has a fair number of verbs that can be used (in the same form, without the addition of any affix) either intransitively or transitively.[14] Some of these are of type S = A, e.g. *knit* in *He is knitting / He is knitting a jumper*, and also *speak, watch, eat, help, know, try*, etc. Others are of type S = O, e.g. *march* as in *The soldiers marched / The officer marched the*

---

[13] As already mentioned, in Dyirbal each verb is strictly transitive or strictly intransitive. Yet there is also an S = O/S = A division, as in Fijian and other languages. Dyirbal has a special 'avoidance' speech style, which must be used in the presence of someone in a taboo relation (it is called by native speakers 'mother-in-law language'); this has the same phonology and grammar as the everyday style but an almost totally distinct lexicon. The avoidance style has fewer lexemes than the everyday style. In a fair number of cases there is just a transitive verb root in avoidance style where the everyday style has non-cognate transitive and intransitive roots. An intransitivised version of the avoidance verb root (by use of the productive 'reflexive' derivational affix) is then used to translate the intransitive root from the everyday style. The interesting point is that some of these transitive/intransitive pairs are of the type S = O (e.g. 'put standing/stand', 'take out/come out') while others are of type S = A (e.g. 'tell/talk', 'follow', 'eat'). (See Dixon 1972: 297, 1982: 102.) Thus, even in this highly ergative language there are lexical pairs of both types S = O and S = A, similar to the situation in English.

[14] These are called 'ambitransitives' or, sometimes, 'labile verbs' (see §3.3 below).

soldiers, and also *walk, move, twist, open, break, burst, cool, grow, hurry*, etc.

One particularly unfortunate use of the term 'ergative' has been as a 'descriptive label' for the 'subject type' in a construction such as *The officer marched the soldiers*. This appears to have originated with Halliday (1967: 44ff.) and was perpetuated by Lyons in a wide-selling and influential textbook (1968: 352):

> the term that is generally employed[15] by linguists for the syntactic relationship that holds between (1) *The stone moved* and (3) *John moved the stone* is 'ergative': the subject of an intransitive verb 'becomes' the object of a corresponding transitive verb, and a new *ergative* subject is introduced as 'agent' (or 'cause') of the action referred to. This suggests that a transitive sentence, like (3), may be derived syntactically from an intransitive sentence, like (1), by means of an ergative, or *causative*, transformation.

The only example quoted in the entry on 'ergative (ergativity)' in Crystal's best-selling *Dictionary of Linguistics and Phonetics* (1991: 124–5) is *The window broke/The man broke the window* with the explanation that for some linguists these 'would be analysed "ergatively"': the subject of the intransitive use of *broke* is the same as the object of its transitive use, and the AGENT of the action is thus said to appear as the "ergative subject"'.

Some of the S=O lexical pairs in English correspond to explicitly marked causatives in other languages, that show a more extensive morphology. In Turkish we find an intransitive *otobüs*(S) *harekit etti* 'the bus(S) started', and a causative explicitly marked by verbal affix *-tir-, şoför*(A) *otobüs-ü*(O) *harekit et-tir-di* 'the driver(A) started the bus(O)' (Lewis 1953: 108). This is plainly a nominative–accusative case system – no affix is used for S or A, but accusative *-ü* marks a definite object. To suggest that the A of a causative is 'ergative' and that 'the bus' in these two sentences is in any sense 'absolutive' (being in S and O functions respectively) would be unbearably confusing. As far as I know no one has used 'ergative' in connection with an overtly marked causative; but there are close parallels to null-marked causatives (and other S=O verbs) in English, where the term has been employed.[16]

---

[15] It is *not* true that this was a term 'generally employed' by linguists, at the time, for this semantic relation. It had been used by Halliday the previous year, in a paper published in a journal of which Lyons was editor.

[16] English has no case marking on nouns but has contrasting nominative (SA) versus oblique (O and prepositional object) forms of pronouns, a residual cross-referencing in 'present' tense (where *-s* marks 3sg. S or A) and a constituent order where S and A precede the verb but O follows – all clear nominative–accusative characteristics.

The use of 'ergative', in this lexical-semantic/causative sense is quite illicit (in addition to being potentially most confusing) in terms of the well-defined use of the term – summarised in this book – by descriptive linguists working on the languages of the Caucasus, South America, Australia, Polynesia, the Tibeto-Burman family and so on (including those working on Basque and Eskimo).

Sadly, the misuse does not stop here. In what Pullum (1988: 585) calls 'a truly crackbrained piece of terminological revisionism', there has arisen the habit – which appears to have begun with the MIT theses of Burzio (1981) and Pesetsky (1982) – of again using the term 'ergative' in connection with pairs of sentences such as *John opened the window* and *The window opened*, but now referring to S and O as 'the ergative set'. Not only is the label 'ergative' being used in an inappropriate context, it is being used for the wrong member of the opposition, in place of 'absolutive'. There is a recent book called *Ergativity in German*, by Grewendorf (1989) dealing with this sort of phenomenon. If the term 'ergative' is used in this way then every language would show 'ergativity' (surely every language has some sort of causative construction). In contrast, only about a quarter of the world's languages (not including German and English) show morphological or intra-clausal ergativity, as discussed at length in Chapters 3 and 4, and only a handful of these show syntactic or inter-clausal ergativity (Chapter 6).

We must mention another illicit use of the term 'ergative' (e.g. by Halliday 1967, Anderson 1968) in relation to pairs of English sentences such as *Mary washed the woollens well* and *The woollens washed well*. It is suggested that here O becomes S and this is then an instance of 'ergativity'. There are several reasons why such an approach is misconceived.[17] Consider the transitive sentence *Mary washed the woollens* (*with Softly*) (*in the Hoovermatic*). The success of the activity can be attributed to Mary and we would say *Mary washed the woollens well* (*with Softly*) (*in the Hoovermatic*). Or it could be considered a feature of the woollens, *The woollens washed well* (*with Softly*) (*in the Hoovermatic*); or to be due to the excellence of the soap mixture used, *Softly washed the woollens well* (*in the Hoovermatic*); or the success of the activity could be considered a feature of the washing machine used, *The Hoovermatic washed the woollens well* (*with Softly*). The points to note are (1) any kind of non-subject NP – not just the object – can, potentially be 'promoted to subject' if its referent is considered responsible for the success or lack of success of the activity

[17] There is fuller discussion in Dixon (1991a: 322ff.).

(this promotion is only permitted in the presence of an appropriate adverb, e.g. *well*, *easily*, *quickly*, or modal or negator or emphatic *do*); (2) promotion does not alter the transitivity of the sentence – there is still an object present when *Softly* or *the Hoovermatic* are promoted to subject and when *the woollens* fill derived subject slot they are still understood to be object of the verb – thus what we get is an O or instrumental or locative NP promoted into A (not into S) slot. Even if O were promoted to S in examples of this type it would still be an illicit circumstance in which to employ the term 'ergative' for the same reasons as those just given in the discussion of causatives and other S = O lexical pairs.

The passive derivation in English really does have O becoming S. One would imagine that those linguists who described *Mary washed the woollens well* / *The woollens washed well* as 'ergative' should also extend the term to *Mary washed the woollens* / *The woollens were washed* (*by Mary*). As far as I know, no one has (yet) done so. I explained at the end of the last section how such a use of the term 'ergative' – like all the uses mentioned in this section – would be not only inconsistent with but also contradictory to the use of the term followed in this book.[18]

There is another way in which the term 'ergative' is used which differs from the standard signification. This is to use 'ergative' to refer to the marking of the syntactic relation A, where this differs from the marking on S, without also requiring that S and O be marked in the same way (e.g. DeLancey 1981).[19] A variant on this is a characterisation such as that given by Tchekhoff (1980: 78): 'An ergative construction is formally recognisable as having a marked agent and an unmarked other modifier together with a neutral verb that is unmarked for voice and thus gives no indication of the part played by its modifiers' (by 'modifier' here may be meant 'argument').[20]

---

[18] 'Ergative' has also been used in relation to discourse structure; again, its sense is at odds with the standard meaning of the term – see notes 2 and 3 to Chapter 8.

[19] Cumming and Wouk (1987) provide a critique of works purporting to show that some Austronesian languages have 'discourse ergativity' but which do not use the term 'ergative' in the standard way.

[20] There is a further use of the term 'ergative' which differs radically from that used here, and from all other uses. Mel'čuk (e.g. 1978: 24–5) works with the following principles: (1) the citation form of a noun is to be called the nominative case; (2) the only core NP (i.e. S) for an intransitive verb is called its subject; (3) for a transitive verb, whichever of A and O is marked in the same way as S is called its subject; (4) if the subject is in nominative case, then we have a nominative construction; (5) if the subject is not in nominative case, we have an ergative construction. By this argumentation, an ergative construction is only found when the citation form of a noun is not that used for S function (see §3.4.3 below). Consider a straightforward ergative language (according to non-Mel'čuk terminology) – S and O would be marked by absolutive case, also used in citation, and thus called

For the remainder of this book, the term 'ergativity' will be used in the standard way, for referring to S and O being treated in the same way, and differently from A. 'Ergative' is then used in relation to A, the marked member of such an opposition, and 'absolutive' in relation to S and O, the unmarked term.

nominative by Mel'čuk; but S and O are also said by Mel'čuk to be subject and so for him this is a nominative (and not an ergative) construction type.

   Job (1985) examined Mel'čuk's (1983), treatment of Lezgian, an ergative language (to everyone save Mel'čuk) from the North-east Caucasian family. Mel'čuk's argumentation forces him to say that there are no transitive verbs in Lezgian, that all verbs 'denote states, not genuine actions; action verbs simply do not exist in the language'. Thus, the verb normally glossed as 'kill' is said by Mel'čuk to mean 'die (maybe from somebody's hand)', and 'eat' is said to mean 'disappear swallowed'. Job shows that this is not an adequate or appropriate characterisation of Lezgian, which is like all other languages in having a full set of transitive verbs. See also Haspelmath (1991), who provides additional arguments against Mel'čuk's position. For instance, one of Mel'čuk's arguments for A NPs not being core constituents was that they could be omitted from a transitive clause; but Haspelmath shows that O NPs can also freely be omitted.

2 Syntactically based and semantically based marking

Before venturing into a detailed examination of kinds of ergative and accusative grammatical patterning, we must distinguish between two different kinds of strategy that languages employ for marking 'who is doing what to who'. These can be called (1) the syntactically based (or 'prototypical') alternative, and (2) the semantically based (or 'direct') alternative. We shall see that labels such as nominative, accusative, absolutive and ergative are only properly applicable to languages of the first type.

For languages of the first type, each verb has a prototypical meaning, and grammatical marking is applied to the verb's arguments on the basis of their function in the prototypical instance. English basically follows this approach. The prototypical meaning of *hit* is that in *He hit me* (implied: with his hand) or *He hit me with a stick*. The agent (who propels the implement) is marked as transitive subject (A), being placed before the verb (and being in nominative case if a pronoun). The target, which the implement comes into contact with, is marked as transitive object (O), and placed after the verb (being in oblique form if a pronoun).

When the verb is used with a non-prototypical meaning the same grammatical marking of arguments applies. *Hit* is categorised as a transitive verb and so there must be a transitive subject stated. In *The falling branch hit me*, the noun phrase *the falling branch* is treated as being in A function, although it is not an agent propelling an implement (nor an implement propelled by an agent).

The transitive subject function prototypically codes a volitional agent. But if an animate being achieves some result by chance, e.g. *John hit Tom accidentally with a stick*, the (here, non-volitional) agent is still marked as transitive subject and an adverb such as *accidentally* is included to indicate that this is a non-prototypical instance of hitting.

It is a rule of English grammar that every non-imperative main clause should have a subject stated. If we wished to describe an instance of hitting in which the identity of the agent is not known, or not considered important, then a passive construction could be used, e.g. *John was hit*, in which underlying transitive object becomes subject of the intransitive, passive clause, and the underlying transitive subject may be omitted.

Turning now to languages of the second type, we find that in any instance of use of a verb its arguments are marked not by a syntactic rule relating to any prototypical scheme, but so as to directly describe its meaning in that instance. Thus, in 'John hit Bill', 'John' would be marked as (volitional) agent and 'Bill' as (affected) patient. In 'John hit Bill accidentally' and 'The falling branch hit Bill', 'Bill' would again be marked as patient but 'John' and 'the falling branch' would not be marked as agent, since they do not exert volitional control over the activity. In 'John hit at Bill (but the implement didn't come into contact with him)' then 'John' would be marked as agent but 'Bill' would not be marked as patient, since he was not affected by the action.

A language of this type deals with each instance of use of a verb separately, looking at the semantic functions of the argument NPs in that instance of use, and marking them accordingly, without reference to a prototypical template. Languages with 'direct marking' may also have more fluid grammatical requirements (compared with English, for instance, where a subject is obligatory in non-imperative clauses). Corresponding to the English *John was hit* we could, in a language of the second type, find 'John' marked as patient, but no statement of any agent (and nothing like a passive derivation).

The remainder of this chapter provides a characterisation of these two alternative methods of marking the arguments of a verb: either according to a syntactic strategy which relates to a prototypical semantic profile for each verb (and ensures that a given verb will always have its arguments marked in the same way, whatever the semantics of a particular situation of use for the verb); or by semantic rules, directly describing the semantics of each situation of use. The alternatives are, of course, idealisations – it is likely that every language mingles 'prototypical' and 'direct' characteristics, to some extent. In English, for instance, a preposition can be inserted before a direct object to mark the fact that it was not affected by an action[1] – compare *John kicked the ball* with *John kicked at the ball* (and missed it); this is 'direct' marking. In Finnish a noun in direct object function can be marked by partitive, or by genitive or nominative case, according to the

---

[1] This is only part of the semantic story behind preposition insertion in English; see Dixon (1991a: 278–80) for a fuller discussion.

semantic character of the clause (the choice between genitive and nominative is conditioned by syntactic factors); similar alternations are found in some other European languages. These are, however, minor matters – both English and Finnish are predominantly of the 'proto-typical' or 'syntactic-marking' type.

2.1   Syntactically based marking

The introductory exemplification in Chapter 1 and most of the detailed discussion in later chapters deal with languages of the first type. These work in terms of the three syntactic relations S, A and O, which serve as intermediaries between meaning and grammatical marking, as shown in the top section of Table 2.1. Thus, a language with syntactically based marking will provide a description of some event in the following way: (a) that verb which most appropriately describes the activity is selected; (b) the NPs describing the participants in the activity are assigned grammatical marking according to the prototypical meaning of the verb. Languages of this type typically show valency-reducing operations such as passive, antipassive and noun incorporation. These can have a syntactic and also a semantic function. After (a) and (b) can be added: (c) syntactic derivations may then be applied, to signal a non-prototypical sense of the verb.

This can be illustrated from three widely separated languages (see also the discussion of the Australian language Yidin[y] in §3.4.1). Polinskaja and

Table 2.1. *Languages with syntactically based marking*

SEMANTICS AND DISCOURSE	BASIC SYNTACTIC RELATIONS	MORPHOLOGICAL/ SYNTACTIC REALISATIONS
prototypical meanings of verbs, and their semantic roles	A S O	grammatical marking of core syntactic relations
the actual sense of a verb in a particular instance of use	valency-reducing derivations, etc.	reassignment of marking as specified by derivations
considerations of discourse structure	clause-combining and sentence-linking operations	equi-NP omission, etc.

Nedjalkov (1987: 262–3) describe how in Chukchee a normal transitive construction, with A NP in ergative case, is preferred if the ability of the referent of the A NP to begin or stop the event at will is pragmatically relevant. In other circumstances the underlying A NP may be coded by absolutive case; this can be achieved by incorporating the object into the verb, which then becomes a derived intransitive with the erstwhile A NP becoming S, and naturally taking absolutive case. Compare:

(1)   *ətləg-e   ən-in   l'ulqəl   rə-gtəkwan-nen*
       father-ERG 3sg-POSS face + ABS CAUS-freeze-3sg + 3sg + AORIST
       father suffered frost-bite on his face

(2)   *ətləg-ən   l'o-nə-gtəkwat-g'e*
       father-ABS FACE-CAUS-freeze-3sg + AORIST
       literally: father got face frost-bitten

The transitive sentence (1) implies that father was aware of the possible consequences of his actions and might have prevented the frost-bite. In contrast, the intransitive sentence (2), with *l'o* 'face' incorporated into the verb, implies that the event could have been accidental, with father having no control over it.

The basic transitive construction in Sinhalese has the A NP in the unmarked nominative case and the O NP generally in the same case (if the O is animate, it can be optionally marked by accusative -*və*). There is a syntactic derivation that marks the verb as being in 'middle voice', puts the underlying A NP into dative or instrumental case (depending on the class of the verb), and leaves the underlying O NP as it is; this is often used to describe some event or state of affairs, for which the referent of the A NP is not in control. Compare a plain transitive clause such as (3) with the middle construction in (4):

(3)   *mamə   vaturə bivva*
       I + NOM water drink + PAST + ACTIVE
       I drink water (e.g. with my meal)

(4)   *maʈə   vaturə pevuna*
       I + DAT water drink + PAST + MIDDLE
       (when I fell into the river) I (accidentally) swallowed water

Some intransitive verbs may have their subject marked either as nominative, to describe purposeful activity, or as dative, to indicate lack of control, e.g.

(5)   *lamɘya   æñḍuva*
        child + NOM   weep + PAST + ACTIVE
        the child wept (in order to attract sympathy or attention)

(6)   *lamɘyaṭɘ   æñḍuna*
        child + DAT   weep + PAST + MIDDLE
        the child wept (involuntarily)

Sinhalese also has a passive, one of whose uses is to indicate potentiality or possibility ('A might/can do something to O'). Taking Sinhalese to be basically of the syntactically based marking type, we see that the middle and passive derivations are used to signal some non-prototypical sense of a verb.[2]

Mam, a Mayan language, also has ergative morphology, and shows both an antipassive and at least four varieties of passive derivation. Two of the latter are used to mark an instance of an activity when the agent is not in control (thus 'Miguel hit Jose' (on purpose) but 'Jose was hit by Miguel' (accidentally)) (England 1983a: 110ff., 199ff. – and see §6.1). Once again, a non-prototypical instance of use of a verb is indicated, within a language that employs syntactically based marking, by a syntactic derivation that works in terms of the basic syntactic relations, A, O and S.[3]

In English an adverb may be included to mark the type of involvement the subject has with an activity, e.g. *accidentally* in *John hit Bill accidentally* (thus showing that although John is coded as transitive subject – which is normally controller of an activity – in this instance he did not exercise volitional control). An adverb such as *nicely* will refer to the success of an activity which is, in unmarked circumstances, taken to be due to the efforts of the subject, e.g. *John played Maple Leaf Rag nicely on that old pianola.* However, in non-prototypical instances the success of an activity may be due to the referent of some constituent other than the subject. As mentioned in §1.3, English has a syntactic derivation whereby a non-subject NP can be promoted to subject slot (the original subject then being omitted) in the presence of an appropriate adverb, if the success of the activity is due to the referent of this NP, e.g. *Maple Leaf Rag played nicely*

[2] Data on Sinhalese is from Gair (1970) and Wijayawardhana, Wickramasinghe and Bynon (forthcoming; and personal communication). It is relevant to ask whether Sinhalese might not be better classed as a language of the second type, with what have been called 'active', 'middle' and 'passive' better described as variant ways of directly marking the semantic effects of the arguments of a verb in a specific instance of use. Theodora Bynon (personal communication) suggests that the language is currently moving from one type towards another, i.e. from a 'syntactic-marking' profile to a direct 'semantic-marking' one.

[3] A reflexive derivation may also be used to mark 'non-control' by the agent in some languages – see the insightful discussion in Geniušienė (1987).

on that old pianola or *That old pianola played Maple Leaf Rag nicely*. This 'promotion to subject' derivation works in terms of the basic syntactic relations, i.e. an NP which is not in subject (S or A) relation may be promoted into subject slot. (There is a full discussion in Dixon 1991a: 322–35.)

The middle portion of Table 2.1 indicates that valency-reducing and other syntactic derivations may be motivated by one of the following factors (among others):

1. to reflect a non-prototypical use of a verb, as in the Chukchee, Sinhalese, Mam and English examples mentioned;
2. to feed a syntactic pivot for operations of subordination and/or coordination (see the discussion in §1.2 and Chapter 6).

Factors 1 and 2 often interrelate. Consider a situation where Bill flings insults at John and, as a consequence, John loses control and punches Bill. According to the prototypical meaning of *punch* the person who delivers the punch should be volitional controller of the activity and mapped onto A relation, i.e. we must say *John punched Bill*. But the fact that, in this instance, Bill was really responsible for what happened, by taunting John to such an extent that he couldn't help what he did, is brought out by passivising *John punched Bill* and using the *get* passive marking which implies that the referent of the underlying O NP did something to bring upon himself what happened (see Chappell 1980; Dixon 1991a: 298ff.), i.e. *Bill got hit by John*. Suppose we want to link this to a clause describing what had happened previously, *Bill taunted John*. The passive then serves a double role, both (a) indicating that in this instance Bill was really responsible for the punch being delivered; and (b) of bringing the underlying O NP (*Bill*) into derived S slot, to meet the pivot constraint by ensuring that the two clauses have a common NP which is in A or S relation in each and can thus be omitted at its second occurrence, e.g. *Bill taunted John and got hit (by John)*. (The *by John* would normally also be omitted since, if nothing else were said, a listener would infer from extra-linguistic knowledge of how people behave that the person who was taunted would deliver the blow.)

2.2   Semantically based marking

Languages of the second type have grammatical marking which directly describes the semantics of the conceptualisation of a particular situation without this having to be related to a prototype and filtered through basic syntactic relations. This is shown in Table 2.2.

In all languages – whether marking of verbal arguments is syntactically or semantically based – verbal clauses can be divided into intransitive and transitive sets, according as they involve one core relation (S), or two (A and O). Again in both types of language, that semantic role of a verb which is most relevant to the success of the activity (if human: which could initiate or control the activity) is linked to A syntactic relation; and that role which is most saliently affected by the action is linked to O relation.

However, in a language of the second type, grammatical marking is not automatically assigned to A, S and O roles, which relate to a verb on the basis of its prototypical meaning and use. Instead, a language of this type marks NPs according to their actual role in a given instance of use of a verb.

This can be illustrated for Manipuri, a Tibeto-Burman language from north-east India. In Manipuri there are three main suffixes to nouns and pronouns: (a) *-nə*, marking the controller of an action (including natural forces like rain, wind and sunshine, which are seen as controlling certain processes or events); (b) *-bu*, marking an animate being affected by an action; and (c) *-də* (with allomorph *-ŋondə*), which can mark something indirectly involved in (or secondarily affected by) an action, e.g. goal, source, experiencer, patient, beneficiary, or can mark a location.

The suffix *-nə* is used with an NP in S or A relation, just when the referent of that NP controls the state of affairs, as it does in (7), (9) and (10) but not in (8) and (11):

(7)   *əy-nə celli*, I(-*nə*) ran
(8)   *əy sawwi*, I got angry
(9)   *əy-nə ma-bu phuy*, I(-*nə*) beat him(-*bu*)
(10)   *ma-nə əy-ŋondə yeŋŋi*, he(-*nə*) looked at me(-*də*)
(11)   *ma əy-bu uy*, he saw me(-*bu*)

Table 2.2. *Languages with semantically based marking*

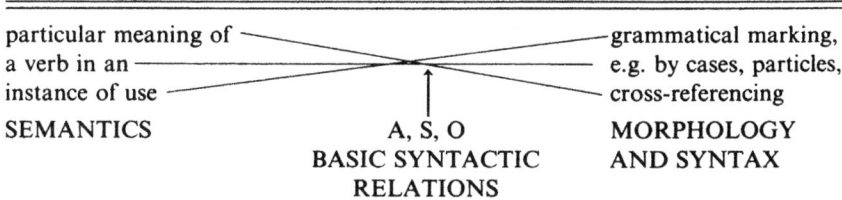

particular meaning of		grammatical marking,
a verb in an		e.g. by cases, particles,
instance of use		cross-referencing
SEMANTICS	A, S, O	MORPHOLOGY
	BASIC SYNTACTIC	AND SYNTAX
	RELATIONS	

Some verbs, both transitive and intransitive, can occur either with or without *-nə* on their A or S NP, depending on whether that instance of the activity is intentional or not, e.g.

(12)   *əy-nə Tombə-bu theŋŋi,* I(-*nə*) touched Tomba(-*bu*) intentionally

(13)   *əy Tombə-bu theŋŋi,* I touched Tomba(-*bu*) unintentionally

It can be seen that the suffix *-nə* is not marking any basic syntactic relation(s). Instead, it has a direct semantic basis, indicating an S or A argument that exercises control over an activity *in that instance.*

The suffix *-bu* marks that animate being seen as most affected by an activity. This can be an O NP, as 'him' in (9), 'me' in (11), 'Tomba' in (12–13) and 'dog' in (14). If the O is inanimate, then *-bu* can affix to an animate indirect object, e.g. to 'him' in (15); compare this with (14), where the O 'dog' is animate and thus takes *-bu,* with the recipient 'him' being here marked by *-də*.

(14)   *əy-nə ma-ŋondə huy-bu pi,* I(-*nə*) gave a dog(-*bu*) to him(-*də*)

(15)   *əy-nə ma-bu sel pi,* I(-*nə*) gave money to him(-*bu*)

In a causative construction (marked by suffix *-hən,* non-future form *-həlli*), the causer NP is necessarily in control and takes *-nə*. The causee (subject of the underlying non-causal clause) cannot take *-nə* but will take *-bu* (since it is 'affected' by being made to do something) unless there is already an animate NP as O or an indirect object which has a stronger claim for this 'affected status' marker, as there is in (18); in this case the causee takes *-də*.

(16)   *ma-nə əy-bu kəp-həlli,* he(-*nə*) made me(-*bu*) cry

(17)   *ma-nə əy-bu layrik pa-həlli,* he(-*nə*) made me(-*bu*) read the book

(18)   *əy-nə ma-ŋondə Tombə-bu il-həlli,* I(-*nə*) made him(-*də*) push Tomba(-*bu*)

Like *-nə, -bu* appears not to be marking any specific syntactic relation(s), but rather to have a direct semantic effect.

In languages of the first type the basic syntactic relations play a crucial role as intermediaries between the semantics of a situation and grammatical marking. In languages of the second type the grammatical marking directly reflects the actual semantic role of a core NP. Information on Manipuri comes from Bhat (1988, 1991, ms.) and Bhat and Ningomba (ms.), who in fact use traditional case labels – nominative for *-nə,* accusative for *-bu* and locative for *-də,* although with explanation that these 'cases' have semantic rather than strictly syntactic use. I consider it best to restrict case labels such as nominative, accusative, absolutive and ergative to languages with syntactically based marking where they indicate syntactic relations, and to use other, semantically based, labels for *-nə*, *-bu* and *-də* in Manipuri.

It appears that the universal syntactic relations A, S and O do still have a place in the grammar of a semantically based marking language like Manipuri, although not so central a role as in a language with syntactically based marking. Suffix *-nə* marks an A or S which is controller in that instance of an activity; for an intransitive verb the controller can only be S, and for a transitive verb it can only be A, from our definition of A as 'that semantic role which could exercise control, if anything could'. Suffix *-bu* marks an animate being affected by an action (carried out by someone else); *-bu* will go onto the O NP if it satisfies the semantic criterion; otherwise this suffix will go onto the indirect object of a verb like 'give', as in (15); if neither O nor indirect object are marked by *-bu* then the suffix may go onto a causee NP, as in (16–17).[4] Although *-nə* and *-bu* mark semantic relations, they are used within a grammatical framework defined by A, S and O.

We mentioned how in languages with syntactically based marking there are often (although not always) a number of valency-reducing derivations (e.g. passive, antipassive, noun incorporation), operating in terms of A, S and O, which can adapt the prototypical grammatical markings to the actual meaning of a given situation, when this diverges from the prototype. From the information available, it appears that languages with semantically based marking generally lack derivations of this kind.[5] Since A, S and O play a less central role in their grammars they would – on a priori grounds – be less likely to have operations that switch around A, S and O. And they have much less need of such manipulation, since they already use grammatical marking directly to reflect the semantics of a given use of a verb (rather than some prototypical use).

It does, however, seem that languages of the second type, like those of the first type, typically show a causative derivation, which involves adding a causer NP to a transitive or intransitive clause of the appropriate semantic kind. This can be periphrastic (e.g. English *She made him give it to the dog*) or it may involve a verbal derivational affix, as in Manipuri.

---

[4] Fuller information on these nominal suffixes is in Bhat and Ningomba (ms.).

[5] Note, though, that Manipuri does have reflexive and reciprocal constructions, marked by derivational affixes *-jə-* and *-nə-* respectively on the verb; here 'one of the two coreferential arguments is generally left unspecified'. Note that 'it is not necessary for the two coreferential arguments to include one that has suffix *-nə-*; it is quite possible for the two arguments to have suffixes *-bu* and *-də*' (Bhat ms.).

Folopa, from the Teberan family of Papua New Guinea, also has characteristics of the second type. Anderson and Wade (1988)[6] describe how core NPs can be marked by the suffix -*nɛ* (or by set I of pronouns) or else left unmarked (corresponding to set II of pronouns). They then point out that some intransitive verbs can take either -*nɛ* or zero on their S NP (these include 'laugh', 'go', 'come', 'get mad') while others allow only zero marking (including 'die', 'grow', 'stand', 'sleep'). And that among transitive verbs some must have -*nɛ* on their A NP (e.g. 'hit/kill', 'send a message'), some may alternate -*nɛ* and zero (e.g. 'eat', 'cook', 'give', 'evaluate', 'get', 'do/say'), while others can never have -*nɛ* (e.g. 'dislike', 'like'). There is a semantic basis to these alternative markings of A and S; the -*nɛ* suffix indicates that the actor is acting independently, is self-motivated, and exerts personal control over the situation, while its lack may indicate that the actor is performing according to his set social obligations, not according to his own independent will (see Foley 1986: 108).

Examples of a transitive verb being used with its A NP marked in two different ways are given at (19–20). In (19) the set II pronominal form, *ɛ*, corresponds to a noun in zero inflection, while in (20) the set I pronoun, *yalo*, corresponds to -*nɛ* on a noun:

(19)   *no-ó   kale naao o   make ɛ   di-ale-pó*
        brother-VOC the   your sago young I(set II) cut down-PAST-INDIC
        brother, I (mistakenly) cut down your young sago tree

(20)   *no-ó naao o make yalo di-ale-pó*
        brother, I (intentionally) cut down your young sago tree

Anderson and Wade assign the label 'ergative' to -*nɛ* and 'absolutive' to zero, but – just as with Bhat's use of nominative and accusative for Manipuri – these syntactic labels seem inappropriate for a language with semantically based marking. The suffix -*nɛ* simply marks whether, in some particular instance of an activity, the S or A NP is an independent, self-motivated controller. It is clear that -*nɛ* in Folopa has a similar function to -*nə* in Manipuri. The inappropriateness of normal case labels for languages with semantically based marking is brought out by the fact that Bhat uses 'nominative' for -*nə* while Anderson and Wade employ 'ergative' for -*nɛ*.

---

[6] In a mimeo draft of this paper, circulated some years earlier, the language is called Podopa (as it is in Foley 1986).

We could use the label 'controller' for both -nǝ in Manipuri and -nε in Folopa, with the understanding that this term has a recurrent central meaning but also slight differences of scope as it is used of different languages (as, indeed, do labels such as 'accusative' and 'ergative').

From the limited information available on Folopa it appears that zero is the unmarked inflection for an NP in S function (some intransitive verbs only take zero, some alternate zero and -nε, none are confined to -nε), and perhaps -nε is the unmarked inflection for A (although there are some transitive verbs, 'like' and 'dislike', which may never take -nε). Discussing Timbe, the only other language in the Teberan family, Whitehead (1981–2: 50) comments that clauses elicited in isolation give the impression that it is an ergative language, with A case-marked by -ne and S by zero. 'In texts, however, there is no more than 60% consistency with this usage; instead it becomes clear that the function of -ne is to indicate the controlling entities.'

In Table 2.1 we indicated that, for languages with syntactically based marking, the basic syntactic relations S, A and O are the basis for operations of clause conjoining. This also applies in Folopa which has a switch-reference system where suffixes on a medial verb indicate whether the subject (S or A) of the following verb has the same or different reference as the subject of this medial verb. Bhat (ms.: 34–5) reports that Manipuri has no syntactic constraints on coordination, i.e. it does not work in terms of a syntactic pivot as do many languages of our first type. It would be in keeping with the low profile of A, S and O in languages with semantically based marking for pivot constraints and markings to be rare (but not unknown – as attested by the switch-reference suffixes in Folopa).

There are undoubtedly other languages, from other parts of the world, which are basically of the second type, with marking of NPs directly mirroring the semantics of each situation of use. But since most languages are of the first type, with the arguments of each verb marked according to a prototypical matrix, irrespective of the semantics of a particular situation of use, linguists have taken this as the only grammatical pattern and tried to describe languages of the second type within this model, then commenting on their aberrant features. It is not easy to identify languages that have direct semantic marking, when they are treated in such a manner.

In a masterly paper, Bashir (1986) points out that Wakhi (or Waxi), a South-eastern Iranian language belonging to the Pamir subgroup (spoken along the border between Afghanistan and Tadjikstan) 'is usually characterised as having a split-ergative system in the process of re-evolution into a nominative-accusative system'. She then points out that case marking is not 'syntactically determined', i.e. does not follow a prototypical pattern, and thus labels such as 'ergative' and 'accusative' are not appropriate.

In Wakhi both transitive and intransitive subjects can be marked in either of two ways, by what have been called NOM(inative) and OBL(ique) cases. John Payne (1980: 182) stated that these two cases were 'in free variation ... in both transitive and intransitive sentences in the upper dialect of Waxi', while Lashkarbekov (1982, 1985) said that the two constructions were functionally equivalent. However, Bashir maintains that the choice of NOM or OBL subject marking is conditioned and that 'the conditioning factors appear to be related on the one hand to the perceived semantics of the action involved rather than to the inherent lexical semantics of a given verb, and on the other to discourse structure.' She gives extensive textual examples in support of the idea that

> an OBL subject will be more likely to appear when one or all of the following conditions obtains: (1) The action is performed as volitional and active rather than as 'passive' or stative; (2) the referential identity of the subject is to be stressed; (3) within a discourse, the subject or topic is 'new' or different from the subject of the preceding action; this new or changed discourse topic is often initiating an action important in advancing the story line of the narrative.

In conclusion, we must again stress that the syntactically based marking and semantically based marking profiles, as described here, are idealisations and that actual languages do appear to mingle both kinds of strategy. Most languages are predominantly of the first type with a few semantic-marking characteristics, while others – like Manipuri, Folopa and Wakhi – are predominantly of the second type. In describing languages of the latter type we need to make some reference to S, A and O; these syntactic relations do not mediate between semantics and grammatical marking in the way they do for languages of the first type, but they are still required for an explanation of some aspects of grammatical behaviour.

The discussion in this chapter has been exploratory, mainly oriented towards alerting other linguists to the existence of languages where the marking on NP arguments is predominantly semantically based. These should be described in their own terms, and not in terms of unprincipled deviations from a template that is appropriate for a language with syntactically based marking. It would not be appropriate, within the context of a book such as this (dealing with syntactic patterns in languages with syntactically based marking) to embark on a full assessment of languages with semantically based marking. Indeed, there is relatively little information readily available on languages of the second type, although I suspect that they are commoner than one might think. Once systematic studies of a number of languages with semantically based marking are available, it will be possible to attempt surer generalisations about them. The main point to be made here is that languages of this second type should not be described as wholly or partly ergative (or accusative). Traditional case labels evolved in the study of languages with syntactically based marking must be confined to such languages.[7]

Nevertheless, we shall have occasion to refer again to the kind of direct marking shown in Table 2.2. What are called 'fluid-S languages', in §4.1.2, are a mixture, being of the first type in the grammatical marking associated with transitive verbs, but of the second type in the way they deal with intransitive verbs, and in their lack of syntactic pivot constraints (that must operate in terms of A, S and O).

Appendix: Both kinds of marking in one language

One possibility I have not yet mentioned is for a language to effectively combine the two possibilities, having one kind of marking for A, S and O (in terms of the prototypical meaning of each verb) and another kind of marking that directly reflects what is happening in each particular instance of use of the verb.

There is a hint that this might be the case in languages of the Muskogean family. In Choctaw-Chickasaw,[8] for example, a set of case markers appears on NPs and is clearly syntactically based – the suffix -*t* (with allomorphic variants) marks A and S. Then there is another, independent

[7] Russian linguists, such as Kibrik (e.g. 1990), would disagree with me on this point, referring to 'semantically ergative/accusative' (in addition to 'syntactically ergative/accusative') languages. Kibrik states (personal communication): 'I think that semantically-motivated sentence constructions are the most prototypic typologically and primary historically.' This indicates a difference in approach. In this book I maintain 'ergative' and 'accusative' as labels exclusively for types of syntactic organisation; and I do not take any stance on which of 'syntactically based marking' and 'semantically based marking' is historically prior (indeed, I would predict that a language could move from one type to the other and back again, given sufficient time – see Chapter 7).

[8] This discussion of Choctaw-Chickasaw (which are dialects of one language and have similar but far from identical properties) is based on Byington (1870), Heath (1977), Munro and Gordon (1982), Doris Payne (1982), Davies (1986). I am aware that there are other source materials (unpublished PhD dissertations by Nicklas, Ulrich and Broadwell, for instance). I have tried here to make some general remarks, rather than give any sort of definitive assessment.

system of marking in the form of cross-referencing affixes to the verb, and it is this which appears to be largely semantically based.

There are three[9] sets of pronominal affixes to the verb (although no more than two can occur in any one verb word), each marking person and number. They have been given various names in the literature – Munro and Gordon (1982) simply use the labels I, II and III, Davies (1986) employs 'nominative', 'accusative' and 'dative', while Doris Payne (1982) prefers 'agent', 'patient' and 'dative'. For intransitive verbs, S can be marked by any of these sets, e.g. 'run' and 'go' take Agent, 'be hungry' and 'be tired' take Patient, while 'be lazy' and 'be crippled' take Dative. Some intransitive verbs may occur, in different circumstances, with different affix sets.

Many transitive verbs also show a great deal of variation in the way their core NPs are cross-referenced. For 'cut' and 'bite', A is marked by Agent affixes and O by the Patient set. For 'doctor' and 'comb', A is again cross-referenced by Agent but O can be either Patient or Dative. For 'want' and 'believe', O is Patient and A can be either Agent or Patient. For 'hate' and 'pity' O is Dative and A can be Agent or Patient. For 'be tired of' and 'forget' there are two quite different patterns – either A is Agent and O Dative, or A is Dative and O Patient.

There is no doubt that this use of the three verbal affix sets to cross-reference arguments of the verb is, at least partly, dependent on the actual meaning of a verb as determined by a particular instance of use. Munro and Gordon (1982: 81–4) mention that the verb *chokma* 'be good' means 'I act good', 'I am good' and 'I feel good' when used with Agent, Patient and Dative first person affixes respectively; and that with Patient affixes *hotolhko* means 'cough' but with Agent affixes it is best glossed 'cough on purpose'. Payne provides a useful preliminary discussion of the uses of the three affix sets: 'Agent affixes ... refer to a participant which is the potentially volitional instigator of the action of the verb.' Patient affixes have a number of uses, including marking

> the majority of S nominals which are less likely to be seen as potentially volitional instigators of the action or state expressed by the verb than would those participants referred to by Agent affixes ... Patient affixes are used to mark Os which are directly affected by the action of the verb, which are highly involved in the action of the verb, or where the action is aimed directly at the O ... [They] can be used to mark the A of some nonvolitional two-argument verbs such as *nokfonkha* 'remember'.

[9] There is a rather minor fourth set, Benefactive, which is an alternative to Dative (see Davies 1986).

She also points out that for many (although not all) verbs that have S cross-referenced by the Dative set, the verb describes a 'temporary or nonpredominant characteristic of the S', e.g. 'feel good', 'be ready', 'be tired/worn out'. Payne's semantic characterisations explain some aspects of the use of pronominal prefixes in this language, but by no means all of them.

There are a number of difficulties in the way of any assessment of the situation in Choctaw-Chickasaw and other Muskogean languages. One is that different sources provide variant information. Byington (1870) gave 'to sleep' as an example of a verb taking either Agent or Patient marking. Heath (1977) stated that he 'encountered no systematic use of variation in case-marking with individual roots for marking nuances, as Byington suggested'. But then Munro and Gordon, Davies and Doris Payne each noted variations in affix choice that have clear semantic bases. It seems that different modern speakers allow different degrees of fluidity (perhaps at least partly due to contact with English, whose marking of core arguments is predominantly syntactically based). Some maintain what may have been the original scheme of marking, which directly reflects the meaning in each situation of use, while others have extracted from this a prototypical pattern, reinterpreting Choctaw-Chickasaw grammar as being more syntactically based.

A good deal of the work on Muskogean languages has treated them as languages of the first type, with some odd characteristics. An alternative would be a thorough descriptively oriented study of the languages from the point of view of the second type, to discover the extent to which their verbal marking of syntactic functions is a direct reflection of the semantics of individual situations of use of a verb, side by side with the prototype-based system of case marking on NPs, which plainly is of the first type. The most fascinating and elusive feature of Choctaw-Chickasaw concerns the meanings and rules for use of the three affix sets – Agent can be used for A and S, and both Patient and Dative for all of A, S and O, in the appropriate circumstances. ('Agent' and 'Patient' may turn out not to be the most suitable labels – but they are certainly better than 'nominative' and 'accusative'.)

Although Muskogean languages appear to operate with both syntactically based and semantically based types of marking, these two systems could not really be said to be superimposed. Jack Martin (personal communication) points out that syntactically based marking is predominantly associated with third person (i.e. free NP constituents) while the semantically based pronominal affixes to verbs largely relate to first and second person (both Agent and Patient are zero for third person and while dative has a non-zero form for third person, it does not distinguish number; all of Agent, Patient and Dative have different forms for first person singular, first person plural, second person singular and second person plural – e.g. Doris Payne 1982: 359).[10] We thus have, effectively, a 'split' between our two types of marking within a single language, the split itself being semantically conditioned.

[10] A similar point is made by Kimball (1991) in the course of an illuminating discussion of types of marking in Koasati.

3   Intra-clausal or morphological ergativity

Every language has intransitive clauses, with a predicate and a single core argument (that we call S) and transitive clauses, with a predicate and two core arguments (A and O). There should always be the means to distinguish A and O. Some languages do this by constituent order (e.g. English), some use cases, particles or adpositions, and some employ pronominal cross-referencing on the verb (many languages employ a combination of these strategies). The marking of core syntactic relations – A, S and O – is generally referred to as 'morphological ergativity' or 'morphological accusativity' since this is generally shown by case inflections or verbal cross-referencing affixes. A more exact label would be 'intra-clausal ergativity/accusativity', since particles and adpositions make use of a syntactic – not a morphological – mechanism, and constituent order is without doubt a matter of syntax.

There must be some means of distinguishing A and O for a transitive clause. The marking of S in an intransitive clause can be the same as A, or the same as O, or different from both. There are thus three basic possibilities:[1]

1. S = O (absolutive), A different (ergative) – an ergative system
2. S = A (nominative), O different (accusative) – an accusative system
3. A, S and O all different – this is a 'three-way' or 'tripartite' system.

[1] John Payne (1980: 155) reports that the Iranian language Rushan uses oblique case marking for both A and O (and direct case for S) in past tenses only; in present tense, direct case is used for S and A and oblique for O. In this language the verb cross-references S or A, never O. Payne indicates how this case-marking system arose and states that younger speakers are making various changes, including generalising the nominative–accusative case marking of present tense into the past tenses (see the discussion in §7.2). This is what we would expect – surely marking A and O in the same way (differently from S) must be an unstable and temporary situation, only encountered as a language moves from one more stable kind of marking to another.

The accusative pattern is, of course, commonest among the languages of the world. The ergative pattern, with which this book is concerned, is by no means uncommon. In contrast, the tripartite alternative is extremely rare. A major reason for this lies in the fact that S is in some ways similar to O and in other ways similar to A (see §3.3), so that languages tend to incorporate one of these patterns of similarity into their grammars ('split-S' and 'fluid-S' languages incorporate both patterns – see §4.1). A further factor may be the desire for economy – there should be distinctive markings for A and O (one of which can be zero) but since S occurs in a different clause type there is no need for a further kind of marking; S can most economically be given the same grammatical treatment as either A or O.

§§3.1, 3.2 briefly survey the available mechanisms for indicating syntactic function, in terms of possibilities 1–3; §3.3 then examines the semantic bases of the alternatives; §3.4 discusses markedness within nominative–accusative and absolutive–ergative case systems.

3.1   Types of marking of core syntactic relations

3.1.1   Case inflections

These have already been illustrated (in §1.2) for Latin and Dyirbal, accusative and ergative languages respectively. The ways in which case is marked on an NP can vary: the inflection can occur just on the head word, or just on a word of a certain word class, or just on the last word, or on every word (or sometimes, on every word *only* if they are non-contiguous, being distributed through the sentence). These details are essentially irrelevant to the present discussion. What is significant is whether case is obligatorily marked on an NP (as in Latin and Dyirbal); or whether it is optional, being included only when ambiguity would otherwise result (see §3.4).

I have said that tripartite systems – in which S, A and O are always marked differently – are rare. John Payne (1980: 175) mentions that Yazgulyam, from the South-east Iranian subgroup of Indo-European, has tripartite marking only in past tense. Sometimes just a small subclass of NP constituents can receive tripartite marking (those from a middle portion of the Nominal Hierarchy – see §4.2). Motu, from New Guinea, has some-times been cited as a language with consistently tripartite marking, on the basis of the slender data provided in Capell (1969: 36, 43, 54); more careful examination of the language indicates that this is not an accurate characterisation.[2] Main clauses in Dhalanji, from Western Australia, have A marked by ergative case, *-lu ~ -ŋgu*, and O by accusative case, *-nha*, while S is unmarked. There is, however, an exception – the first person singular pronoun has the same form for S and A (but does add *-nha* for O) (Austin 1981c: 216). We can reconstruct an earlier stage of the language in which pronouns showed no inflection for S and A but added *-nha* for O, while nouns had no inflection for S and O but added *-lu ~ -ŋgu* for A; these A and O case markings have now been generalised across all NP constituents, save the first person singular pronoun. A group of Australian languages from south-east Queensland, including Wangkumara (Breen 1976) and Galali (McDonald and Wurm 1979) have also been reported to have distinct marking for S, A and O across all NP constituents.

3.1.2   *Particles and adpositions*

Particles and adpositions (i.e. prepositions and postpositions) can be used to mark syntactic function and show exactly the same possibilities as case systems. Since a particle or adposition usually has the phonological status accorded to a 'separate word', there will normally be only one occurrence of the particle in an NP, whereas a case inflection may be added to each word; but this is not significant for the present discussion. What can complicate the syntactic picture is the tendency of particles to combine information about syntactic function and 'topic', as in Japanese (e.g. Kuno 1973: 37–123; Shibatani 1990: 333–57).

An ergative system of function-marking particles is found in Tongan, from the Polynesian subgroup of Austronesian (Churchward 1953: 68):

(1)   *na'e lea* [*'a Tolu*]ₛ Tolu spoke
(2)   *na'e lea* [*'a e talavou*]ₛ the young man spoke

---

[2] As Lister-Turner and Clark (1930: 34ff.) point out, the syntactic function of an NP in a Motu sentence is 'indicated by the demonstrative adjectives or articles *ese, se, be,* and *na*; by suffixes; by prepositions; and sometimes by the position of the word in the sentence'. The ergative particle *ese* is used when it is not clear on semantic or other grounds which NP is A, and which is O (see §3.4.1). The particle *na*, said by Capell to mark S function, has complex behaviour which is far from being fully understood – it can be used as the copula in verbless sentences; it may occur after an S NP; and it is occasionally found after an O NP, most commonly when the constituent order is OAV rather than the more usual AOV. In addition, *na* is sometimes encountered after an A NP, with the sequence *ese na* being attested. The use of *na* characterises the western dialect; it is used much less in eastern Motu. (I am grateful to Andrew Taylor for all this information.)

(3)   *na'e tāmate'i* [*'a e talavou*]$_O$ [*'e Tolu*]$_A$ Tolu killed the youth
(4)   *na'e tāmate'i* [*'a Tolu*]$_O$ [*'e he talavou*]$_A$ the youth killed Tolu

A sentence in Tongan begins with the predicate, which includes a tense
marker (here *na'e* 'past') and then a verb – intransitive *lea* 'speak' in (1–2)
and transitive *tāmate'i* 'kill' in (3–4). An S or O NP is introduced by the
absolutive particle *'a* and an A NP by the ergative particle *'e* (note that *'*
indicates a glottal stop). A common noun, such as *talavou* 'young man'
will be preceded by an article, here the definite article *e ~ he*. Note that the
A and O NPs can occur in either order following the predicate in (3–4),
their functions being fully specified by the case particles *'a* and *'e*.

A fairly small number of languages use particles or adpositions for
marking core syntactic functions. There are accusative and ergative
examples but no examples are known of a tripartite system.

3.1.3   Cross-referencing

A verb or verbal auxiliary may include bound affixes etc., which provide
information about the person and/or number and/or gender etc. of NPs in
certain syntactic functions. There is tremendous variation as to how much
information is 'cross-referenced' in the verb, and how it is realised.[3]
English shows minimal cross-referencing (a relic of a more extensive
system in earlier stages of the language): most verbs have two 'present-
tense' forms, indicating whether or not the subject is third person singular
(e.g. *walks* vs. *walk*).

The patterning of bound pronominal affixes in the verbal word can be
taken as evidence of intra-clausal accusativity or ergativity, just like the
patterning of case inflections. If a certain affix cross-references an NP that
is in S or A function, with a different affix referring to an NP that is in O
function, then the language can be characterised as 'nominative–
accusative' at this level.

Consider some sample sentences in Swahili (from the Bantu subgroup of
Niger-Congo):

(5)   *tu-li-anguka*, we fell down
(6)   *m-li-anguka*, you all fell down

---

[3] Familiar cross-referencing systems involve person and number, or person alone.
Frajzyngier (1984a, b) describes how the verb in some Chadic languages (and perhaps also
in proto-Chadic) agrees with S or O just in number.

(7)   *m-li-tu-ona*, you all saw us
(8)   *tu-li-wa-ona*, we saw you all

These reveal a pronominal prefix paradigm:

(9)   S/A   O
         we   *tu-*   *-tu-*
         you all   *m-*   *-wa-*

Note that the same form, *-tu-*, is used to cross-reference S, A and O in the first person plural. The existence of one form for S/A, but another for O, in the second person plural (as well as in second person singular and third person singular) establishes an 'accusative' pattern. Perhaps the most important detail here is the *position* of the pronominal affix within the word: bound forms which cross-reference S or A occur word-initially, whereas the affix which refers to the O NP comes between tense (here, 'past' *-li-*) and the root.

We will now give examples from two languages that have an 'ergative' system of cross-referencing, where one affix cross-references S or O, and another affix relates to A. First, Abaza of the North-west Caucasian family (Allen 1956):

(10)   *d-θád*,   he/she's gone
(11)   *h-θád*,   we've gone
(12)   *h-l-bád*,   she saw us
(13)   *h-y-bád*,   he saw us
(14)   *d-h-bád*,   we saw him/her

Here we have a pronominal prefix paradigm:

(15)   S/O   A
         we   *h-*   *-h-*
         he   ⎫   *d-*   ⎰ *-y-*
         she   ⎭   ⎱ *-l-*

As with Swahili, some of the forms are identical between the two columns. The fixed order of prefixes (S–V, O–A–V) enables us to tell that *-h-* is referring to a first person plural A in (14) and S or O in (11–13).[4]

---

[4] In fact the forms of S/O and of A bound pronominals differ only for third person and for 'relative' choices. Note also that as many as four NPs may be cross-referenced on the verb in Abaza – e.g. causative agent, subject, object and indirect object, as in 'The old man couldn't make the boys give the girl her dog back' (Allen 1956: 139 and personal communication).

Languages of the Mayan family also have one set of affixes cross-referencing A (it is a tradition in Mayan studies to label this 'set A') and another set ('set B') cross-referencing S and O. The examples here are taken from Sacapultec Maya (Du Bois 1987b: 205). Note that each verb begins here with the 'completive aspect marker' *š-*, and ends with a 'transitivity marker', intransitive *-ek* on *-ak-* 'enter' in (16–17) and transitive *-aŋ* on *-č'iy-* 'hit' in (18–19).

(16)   *š-at-ak-ek*, you(sg.) entered
(17)   *š-∅-ak-ek*, he/she entered
(18)   *š-at-ri-č'iy-aŋ*, he/she hit you
(19)   *š-∅-a:-č' iy-aŋ*, you(sg.) hit him/her

The prefix paradigm is:

(20)   S/O (set B)   A (set A)
        you(sg.)   *-at-*   *-a:-*
        he/she   *-∅-*   *-ri-*

Again, the order of prefixes is fixed; the set B form always precedes the set A choice, with a transitive verb. The interesting point here is that there is just one zero term in the pronominal prefix systems, and it marks third person singular in set B. Note how this correlates with the occurrence of zero in ergative case-marking systems – it is always absolutive that has zero realisation (or a zero allomorph), never ergative.[5]

Some accusative languages, such as those of the Indo-European family, cross-reference S and A on the verb, but not O. In similar fashion, some ergative languages cross-reference S and O, but not A (e.g. Canelo-Krahô from the Jê family, in Central Brazil – Popjes and Popjes 1986; and Avar, from the North-east Caucasian family – Černý 1971; Charachidzé 1981). The Nilotic language Päri shows a number of ergative features, including A being cross-referenced on the verb in one type of construction, but never S or O; see examples (23–5) in §3.2. (Andersen 1988). However, I do not know of any accusative language that consistently cross-references O, but not S or A.

In some languages what were originally distinct affixes cross-referencing A and O have merged into a single portmanteau form which is not synchronically analysable. In such a language we would have to admit that S is marked in a different way from A and O, as a rather special kind of

---

[5] This also shows that third person singular is the unmarked person/number combination (as it also is in the diachronic restructuring of paradigms – see Kuryłowicz 1964: 148ff.; Arlotto 1972: 154–8).

tripartite marking. But in almost all such cases the portmanteau forms have developed from an agglutinative structure in which there were segmentable A and O affixes, and one of them was identical or closely similar to the S set of cross-referencing forms. (See, among many other examples, Hinton and Langdon 1976.)

I know of no language that has different, segmentable, sets of verbal affixes for each of S, A and O across all tenses and aspects. However, in the Mayan language Chorti (Quizar and Knowles-Berry 1988) prefix set A is used for A function, set B for O and a set C for S in imperfective aspect; but in the perfective there is the familiar absolutive–ergative pattern, with set B used for both S and O, and set A for A.

In cross-referencing languages such as Swahili, Abaza and Sacapultec Maya a clause can – as in the examples given – consist just of a verb word, since this includes specification of core NPs. Such clauses can of course be expanded by NPs providing more information about the referents of S, or of A and/or O.

Cross-referencing affixes typically provide information about the person and/or number of the core arguments of the verb. This can provide a unique specification in the case of first and second persons but not for third person. Many languages do have a number of third person verbal affixes, showing gender or noun class (Swahili, for instance, has no less than sixteen choices combining information about noun class and number). But there are always instances where both A and O belong to the same gender or noun class, and one cannot tell from the forms of cross-referencing affixes who is doing what to who. For a sentence like 'girl man he(A)-her(O)-hit' we know the meaning can only be 'the man hit the girl' whereas in the case of 'man boy he(A)-him(O)-hit' it could be either 'the man hit the boy' or 'the boy hit the man'. Thus, a cross-referencing system – however fully articulated – is never an absolutely sufficient marker of syntactic function. There should always be some 'back-up' grammatical mechanism, e.g. an optional accusative or ergative marking on NPs (see §3.4) or a constituent order in which A and O NPs occur in fixed order (perhaps only in the circumstance that syntactic function is not recoverable from cross-referencing in the verb, or from contextual information).

3.1.4 *Two cross-referencing mechanisms*

Most languages that show cross-referencing have means for cross-referencing two NPs (just occasionally they may cross-reference three or even four NPs – see note 4 on Abaza). That is, in the verb of a transitive clause there will be one bound pronominal series cross-referencing A and one cross-referencing O, as in our Swahili, Abaza and Sacapultec Maya examples. S may be cross-referenced by the same series as A (an accusative pattern) or by the same series as O (an ergative pattern). Cross-referencing systems that refer to both A and O are found in many of the languages of Africa, Australia, North and Central America and the Caucasus.

What is much less common, across the languages of the world, is for the verb to cross-reference just one core argument. This is found among languages of the Indo-European family (where S is cross-referenced on an intransitive and A on a transitive verb). The Amazon basin, in South America, contains an amazing genetic diversity of languages, yet many of them share a number of areal features. One is that there should be just one pronominal affix to a verb. With a transitive verb this sometimes refers to A and sometimes to O, giving rise to a number of complex types of 'split-ergativity', that we survey in Chapter 4.

In Gavião (which is spoken in the Brazilian state of Rondônia and belongs to the small Mondé family within the Tupí stock) canonical clause structure contains one or more verbs preceded by an auxiliary (although the verb can be fronted to precede the auxiliary). The auxiliary must either be preceded by an explicit NP in S or A function, or it takes a pronominal prefix indicating person and number of S or A. A transitive verb root must either be preceded by an explicit NP in O function (this comes between auxiliary and verb) or it takes a pronominal prefix which indicates person and number of O. If the verb is intransitive, it has a prefix cross-referencing S. Thus we get the possibility of a single pronominal prefix onto each of auxiliary and verb – the auxiliary prefix refers to S or A and the verb prefix refers to S or O. The two prefix paradigms have exactly the same form except that third person singular on a verb (copying third singular S prefix on the auxiliary) has a different form from the regular third person singular prefix. (Data from Moore 1984 and personal communication.)

Thus, while Gavião maintains the areal feature of allowing only one pronominal prefix per word, it manages to refer to both A and O by requiring each verb to be accompanied by an auxiliary and making two choices from the prefix system, one on the auxiliary for A and one on the verb for O.[6]

Let us now look at cross-referencing in Jarawara, from the small Arawá

---

[6] Surui, another language from the Mondé family, behaves in a similar way – see Van der Meer (1985).

family,[7] in the Brazilian state of Amazonas (although Jarawara is spoken just a few score miles from Gavião there is no proven genetic relationship). Here there are two systems of cross-referencing on the verb and both are obligatory, irrespective of whether or not A, S and O are shown by NPs (unlike Gavião, where the pronominal prefixes are not used when there are explicit NPs). The centre of each clause is the predicate which begins with two obligatory bound pronominal slots (some of the fillers are words and others are prefixes); the fillers of the first slot cross-reference O and those of the second slot S or A. There is then a verb root and (for one class of verbs) an auxiliary. A number of suffixes (all optional) attach to auxiliary or verb; most of the suffixes come in two forms, feminine and masculine.[8] There are two varieties of transitive construction, one where the A argument continues an established topic (the 'A-construction') and one where the O argument continues an established topic (the 'O-construction'). The verbal suffixes cross-reference the gender of S in an intransitive clause, of A in an A-construction, and of O in an O-construction. The following examples illustrate this gender agreement (note that third person singular has zero realisation in both O and S/A pre-verbal slots, so these sentences do not illustrate the exclusively nominative–accusative predicate-initial cross-referencing system):

(21)   *jomee   to-ko-me,*   *fana*
        jaguar AWAY-go-RETURN + MASC woman
          kabe-hino-ka
          eat-PAST + MASC-DECL + MASC
        the jaguar went back and ate the woman

(22)   *fana   to-ko-ma,*   *jomee*
        woman AWAY-GO-RETURN + FEM JAGUAR
          hi-kaba-hani-ke
          PREFIX-eat-PAST + FEM-DECL + FEM

        the woman went back and the jaguar ate her

The first clause in (21) is intransitive with a masculine S NP, *jomee* 'jaguar', and the 'return' suffix to the verb takes masculine form, *-me*. In the first

---

[7]   A similar set of two cross-referencing systems is found in other languages from the Arawá family, e.g. Chapman and Derbyshire (1991) on Paumarí.

[8]   Feminine is the unmarked term from this two-term system. All pronouns are cross-referenced as feminine. Animate plural must be marked by a third person plural pronoun within the predicate and so animate plural NPs (whether the head noun is feminine or masculine) are cross-referenced as feminine. Masculine forms of verbal suffixes are thus used only for singular animate masculine (including sun, moon and star) and all inanimate masculine (for which no number distinction applies).

clause of (22) the S NP is feminine and here the 'return' suffix has feminine form, -*ma*. The second clause of (21) is an A-construction with the A NP again *jomee* 'jaguar' (it is not repeated in this clause); here the immediate past non-eyewitness tense marker shows masculine form -*hino*- (with the preceding stem-final *a* changing to *e*) and the declarative verbal suffix also shows masculine form -*ka*. In (22) the second clause is an O-construction, marked by prefix *hi*-(more specifically, this is used when both A and O are third person, in an O-construction); the A NP is stated as *jomee* and the O NP, which is not explicitly stated, is taken to be identical to the S NP of the first clause, i.e. *fana* 'woman'. The verb *kaba* 'eat' in (22) bears the feminine form of the immediate past non-eyewitness tense, -*hani*-, and also the feminine form of the declarative suffix, -*ke*, showing that it is here cross-referencing the O NP. (Note that for the 'return' suffix final *a* is feminine and final *e* masculine while for the 'declarative' suffix this vowel alternation is reversed.) (Data on Jarawara from Vogel 1989 and my own field work.)

There are also two mechanisms for cross-referencing in Koiari, a Papuan language from New Guinea. Tom Dutton reports (personal communication) that verbs in Koiari have suffixes indicating number (singular or plural) of S or O, followed by a tense/aspect suffix which also encodes some information concerning the person and number of S or A.

We saw that languages such as Swahili, Abaza and Sacapultec Maya have two bound pronominal slots in the verb, but these operate as a *single* system; one cross-references person and number (and perhaps gender) of A and the other provides similar information about O (with S falling together with one of these). In Jarawara, however, we have *two* independent cross-referencing systems, conveying different sorts of information (person and number for the pre-verbal system, gender for the post-verbal one) and operating on different grammatical principles (O marked in one slot and S or A in the other for pre-verbal slots; either S and A, or S and O, marked in the same way by suffixes). Koiari operates on similar principles. Gavião is somewhere between these – it has a single system (which always refers to person and number) that can apply twice in each clause, once cross-referencing S or A, the other time S or O.

Whereas the cross-referencing systems discussed in §3.1.3 can be simply characterised as accusative or ergative, in Jarawara, Koiari and Gavião we have *two* mechanisms related to the verb for referring to core arguments – one system organised on an accusative and the other on an ergative or partly ergative basis. We return to these examples at the end of §4.2 and comment on the semantics of the two cross-referencing mechanisms.

Although intra-clausal marking of syntactic function can be achieved either by case or other indicators on NPs or by cross-referencing to a verb (and although both kinds of system can be either accusative or ergative) these two mechanisms are by no means equivalent. For instance, there is no possibility of 'double case marking' to parallel the two cross-referencing systems discussed here. When surveying kinds of 'split-ergative' systems, in Chapter 4, we will be careful to note the type of intra-clausal marking involved, and to see whether a particular sort of conditioning for the split system can apply equally well to both types (see also §3.4.4).

3.2   Intra-clausal constituent order ('word order')

It is the fashion in linguistics nowadays for one of the first questions about any language to be 'what is its word order?' (by which is meant 'what is the order of core constituents in a simple clause?', these constituents generally being phrases rather than just words). In fact languages fall into two fairly distinct groups: (a) those, like English, for which constituent order is a critical indicator of syntactic function; and (b) those that have other means of showing syntactic function.

Sometimes languages of type (b) do have a fairly rigid constituent order. But for many languages of this kind constituent order is relatively free, and may be used to highlight a 'topic', distinguish between 'given' and 'new' information, or fulfil other para-grammatical purposes. There is generally an underlying constituent order which may appear when other parameters are on 'neutral'. Dyirbal, for instance, allows any ordering of A, O and verbal complex in texts although there are underlying orders that tend to come out in elicitation – this is AOV if both A and O are pronouns or if A is a pronoun and the head of the O NP is a noun, and OAV if O and A both involve nouns, or if O is a pronoun and A has a noun head. In many languages only a small proportion of clauses in texts have a transitive verb and two explicitly stated NPs. Fijian is like this – only 2–3 per cent of clauses in a text sample had both A and O NPs, and of these about half were VOA and about half VAO; in elicitation, consultants would most often – although not always – opt for VOA unless O was a complement clause, in which case only VAO was acceptable (Dixon 1988a: 242–3, 273).

For languages of type (a), with syntactic function shown by constituent order, we could suggest that a combination SV/AVO or VS/OVA would be an indication of accusativity, and SV/OVA, VS/AVO of ergativity.[9] Note that this sort of categorisation would not be so easy for verb-final or verb-initial languages. With orders SV and AOV one could argue either that S and O are treated in the same way, since they both immediately precede the verb; or that S and A are equivalent, since they both occur initially; and similarly for SV/OAV, VS/VAO and VS/VOA. The only way in which a verb-initial or verb-final language could be characterised as accusative or ergative in terms of constituent order would be if some criterial evidence came from the placement of peripheral constituents – see paragraph 3 below.

With case marking and cross-referencing we mentioned a third alternative to ergative and accusative patterning (albeit found very rarely), the tripartite system where S, A and O are all marked differently. This would only be possible in terms of constituent order if both A and O occurred on one side of the verb and S on the other, i.e. SV/VAO, SV/VOA, VS/AOV, VS/OAV. I have not been able to discover a language with such orderings.[10]

In fact I know of no language of type (a) – in which constituent order is the only or major mark of core syntactic functions – that has an ergative pattern, SV/OVA or VS/AVO. (But see the discussion of Tolai in §4.1.1.)

What about languages of type (b) where syntactic function is shown by case inflection (or particles or adpositions) on an NP, or through cross-referencing on the verb? Surely some of these languages should have a preferred constituent order on an ergative pattern. In fact, languages with intra-clausal ergativity seem seldom to have a preferred verb-medial constituent order. There are just a handful of examples:

1. *SV/OVA*. In Päri, a Western Nilotic language spoken in southern Sudan, absolutive case, with zero realisation, is used on S and O, and ergative case, *-i* ~ *-ɛ*, on A in independent indicative clauses. Intransitive

---

[9] It is common practice, when discussing 'word order', to use the symbol 'S' for both intransitive and transitive subjects. This leads to no difficulties for languages where S and A (in my notation) both occur on the same side of the verb, but it does give rise to confusion for languages with configurations such as SV/OVA, VS/AVO or even a language like Sanuma (see paragraph 3 below) with SV and AOV but with peripheral constituents preceding S and following A. If one wants to undertake a universal investigation there is no alternative to using separate symbols for S and A.

[10] In Williams (1989a: 117) there is reference to 'the SV order of intransitives and the VSO order [i.e. VAO in my symbolisation] in some of the languages of the Biu-Mandara branch [of the Chadic family]'. However, further investigation reveals that SV and VAO orders are found in *different* languages, never in the same language (Williams 1989b; Kemp Williams and Zygmund Frajzyngier, personal communication).

clauses have the order SV, as illustrated in (23), and for transitives the unmarked order is OVA, as in (24). There is a variant transitive order in which A is topicalised: this involves the A NP being fronted to the beginning of the sentence and losing its ergative inflection, and the verb now taking a suffix which cross-references A, as in (25).

(23)   *ùbúr   á-túuk`*
       Ubur COMPLETIVE-play
       Ubur played

(24)   *jòobì   á-kèel   ùbúrr-ì*
       buffalo COMPLETIVE-shoot Ubur-ERG
       Ubur shot the buffalo

(25)   *ùbúr jòobì   á-kèel-é*
       Ubur buffalo COMPLETIVE-shoot-3sgA
       Ubur shot the buffalo

Thus we always get SV and OV, with A having the possibility of following or preceding the OV unit. (Data from Andersen 1988.)[11]

In Kuikúro, a Carib language from Brazil, there is again ergative inflection on the noun and ergative cross-referencing on the verb. Here the neutral constituent order is SV and OVA although AOV is also possible: once more SV and OV are the basic units, with A having a degree of mobility (Franchetto 1990). A similar pattern is found in two other South American languages: Macushi, also from the Carib family (Abbott 1991), and Maxakalí, from the Macro-Jê stock (Harold Popovich, personal communication).

Nadëb (Maku family), spoken in northern Brazil, shows many ergative features (see §§4.2, 5.3.1, 6.3). Helen Weir (personal communication) regards the basic constituent orders as SV and OAV, although VS and AVO are also possible. Here A must immediately precede V, O can either precede or follow the AV sequence while S can either precede or follow V – S and O are treated in the same way, and differently from A.

2. *VS/AVO*. Huastec, a Mayan language from Mexico, shows ergative cross-referencing with the familiar Mayan series of clitic pronouns to the verb. Here the most frequent constituent orders are VS and AVO; as with all type (b) languages, variation is possible from these most common

---

[11] Andersen (1988: 320) mentions that ergative case marking and SV/OVA orders are also found in Jur Luo, another Western Nilotic language – see Buth (1981).

orders (Edmonson 1988). Similar remarks apply to Paumarí from the small Arawá family in the Amazonian basin (Chapman and Derbyshire 1991).[12]

3. *Other patterns*. Sanuma, from the Yanomami family (in northern Brazil and southern Venezuela) has ergative inflection on nouns and plural pronouns. There are fairly rigid constituent orders SV and AOV which, as mentioned above, could not in themselves be taken as evidence of ergativity or accusativity. However, peripheral NPs (which we can show as X) must precede S in an intransitive clause and come between A and O in a transitive one, i.e. XSV, AXOV. We now do have an ergative pattern – both S and O come between peripheral constituents and the verb, while A precedes the peripherals (Borgman 1990).

It will be seen that all the languages quoted here as having some kind of ergative pattern in their constituent ordering show other ergative features, at the level of intra-clausal marking. Indeed, since constituent order fulfils a wide variety of pragmatic as well as grammatical functions, we should hesitate to characterise a language as 'ergative' on the basis of constituent order alone.

3.3   Semantic basis

I remarked, in §1.1, on the notable consistency with which languages map semantic roles, from different semantic types of verbs, onto the basic syntactic relations A and O. It is the Agent for an AFFECT verb, Donor for a GIVING verb, Speaker for a SPEAKING verb, Perceiver for an ATTENTION verb, and so on, that is placed in A function. This can be explained in terms of a semantic principle: that role which is most likely to be relevant to the success of the activity will be identified as A. Most often the role mapped onto A will be human and then 'most relevant to the success of the activity' equates with 'could initiate or control the activity'. I also mentioned that if there are just two core roles then the one not identified as A will be mapped onto O. Some verbs have more than two core roles and then that role which is most saliently affected by the activity will be mapped onto O (examples were given in §1.1).[13]

[12] Boas (1911: 298) gives basic orders VS/AVO in Tsimshian, from western Canada. However, Rigsby (1975: 353) suggests that in Nass-Gitksan, a Tsimshian dialect, the order AVO, which applies only in embedded clauses, can be derived from the basic main-clause ordering VAO.
[13] In English and in many (but by no means all) other languages there are two syntactic frames open to *give*, one with the Gift as O and one with the Recipient as O (in both cases the Donor is A). Whichever of Gift and Recipient is most specific and individuated is likely

There is no comparable semantic basis attached to the assignment of the S role (and this is basically why some languages are accusative, some ergative and others a mixture of the two). It is simply the case that for intransitive verbs with a single core role, this is mapped onto S. For some intransitive verbs the referent of the S NP would be likely to be controller of the activity, e.g. 'jump', 'speak'; this subtype of S can be called S_a. For other verbs the referent of the S NP is not likely to control the event but may be affected by it, e.g. 'break', 'die', 'yawn' – this can be called S_o.

A nominative–accusative system uses only one type of grammatical marking (cases, cross-referencing, etc.) for A and S functions, making no distinction at all between S_a and S_o. The semantic relation that holds for verbs like 'jump' and 'speak' is generalised to hold, as a *grammatical* relation, for all intransitive verbs. Similarly, an absolutive–ergative system generalises from the semantic relation that holds for verbs like 'break' and 'die', and provides *grammatical* identification of O and S over all intransitive verbs; it too ignores the putative distinction between S_a and S_o.

Our examples have been of clearly 'controlled' or definitely 'non-controlled' verbs. But these lie at the extremes of a continuum, with most intransitive verbs somewhere in between. With 'laugh', the activity is sometimes involuntary, but at other times contrived and controlled. 'Vomit' is similar although here there are differences between cultures – in some societies it is in certain circumstances desirable to vomit and people have various ways of bringing this about; in others the action is generally involuntary. Whether or not an action is controlled often depends on the semantic nature of the referent of the S NP. As Lyons points out (1968: 350–65), in his exemplary discussion of this topic, *It moved* would be taken as non-agentive, while *He moved* could be either agentive or non-agentive (Lyons suggests 'ideal' representations *He moved* for the agentive and *Him moved* for the non-agentive sense, relating to *he* as the transitive subject (agentive) pronoun and *him* as the transitive object (affected) pronoun, as in *He hit him*). Thus, for many intransitive verbs, it is difficult to decide whether they basically belong to the 'controlled' or 'non-controlled' class, i.e. it is difficult to determine whether the S NP is of subtype S_a or S_o. Most

to be preferred as O, e.g. *John gave his favourite armchair to some charity* sounds more felicitous than *John gave some charity his favourite armchair*, whereas *John gave his girl-friend lots of things* sounds better than *John gave lots of things to his girl-friend*. The alternatives here are still acceptable, which is not the case when the Recipient is really vague, e.g. *good causes*; one would have to say *John gave all his money to good causes*, the alternative construction *John gave good causes all his money* being judged as un-grammatical by speakers of English. (See also the discussion in §5.1.)

languages avoid decisions in this area of semantic fuzziness by simply marking all S like A (the accusative scheme) or all S like O (the ergative one).

There are other ways in which S is sometimes linked with A and sometimes with O. Discussing lexical semantics, in §1.3, I mentioned ambitransitive pairs of verbs (sometimes called 'labile' verbs) which occur in many languages, some being of type S = A (e.g. *knit, eat* in English) and others of type S = O (e.g. *break, trip*).[14] In an accusative language pairs of the first type can be described in terms of a transitive verb from which the object NP may be optionally omitted, e.g. *She is knitting (a scarf)*, because A and S are treated in the same way in the grammar – whereas S = O pairs appear grammatically more significant since the case marking etc. associated with the NPs differs, e.g. *She tripped, The boy tripped her.*[15] Exactly the reverse applies in an ergative language – an S = O pair can be described as a transitive verb from which the A NP can be omitted (since S and O receive the same marking) but here an S = A pair appears to involve considerable grammatical differences. This can be illustrated with a hypothetical example from a language which is like English except that S follows the verb, like O, and has the same pronominal form as O. There is then similarity between the S = O pair *Tripped her* (i.e. 'she tripped') and *The boy tripped her* but considerable difference between the S = A pair *Is knitting her* (i.e. 'she is knitting') and *She is knitting a scarf*. In fact, the basic semantic statuses of the two sorts of transitive/intransitive pairs are the same in each language; it is just that the grammatical orientation of a language makes them seem (at a fairly superficial level) to be different. (This is discussed further in §8.2.)

When we look at recurrent grammatical properties, and the nature of discourse organisation, there are again some links between S and A and some between S and O. A 'topic', running through a considerable slab of discourse, is most likely to be human, and humans are typically found as S or A; grammatical identification of S with A can simplify discourse tracking. In Chapter 5 we discuss 'subject properties' (based in part on Keenan, 1976), most of which link S and A. On the other side of the

---

[14] Note that there is no correlation between presence or absence of control and S = A/S = O. Of the S = O verbs in English, *trip* and *break*, in their intransitive use, imply lack of control, whereas *walk* (e.g. *The dog walked in the park / John walked the dog in the park*) implies control. Whether a verb is S = O or S = A depends to a considerable extent on its semantic type and subtype membership – see Dixon (1991a: 267–97).

[15] It is perhaps because such S = O pairs appear significant within the context of an accusative-oriented grammar that a number of linguists have recently described this as a type of 'ergativity' (as discussed and regretted in §1.3).

picture, Du Bois (1987a, b) has shown that new information is most likely to be introduced into a discourse in S or O function (see §8.1). Keenan (1984) supplies a useful list of properties that S and O share, e.g. noun incorporation typically involves S or O (seldom A); if a verb has multiple senses these may relate to the nature of the S (e.g. *The horse/ watch/tap/exhibition is still running*) or of the O (e.g. *John cut his arm/his nails/the cake/a tunnel through the mountain/all his classes*) but not of the A argument. Durie (1986) surveys languages which have different forms for some verbs depending on whether one of the arguments is singular or plural, and finds that the critical argument is always S or O, never A.[16]

There are thus a considerable number of ways in which S aligns with A, and also a fair number in which it aligns with O. This explains why many languages are basically accusative (exploiting the S/A similarities) while a fair number are overridingly ergative (exploiting the S/O parallels) in intra-clausal marking. It also explains why there are very few languages with a consistently tripartite system, marking S differently from both A and O. There are good reasons to treat S in the same way as A or in the same way as O or – as we shall soon see – sometimes like one and sometimes like the other.

Many languages employ a mixture of accusative and ergative strategies for intra-clausal marking of syntactic functions. These are generally called 'split-ergative', by which is meant 'split-ergative–accusative'.[17] These splits can be conditioned by one or more of a variety of factors.

First, and most obvious, there can be a split according to the semantic nature of verbs; some languages avoid marking *every* S like A or like O and effectively recognise two subclasses of intransitive verbs (which may or may not overlap).

A second type of split is conditioned by the semantic content of the NPs involved. Something that can function as controller of an action (a human, or perhaps a higher animal) is unmarked in its normal S or A function, but an NP of this kind receives a non-zero marking in O function; similarly,

---

[16] To Durie's examples can be added Sumerian (Thomsen 1984: 131–6), Meryam Mer, spoken on the eastern Torres Strait islands between Australia and New Guinea (Piper 1989: 81) and the Brazilian languages Gavião (Moore 1984), Nadëb (Helen Weir, personal communication) and Maxakalí (Harold Popovich, personal communication) as well as other languages from the Macro-Jê stock (Weisemann 1986: 360). See also Sapir 1917.

[17] 'Split-accusative' should be an equally appropriate label. Of course, 'split-ergative' is used simply because accusativity is the familiar pattern which linguists until recently thought was the basic structure for all languages (some probably still do think this), with ergativity being regarded as a novel and unusual arrangement. (If the study of linguistics had evolved among speakers of Eskimo or Basque, instead of among speakers of Greek, Latin and Sanskrit, things might have been different.)

something inanimate, which would not normally initiate or control any activity, may be unmarked in S or O function, but receive a positive marking if it does happen to occur in A function.

A third type of split can be conditioned by a further component of a sentence – the tense or aspect or mood choice. Something that is complete can be viewed either from the point of view of the patient ('something happened to X') or of the agent ('Y did something'); but a prospective activity is best viewed in terms of a proclivity of an agent. In the latter case, there is pressure for S and A to be dealt with in the same way.

Chapter 4 discusses each of these types of conditioning factor for split-ergative systems. But before dealing with these, we need to consider the question of 'markedness' within both ergative and accusative systems.

3.4   Markedness

The idea of markedness is used in linguistics in a number of different ways. One term in a system can be unmarked in form, compared to the other(s). In English, for instance, singular number is always shown by a zero suffix, while plural is generally shown by orthographic -*s*, e.g. *dog* versus *dog-s*; singular is formally unmarked within this system. We also have functional markedness. Compare *I* and *me* in English; *I* is only used in subject function whereas *me* – the functionally unmarked term – is used in all other circumstances: as object of a verb, after a preposition, and when making up a sentence on its own (e.g. *Who wants to go? Me!*).

Formal and functional markedness often do coincide. Referring back to Table 1.1 in §1.2, in Dyirbal the pronoun *ŋana* 'we all' is both formally and functionally unmarked with respect to *ŋana-na*, and *yabu* 'mother' is also formally and functionally unmarked with respect to *yabu-ŋgu*. But the two parameters do not always coincide. In English, *me* is functionally unmarked with respect to *I* but in terms of form both pronouns are equally marked. Singular is formally unmarked on nouns but it is not at all clear that it is the functionally unmarked term from the English number system. (It is not impossible that a system should have two terms, one being unmarked formally and the other being unmarked functionally, although I have no example to hand of such a thing.)

Turning now to case systems, there is a clear, overall generalisation: that case which covers S[18] (i.e. absolutive or nominative) is generally the

---

[18] The case which covers S is also always used as topic of an equational sentence which shows only a copula or (in many languages) no verb at all.

unmarked term – both formally[19] and functionally – in its system. In terms of form: if any case has zero realisation, or a zero allomorph, it will be absolutive or nominative. At the functional level, if any NP is obligatory in a clause it will be absolutive or nominative (while NPs in ergative or accusative case may be omittable, under specifiable circumstances). And the absolutive or nominative form of a noun will be used in citation.[20]

Absolutive will mark S and O functions and nominative S and A; these are generally the only syntactic functions of these cases. Ergative is sometimes confined to marking A function (e.g. Basque, a number of Australian languages, including Yidin^y, and a number of North-east Caucasian languages, including Ingush) but in many languages this case form has a number of further functions – instrumental in Dyirbal and many other Australian languages, in North-east Caucasian languages such as Avar and Andi, in Chukotko-Kamchatkan, in a number of Papuan languages (Foley 1986: 107) and in both Classical and Modern Tibetan (Andersen 1987; Betty Shefts Chang, personal communication); locative in a handful of Australian languages and in Kuikúro from the Carib family (Franchetto 1990); genitive in Eskimo, Lak from the North-east Caucasian family and Ladakhi from the Tibeto-Burman family (Koshal 1979); generalised oblique in Burushaski and certain Iranian languages; and so on.[21] In Alutor, from the Chukotko-Kamchatkan family, ergative coincides in form with locative for proper nouns and with instrumental for common nouns (Mel'čuk 1978). For the Tibeto-Burman language Limbu, ergative, instrumental and genitive all have the same formal realisation (van Driem 1987: 39).

In a similar fashion, accusative case often has syntactic functions additional to that of marking O – in Latin (as in other Indo-European

---

[19] This generalisation goes back to Greenberg's (1963: 95) 'Universal 38. Where there is a case system, the only case which ever has only zero allomorphs is the one which includes among its meanings that of the subject of the intransitive verb.'

[20] It is the unmarked case form that is employed in citation (indeed, this is one criterion for functional markedness). But one or two languages customarily mark A, S and O by non-zero inflections, and employ the bare stem in citation. In Creek, for example, nominative (S/A) is -*t* and accusative (O) is -*n*; the bare stem is used in citation and for a title, spoken at the beginning of a story. But a bare stem is sometimes found at an A, S or O slot within a sentence, if the function of the NP is clear from the context etc. (data on Creek from Mary Haas). It seems that the Creek inflections -*t* and -*n* are *usually* included on core NPs, but they are *never* used in citation. All known languages which have *obligatory* inflections for A, S and O must use one inflectional form (never the bare stem) in citation.

The use of case in Kemant, a Cushitic language, shows some similarities to the Creek situation (see Hetzron 1976: 16ff.); but insufficient detail is available to check whether the bare citation form can be used in core function, in place of a normal inflected form.

[21] Some of these data is based on Klimov (1973) and Comrie (1981a), which contain further examples of additional functions of an ergative case form.

languages) it also covers 'place to which there is motion', 'extent in time and space' and certain 'adverbial relations' (Kennedy 1962: 119–22). The accusative case form is also used to cover dative function in Dravidian languages such as Koṇḍa (Krishnamurti 1969: 254–7) and Pengo (Burrow and Bhattacharya 1970: 38–9). In Pengo it may, in addition, be used to 'express cause', 'express the time during which or at which something takes place', for comparison, and sometimes 'in genitive function with nouns denoting persons'. In Assyrian, the accusative ending was also used for genitive in non-singular numbers (Mercer 1961: 46). Many other languages could be mentioned but these examples should suffice to indicate that while the unmarked cases – absolutive and nominative – are almost always used only for basic syntactic relations, the marked case forms – ergative and accusative – often (but not always) have wider uses.

I said above that the case which includes S is 'generally' the unmarked one. It seems that absolutive is always unmarked with respect to ergative[22] and nominative is almost always unmarked with respect to accusative. There is a further possibility, less common but quite adequately attested, whereby nominative can be morphologically marked with respect to accusative. We now discuss these possibilities one at a time.

3.4.1   *Absolutive unmarked, ergative marked*

It is not uncommon to find an ergative case inflection described as 'optional'. For Motu, an Austronesian language of coastal New Guinea, '*ese* is the transitive subject particle ... it need not appear when there is no possibility of the object NP being taken as the subject' (Taylor 1970: 30). In 'The boy saw the girl', *ese* will be included after 'the boy'; but this particle is not required, and is unlikely to be included, in 'The snake bit the boy'. Similar descriptions apply to the ergative marker in a number of Papuan languages (spoken in the same geographical region as Motu, but not genetically related), e.g. Dani (Bromley 1981; Foley 1986: 107) and Hua (Haiman 1980).

Another example is Murinypata, a non-Pama-Nyungan language from north Australia. Here there are pronominal prefixes to the verb, cross-

---

[22] One hypothesis concerning 'ergativity' in proto-Indo-European suggested that absolutive was marked by -*N* and ergative by zero. Rumsey (1987b: 25–6) uses the information that no attested language has zero marking for ergative and non-zero for absolutive to show that the hypothesis is implausible.

referencing S/A and O NPs by (roughly) person, number and gender. There is also an ergative inflection on nouns, *-te* ~ *-ɹe*; but this is normally used only when information about which NP is in A, and which in O function, is not inferrable from either (a) the cross-referencing prefixes or (b) the semantic nature of the NPs and of the verb, and the pragmatic context. Thus, although ergative case *can* always be used as an A NP, it is less likely when one of A and O is masculine and the other feminine, since they are then distinguished by the cross-referencing system. If both A and O are third person and of the same gender then ergative may again be omitted from a sentence like 'dog bites man' (since 'dog' is here the expected A) but would be included in 'man bites dog'.[23] Note that, although Murinypata has an ergative nominal inflection, verbal prefixes work on a 'nominative–accusative' paradigm, with one series for S or A, and another for O reference. (Data on Murinypata are from Walsh 1976a, b and personal communication.)

The status of ergative as the marked case is supported by examples such as these. The ergative particle (in Motu) or inflection (in Murinypata) is normally used only when the identity of the A NP can *not* be inferred from any other grammatical or semantic information in the sentence.

In most languages in which the ergative occurs, it is obligatory; an NP of a certain semantic type (see §4.2) *must* take ergative inflection when it is in A function. But there can still be evidence that it is grammatically the marked case, as in Yidinʸ, from North Queensland. Yidinʸ appears to work on these principles: (a) that NP which is marked by ergative case is the 'controlling agent' of a transitive action; and (b) that NP which is the controlling agent of a transitive action is (if non-pronominal) marked by ergative case. Any deviation from this is shown by a derivational affix *-:ji-n* on the verb (coming between the verb root and the final tense-type inflection).

Consider a regular transitive sentence in Yidinʸ:

(26) *waguja-ŋgu jugi-∅   gunda-l (galba:n-da)*
      man-ERG   tree-ABS cut-PRES axe-INST
      the man is cutting a tree (with an axe)

Absolutive case (covering S and O functions) has zero realisation; ergative is here *-ŋgu* and instrumental *-da*. (In fact, instrumental has the same realisation as locative, but there are important syntactic criteria for

---

[23] Another Australian language reported to use 'optional ergative' is Dalabon (Capell 1962: 111). McGregor (1989) describes discourse conditions on the occurrence of ergative marking in the Australian language Guniyandi.

distinguishing the two cases.) Present tense is -*l* with verbs from the predominantly transitive -*l* conjugation, here *gunda-l* 'cut'. (The occurrence of vowel length in these examples is inserted or deleted by regular phonological rules; see Dixon 1977a, b.)

For (26), both (a) and (b) are satisfied: *waguja* 'man' is the controlling agent of the activity, and *is* marked by ergative case. But consider (27), the antipassivised counterpart. Here the underlying A NP is brought into derived S function (normally, to meet syntactic conditions on subordination and coordination), and the underlying O NP receives locative inflection; a number of grammatical tests show that an antipassive construction must be considered intransitive (Dixon 1977a: 274, 252–4).

(27)   *wagu:ja-∅ gunda-:ji-ŋ jugi-:l   (galba:n-da)*
        man-ABS   cut-:*ji*-PRES tree-LOC axe-INST
        the man is cutting a tree (with an axe)

Here condition (b) is broken: *waguja* is still the controlling agent of the verb but, in this derived intransitive construction, it does not receive ergative marking. The infringement of this condition is shown by -:*ji-n* on the verb. (Note that -*ŋ* is the present-tense inflection on the predominantly intransitive -*n* conjugation; -:*l* is the locative inflection on *jugi* 'tree'.)

Similarly, a reflexive sentence – with the agent intentionally doing something to himself – is also a derived intransitive:

(28)   *wagu:ja-∅ gunda-:ji-ŋ   (galba:n-da)*
        man-ABS   cut-:*ji*-PRES axe-INST
        the man is cutting himself (with an axe) (on purpose)

Here *waguja* is in derived S function and absolutive case; but it is the underlying A (and also the underlying O) of an underlying transitive verb; -:*ji-n* is again included, to indicate that the controlling agent is not in ergative inflection, i.e. that condition (a) is broken.

It is important to note that a construction like (28) indicates a purposeful reflexive activity. In English *The man cut himself* could also be used of an accidental injury; this must be rendered in Yidin[y] by (29), which differs from (28) primarily in that *galban* 'axe' takes ergative -*du*, rather than the instrumental inflection -*da* (the allomorphs that occur after a stem ending in *n*).

(29)   *galba:n-du wagu:ja-∅ gunda-:ji-ŋ*
        axe-ERG   man-ABS   cut-:*ji*-PRES
        an axe cut the man (= the man cut himself on an axe, accidentally)

Here the man could have injured himself by accidentally standing on the axe, or letting it drop on his foot, or nicking himself in the neck while swinging it back.

Now (29) is, by an array of syntactic tests, a transitive sentence. Indeed, it contains an ergative (A) and an absolutive (O) NP. But the ergative inflection is not here marking a 'controlling agent' (there is *no* controller, for an accident of this sort), and condition (a) is broken; thus the verb is marked by -*:ji-n*.[24]

As a final example we can contrast the following:

(30)   *waguja-ŋgu bana-∅   wawa-l*
         man-ERG   water-ABS   see-PRES

(31)   *waguja-ŋgu bana-∅ wawa-:ji-ŋ*

Sentence (30) is, like (26), a normal transitive construction,[25] 'The man sees the water', with the presumption that he was looking for some water, and found it. Sentence (31) is also transitive; unlike (29), it has an ergative NP with human reference that *could* be the controlling agent. But the insertion of -*:ji-n* into the verb of (31) indicates that in this instance the man did not simply do what he had set out to do. In contrast to (30), it means 'The man sees the water accidentally': he may have been, say, chasing a dog or looking for a place to defecate, when he came across a stream of fresh water. In (29), the NP *could* not have controlled the activity; in (30–1) he *could* - but, just in case he achieves some result by pure chance, - *:ji-n* is inserted in (31), to mark the non-satisfaction of condition (b).

It will be seen that - *:ji-n* has a wide range of uses.[26] In (27–8) it marks a derived intransitive construction (antipassive in (27), reflexive in (28)); in

---

[24] In fact, - *:ji-n* is used to mark an inanimate agent only with transitive verbs from the AFFECT semantic class ('hit', 'cut', 'split', 'spear', 'burn' etc.; full details are in Dixon 1977a: 287).

[25] Like Dyirbal (§1.2), Yidin^y has absolutive–ergative case marking for nominals, but a nominative–accusative paradigm for first and second person pronouns. Thus the S/A form of the first singular pronoun is *ŋayu*, the O form is *ŋan^van^v*. The transitive/intransitive status of the sentences given here can be seen from examination of the pronominal equivalents:

(26') *ŋayu jugi gundal (galba:nda)*, I am cutting a tree (with an axe)
(27') *ŋayu gunda:jiŋ jugi:l (galba:nda)*, I am cutting a tree (with an axe)
(28') *ŋayu gunda:jiŋ (galba:nda)*, I am cutting myself on purpose (with an axe)
(29') *galba:ndu ŋan^van^v gunda:jiŋ*, an axe cut me (= I cut myself on an axe, accidentally)
(30') *ŋayu bana wawal* I see the water (that I was looking for)
(31') *ŋayu bana wawa:jiŋ* I see the water (by chance)

[26] An additional, minor use of - *:ji- n* is to mark some activity as 'continuous'; in this sense, it can be added to a transitive or an intransitive stem, and preserves the transitivity. There appears to be no connection between this sense and those given above (a full discussion is in Dixon 1977a: 273–93).

(29) and (31) it indicates that, in a transitive construction, the referent of the ergative NP does not control the activity. These apparently diverse syntactic and semantic effects can be related as involving non-satisfaction of conditions (a) and (b). It appears that the Yidin^y ergative definitely *marks* one NP in a transitive construction as 'controlling agent' for the activity described by the verb. Here the ergative contrasts with the (functionally and formally) unmarked absolutive case, which appears on S and O NPs.

In many ergative languages, the absolutive NP must obligatorily be included in each sentence, but an ergative NP may be omitted (this holds for Dyirbal and for Eskimo – Woodbury 1975: 113); this provides further support for absolutive as the unmarked and ergative as the marked case. In every ergative language known to me, the absolutive is the sole citation form.

3.4.2   Nominative unmarked, accusative marked

In most languages that have a nominative–accusative case system, it is the nominative that is morphologically unmarked. If any case has zero realisation (or a zero allomorph) it will be nominative, and this is the form used in citation; as a non-Indo-European example we can mention the Dravidian language Telugu (Krishnamurti and Gwynn 1985: 87). Sometimes both nominative and accusative involve a non-zero inflection, as in the Latin forms of 'slave' from the examples of §1.2, nominative *serv-us* and accusative *serv-um*; it is still the nominative form which is used in citation. If any NP is obligatory in a clause, it will be the one in nominative case. Accusative is then the marked case. Paralleling the ergative examples above, there are instances where an O NP need not (and does not) receive accusative marking when other factors show which NP is in A and which in O function. Thus in Finnish the O NP usually receives the accusative/ genitive inflection, but in a first or second person imperative construction or in an impersonal construction there is no overt expression of the subject, and here the O NP does not take the accusative/ genitive ending. However, in a third person imperative (e.g. 'Let him eat the fish'), there can be overt expression of the subject, and here the direct object *is* in the accusative case (Comrie 1975a: 115–1; Moreau 1972).[27]

---

[27]   The Finnish accusative has (to my mind, rather misleadingly) been termed 'anti-ergative' by Comrie (1975a). Comrie uses 'anti-ergative' for an object inflection that applies only when a subject is present; this is seen as the mirror-image of ergative, which is a 'subject'

A similar situation prevails in other Balto-Finnic languages (Collinder 1965: 54–5), in Australian 'nominative–accusative' languages like Ngarluma (O'Grady, Voegelin and Voegelin 1966: 102), Lardil[28] (Klokeid 1976: 197) and Kayardild (Evans 1987), and in Southern Paiute (Sapir 1930: 179–81, 235) and other Uto-Aztecan languages.[29] In each of these languages, the nominative is morphologically and phonologically unmarked, whereas the accusative involves a non-zero affix. Thus the accusative can be thought of in terms of a special marking of the object that can be omitted whenever its identity can be inferred in certain other ways; if the subject of an imperative must be second person, then (whether or not this subject is expressed) any non-second person core NP must be in O function.

Discussing Jaqaru (spoken in Peru) from the Aymara family, Hardman (1966: 93) mentions that the accusative suffix -*ha* 'is used only in emphatic or unclear situations, frequently when the verb is omitted'.

3.4.3 Marked nominative

We began with the thesis that morphological marking can be used for either A or O function. S is normally unmarked, since there is no other core NP in an intransitive clause from which it must be distinguished; it then falls together with the unmarked transitive function. In §3.3 we noted some properties that link S with O, and others that link S with A, including here the important property of being the NPs whose referents can control and/or initiate an event, if anything can. A and S are joined together, at the underlying syntactic level, in the universal category of 'subject' (discussed in some detail in Chapter 5).

It is, in view of this, natural that the positive marking on A in transitive sentences should be extended to cover S function. This type of system differs from those of §§3.4.1–2 in that it is the marked transitive case, not the unmarked case, which is used for S in an intransitive sentence. One case does cover A and S functions, and another case O function, so this kind of

---

inflection applying only when an object is present (i.e. only in transitive sentences). This ignores the crucial difference between transitive and intransitive sentence types, and conflates A and S functions. I attempt to demonstrate throughout this book, however, that A and S must be clearly distinguished if any progress is to be made in an investigation of ergativity and in a general theory of case marking.

[28] The situation in Lardil is slightly more complex, in a rather interesting way; details are in §4.2. See also §7.2.

[29] For discussion of the syntactic circumstances in which an object NP can be marked with 'nominative' in North Russian dialects, see Timberlake (1974).

system could be termed 'nominative–accusative'. It is, however, radically different from the kind of nominative–accusative system discussed under §3.4.2; there the O function was marked by a non-zero accusative case, but here it is the A function in a transitive sentence that is marked. As far as transitive sentences go, the present type is – on semantic grounds – most similar to the ergative case system, dealt with under §3.4.1. But since the 'special A-marking' is extended – so that it is in fact a 'special subject marking' – there are distributional (although scarcely semantic) similarities to the 'unmarked nominative/marked accusative' type of morphology.

Midway between the type of §3.4.1, marked case for A function, and the present type, marked case for A and S functions, there are some languages where a marked case is used for all A NPs in transitive sentences and for *some* S NPs – just those where the S NP does have agentive force (see the discussion in §4.1). In the latter circumstance it is usually said that the 'ergative case' *can* also be used to mark intransitive subject. This terminology could appropriately be taken further; the name 'extended ergative' (rather than 'marked nominative') could be used when we encounter a marked case employed for A and for *all* instances of S function. Using labels of this type would ensure that 'ergative' and 'accusative' are always used to name marked case choices, and 'absolutive' and 'nominative' unmarked choices.

This is not an easy terminological question. On balance, it seems wisest to maintain the standard use of ergative to refer to marking just of A function (contrasting with absolutive, that marks S and O in the same way). We shall thus prefer the label 'marked nominative' over 'extended ergative'.

Languages showing the 'marked nominative' include some members of the Cushitic family, from north-east Africa. Here it is the unmarked 'accusative' case that is used in citation forms – and, interestingly, as the complement of the verb 'to be'.[30] A similar situation is found in Zayse, from the related Omotic family (Hayward 1990a: 241) and in some languages (spoken in Morocco and Algeria) from the Berber family, another branch of Afroasiatic (Sasse 1984; Chaker 1988). The Nilotic language family is found in the same geographical area as Cushitic and

---

[30] E.g. Oromo, Dasenech and Kambata (Bender 1976: 182, 205, 253). Other Cushitic languages have a marked nominative only in *some* noun classes, or use the zero accusative only for *indefinite* objects. A further group appears to have non-zero inflection for both nominative and accusative, with accusative being used in citation (information from Robert Hetzron and Richard A. Hudson).

Omotic but is not genetically related to them; it is interesting to note that some Nilotic languages have a case system marked by tone in which accusative is the unmarked term, e.g. it is used in citation (see Andersen 1988: 321; Tucker and Bryan 1966: 443–94; Dimmendaal 1985). The Nilotic language Päri has an ergative pattern in most construction types but a 'marked nominative' in imperatives and in most types of subordinate clauses. Andersen (1988) suggests that the simple ergative pattern in main clauses developed from an earlier 'marked nominative' system (see §7.1).

A further example of 'marked nominative' is found in the Yuman family of California. Proto-Yuman used the stem form for 'object', but added a suffix -č for (transitive and intransitive) subject; this system is followed in most modern Yuman languages. Thus in Mojave 'nouns are usually cited in their unmarked form, often with a -ə vowel added, but sometimes they are cited with -č (N + č may constitute an elliptical 'It's a ... " sentence, which could explain this)' (Pamela Munro, personal communication.) Wappo (from the small Yukian family, in north-west California) appears to be another language of this type; Li, Thompson and Sawyer (1977) suggest that an original A marker has been extended to cover S function in main clauses, but not yet in relative clauses or equational sentences. (If this hypothesis is correct, 'extended ergative' would be a diachronically appropriate label for the marked 'subject' inflection.) From South America, Urban (1985) mentions a 'marked nominative pattern' just in active aspect for the Jê family language Shokleng (see §4.5).

Having the unmarked nominal case only for O function (and as the normal citation form) appears to be a well-established grammatical characteristic of the Cushitic, Omotic, Berber, Nilotic and Yuman families. In other languages, phonological changes may lead to an accusative form being phonologically unmarked with respect to nominative; but this may never correlate with morphological marking, and is then likely to be a transient stage of development. An example of this is found in some of the older Germanic languages – where, for example, the Indo-European masculine nominative *-os still appears as -s or -r, but accusative *-an has completely disappeared (the -n was lost first, and then the -a; -a is still found in Runic Norse). There is no evidence that accusative ever functioned as the unmarked case (that it was ever, say, employed in citation).[31]

---

[31] In taking into account the 'evidence' of citation it is important to distinguish between the free and bound forms of, say, pronouns. Both German and French are accusative languages. In German subject pronouns have the status of words and are used in citation (as also in the answer to a question such as 'Who wants to go?' where one would say *Ich* 'I'). In French both subject and object pronouns (e.g. *je*, *me*) exist just as bound clitics to

Further changes have led to nominative and accusative falling together (Meillet (1917) 1970: 91ff.).

It is interesting to compare the 'marked nominative' systems of Yuman and Cushitic, and the regular 'unmarked nominative' system of Germanic (with unusual phonological realisation), with case marking in Maidu, a Californian Penutian language. Here 'subject case' involves the addition of *-m* to the 'object' form. Shipley (1964: 29–30) reports that older speakers employ the 'subject' form for naming (i.e. citation), but that younger speakers use the 'objèct' form; each speaker is quite consistent in his citation forms. An immediate suggestion here is that Maidu was originally of the Germanic type, with nominative as the functionally unmarked case (we would then wonder whether, in an earlier stage of the language, accusative would have had some non-zero realisation), but that the youngest generation of speakers has extended formal markedness to apply also at the functional level, making Maidu more like Cushitic and Yuman in this respect. (We would of course need to know a good deal more about the use of cases in Maidu to be sure of this shift in markedness. Note also that the 'younger speakers' referred to by Shipley were the remnant last generation, speaking a language on the point of extinction. We cannot say that this provides a natural example of language change, under normal conditions of use.)

In summary, we have distinguished three kinds of 'markedness' among case inflections covering the three core syntactic functions A, O and S. Basically, either of the transitive functions can be marked. If O is marked (by 'accusative case'), then the unmarked 'nominative case' is used for S and A functions, and is used in citation etc. If A is marked (by 'ergative case'), then both O and S may be shown by the unmarked 'absolutive case', which will again be used for citation. But the marking on A can also be extended to cover S, with the unmarked case being confined to O function and most instances of citation. Strictly speaking, none of the terms 'nominative', 'accusative', 'absolutive' or 'ergative' are really appropriate for this third possibility. I will employ 'marked nominative' as less

---

the verb; only the oblique form of a pronoun (e.g. *moi*) has existence as a word and it is this that is used in citation (or in answer to question such as 'Who wants to go?'). English also has an accusative grammar but uses the accusative/oblique form of a pronoun (e.g. *me*) in citation or in a one-word answer to a question. Commenting on this, Jespersen (1933: 248) quoted Sweet (1875–6: 495) and himself added the bit in square brackets: 'the real difference between "I" and "me" is that "I" is an inseparable prefix used to form finite verbs [also a "suffix": *am I*, etc.], while "me" is an independent or absolute pronoun which can be used without a verb to follow'. To this one must add that an adverbal can come between subject and verb, e.g. *I really think so.*

potentially confusing than 'extended ergative'. (It is interesting that a 'marked nominative' marking system can develop into an ergative one – see §7.1 on Päri – or vice versa, as mentioned above for Wappo.)

The extension of 'marked A case' to S can be explained in terms of the universal syntactic–semantic identification of A and S as 'subject' (see Chapter 5). There is a more slender semantic link between O and S, so that the fourth logical possibility – ' marked O case' being extended also to cover S – appears not to occur.[32]

3.4.4 *Marking in cross-referencing systems*

In §3.1 we noted that languages can be characterised as ergative or accusative at the intra-clausal or morphological level in terms of case inflections (or particles or adpositions) on NPs, or in terms of bound pronominal-type affixes (usually attached to the verb) which cross-reference certain features of core NPs. The discussion in §3.3, on the semantic basis of morphological marking, applied equally to the two possibilities. However, the present discussion of 'markedness' applies only to case inflections.

Some form of a noun – either just the root, or else a particular non-zero inflectional form – must be used in citation. In many languages, one NP (in a particular case) must be present in each sentence. There is often a restriction (in terms of derived syntactic function and/or case inflection) on the NPs that can act as 'pivots' in subordination or coordination. All these considerations, and others besides, will provide criteria for recognising functional markedness in case systems. In addition, one case often has zero realisation: in most instances, this formal markedness correlates with functional markedness (the Germanic example quoted in §3.4.3 is one of the few exceptions).

One way in which we might talk about 'markedness' with respect to pronominal affixes is in terms of *which* among A, S and O is cross-referenced, in a language with only partial cross-referencing of core NPs.

---

[32] Australia offers examples where the accusative case is extended to cover S as well as O function for *some types* of nominal constituent only. For instance, in the Western Desert language, the pan-Australian accusative suffix -*nʸa* marks O and also S functions on proper names (Dixon 1980: 308). Note that in proto-Australian an accusative inflection occurred only with pronouns, demonstratives and proper nouns (as in most modern Australian languages) and marked just O function; common nouns used the bare stem – absolutive case, with zero inflection – for S and O functions.

In the Paleo-Siberian language Yukagir the suffix -*leŋ* can be added to a focussed NP if it is in S or O relation (Comrie 1981a: 261), but this is scarcely an example of 'marked absolutive'.

If only A and S are cross-referenced, this could be taken as evidence for an (unmarked) nominative/(marked) accusative system.[33] Note that this is a further interpretation of the idea of markedness and that here the unmarked term is the one that has some positive realisation; this is the inverse of the situation with cases, where an unmarked case is the most likely candidate for zero realisation.

There may be one or more forms in a cross-referencing paradigm that have zero realisation (usually including third person singular), though this is evidence about a quite different type of markedness, i.e. formal markedness within person/number systems. But if there are more zero forms in the A than in the O prefix paradigm (as Rumsey 1982 reports for the Australian language Ungarinjin), this could conceivably be taken as evidence for A being relatively unmarked with respect to O.

For many languages, each affix that cross-references S, A or O has non-zero form; even for those with some zero forms, the criteria for kinds of 'markedness' outlined in the last two paragraphs are slim, and need corroboration from other types of grammatical criteria. This contrasts with the several strong criteria available for deciding on markedness within a system of case inflections. This discrepancy in the recognition of markedness constitutes an important difference between cases and cross-referencing affixes.[34] A further difference between the two kinds of intra-clausal marking was mentioned in §3.1.3 – case-type systems on NPs can *always* mark which NP is in A function, and which in O, without reference to any other grammatical information, but cross-referencing pronominal

---

[33] Latin and English are essentially of this type. The Caucasian language Avar represents the other type of system – where, roughly, S and O are cross-referenced in the verb, but not A (Anderson 1976: 4; Černý 1971).

[34] One is tempted to take the generalisation 'the case which covers S is most likely to be unmarked and have zero realisation', and analogise it to cross-referencing systems, suggesting 'the bound pronominal paradigm which covers S is more likely to include (more?) zero realisations than the paradigm which does not cover S' – as does apply for Sacapultec Maya in (20) above. This would be worth investigating, but the inherent difference between case and cross-referencing mechanisms makes me hesitant to predict that it would necessarily follow.

Ortiz de Urbina (1989: 7) comments on differences in markedness for case marking and for cross-referencing:

while Jacaltec shows third person unmarked absolutive markers on the verb, Basque ... has [zero as one allomorph for absolutive case on nouns but, on the verb,] unmarked third person ergative markers and marked absolutives ... On the other hand, in some accusative languages with object person agreement like Cuzco Quechua, where the accusative noun is marked by -*ta* and nominative is unmarked, third person accusative is unmarked on the verb, while nominative is marked: compare *riku-∅-ni* 'I see him, it' and *ruku-wa-n* 'he sees me'. Thus, markedness in the person marking system may differ from the case marking system, presumably due to the fact that both case and person are involved in the former.

affixes to verbs provide only limited semantic information about core NPs (person, number, often also gender/noun class) and there should be some 'fall-back mechanism' to mark what is A and what O when these cannot be distinguished by the cross-referencing system.

These are fundamental differences. If we describe a language as 'ergative' in terms of case inflection, or in terms of the paradigm of cross-referencing affixes, we are describing distinct types of grammatical phenomena. We cannot expect that the types of conditioning for 'split-ergative systems' will necessarily apply equally to case systems and to cross-referencing systems.

4 *Types of split system*

Many languages mix nominative–accusative and absolutive–ergative types of intra-clausal marking. This chapter surveys the kinds of factor that condition these splits. They can relate to the semantic nature of the main verb (§4.1), to the semantic nature of the core NPs (§4.2), to the tense or aspect or mood of the clause (§4.3), or to the grammatical status of a clause, whether it is main or subordinate, etc. (§4.4). Some languages show just one conditioning factor while others combine two or more of the parameters (§4.5).

4.1 Split conditioned by the semantic nature of the verb

There must be contrastive marking for A and O (if a transitive clause is not to be ambiguous). In §3.3 we discussed ways in which S is like A, and other ways in which S is like O, in terms of universal semantic and discourse features and universal grammatical properties. This appears to be the major explanation for the rarity of tripartite systems, where S is marked differently from both A and O. There are pressures to identify S with A (as in an accusative language) or S with O (as in an ergative language). And some languages pursue a middle course, marking some S like A and some like O; such languages fall into two kinds, 'split-S' and 'fluid-S'.

We noted that there is a semantic basis to the assignment of A and O to semantic roles in a transitive clause. S, in contrast, simply marks the sole core NP in an intransitive clause. Since each grammar must include semantically contrastive marking for A and O, this can usefully be applied also to S – those S which are semantically similar to A (exerting control over the activity) will be S_a, marked like A, and those S which are semantically similar to O (being affected by the activity) will be S_o, marked like O.

Languages that distinguish between S_a and S_o, as subtypes of S, are of two kinds. The first kind are like ergative and accusative languages in

70

having syntactically based marking of core constituents, the first of the alternatives discussed in Chapter 2. Each verb is assigned a set syntactic frame, with case marking or cross-referencing always being done in the same way, irrespective of the semantics of a particular instance of use. We call such a system 'split-S'. The second kind employs syntactically based marking for transitive verbs, but employs semantically based marking (the second alternative from Chapter 2) just for intransitive verbs – an intransitive subject can be marked as S_a (i.e. like A) or as S_o (like O), depending on the semantics of a particular instance of use.[1] We can call this a 'fluid-S' system. These two kinds of verb-conditioned split will now be discussed in turn.

4.1.1   Split-S systems

The identifications between S, A and O in accusative and ergative systems can be shown graphically, as in Figures 4.1 and 4.2. In Figure 4.3 we show the system in a split-S language. Intransitive verbs are divided into two sets, one with S_a (S marked like A) and the other with S_o (S marked like O).

For the Siouan language Mandan, Kennard (1936) distinguishes verbs which indicate an 'activity' from those which indicate a 'state or condition'. The first class (of 'active verbs') can be transitive, occurring with subjective and objective pronominal suffixes (e.g. 'ignore', 'tell', 'give', 'see', 'name'), or intransitive, occurring just with subjective suffixes (e.g. 'break camp', 'enter', 'arrive', 'think it over', 'go'). The second class (of 'neutral verbs') takes only the objective prefixes, they include 'fall', 'be lost', 'lose balance' and verbs covering concepts that would be included in an adjectival class for other languages such as 'be alive', 'be brave' and 'be strong'. One might prefer to say that S_a (intransitive 'active') verbs refer to an activity that is likely to be controlled, while S_o ('neutral') verbs refer to a non-controlled activity or state.

---

[1] Languages thus fall into three types: (1) syntactically based marking in transitive and intransitive clauses (in ergative, accusative and split-S systems); (2) semantically based marking in transitive and intransitive clauses (languages like Manipuri, Folopa and Wakhi for which, I maintained in Chapter 2, labels such as 'ergative' and 'accusative' are inappropriate); and (3) 'fluid-S' languages in which transitive clauses show syntactically based and intransitive clauses semantically based marking. Theoretically, we could envisage a fourth type, in which intransitive clauses show syntactically based marking (S always being marked in the same way) and transitive clauses semantically based marking (e.g. the A NP receives a specific mark only when it refers to a volitional agent and/or the O NP receives a specific mark only when it is an affected patient). This putative fourth type is not attested in any language and I predict that it would never be encountered. There is more reason to mark A and O in a transitive clause (to avoid the possibility of ambiguity) than to mark S in an intransitive clause, and especially to provide syntactically based marking of A and O, that will give an unequivocal indication of which NP is in A and which in O function.

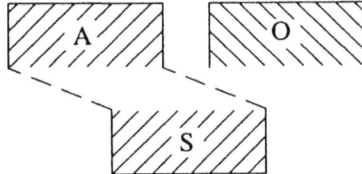

Figure 4.1 Accusative system

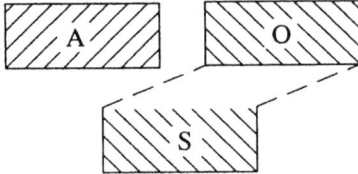

Figure 4.2 Ergative system

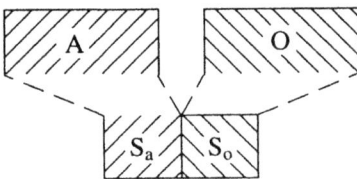

Figure 4.3 Split-S system

Note that in a split-S language like Mandan each intransitive verb has fixed class membership – either S_a or S_o – generally on the basis of its prototypical meaning. If one wanted to use a verb which deals with a prototypically non-controlled activity to describe that activity done purposely, then it would still take the S_o marking (and something like an adverb 'purposely' could be added). And similarly for a verb which describes a prototypically controlled activity used to refer to that activity taking place accidentally – S_a marking would still be used (according to the prototypical pattern) together with something like an adverb 'accidentally'.

Guaraní, a Tupí-Guaraní language from Paraguay, provides a further example of split-S marking.[2] Gregores and Suárez (1967) distinguish three

[2] A more complex (and also more interesting) example of split-S marking occurs in Tunica. Haas (1940) first distinguishes 'active' from 'static' verbs. Active verbs all take a prefix indicating person/number of the subject (A or S), and also the mood of the clause; they can be subdivided into transitive verbs, which also take an object prefix, and intransitive verbs, with no object affix. Static verbs (a small class – only some thirty members are known) take a different prefix, cross-referencing the S NP.

Now the static prefix is identical to the prefix on nouns that marks inalienable possession (e.g. 'my father'). The object prefix on a transitive verb is identical to the alienable possessive prefix on nouns (e.g. 'my hog'). Furthermore, alienable prefixes appear to be classes of verb. 'Transitive verbs' (e.g. 'give', 'steal', 'know', 'order', 'suspect', 'like') take prefixes from both subject and object paradigms (i.e. A and O). 'Intransitive verbs' ('go', 'remain', 'continue', 'follow', 'fall') take subject prefixes (i.e. S_a). Both of these classes can occur in imperative inflection, unlike the third class, which Gregores and Suárez call 'quality verbs'; these take prefixes (S_o) which are almost identical to object prefixes on transitive verbs. Most quality verbs would correspond to adjectives in other languages, although the class does contain 'remember', 'forget', 'tell a lie' and 'weep'.[3]

Split-S languages are reported from many parts of the world – they include Cocho, from the Popolocan branch of Oto-Manguean (Mock 1979), Ikan, from the Chibchan family (Frank 1990), many modern languages from the Arawak family and quite possibly proto-Arawak (Alexandra Y. Aikhenvald, personal communication), many Central Malayo-Polynesian languages of eastern Indonesia (Charles E. Grimes, personal communication) and probably also the language isolate Ket from Siberia (Comrie 1982b).[4] The most frequently quoted example of a split-S language is undoubtedly Dakota, another member of the Siouan family (Boas and Deloria 1939; Van Valin 1977; Legendre and Rood 1992; see also Sapir 1917; Fillmore 1968: 54). There are many other languages of this type among the (possibly related) Caddoan, Siouan and Iroquoian families, e.g. Ioway-Oto (Whitman 1947) and Onondaga (Chafe 1970).

Mithun (1991a) provides a detailed and perceptive study of the semantic basis of the S_a/S_o distinction in Lakhota (a dialect of Dakota), Caddo (from the Caddoan family) and Mohawk (from the Iroquoian family) – prototypical S_a (like A) 'perform, effect, instigate and control events', while prototypical S_o (like O) are 'affected; things happen or have happened to them' (Mithun 1991a: 538). She also reconstructs the ways in

---

derived from inalienable prefixes by the addition of -$(h)k$. Thus the static S prefix does not coincide with the O prefix; but it has the same formal relation to it as inalienable nominal prefixes have to alienable ones. This suggests tempting lines of philosophical speculation, e.g. that an S NP is more closely attached to ('inalienably possessed by') an intransitive verb than an O NP is to a transitive verb.

[3] Kennard and Gregores and Suárez would have been trained to think of nominative–accusative as the 'normal' grammatical system, and thus to expect S to be treated in the same way as A. It is in view of this that they refer to the S_a class as 'active' (like transitives) or as plain 'intransitive' respectively. A more neutral approach would be first to distinguish transitive from intransitive verbs and then to divide the latter class into S_a and S_o (or whatever other names might be preferred).

[4] Moravcsik (1978) provides a comprehensive survey of the rather limited instances in which accusative marking may be used for intransitive subject (i.e. a split-S pattern) in Finnish, Hungarian, Turkish, Amharic and a number of well-known European languages. Aikhenvald (1986) mentions that there are limited instances of a split-S pattern in Berber languages.

which semantic parameters underlying the S_a/S_o distinction may have shifted over time.

The essential function of a language is to convey meaning; grammar exists to code meaning. The great majority of grammatical distinctions in any language have a semantic basis. But there are always a few exceptions. As a language develops many factors interrelate – phonological changes which can lead to grammatical neutralisation; loans and other contact phenomena – and can lead to a temporary loss of parallelism between grammar and meaning.[5] Mithun (1991a: 514) mentions that the Guaraní verb *avuří* 'to be bored' is S_a when we would expect it to be S_o from its meaning. But this is a loan from the Spanish verb *aburrir* (*se*) and Guaraní has a convention of borrowing Spanish intransitive verbs as S_a items and Spanish adjectives as S_o verbs. Note that there is a native Guaraní verb *kaigwá* 'to be or become bored' which is in the S_o class.

There are split-S languages where the two intransitive classes do not have as good a semantic fit as those in Mandan and Guaraní. Thus in Hidatsa, another Siouan language (Robinett 1955), the S_a class includes volitional items like 'talk', 'follow', 'run', 'bathe' and 'sing', but also 'die', 'forget' and 'have hiccups', which are surely not subject to control. And the S_o class includes 'stand up', 'roll over' and 'dress up', in addition to such clearly non-volitional verbs as 'yawn', 'err', 'cry', 'fall down' and 'menstruate'.

One must of course allow for cultural differences. As mentioned in §3.3, in some societies vomiting plays a social role and is habitually induced, while in other societies it is generally involuntary; the verb 'vomit' is most likely to be S_a in the first instance and S_o in the second. In some societies and religions people believe that they can to an extent control whether and when they die, so the verb 'die' may well be S_a. But even taking such factors into account, there is seldom (or never) a full grammatical–semantic isomorphism. The S_a/S_o division of intransitive verbs in a split-S language always has a firm semantic basis but there are generally some 'exceptions' (with the number and nature of the exceptions varying from language to language). As Harrison (1986: 419) says of Guajajara, a split-S language from the Tupí-Guaraní family: 'semantically, a few verbs seem to be in the wrong set'.

---

[5] A good example of this concerns noun (gender) classes. Such a system probably always begins with a clear semantic basis but processes of change later obscure this, at least in part (as has happened in many Bantu and other Niger-Congo languages – see Givón 1972, 1970; Creider 1975; Denny and Creider 1976; Hinnebusch 1989: 466–7).

The size of the S_a and S_o classes varies a good deal. Merlan (1985) quotes examples of languages with a small closed S_o class and a large open S_a class (e.g. Arikara from the Caddoan family) and with a small closed S_a class and a large open S_o class (e.g. Dakota). In other languages both classes are open (e.g. Guaraní).

In some split-S languages the distinction between S_a and S_o extends far beyond morphological marking. Rice (1991) shows how, in the Northern Athapaskan language Slave, causatives can be based on S_o (her 'unaccusative') but not on S_a (her 'unergative'); passive on S_a but not on S_o; noun incorporation can involve O or S_o, but not S_a; and so on.

It might be thought that a split-S language could be described without recourse to an S category, that instead of what I posit as the universal set of syntactic primitives, S, A and O, we should perhaps use four primitives for a split-S language: S_a, S_o, A and O. Or perhaps just two, A and O, with the proviso that a transitive clause involves A and O and that there are two kinds of intransitive clause, one with just A and the other with just O.

Careful study of the grammars of split-S languages shows that they do work in terms of a unitary S category with this being subdivided, for certain grammatical purposes, into S_a and S_o. Many languages from the Tupí-Guaraní family have, in main clauses, prefix set 1 cross-referencing A or S_a, and prefix set 2 referring to O or S_o. But in subordinate clauses set 2 is used for O and for all S (i.e. both S_o and S_a). (Jensen 1990; see §4.5 below). Seki (1990) lists a number of other ways in which S_a and S_o are grouped together by the grammar of Kamaiurá, a Tupí-Guaraní language. Wichita, a Caddoan language, has a split-S system with one class of intransitive verbs (e.g. 'go') taking the same prefix as A in a transitive clause, and a second class (including verbs such as 'be cold' and 'be hungry') taking the same prefix as transitive O. Rood (1971) notes two grammatical processes that group together O and S (and take no account at all of the distinction between S_a and S_o): many O or S (but no A) NPs can optionally be incorporated into a verb word, and a single set of verbal affixes indicates plural O or S (another set is used for plural A). Finally, S and A behave the same way in constituent ordering: an O NP (if there is one) will generally precede the verb, and then the subject (A or S NP) can either precede or follow this complex.[6]

---

[6] Rood points out (personal communication) that there are distinct S_a and S_o prefixes only for first and second persons, but the processes of incorporation and pluralisation which group together S and O apply only to third person forms. He suggests that this could be evidence for a split according to the Nominal Hierarchy (§4.2) – with, roughly, S_a being grouped with A for first and second persons, but included with S_o and O in an 'absolutive' grouping for other nominal constituents.

Rood also points out (modifying his statement in Rood 1971: 101) that constituent

Split-S marking relates to the nature of the verb. It is scarcely surprising that for most languages of this type morphological marking is achieved by cross-referencing on the verb (as it is for all the languages mentioned above). There are, however, some split-S languages which have syntactic function shown by case markings on an NP, e.g. Laz from the South Caucasian family (Holisky 1991).

Yawa, a Papuan language from Irian Jaya, combines NP marking and cross-referencing. A pronominal-type postposition, inflecting for person and number, occurs at the end of an NP in A function, whereas S and O are marked by prefixes to the verb. This is a split-S language in that S_o intransitive verbs take the same prefix as marks O with a transitive verb, whereas S_a verbs have a prefix that is plainly a reduced form of the postposition on NPs in A function. Singular forms are (dual and plural follow the same pattern):

	A postposition	S_a prefix	O/S_o prefix
1sg.	*syo*	*sy-*	*in-*
2sg.	*no*	*n-*	*n-*
3sg. masc.	*po*	*p-*	$\emptyset$
3sg. fem.	*mo*	*m-*	*r-*

It will be seen that although intransitive verbs divide into an S_o class (which is closed, with about a dozen members, e.g. 'to be sad', 'to remember', 'to yawn') and an S_a class (which is open and includes 'walk' and 'cry'), Yawa does work in terms of the S category – there is always a prefix indicating S (rather than S_a being marked by a postposition, as A is). (Data from Jones 1986.)

There are also examples of a split-S system where syntactic functions are marked by constituent order. Tolai, an Austronesian language spoken in New Britain, Papua New Guinea, has, in transitive clauses, the A NP before the verb and the O NP following it. Intransitive clauses have a single core NP – this must precede the verb for one set of verbs (e.g. 'go', 'sit', 'say', 'eat', 'be sick', 'be cold') and must follow the verb for another set (e.g. 'flow', 'fall', 'burn', 'cry', 'grow', 'be big', 'be nice'). We thus have a contrast between S_a and S_o realised through constituent order. (Data from Mosel 1984.)

order in Wichita shows considerable fluidity: although AOV and OVA are the most frequent, and represent 'the first interpretation of sentences with two NPs, neither incorporated', OAV and AVO have been encountered.

A very similar pattern is apparent in Waurá, an Arawak language spoken on the Upper Xingu River in Brazil. Here a transitive clause shows basic constituent order AVO; the verb has a pronominal prefix cross-referencing the A NP, as in (1). There are two classes of intransitive verbs. One (which includes 'work', 'flee', 'walk', 'fly') has an S_a NP that precedes the verb, and there is a verb prefix cross-referencing it, as in (2). The other (which includes 'catch fire', 'die', 'be full', 'be born' and 'explode') has an S_o NP that comes after the verb; there is no cross-referencing prefix on the verb. This is illustrated in (3).

(1) *yanumaka ɨnuka   p-itsupalu*
     jaguar   3sg + kill 2sgPOSS-daughter
     the jaguar killed your daughter

(2) *wekɨhɨ katumala-pai*
     owner 3sg + work-STATIVE
     the owner worked

(3) *usitya   ikítsii*
     catch fire thatch
     the thatch caught fire

Thus, S_a behaves exactly like A, and S_o like O. (A full discussion is in Richards 1977; see also Derbyshire 1986: 493–5.)

In conclusion, we can note that some scholars maintain there to be three basic types of system for marking syntactic function: accusative, ergative and split-S (often called 'active' or by a variety of other names – see, for instance, Dahlstrom 1983; Klimov 1973). Mithun (1991a: 542), for example, insists that split-S systems are 'not hybrids of accusative and ergative systems'.[7] Despite such scholarly opinions, it is a clear fact that split-S systems do involve a mixture of ergative and accusative patterns – S_a is marked like A and differently from O (the criterion for accusativity) while S_o is marked like O and differently from A (the criterion for ergativity). I would fully agree with Mithun that split-S systems 'constitute coherent, semantically motivated grammatical systems in themselves'. So do other kinds of split-ergative grammars, e.g. those to be described in §4.2 which involve a split determined by the semantic nature of NPs. The fact that a grammatical system is split does not imply any lack of coherency or stability or semantic basis. There are two simple patterns of syntactic

---

[7] 'Hybrid' is a loaded and unfortunate term to use here, as if there were pure systems and anything deviating from one of them must be inferior. There are simple systems (accusative and ergative) and more complex ones (combinations of these two); all are likely to be balanced systems but the more complex ones can have greater subtlety of expression.

identification, accusative and ergative, and many combinations of these, as exemplified throughout this chapter. The various ways of combining ergative and accusative features can all yield systems that are grammatically coherent and semantically sophisticated.

The one difficulty we do have is what 'case names' to use for A and O in a split-S language. Since each of A and O is like S for some intransitive verbs and unlike S for others the labels nominative/accusative and absolutive/ergative are equally applicable – to choose one of these sets over the other would be unmotivated. Using ergative for A and accusative for O is one possibility, although one might also want to take into consideration the relative markedness between A-marking and O-marking in each particular language. One solution is not to employ any of ergative, absolutive, accusative or nominative for a split-S language but just stick to the terms A-marking and O-marking.

4.1.2   *Fluid-S systems*

In Chapter 2, I discussed languages with semantically based marking, where grammatical marking on core NPs directly reflects the semantics of a particular situation, rather than being filtered through a prototypical template, as happens with languages that work with syntactically based marking (whether these be ergative, accusative, split-S or involving some other type of split).

There is a fascinating group of languages which has syntactically based marking for transitive verbs – always marking A and O in the same way for a given verb – but uses semantically based marking for intransitive verbs – with direct marking reflecting the semantics of each particular instance of use. The typical situation in such a language – which I call 'fluid-S' – is for each intransitive verb to have the possibility of two kinds of marking for its core NPs – one (S_a, the same as on a transitive A) to be used when the referent of the S NP controls the activity, and the other (S_o, the same as on a transitive O) when control is lacking.

A main purpose of case-marking/cross-referencing is to distinguish A from O; two contrastive markings are needed for this. But an intransitive clause has a single core NP whose syntactic function is clear; both syntactic markings from a transitive clause can profitably be employed. In a split-S language the A-type and O-type markings are allocated to S syntactically; the S_a/S_o division has a semantic basis, of course (as does the prototypical identification of A and O in a transitive clause) but there is no choice

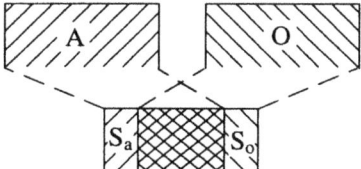

Figure 4.4 Fluid-S system

involved for an individual verb. In a fluid-S language the A-type and O-type markings are allocated to intransitive clauses semantically, with each intransitive verb having the possibility of either choice, depending on the semantics of each particular context of use. In practice, some verbs refer to activities that are always likely to be controlled and these are always likely to be marked as S_a; other verbs refer to activities or states that are likely never to be controlled and these are always likely to be shown as S_o. But there will be many verbs in a middle region, referring to activities where there can be control or lack of control, and these may accordingly be marked either as S_a or S_o. This is shown in Figure 4.4. (Note that for a fully fluid-S language every intransitive verb has the *potentiality* of taking either marking; it is just that some verbs are more likely than others to exercise this choice.)

One of the most cited examples of a fluid-S language is Bats or Batsbi (or Tsova-Tush, the designation now preferred by native speakers) from the North-east Caucasian family. Schiefner (1859) was the first to provide this characterisation of Bats, quoting a single verb that had variable marking: 'I fell' with A-type marking on its subject implies 'it was my own fault that I fell' and with O-type marking implies that there is 'no implication that it was my fault'. (The marking is shown on the NP itself, and this is then cross-referenced on the verb – Holisky 1987: 105.) The next field work was by Dešeriev (1953), who quoted six verbs with variable marking but said that his informant didn't accept Schiefner's example, and suggested that variable marking was perhaps being lost.

Holisky (1987) undertook a masterly piece of field work from which she found that fluid-S marking is still in operation in Tsova-Tush, with S_a being employed whenever the referent of the S NP is 'a human participant to whom is ascribed volition and conscious (mindful) control with respect to the situation denoted by the verb', and S_o used in other circumstances. Holisky checked 303 intransitive verbs with native speakers to see whether S_a or S_o or both were acceptable, and, if both, which was preferred. Thirty-one verbs were accepted only with S_o – these refer to states or activities that cannot be controlled, e.g. 'tremble', 'be hungry', 'be ripe, grow up'. Seventy-eight verbs were acceptable only with S_a – they refer to activities that must be controlled, e.g. 'walk, wander', 'talk', 'think'. The remainder were said by Holisky's consultants to be acceptable with S_a or S_o marking. For some of these S_o was preferred since there is unlikely to be control, e.g. 'die', 'burn', 'become old'; for others S_a was preferred since there normally is control, e.g. 'wash', 'laugh out once', 'begin'; and for a middle set either S_a or S_o marking were considered equally likely, e.g. 'lose weight', 'slip/slide', 'be late', 'get lost', 'get drunk'.

The results Holisky obtained were determined partly by speakers' world-view and by other pragmatic factors. She mentions 'when I constructed the first person form for the verb "get poor" in Tsova-Tush using [S_a] marking, my consultant did not say *categorically* that it wasn't possible. She said it isn't possible because you would never want to be poor' (Holisky 1987: 115).

The other languages in the small Nakh branch of the North-east Caucasian family, Chechen and Ingush, employ a variety of case-marking patterns (e.g. Nichols 1982, forthcoming) but – interestingly enough – do not show a fluid-S system for intransitives. (It is likely that Tsova-Tush developed its fluid-S strategy fairly recently.) On the basis of information in Kibrik (1985) it seems that Tabassaran, from the Dagestanian branch of the North-east Caucasian family, also shows a fluid-S profile.

Acehnese, a western Austronesian language from north Sumatra, behaves in a similar way to Tsova-Tush. Transitive verbs have grammatical marking assigned to A and O NPs on a prototypical basis, as in languages with syntactically based marking. But A and O markings are then used to provide marking for the core NP, S, of an intransitive verb in a way that directly reflects a particular situation of use. Durie (1985: 63ff.) reports that intransitive verbs such as 'get up', 'cough', 'vomit', 'think', 'dream' and 'want, like' only take S_a marking; another set, including 'explode', 'fall', 'be sad' and 'be delicious' only take S_o; and a further set may take either marking, depending on the meaning of the verb in a particular instance of use, e.g. 'be disgusted', 'begin', 'stop', 'suspect', 'be obedient'.

Spoken Tibetan provides a further example of a fluid-S language. Chang and Chang (1980: 21) explain how S_a marking 'is used to signify either the achievement or the guarantee of an act directed towards a goal'. For example, in 'I went to Lhasa' the first person singular pronoun can be marked as S_a, implying that I went there purposely, or as S_o, perhaps referring to my having been taken there as a child.

Fluid-S characteristics have been reported for at least one language from South America – Baniwa do Içana (spoken on the Upper Rio Negro, Arawak family). Here information as to syntactic function of core arguments is provided by cross-referencing – a transitive verb shows a pronominal prefix referring to A and a suffix referring to O. One group of intransitive verbs (e.g. 'go for a walk') has S_a cross-referenced by the A prefix while another class (e.g. 'die', 'be lost') has S_o cross-referenced by the O suffix. And there are a number of intransitive roots that can occur with S_a or S_o; for instance -*aku* with S_a marking means 'speak' whereas with S_o marking the meaning is 'make a noise (including people talking nonsense)'. Interestingly, the verb -*idza* means 'weep' with S_a marking, and 'rain' with S_o. (Data from Taylor 1991 and Alexandra Y. Aikhenvald, personal communication.)

There are also some fluid-S languages reported from North America. In Eastern Pomo, a Hokan language of northern California, there are some intransitive verbs (e.g. 'fall', 'sneeze') whose S NP always receives case inflection typical of an O NP in a transitive sentence: these describe an event that *cannot* be controlled. At the opposite end is a group of intransitive verbs (e.g. 'sit', 'go') where the patient *always* exercises control; the S NP receives marking that applies to the A NP in a transitive sentence (at least for pronouns, kin terms and proper nouns). Between these two extremes is a further group of intransitive verbs whose S NPs can be inflected like an A or an O NP, depending on whether the participant referred to does or does not exercise control, e.g. 'slide/slip' (McLendon 1978).

In Eastern Pomo, fluid-S marking is expressed by case inflections; in Tsova-Tush by case markers which are iconic with cross-referencing markers on the verb; in Tabassaran only by cross-referencing. Another language to show a fluid-S system by cross-referencing is Crow, from the Siouan family (Kaschube 1967; Avery Andrews, personal communication).[8] The class of intransitive verbs which appear only with S_a marking includes 'run'; the class with S_o marking includes 'fall over'; and the class that can take either S_a or S_o – depending on whether or not volition is involved – includes 'go'.[9]

---

[8] See also Hoijer (1933: 70) on Tonkawa, a language isolate from Texas.

[9] There are some complications in Crow. There is a class of verbs (e.g. 'to not know') that are semantically non-agentive but take agentive prefixes, except for first person plural (this pattern of prefixation is also shown by a class of prepositions, with respect to their objects). The verbs 'to tattle' and 'to tell lies' take non-agentive (O) prefixes although they behave syntactically like agentive verbs (intransitive verbs taking A prefixes).

Different languages show different kinds of structural complexity – for instance, a simple morphology may co-occur with a complex set of syntactic rules. These tend to balance out, leading to the implicit tenet of modern students of linguistics: in terms of *overall* structural complexity, all languages are roughly equal.

As an example of this, some particularly useful grammatical convention may lead to a reduction in the number of distinct lexemes needed. This is certainly the case with fluid-S marking. Like Eastern Pomo, Tsova-Tush has a single verb root that can be 'glossed 'slip' when used with S_o marking and 'slide' when used with S_a (Holisky 1987: 125). In contrast, English requires two distinct lexemes, one describing an involuntary action, *slip*, and the other something which may be done voluntarily, *slide*.

For an intransitive verb like 'slip/slide', 'get lost' or 'get fat', a fluid-S language can always show – by choice of grammatical marking – whether control is involved. But this is not possible for transitive verbs, which still operate with syntactically based marking. Consider 'see'; here the Perceiver will always receive the same grammatical marking, regardless of whether the Impression came into his span of attention accidentally, or as a result of effort on his part. Acehnese deals with this by having an 'uncontrolled' verbal prefix *teu-* which is added to a transitive verb root referring to something that is normally controlled when it is used to describe something that happens by chance, e.g. 'I accidentally saw him'; *teu-* derives an intransitive verb, with an S_o subject (Durie 1985: 72–8). (Note that for a transitive verb without the *teu-* prefix, the referent of the A NP is, if animate, always taken to be in control; there are a few A NPs that refer to natural forces, e.g. 'lightning', but a noun such as 'stone' could never be in A function in this language.) The use of prefix *teu-* in Acehnese appears roughly parallel to the use of verbal suffix *-:ji-n* to mark an activity as 'uncontrolled' in Yidinʸ, a language with full syntactically based marking, as described in §3.4.1. (See also the discussion in §5.1, for an account of further strategies for dealing with this sort of variation, by using alternative case frames.)

Before concluding this section I must again stress that there is a fundamental difference between the two systems (which are often confused) – fluid-S, where each intransitive verb has the potentiality of taking either of two markings, to directly reflect its context of use; and split-S, where intransitive verbs are divided into two sets, roughly on semantic grounds, but each still has a single syntactic frame available, according to its prototypical assignment. I said in Chapter 2 that the syntactically based marking and semantically based marking types are idealisations, with many languages combining features of each. Nevertheless, most languages with a split conditioned by the semantic nature of the verb are either clearly fluid-S or else clearly split-S. It is not uncommon for a split-S language to have a handful of verbs that can take either S_a or S_o marking,[10,11] but this is often a case of lexicalisation. For instance, Tupínambá the language spoken along the eastern coast of Brazil at the time of the Portuguese invasion in the sixteenth century, is said to have had just a few verbs that could take S_a, then meaning 'do something,' or S_o, then meaning 'able to do it, know how to do it', e.g. 'speak' (S_a)/'know how to speak, can speak' (S_o) (Rodrigues 1953: 135). In Guaraní there are about a dozen verbs that can take S_a or S_o, e.g. *che-karu*, 'I (S_o) am a big eater'; *a-karu* 'I (S_a) am eating'. The contrast is not productive – 'move' and 'burn' must be S_a (whether or not the activity is controlled) while 'be tired' and 'be happy' can only be S_o (Velázquez-Castillo, 1991).[12]

A great variety of names have been given to split-S and fluid-S systems, including Sapir's (1917) 'active/inactive'. Mithun (1991a: 511) lists: active, active–neutral, active–stative, stative–active, agentive, agent–patient and split-intransitive, to which can be added agentive/patientive (Kibrik 1985), active/non-active and unaccusative/unergative (see the Appendix, pp. 232–6). One of the difficulties with these labels is that they tend to be used indiscriminately for both split-S and fluid-S; or, if a distinction is made, different linguists may use the same label for different systems. It is partly because of this terminological confusion that I here use the self-explanatory labels 'split-S' and 'fluid-S'.

4.2   Split conditioned by the semantic nature of NPs

The kinds of split systems discussed in §4.1 were conditioned by the reference of the verb. Some intransitive verbs refer to events that are likely to be (or that must be) controlled, others to events or states that are seldom (or, perhaps, never) controlled, and – for fluid-S languages – a third class

---

[10] See also Kashmiri, as described in Koul (1977).

[11] Tolai appears to be basically a split-S language (where this is marked by constituent order, as described above) but some intransitive verbs can be treated either as S_a (with S preceding verb) if the S refers to a person, or as S_o (with S following verb) if the S refers to a body-part, e.g. *a tutana i vana* ('the man he went') but *i ga vana ra polo ura ra pi* ('it TENSE go the liquid down-to the ground') 'the liquid of his body flows down to the ground' (Mosel 1984: 148, 150).

[12] In §8.1 I mention a rather different kind of S_a/S_o distinction, motivated by discourse factors, in two Peruvian languages, Yagua and Pajonal Campa (Thomas Payne 1985).

refers to events that may or may not be controlled, according to the particular circumstance.

We now consider a second kind of split, that conditioned by the referents of the core NPs. If pronouns and nouns have different systems of case inflection, then the pronoun system will be accusative, and the noun system ergative, never the other way around. In fact, we can be more specific than this, setting up a hierarchy of types of NP constituent, in terms of which accusative/ergative splits are motivated. This relates to the fact that certain kinds of NPs are very likely to be the controller of an event, others less likely, others most unlikely.

Some type of grammatical marking is needed to distinguish A and O in a transitive clause. It is useful to look at the different kinds of words that can be head of an NP and consider whether they are more likely (over the full range of transitive verbs for a language) to be in A rather than in O function, or whether the reverse holds, or – in the middle ground – whether A and O are about equally likely.

For many verbs the A NP is normally human (e.g. 'believe', 'tell', 'decide'); for others it may be human or animate (e.g. 'bite', 'see'); very few, if any, verbs are restricted to an inanimate A. There is more variety with regard to O: for a verb like 'see' anything could be O; for 'shoot' or 'spear' the O is likely to be animate or human; for 'pick up' or 'roll' it is most likely to be inanimate. Averaging out over all types of verbs, there is no doubt that human NPs are more likely to be in A than in O function, and that inanimates are more likely to be in O function than in A, with non-human animates falling between these.

Inanimate things are generally referred to by common nouns, but for humans each language provides a number of grammatical alternatives. There is always a class of first and second person pronouns, with 'shifting reference'. And there are always demonstrative pronouns, which are most frequently used to refer to humans. And there are proper names.

Most discourse, in any language, is oriented to the people involved in the speech act – preeminently to the speaker, then to the addressee, then to other specific people, referred to by demonstratives or third person pronouns, or by proper names, or just by common nouns with human reference. Put very roughly, a speaker will think in terms of doing things to other people to a much greater extent than in terms of things being done to him. In the speaker's view of the world, as it impinges on him and as he describes it in his language, he will be the quintessential agent. (Note the use of the label '*first* person' to refer to the speaker in the Greek-based

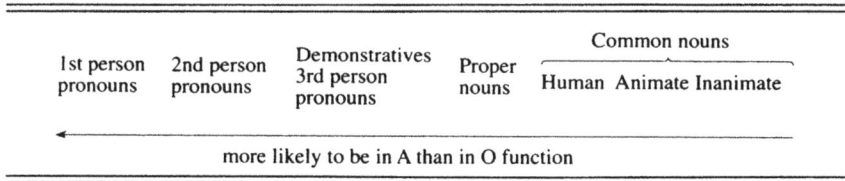

Figure 4.5 The Nominal Hierarchy

grammatical tradition.) That is, a first person pronoun is more likely than any other NP constituent to be in A rather than in O function. Next most likely as A is second person pronoun, then demonstratives and third person pronouns, followed by proper names.

We can represent this Nominal Hierarchy in diagrammatic form, as Figure 4.5. Those participants at the left-hand end of the hierarchy are most likely to be agents, to be in A function, and those at the right-hand end are most likely to be patients, to be in O function.

It is plainly most natural and economical to 'mark' a participant when it is in an unaccustomed role. That is, we could expect that a case-marking language might provide morphological marking of an NP from the right-hand side of the hierarchy when it is in A function, and of an NP from the leftmost end when in O function (as an alternative to providing ergative marking for *all* A NPs, of whatever semantic type, or accusative marking for *all* O NPs).

A number of languages have split case-marking systems exactly on this principle: an 'ergative' case is used with NPs from the right-hand end, up to some point in the middle of the hierarchy, and an 'accusative' case from that point on, over to the extreme left of the hierarchy. The case marking of Dyirbal, mentioned in §1.2, provides a straightforward example, as shown in Table 4.1, with boxes around the ergative and accusative forms.

Here we have accusative *-na* versus the unmarked nominative *-∅* for first and second person pronouns, but ergative *-ŋgu* opposed to the unmarked absolutive *-∅* for the rightmost three columns.[13]

---

[13] The situation is in fact slightly more complex than this. The interrogative/indefinite form *wanʸa* 'who, someone' has distinct forms for S, A and O functions; and proper names, as well as some nouns with human reference, can optionally take *-nʸa* (cognate with pronominal accusative *-na*) in O function only. (This suggests that they should be placed to the left of 'third person pronouns', as least as far as Dyirbal is concerned.)

Australian languages that do have mutually exclusive ergative and accusative marking, with no overlap of any sort in the middle of the hierarchy, include Kuku-Yalanji (H. Hershberger 1964, R. Hershberger 1964, Patz 1982); and Ngiyambaa (Donaldson 1980). See also the revealing discussion of this point in Blake (1987a), and his tabulation of the varying extent of accusative marking in a selection of Australian languages (p. 21).

Table 4.1. *Dyirbal*

A	-∅	-ŋgu	-ŋgu	-ŋgu
S	-∅	-∅	-∅	-∅
O	-na	-∅	-∅	-∅
	1st & 2nd person pronouns	3rd person pronouns	proper names	common nouns

Table 4.2. *Cashinawa*

A	-∅	*habũ*	*nasalisation*
S	-∅	*habu*	-∅
O	-a	*haa*	-∅
	1st and 2nd person pronouns	3rd person pronoun	proper names and common nouns

We can think of O-marking, extending in from the left, and A-marking, coming in from the right, as essentially independent parameters. They can overlap, so that something in the middle portion of the hierarchy will have different forms for all three of the core functions S, A and O.[14] Consider Cashinawa, a Panoan language from Peru, shown in Table 4.2.[15]

In the right-hand column, an NP with a noun as head receives ergative case marking (realised as nasalisation of the last vowel in the final word of the NP) when the noun is in A function, and takes absolutive case (with zero realisation) when in S or O function. In the left-hand column, first and second person pronouns have an accusative suffix *-a* only for O function, and zero marking (nominative case) when in A or S function. In the middle of the hierarchy, the third person pronoun has both types of marking, showing three different case forms (note that the root is *habu* for S function, with nasalisation added in A function as it is for nouns; in O function the pronominal accusative *-a* is added to a shorter root *ha-*).

---

[14] There are examples of ergative case covering the whole length of the hierarchy, with accusative being more limited in application. In Waga-Waga, from south-east Queensland, all NP constituents take the ergative inflection; accusative marking applies to pronouns, proper nouns, all common nouns with human reference, and just a few common nouns with non-human reference (Wurm 1976). Here there are separate forms for S, A and O at the left and middle of the hierarchy, but an absolutive–ergative system at the far right (and no simple nominative–accusative case marking in any part of the hierarchy).

[15] Analysis of Cashinawa is inferred from data provided in Merrifield et al. (1965: 140–3); I am grateful to Robert E. Cromack for supplying additional data.

Table 4.3. *Yidinʸ*

A	∅	ERG	ERG	ERG	ERG
S	∅	∅	∅	∅	∅
O	ACC	ACC	(ACC)	∅	∅
	1st and 2nd person pronouns	human deictics, interrog.	inanimate deictics, proper names, kin terms	inanimate interrog.	common nouns and adjectives

There are many other languages where A and O markings overlap for some part of the middle of the hierarchy, rather than ergative marking stopping at the place where accusative begins. (Note, though, that the A and O markings, extending in from opposite ends of the hierarchy, should at least meet if A and O are to be distinguished by case marking; if they did not meet other means would have to be employed to distinguish A and O for the class of NPs that show neither accusative nor ergative affixes, or else we would simply get ambiguity.) In Yidinʸ (cf. §3.4.1), for example, first and second person pronouns have a nominative (-∅)/accusative (-n^y ~ -:n^y) paradigm, while at the other end of the scale, common nouns show absolutive–ergative marking (-∅ versus -*ŋgu* ~ -*du* etc.). But in the middle region, there are separate forms for A, S and O functions for deictics that have human reference and for the human interrogative/indefinite form 'who, someone'. Deictics with inanimate reference can use the unmarked S form for O function, *or* they can use a special O form (in accusative -:n^y). Proper names of people and kin terms can optionally add an accusative suffix -$n^y a$ (as happens, for instance, in (40) from §8.2). The inanimate interrogative/indefinite 'what, something' has one form for S and O functions, exactly like nouns. This is summarised in Table 4.3. Note that the ergative case in Yidinʸ marks any common or proper noun, or deictic or interrogative/indefinite, when it is in A function (that transitive function whose reference *could* be controller/initiator of the action in a prototypical situation). But in addition, as described in §3.4.1, the verbal affix -:*ji-n* is brought in when the A NP is inanimate (and thus *incapable of being* the controller) or when the A NP is human but *is not in this instance* controlling the activity.

The Nominal Hierarchy, in Figure 4.5, also helps explain case splits outside the field of 'ergative languages'. Thus, in most Indo-European languages, pronouns and nouns from masculine and feminine declensions have distinct nominative and accusative forms; but neuter nouns have a single form for S, A and O functions. We can say that accusative marking extends only so far in from the left of the hierarchy, but there is no ergative marking on the right. (One presumes that a transitive sentence whose A and O NPs both involved neuter nouns would have to resort to something like constituent order to decide which was A and which O; such sentences are, of course, quite uncommon.) And in English most pronouns have nominative (SA) versus oblique (O, and other function) forms, while nouns lack inflection for core argument functions.

For all of the examples quoted so far, first and second person pronouns pattern in the same way but are clearly to the left of third person pronouns/demonstratives etc. on the hierarchy. The same situation is found in Sumerian (Thomsen 1984: 49–51; Michalowski 1980), in Coast Salish languages (Jelinek and Demers 1983) and in many Caucasian languages (e.g. Comrie 1981a: 211).

It has been suggested (DeLancey 1981;[16] Wierzbicka 1981) that no distinction should be made between first and second person on the hierarchy. There are, however, a considerable number of languages which provide data in favour of first person being at the extreme left, separated off from second person. These include:[17]

(a)   Derbyshire (1987: 319) reports:

> in all the cases I have seen reported for Amazonian languages, the person/agentivity hierarchy (Dixon 1979a and Silverstein 1976) follows this pattern: first person outranks second, second outranks third; when the higher-ranked person in a transitive clause is the subject, the nominative–accusative pattern is followed; when the higher-ranked person is the object, the pattern is ergative–absolutive.

---

[16] DeLancey (1987: 807) appears to have reconsidered his position, stating 'in a number of modern [Tibeto-Burman] languages the verb also marks in transitive clauses whether the subject is higher or lower than the object on a 1st > 2nd > 3rd or 1st = 2nd > 3rd person hierarchy, and this 'direct/inverse' marking system is probably also to be reconstructed for the Proto-Tibeto-Burman verb'.

[17] Note that Hetzron (1990: 582) invokes the Nominal Hierarchy, with first person to the left of second person, to explain the development of pronoun systems in Afroasiatic languages. See also DeLancey (1989) on verb agreement in proto-Tibeto-Burman.

Note that this also correlates with Kuno's 'Speech Act Participant Empathy Hierarchy': Speaker ⩾ Hearer ⩾ Third Person. Kuno (1976: 433) suggests that 'it is easiest for the speaker to empathize with himself (i.e. to express his own point of view); it is next easiest for him to express his empathy with the hearer; it is most difficult for him to empathize with the third party, at the exclusion of the hearer or himself'. There is, of course, considerable difference between 'empathy' and 'potentiality for being A rather than O', but both perhaps relate to the egocentric nature of the way humans see the world, and use languages.

Note that Derbyshire's sample includes representatives of the Arawak, Carib, Jê, Panoan, Tacanan, Tupí and Yanomami families as well as a number of language isolates. The hierarchy 1 > 2 > 3 for Tupí languages is also referred to by Jensen (1990), Seki (1990) and Monserrat and Soares (1983). The operation of this hierarchy in the Carib language Kuikúro and in the Tacanan language Cavineña are described in §4.5 below.

(b)   In Nadëb (Maku family), from north-west Brazil, second and third person pronouns have distinct forms for S/O and for A while first person pronouns have a single form for all three functions. This indicates 1 > 2, 3 on the hierarchy (Helen Weir, personal communication).

(c)   Discussing bound-pronominal cross-referencing forms in the Australian language Ndjebbana, McKay (1990) shows that first person singular has one form for S/A and another for O while second person singular has one form for S/O and another for A, again indicating 1 > 2.

(d)   Nedjalkov (1979: 259) states that 'the degree of ergativity in Chukchee verb-agreement increases in the following "direction": first > second > third'.

(e)   In some languages person and number intertwine but there is still evidence for 1 > 2. Foley (1991: 201) shows that in the Papuan language Yimas first person dual has a nominative–accusative paradigm, first person singular and plural and second person show a tripartite system, while third person has an absolutive–ergative paradigm. (Foley also shows that the order in which cross-referencing prefixes occur on the verb is motivated by the hierarchy 1 > 2 > 3.) We mentioned in §3.1.2 that in the Australian language Dhalanji the first person singular pronoun has a nominative–accusative paradigm while all other NP constituents employ a tripartite system in main clauses.

(f)   The NP hierarchy explains an oddity in the case system of Lardil (spoken on Mornington Island, Australia), which is basically an accusative language. We mentioned in §3.4.2 that for Lardil the accusative case is marked on O NPs except in imperative constructions. There is in fact an exception to the exception: accusative *must* be marked on a first person pronoun, even in imperative sentences. Since first person is on the extreme left of the hierarchy, it is the strongest candidate for accusative marking: it receives this marking even when accusative case is suspended for all other pronouns and nouns, in imperative constructions. (Data on Lardil are from Klokeid 1976: 197.)

I am not suggesting that the Nominal Hierarchy in Figure 4.5 will explain every detail of split marking in every language. There are always likely to be odd exceptions.[18] Just occasionally we get personal names > demonstratives (as in some Australian languages) and there are a few languages with 2 > 1 (a number of languages from the Algonquian family, including Ojibwa (Grafstein 1984) and southern Cheyenne (Charles E. Grimes, personal communication)). But the hierarchy does explain the great majority of marking systems split according to the nature of the NP.[19] And it is certainly the case that for the great majority of languages which distinguish between first and second person, it is first person that is furthest to the left, in keeping with my a priori impression that the speaker is, for him- or herself, the quintessential agent.

I mentioned that split-S and fluid-S marking, which relate to the semantic nature of the verb, are *most often* realised by cross-referencing on the verb, although they are realised through case marking in some languages. We should expect that splits according to the semantic nature of NPs would *most often* occur in languages that mark syntactic function on NPs. This does appear to be the case, although there are some split-by-NP-type languages that employ cross-referencing, e.g. Chukchee (Nedjalkov 1979), Coast Salish (Jelinek and Demers 1983) and Chinook (Silverstein 1976).

A more common phenomenon is for bound prefixes to indicate the *relative* positions of A and O on the hierarchy. We should expect A to be further to the left than O; choice of verbal affixes may depend on whether or not this does hold. In Algonquian languages, for example, each

[18] Exceptions to the hierarchy include: in the Australian language Arrernte the first person singular pronoun has an ergative, but all other pronouns an accusative paradigm (Wilkins 1989: 124). In Nganasan, from the Samoyedic group of the Uralic family, pronouns show no case distinctions while nouns inflect on an accusative pattern (information from Yakov Testelec). There may be other sorts of explanations in these and other cases, or they may just be exceptions. (Almost all typological generalisations in linguistics indicate majority – rather than absolute – patterns.)

[19] And it can be used as a check on diachronic hypotheses. Rumsey (1987a, b) follows earlier scholars in maintaining that any reconstructed proto-system must be typologically plausible: that is, it must accord with the kinds of systems that can be observed to occur in actually attested languages. Following Silverstein's (1976) work, Rumsey states that 'no language with ergative case marking for personal pronouns and animate nouns lacks ergative marking for inanimate nouns'. He then shows that some of the hypotheses concerning a putative ergative system in proto-Indo-European must be rejected since they yield typologically implausible systems.

transitive verb selects one of four suffixes: (a) *-a·*- denotes 'action by first or second person on third, and by third person proximate on third person obviative': (b) *-ekw*-, the inverse of (a), denotes 'action by third person on first or second person, and by obviative on proximate'; (c) *-eθe(ne)*-, denotes 'action by first person on second person'; (d) *-i*- denotes 'action by second person on first person' (Goddard 1967: 67).[20]

The Algonquian type of marking is not to be taken as a kind of ergativity. Rather, 'ergativity' is just one part of the wider field of 'surface marking of syntactic-semantic functions' and this shows that the Nominal Hierarchy has relevance over the wider field.

There is one other parameter that relates to the Nominal Hierarchy in Figure 4.5 – this is definiteness. Pronouns always have definite reference, and so do demonstratives. An NP referring to a human is more likely to be definite than one referring to a non-human (compare *The boss sacked me* with *A crocodile bit off my leg*) and an animate NP is more likely to be definite than an inanimate one (compare *I saw your dog* with *I saw a flash of lightning/a coconut tree*). The further to the left on the hierarchy an NP is, the more likely it is to be definite (at the extreme left it is always definite) and the farther to the right it is the more likely it is to be indefinite. There are thus two parameters that relate to the hierarchy: the accusative/ergative split, and definiteness. Relating them to each other, we can say that an accusative system (in which S and A are treated in the same way) correlates with definiteness, while an ergative system (in which S and O are treated in the same way) correlates with indefiniteness (see Jelinek, forthcoming).[21] This is a significant point, to which we shall return in §8.1.

The hierarchy in Figure 4.5 is based on that in Silverstein (1976). However, Silverstein also included number specification on his scheme. This is, it seems to me, a quite different parameter from the referential nature of the NP (as shown in Figure 4.5) and should be kept separate.

The interrelation of reference and number can be illustrated from Arabana (spoken in South Australia) in Table 4.4 (see Hercus, forthcoming). There is absolutive–ergative inflection of common nouns, and a

---

[20] DeLancey (1981: 643) quotes data from the Algonquian language Potawatomi as showing second person to the left of first person on the hierarchy, to assist his point that first and second person occupy essentially the same position and should not be separated. He also quotes data from Jyarong, a Tibeto-Burman language of Szechwan in which 'first person slightly outranks second, while both strongly outrank third'.

[21] Some languages only show case inflection on definite (not on indefinite) nouns: this can apply both to ergative (e.g. the North-west Caucasian Kabardian) and to accusative languages (e.g. Aari from the Omotic family – Hayward 1990b: 442). See also Mallinson and Blake (1981: 62).

Table 4.4. *Arabana*

A	-∅	*aḏu*	*-ru ~ -ri*	*-ru ~ -ri*
S	-∅	*anḏa*	-∅	-∅
O	*-ṇa*	*aṇa*	*-ṇa*	-∅
	non-sg. pronouns	sg. pronouns (exemplified here by 1st)	proper nouns	common nouns

nominative–accusative paradigm for non-singular pronouns (of all three persons), but three distinct forms for proper nouns and for singular pronouns. (Singular pronouns are not readily analysable; the actual first person singular forms are cited in the table.)

There is surely no justification for conflating reference and number into a single hierarchy. On what basis could one say that non-singular pronouns have the greatest likelihood – greater than singular pronouns – of being A rather than O?

Quite different factors are involved in a number split. If different kinds of morphological distinction are made for singular and non-singular pronouns (or nouns), then there are likely to be more distinctions in the singular than in the plural. This explains the Arabana system – singular pronouns have different forms for each of S, A and O while plural pronouns have the same form for S and A and a different one for O. (A similar pattern can be constructed for proto-Australian, which modern Arabana may directly reflect – Dixon 1980, Chapter 11.[22])

For Kalaw Lagaw Ya, the western language of the Torres Strait between Australia and New Guinea, Comrie (1981b) describes the kinds of marking shown in Table 4.5. It will be seen that in each column there are more distinctions made in the singular than in the plural (dual patterns with the plural for pronouns and with the singular for nouns). The different markings on non-plural names and common nouns accord with the Nominal Hierarchy, but those on singular pronouns do not. We must simply note a tendency (especially marked in Australian languages) to have maximal differentiation of syntactic function for singular pronouns.

---

[22] Note that in Bandjalang, from north-east New South Wales, non-human nouns have an ergative pattern, first person plural has an accusative pattern, while all other pronouns, and human common nouns, show a tripartite system (Crowley 1978). There is surely no justification for saying that first person plural has the greatest potentiality for use in A rather than in O function. It is just that one of the plural pronouns makes fewer grammatical distinctions than does the corresponding singular.

Table 4.5. *Kalaw Lagaw Ya*

singular	A,S,O all different	S = A, O different	S = O, A different
dual	A = S = O		
plural		A = S = O	A = S = O
	pronouns	names	common nouns

In some languages different factors may explain inconsistencies in the marking of syntactic function across different numbers. For Chukchee, Nedjalkov (1979: 259) shows that ergativity is marked most strongly in the plural and says 'this is consistent with the fact that the plural number forms are usually more regular with respect to the marking of different properties (ergative verb-agreement as well) than the singular ones'.

The Nominal Hierarchy in Figure 4.5 and the somewhat vague remarks I have made about number explain most NP-conditioned splits, but not all of them. In the New South Wales language Gumbaynggir first person dual and second person singular pronouns are like nouns in having one form for S/O and another for A, but first person singular and plural and second person dual and plural have distinct forms for each of S, A and O (Eades 1979). We mentioned above that in Yimas first person singular and plural show a tripartite system while for first person dual S and A fall together. There may well be diachronic explanations for exceptions of this type, e.g. phonological changes may have blocked a certain change in a particular environment, or some new category (e.g. dual) may have developed recently. In Diyari, from South Australia, male personal names and singular common nouns inflect on an ergative pattern; female personal names, non-singular common nouns, singular first and second person pronouns and all third person pronouns have a tripartite system, while non-singular first and second person pronouns show an accusative paradigm (Austin 1981a). The difference in marking between singular and non-singular first and second person pronouns is explainable, but not that between singular and non-singular common nouns, where more distinctions are made for the non-singulars.

In §3.1.4 I mentioned that a single language can have two cross-referencing mechanisms; one relating to S or A and the other to S or O. Moreover, different kinds of information may be cross-referenced by the two systems. The examples we quoted were:

Jarawara
1. person and number of S/A
2. gender of S/O or of S/A (depending on construction type)

Koiari
1. person and number of S/A
2. number of S/O

There is surely a semantic basis to these assignments, which interrelates with the hierarchy in Figure 4.5. We would expect person (associated with pronouns, at the left of the Nominal Hierarchy) to identify most closely with S/A, and for gender (always associated with nouns, to the right of the hierarchy in Figure 4.5, less often with pronouns) to identify most strongly with S/O, while number (which relates both to pronouns and nouns) would come between them. That is:

```
        person        number          gender
S/A ———————  ———————————————————— >
              < ———————————————— S/O
```

This explains the facts concerning Jarawara and Koiari (note that there is no category of grammatical gender in Koiari). It also correlates with the observation in §3.3 that languages which have different forms for some verbs depending on the 'number' of an argument NP always relate to S or O (never A). (And see note 3 to Chapter 3.)

Information on other languages with two cross-referencing mechanisms would be needed to confirm this additional hierarchy and to articulate it more finely.

Finally, we can mention that there are languages known where an ergativity split is conditioned partly by the semantic nature of the verb (§4.1) and partly by the semantic nature of NPs. These are discussed, together with other examples of combinations of types of split, in §4.5.

4.2.1 'Bound' versus 'free' split

A further kind of split mentioned in the literature on ergativity consists in different kinds of marking on *free*-form nominals (i.e. case or similar marking on NPs) and in cross-referencing *bound* affixes. This is best regarded not as a distinct kind of conditioning, but as a secondary phenomenon, explainable in the same terms as NP-conditioned split.

In §3.1 I discussed the two major kinds of morphological marking: some languages use cases exclusively, while others only employ cross-referencing verbal affixes (and some use both mechanisms). I mentioned that a language can be characterised as 'ergative' in terms of either type of marking.

These two morphological mechanisms may yield the same ergativity value. Thus, in Latin, one case marks S and A NPs, and a different case marks O NPs; the verb cross-references just S and A. In Avar, a North-east Caucasian language, nouns take ergative–absolutive (-*as:* ~ -*aɬ:*/∅) case inflections, and verbs cross-reference gender and number only for S and O NPs (Anderson 1976: 4; Simon Crisp, personal communication). But the two morphological mechanisms may also be in conflict. We saw in §3.4.1 that, in Murinypata, one verbal prefix is used to cross-reference S and A NPs and another for O NPs (a 'nominative–accusative' pattern), while NPs in A function can take ergative inflection (but there is no inflection for S or O functions).

Plainly, this is a 'split' of a different kind from those discussed above. It might seem at first glance that the split is not conditioned by the semantic nature of any sentential constituent, but is instead a 'meta-split' – depending entirely on the different *grammatical* ways of realising S/A/O identification. However, a close examination of the phenomenon yields a semantic explanation.

Cross-referencing affixes index a limited amount of information. They can make choices from a number of grammatical systems: basically, person, number and gender. These systems provide a full characterisation of pronouns, but supply only quite limited data on nouns. Verbal cross-reference makes free-form pronouns in core functions virtually redundant (they tend to be used rather infrequently, mainly for special emphasis); but at best it can only indicate the gender and number of a noun in a core syntactic function.

Cross-referencing systems are thus basically pronominal (with the affixes having developed from free-form pronouns, in some earlier stage of the language). We would expect them to be on a nominative–accusative pattern, since this characterises pronouns, at the extreme left of the hierarchy. Case marking on NPs is under no such constraint, and can be either nominative–accusative or absolutive–ergative. What we can predict is that, if there is a 'split' of this kind, then bound prefixes will be accusative, and case marking on free forms will be ergative. This is exactly what is found. Both case-marking and cross-referencing affixes can be accusative, or both can be ergative; but if there is a split, then bound forms will be accusative and free forms ergative (as in Murinypata) – never the other way around. We can thus regard this type of 'meta-split' as a corollary of the type discussed in §4.2; it can be given a semantic explanation in terms of the Nominal Hierarchy.

Another example is Gahuku, a Papuan language, where the verb has a prefix cross-referencing S and A and a suffix cross-referencing O, while nouns have an ergative case *-qmo* to mark A function and absolutive case, with zero realisation, for S and O (Deibler 1966).

A language with bound pronominal forms attached to the verb will almost always also have free pronouns, functioning in independent NPs. Free and bound pronouns can be organised on the same syntactic basis or they can vary – free-form pronouns may be ergative in their inflection while bound pronominal markers are accusative. This is so in Warlpiri, among other Australian languages. The following fairly certain chain of historical development (see Hale 1973; Dixon 1980: 333–49) provides an explanation:

(a)   Originally there was a simple split case-marking system, conditioned by the semantic content of NPs. Pronouns (for all persons) followed a nominative–accusative paradigm, and nouns an absolutive– ergative pattern. At this time there were no bound pronominal affixes.

(b)   A system of cross-referencing suffixes developed, on the verbal auxiliary, as reductions of free-form pronouns; these followed the free pronouns in having a nominative/accusative paradigm. Since full pronominal information was now obligatorily included in the auxiliary, the use of free-form pronouns diminished (and was only necessary for emphasis etc.).

(c)   Warlpiri morphology was simplified, in that the absolutive–ergative case system on nouns was generalised to apply to free pronouns. The original 'nominative' pronominal forms now receive ergative inflection in A function.

This series of changes can be tabulated:

	Bound pronouns	Free pronouns	Nouns
Stage 1	(none)	accusative	ergative
Stage 2	accusative	accusative	ergative
Stage 3	accusative	ergative	ergative

In modern Warlpiri, information on the core participants in an activity is obligatorily shown by bound-form pronouns, and these have a nominative–accusative pattern, while nouns (within an NP) have absolutive–ergative inflection; this is all as predicted by the Nominal Hierarchy. Free-form pronouns in A, S or O function have a secondary role, being used only for emphasis: they are similar in some ways to proper names and have, like them, assumed an ergative pattern (so that *all* NP constituents now have the same absolutive–ergative inflectional pattern).

4.3   Split conditioned by tense/aspect/mood

Each natural language has several varieties of 'shifters'. The pronominal system involves orientation to speaker 'I' and addressee 'you'. There will also be a deictic/demonstrative series, including terms like 'this' and 'that', 'here' and 'there'. The other area in which shifters are always encountered is time reference. The focus here is primarily 'now', the moment of speaking; there is also always a secondary focus 'today'. Relative to these shifting origins, languages show either a grammatical system of tense inflection, or a lexical class of time qualifiers, or both.[23]

Just as one type of ergativity split can be explained in terms of a semantic hierarchy extending from 'I', through 'you' and other shifters, to nominal referents that are increasingly distant from the speaker (§4.2), so a further type of ergativity split can be explained with reference to the different ways of regarding events that are established facts (roughly, completed before 'now') versus those that are merely prospective possibilities.

There are two different ways of viewing time: first, as a gradually unfolding scale, with 'now' as a point which moves along it at a steady rate, as in Figure 4.6.

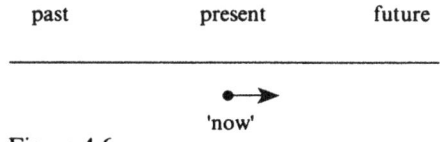

Figure 4.6

Alternatively, time can be viewed by looking in both directions from the constant origin 'now', as in Figure 4.7.

---

[23] Tense systems are always relative to 'now', but can sometimes also involve 'today'; see Hymes (1975). Time qualifiers appear always to refer to 'today' – including items like 'yesterday', 'tomorrow' – but sometimes also involve 'now' (in the latter case, the class contains items 'earlier today' and 'later today'). (Further discussion and exemplification from the Australian language family are given in Dixon 1977a: 498–500.)

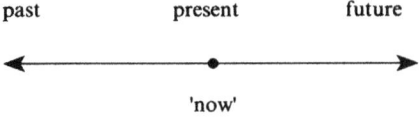

Figure 4.7

From the perspective of Figure 4.6, the speaker moves through time and the guessable but essentially unknowable future becomes the established past. Tense systems in a few languages appear to operate according to Figure 4.6, according equal grammatical status to 'past', 'present' and 'future' (Ancient Greek was of this type). But most languages treat 'future' in a quite different way from 'past', according to the perspective of Figure 4.7. For example, English which has an inflection for past tense but employs an array of modals for future reference – one must indicate whether something should or might or could happen, or is predicted to happen, etc.

Every language has some syntactic means for linking descriptions of a series of connected actions. There are basically two ways in which such a series can be viewed:

(a)   It may simply be seen as a series of actions that all happened to involve a certain participant. Here no causal connection between the events need be stated (or implied): it is simply that the events *are* documented, and that they *are* linked through a common participant – looking backward from 'now', in Figure 4.7, to a series of known and documented events.

(b)   It may be seen in terms of an agent initiating and controlling a series of interconnected actions: he undertakes X so that he can then engage in Y, as a result of which Z will follow, etc. The common participant to the events must, in this view, be the referent of S and A NPs in the sequential clauses. Here the events follow a causal sequence, moving forward through time; this viewpoint is compatible either with Figure 4.6 or with the future perspective in Figure 4.7.

I have suggested that (b), which demands syntactic identification of S and A as controlling 'agent', is the expected alternative for future-time discussion, and can also be employed for past time, as in Figure 4.6. But with (a) we could equally well get either S/A or S/O as syntactic pivot; this viewpoint is most plausible in past time.

An analogy may help here. The classic crime thriller begins with a series of events that have all befallen some participant – a victim, a sum of money, or whatever. The detective notes the events and the connection between them. He then tries to establish the agent and the chain of causality. Effectively, he begins with viewpoint (a), and then reinterprets the events from viewpoint (b). Once this is successfully done, he can project the modus operandi of the criminal into the future, predict his likely actions, and perhaps trap him.

These different syntactic orientations for known events, on the one hand, and for potential happenings, on the other, can aid in predicting the form of a morphological split conditioned by tense or aspect. If absolutive–ergative marking is found in one part of the system, we would expect it to be in past tense or in perfective aspect, where a series of completed events could be related to O and S as pivots. In non-past tense or in imperfective aspect, nominative–accusative marking would be expected. Something that has not yet happened is best thought of as a propensity of the potential agent ('That man might hit someone', rather than 'That person might get hit by someone'); this must involve A and S NPs as pivot.[24]

This is exactly what is encountered. Many languages can, of course, have nominative–accusative marking in all aspects and tenses, and others have absolutive–ergative marking unimpeded by aspect or tense (it may be conditioned by one of the factors mentioned in §§4.1–2). But if a split is conditioned by tense or aspect, the ergative marking is *always* found either in past tense or in perfective aspect.[25]

The language isolate Burushaski shows this type of split. Here a noun or singular pronoun in A function is obligatorily marked for ergative case (with the suffix -ε), only if the transitive verb is in a past-based tense (i.e. preterite, perfect, pluperfect past participle or static participle active); if the verb is in any other tense, ergative will not be used (Lorimer 1935: 64; see also Tiffou and Morin 1982).[26] In non-past tenses, there are no inflections for A, S or O (as there are none for S or O in past tenses):

[24] Regamey (1954) provided one of the earliest and most insightful discussions of this topic.
[25] Gildea (1992: 256ff.) notes that while some languages of the Carib family follow the generalisation here, others are apparent exceptions to it, e.g. in Cariña an ergative pattern is only found in the future. However, he argues that this is 'a function of idiosyncratic diachronic development rather than synchronic functional demands'. As Gildea reconstructs the history of Carib languages, an ergative pattern developed first in future tenses (from nominalisations) but soon spread into past tenses. At a transitional stage of development there was an exception to the generalisation, but the final result – he maintains – accords fully with the generalisation.
[26] Lorimer mentions two further peculiarities: ergative *must* be used on the A NP of *henʌs* 'to know' in non-past tenses, and it *can* be used on the A NP of *senʌs* 'to say' in non-past tenses. He mentions that ergative is permissible with other transitive verbs in non-past tenses, but is seldom used there; it is obligatory with all transitive verbs in past-based tenses.

Burushaski shows a split of ergative in past tenses versus no case marking in non-past. (It appears that, in non-past tenses, A and O are distinguished partly through constituent order and partly through pronominal prefixes; the latter cross-reference S NPs for intransitive verbs; indirect objects for ditransitive verbs like 'give', 'tell' or 'say to'; and direct objects for transitive verbs like 'strike', 'see' and 'kill'; Lorimer 1935: 192ff.)[27]

Many other examples in the literature show this type of split; generally (by contrast with Burushaski), explicit nominative–accusative marking occurs in non-past/perfective sentences. Ergative–absolutive marking occurs only in past tense for Iranian languages (see Noda 1983 on Middle Persian; John Payne 1980 on the Pamir subgroup; and Comrie 1981a: 173–7; Garrett 1990) and Kashmiri (Hook 1985); only in perfective aspect for Hindi (Allen 1951; Kachru 1965), Rājāsthanī (Allen 1960), Sumerian (Michalowski 1980) and a number of Mayan languages (e.g. Bricker 1978; Larsen and Norman 1979; Hofling 1984); and only in the compound perfect for Classical Armenian (Comrie 1981a: 181).

In some instances the marking involves case inflections (e.g. Burushaski, Hindi). There is generally positive marking for A function in past/ perfective, and for O function in non-past/imperfective – creating a genuine 'accusative' versus 'ergative' split; absolutive/nominative then has zero realisation. In other languages, the marking is shown by verbal affixes: in Yucatec, A is cross-referenced by a prefix and O by a suffix, while S is marked by the prefix system in incomplete aspect and by the suffix in completive aspect. In Chukchee the verb has cross-referencing affixes, whose 'degree of ergativity', Nedjalkov (1979) reports, increases in the following direction 'imperfect → aorist → perfect'.

As mentioned in §3.1.3, the Mayan language Chorti has set A of verbal affixes cross-referencing function A and set B cross-referencing S and O in the perfective; in the imperfective A, S and O are all marked differently, by sets A, C and B respectively (Quizar and Knowles-Berry 1988). In this language S and O are marked in the same way (an ergative system) only in perfective aspect.

---

[27] Alan Rumsey (personal communication) has pointed out a universal tendency: the NPs which are most likely to be cross-referenced on the verb are those which are highest on the Nominal Hierarchy. Many languages have just two NPs cross-referenced: one is the NP in S or A function, while the other is the indirect object (if there is one) or direct object (in the absence of an indirect object). In most sentences, the referent of the indirect object will be higher than that of the direct object. Languages behaving in this way include the Australian Walmatjari (see §6.2.3), Rembarnga (McKay 1975), and Ungarinjin (Rumsey 1982); Lakhota from the Siouan family (Van Valin 1977: 7); and Chukchee (Comrie 1979), among many others.

Newari shows a further variation on the basic tense/aspect split. Here ergative marking is obligatory in perfect/past and future/irrealis but is optional in durative/progressive (Givón 1985; see also Genetti 1988). It may be that durative/progressive is the temporal domain in which the agent's control is likely to predominate. This would interrelate with a type of ergativity split that is conditioned by mood – imperative constructions may show accusative marking while most or all other moods are ergative. Such a split is found in Sumerian (Michalowski 1980) and in the Nilotic language Päri (Andersen 1988). Imperatives place particular emphasis on the control of an activity, by A or S. In §4.5 we discuss the marking systems in Kuikúro, where ergative can be optional if the clause is in an 'interactive' mood (imperative, hortative or intentional) but always obligatory if the mood is 'descriptive'.

There is another sort of ergativity split, not conditioned by mood but by a parameter closely related to mood. In Marubo, a Panoan language (spoken where Columbia, Peru and Brazil meet), ergative inflection is used in positive but not in negative clauses (syntactic function in negative constructions is shown just by constituent order, AOV). (Information from Raquel Costa, private communication.)

In summary, it will be seen that ergative marking is most likely to be found in clauses that describe some definite result, in past tense or perfective aspect. An ergative system is less likely to be employed when the clause refers to something that has not yet happened (in future tense), or is not complete (imperfective aspect) or did not happen (negative polarity), or where there is emphasis on the agent's role (imperative or hortative moods).

Splits conditioned by tense, aspect or mood do co-occur with other kinds of splits. Illustrations will be provided in §4.5.

4.4   'Main' versus 'subordinate' clause split

The literature on ergativity contains some mention of a split conditioned in another way: morphological marking may differ between 'main' and 'subordinate' clauses. At first this appears to be a grammatically conditioned split, of a quite different type from the semantically motivated splits dealt with above. However, closer consideration shows that this type of division can be related to tense/aspect-type and to NP-conditioned splits, and that it does have a semantic basis.

The term 'subordinate clause' covers a variety of phenomena with different kinds of semantic implication. Thus 'purposive (= infinitival) clauses' normally refer to some attempt at controlled action; clauses of this kind generally have an A·or S 'agent' NP that is coreferential with some NP in their main clause ('We went to pick fruit', 'We went to play', 'I told you to pick fruit', etc.) For this type of subordinate construction, we would surely expect S and A to be treated in the same way within the complement clause.

Then there are relative clauses, and non-purposive complement clauses, most commonly detailing some action that takes place at the same time as (or previous to) the event referred to by the main clause: 'I kissed the child who had fallen over', 'I heard the man cutting wood', 'I saw the child being spanked by its mother'. Here the subordinate clause simply describes some event (usually an actual or completed event) that is related to an NP in the main clause: any syntactic orientation is possible.

Now if there were a split in morphological marking between main clause and purposive clause, we should expect the subordinate clause to show 'accusative patterning' – while the main clause would, if it differed from the subordinate clause, require an 'ergative pattern'. But if it were relative clauses that entered into a split, we might expect the subordinate clause to show 'ergative' characteristics – and the main clause would, if it differed from subordinate clauses, be of the 'accusative' type. (In the great majority of languages, of course, the same marking conventions apply to all clauses, whatever their grammatical status.)

The point at issue here is that purposive clauses are like main clauses in future tense (or imperfective aspect): they express some potential event as a propensity of the (A or S) agent, and thus demand accusative marking. However, relative clauses resemble past tense (or perfective) main clauses in simply describing something that has happened or is happening. Main clauses, for which either accusative or ergative marking is appropriate, must show the type of marking *opposite* to that of the subordinate clause, *if* there is a split.

There is another type of conditioning factor to be considered in relation to relative clauses. Many relative clauses have a 'restrictive' meaning, serving to specify more fully the referent of the noun they qualify (e.g. 'The man who lives in that big house ... '). Restrictive relative clauses can only be used with nouns or plural pronouns, not with first or second person singular pronouns, which are already fully specified. In some languages (including English) relative clauses are almost never used with singular pronouns. (There is further discussion of this in §8.2.) That is, relative clauses tend to be associated with items from the right-hand end of the

Nominal Hierarchy, which is in turn associated with ergative marking. This reinforces the conclusion drawn from the tense–aspect character of relative clauses, that they have an ergative bias.

Only a few examples of main/subordinate clause splits are known but they do, by and large, support the sorts of orientation predicted on semantic grounds. In the Nilotic language Päri, S is generally treated like O but in purposive clauses (as in imperative – §4.3), S is instead treated like A. (Andersen 1988 suggests that this is best described as an 'extended ergative' pattern.) In Shokleng, from the Jê family of Brazil, main clauses can be ergative or accusative (this is an aspectually conditioned split) but subordinate clauses are always ergative in their cross-referencing. Interestingly, all subordinate clauses in Shokleng behave in the same way, whether they are relative clauses, 'when' or 'after' time clauses, conditionals or purposive complements. My prediction would have been that purposive complements should be accusative – here, however, we appear to have a language that is basically ergative, with accusativity coming in just for 'active' (i.e. non-stative) aspect in main clauses, but there being no split within subordinate clauses (Urban 1985).

Another example comes from Tsimshian (Boas 1911).[28] Here subordinate ('subjunctive') clauses – e.g. 'Then he heard *him come again*', 'His mother was glad *when she saw him*' – consistently show an ergative pattern of cross-referencing; a 'subjective' verbal prefix refers to A, and an 'objective' prefix to S or O. But in main ('indicative') clauses, 'objective' is used for A cross-reference, as for O, when first or second person is acting on third person; subjective prefixes are used for the A NP in a main clause only when third person is acting on first or second person (as predicted, in terms of the Nominal Hierarchy). Tsimshian subordinate clauses clearly show 'ergative' marking, while main clauses demonstrate a split between 'ergative' marking and no marking at all, the split being conditioned by the Nominal Hierarchy.[29]

[28] I am grateful to Michael Silverstein for drawing this to my attention.
[29] In Mayan languages, set A of pronominal affixes typically cross-references A, while set B cross-references S and O. There appears to be a diachronic shift, beginning in subordinate clauses, that involves the extension of use of set A (see §7.2). In Jacaltec (Craig 1976, 1977; Larsen and Norman 1979) set A refers to A and S in 'aspectless' subordinate clauses. In Mam, set A has been extended to cover S and O, as well as A, in some types of subordinate clauses (England 1983a, b). See also Hofling (1984). It is likely that these uses of A are best described as 'extended ergative' (or 'marked nominative', see §3.4.3). Note that Larsen (1981) suggests that subordinate clauses in the Mayan language Aguacatec, in which S and A are marked in the same way, can be regarded as 'derived verbal nouns and, thus, the ergative prefixes cross-referencing their respective Ss and As may be viewed as being formally noun possessors'.

It is clear that to talk simply of 'main clause' versus 'subordinate clause' split is misleading. Any analysis of this phenomenon will have to take account of the types of subordinate clause involved and their semantic function. The data available provide initial support for my a priori semantic prediction that purposive clauses are most likely to be accusative, and relative clauses to be ergative, if these clause types do enter into a split. We now need further detailed and reliable data on these kinds of split in other languages.

4.5   Combinations of different kinds of split

Most languages that show a split-ergative system do just operate with one conditioning factor: (1) the semantics of the verb; or (2) the semantics of the core NPs; or (3) tense and/or aspect and/or mood of the clause; or (4) main/subordinate status of the clause. But there are some that involve a combination of two or even three conditioning factors (so far no language that requires all four has been reported). Every combination of the four parameters is attested.

Balochi, a north-western Iranian language, combines (2) and (3) – ergative is marked only on third person pronouns and nouns, and only in perfective aspect (Farrell, forthcoming). A similar system is suggested by Bricker (1986) for the grammar of the Mayan hieroglyphs.[30] The same combination occurs in Burushaski, where ergative case is found only in past-based tenses and only on nouns and singular pronouns; non-singular pronouns have a single form for S, A and O in all tenses. Sumerian has ergative marking only on nouns (not on first or second person pronouns) and then only in perfect aspect (Michalowski 1980).

The interrelation of factors (1) and (3) is found in Mawayana, an Arawak language from northern Brazil. There are two classes of intransitive verb. One (which includes 'be red') always has an S_o, marked by a verbal suffix which is identical with the suffix cross-referencing O on a transitive verb. For the other class of intransitive verbs (which includes 'sleep') there is a split according to tense–aspect; roughly, the same S_o suffix appears to be used in present continuous and near past clauses, but an S_a pronominal prefix – identical with the prefix marking A on a

---

[30] Loma, a Mande language from Liberia, has a split-S system in the perfective – with set 1 of free pronouns used for A and S_a and set 2 for O and S_o – but in the imperfective no distinction is made, set 2 being used for all of A, O and S. A and O are then distinguished in terms of constituent order, AOV (Rude 1983).

transitive verb – in remote past and future clauses. (Personal communication from Alexandra Y. Aikhenvald, based on Howard 1986.)

In the Carib language Kuikúro, an ergative construction must be used in certain circumstances, it is optional in others, and is not allowed in others. There are two interrelating criteria – whether the mood of clause is 'interactive' (i.e. imperative, hortative or intentional) or 'descriptive', and the reference of the A NP (Franchetto 1990):

interactive moods	A is first person singular or first plural inclusive: ergative not allowed	A is second person or first plural exclusive: ergative optional	A is third person: ergative obligatory
descriptive mood	ergative obligatory for all types of A		

The use of ergative in interactive moods perfectly accords with the Nominal Hierarchy as far as singular pronouns are concerned. The placement of first person plural forms is also semantically natural – first exclusive is effectively a combination of first and third persons and it falls into the middle column, between those of first singular and of third person. First inclusive is a combination of first and second persons and it naturally falls to the left of first exclusive, in the first column. As mentioned in §4.3, the fact that ergative marking can only be omitted when there is an order, or an invitation ('let's ... ') or a stated intention is in keeping with our generalisations concerning aspect and mood-type splits.

Yukulta, from the Tangkic subgroup of Australian, shows a split system which is also conditioned partly by tense/aspect-type considerations and partly by the semantic nature of NPs. Keen (1983) recognises two kinds of transitive construction, with the following inflections:

	A	O	Verb marked by
	A	**O**	Verb marked by
(a)	ergative	absolutive	transitive suffixes
(b)	absolutive	dative	intransitive suffixes

Ergative is basically -*ya*; dative is -*n^{y}d^{y}a* ~ -^{y}*i*; and absolutive has a number of allomorphs, one of which is zero (with a vowel-final stem of more than two syllables).

Construction (a) is used with statements of past fact and of future intention; but (b) is required in all other cases, i.e. for negative sentences in past tense ('He didn't do it') and for future irrealis (e.g. wishing). We see that this split is not simply in terms of past/future tense, but in terms of things that have happened (or are promised to happen) versus those that have not happened or might conceivably happen. Construction (b) must also be used, whatever the tense/polarity choice of the sentence, if (i) A is third person and O is first or second person, or if (ii) A is second person and O is non-singular first person.[31] This second conditioning factor appears to deal with the relative positioning of A and O NPs on the Nominal Hierarchy, somewhat as in Algonquian; it is explainable in terms of the discussion there, except for the odd specification of *non-singular* first person under (ii).[32]

Factors (3) and (4) are combined in Shokleng. As mentioned in §4.4, subordinate clauses in this language are always ergative. In main clauses that are marked with the 'stative' aspectual particle, an ergative postposition *tõ* marks an A NP while S and O are left unmarked. When a main clause includes the 'active' particle, S and A are marked by the nominative postposition *wũ* with O being left unmarked. (Urban, 1985, suggests that this should be regarded as 'marked nominative' – see §3.4.3.) Tsimshian, mentioned in §4.4, combines (2) and (4).

We can now turn to languages where three of the conditioning factors interrelate. Georgian combines (1), (2) and (3): there is a split-S pattern only in the aorist and perfect series and here the 'ergative' marking (on A and S_a) is only found on nouns and third person pronouns, not on first and second person pronouns (see Merlan 1985: 341–4 for a useful summary, Vogt 1971 and Harris 1981 for fuller accounts). Cavineña, a Tacanan language of northeastern Bolivia, combines all of (2), (3) and (4). Here the Nominal Hierarchy applies in fully articulated form. A noun in A function always takes the ergative case suffix *-ra*, whereas a pronoun in A function often omits *-ra*. Camp (1985) reports:

> This is how it works. If the overt noun is ergative, then the absolutive pronoun is the object ... However, if the noun is absolutive, then the absolutive [i.e. zero-marked] pronoun is the subject ... When subject and object are both expressed by pronouns, cases are determined by a ranking

---

[31] Blake (1976) mentions similar phenomena in two other Queensland languages, Kalkatungu and Pitta-Pitta – see §7.2.

[32] It is interesting that the ergative construction is used here for future intention – it may be that for speakers of Yukulta intention is looked upon as something definite (as definite as past fact) as opposed to, for instance, wishing. (Or, there may be some other explanation.)

on topicality; first person outranks second, which outranks third. This ranking manifests itself in the obligatory use of ergative case pronouns in certain preferential combinations. It also manifests itself in the ordering of subject and object pronouns when they are contiguous ... When a pronoun occurs as the subject of a transitive clause, that pronoun appears in the ergative case when it is a lower-ranked subject interacting with a higher-ranked object.

This applies to transitive clauses of 'high activity'. However, 'in transitive sentences of low activity, that is negation,[33] potentiality, intention, sensation and contrary to fact, if the agent is expressed by a pronoun, that pronominal form is usually ergative. The pronominal subject of a dependent transitive clause, if expressed, can only be in the ergative case'. We see that ergative marking is used most in dependent clauses, and in mood types that downplay the role of the agent (including intention – compare with the set of conditions given above for Yukulta), and in neutral mood the use of ergative marking is conditioned by the Nominal Hierarchy.

Finally, there are splits conditioned by a combination of factors (1), (2) and (4) in some languages of the Tupí-Guaraní family. Jensen (1990: 12ff.)[34] details four sets of pronominal prefixes to verbs – roughly, set 1 cross-references A and S_a, set 2 refers to O and S_o (and see §4.1.1), and set 3 marks the S_a of a serial verb which is coreferential with S or A of the main clause. The function of set 4 will be described below.

In intransitive main clauses, set 1 is always used for S_a and set 2 for S_o. Choice of prefixes in a transitive main clause is conditioned by the Nominal Hierarchy, 1 > 2 > 3 as follows: (a) if O is third person, use set 1 for A and set 2 for O; (b) if O is higher than A on the hierarchy then O is as before cross-referenced by set 2, and A is not marked on the verb; (c) if A is first person and O second person then set 4 of prefixes is used – this series contains only two prefix forms, distinguishing between singular and plural second person O. In subordinate clauses, which are always temporal or conditional, set 2 is used for O and for all S (S_a as well as S_o), with A not being cross-referenced.

---

[33] Note that in Marubo and Yukulta ergative marking is not used in negative clauses, contrary to the situation in Cavineña. This indicates that although the same kinds of semantic considerations are likely to underlie ergativity splits in different languages, the actual details of the semantic criteria will vary from language to language, and will depend on the semantic organisation of the grammar and lexicon for each particular language.

[34] See Seki (1990) and Harrison (1986) for descriptions of the situations in two individual languages of the Tupí-Guaraní family.

Thus we have subordinate clauses having a fully ergative pattern while main clauses are basically split-S but with the decision concerning which core constituent(s) are cross-referenced on the verb, and by which prefix set(s), determined by the Nominal Hierarchy.

4.6   Summary

In this chapter, each type of split of intra-clausal marking (whether realised by case inflections, or particles or adpositions, or cross-referencing, or constituent order) has been explained in semantic terms. Some splits are motivated by the semantic content of intransitive verbs, others by the semantic content of A and O NPs within a transitive clause, and others by the tense, aspect or mood of the clause. Differences of marking between main and subordinate clauses have been related to tense/aspect-type and to NP-type distinctions, while differences between case marking and bound affixes were just related to the hierarchy that underlies NP-conditioned splits.[35] Case marking is also, of course, syntactically motivated. In Chapter 8, I will summarise the varying pressures on morphological marking – universal and language-particular syntactic requirements (discussed in the next two chapters), as well as the semantic preferences described here.

We could, in conclusion, enquire which type of split is most superficially ergative – and, at the other extreme, which type is most likely to correlate with ergativity at the syntactic level. Any answer to this question must at present be quite tentative: detailed investigation of the morphology and syntax of a large number of 'ergative' languages (in terms of the distinctions stressed in this book) would be required before we could make any firm statement. But I am prepared to advance a preliminary hypothesis. Syntactic processes typically operate with NPs as pivots, and a particular case marking is perhaps more likely to correlate with some syntactic property than is a corresponding pattern among bound affixes. Since case marking is most strongly associated with splits conditioned by the semantic

---

[35] Klaiman (1987) provides an inclusive survey of ergative characteristics in South Asian languages, in terms of nominal case marking, clitic pronominals, nominal agreement on main verbs and nominal agreement on auxiliary verbs, also taking account of tense/aspect-conditioned splits. She draws correlations between the occurrences of these different ergative marking mechanisms. For instance: no South Asian language has an ergative split conditioned by the semantics of core NPs unless it also has a split conditioned by tense–aspect; none has ergative cross-referencing on main verbs unless there is a tense–aspect-conditioned split.

nature of the core NPs, it may be only among languages of this type (e.g. Dyirbal, §1.2) that we will find the strongest examples of 'ergativity' at the syntactic level.

Appendix: Inventory of types of split

It is useful to consider the various logical possibilities for types of split and to see whether examples are known for all of them. Below, a slash indicates the split; where two function letters are juxtaposed they are marked in the same way, and where another function letter is separated by a hyphen it is marked in a different way, e.g. AS-O/A-S-O indicates that A is marked in the same way as S and differently from O on one side of the split, while on the other side A, S and O are all marked differently.

Split conditioned by semantic nature of NPs

(a) Part accusative: AS-O/ASO, e.g. Latin.

(b) Part ergative: ASO/A-SO, e.g. Burushaski.

(c) Part accusative, remainder ergative (complementary distribution of ergative and accusative marking): AS-O/A-SO, e.g. Kuku-Yalanji, Ngiyambaa.

(d) Part accusative, part ergative (overlapping distribution of ergative and accusative marking): AS-O/A-S-O/A-SO, e.g. Cashinawa, Yidin^y.

(e) All accusative, part ergative (distribution of ergative entirely within distributional scope of accusative): AS-O/A-S-O, no example known.

(f) All ergative, part accusative (distribution of accusative included entirely within distributional scope of ergative): A-S-O/A-SO, e.g. Waga-Waga.

(g) Part accusative, part ergative, part neither (middle area where neither accusative nor ergative applies): AS-O/ASO/A-SO, no example known.[36]

[36] In the Australian language Gurinji, nouns show an ergative paradigm (A-SO), free pronouns have the same form for all three core functions (ASO) and bound pronominal clitics follow an accusative pattern. (AS-O). We do get an AS-O/ASO/A-SO system, but only through combining the free/bound parameter with the Nominal Hierarchy. (Data from Patrick McConvell.)

It is interesting to speculate whether the apparent absence of a split system of type (g) is just an accidental gap (and we might expect an example to turn up, as more languages are studied) or a real gap – something which just cannot occur, so that a theoretical explanation should be provided for why it cannot occur.

Split conditioned by tense/aspect/mood.
No languages showing this kind of split are known to have more than two kinds of marking (unlike (d) and (g) above, which show three kinds).

(a)	Part accusative: AS-O/ASO, e.g. Lardil.
(b)	Part ergative: ASO/A-SO, e.g. Burushaski, Classical Armenian, Marubo.
(c)	Part accusative, remainder ergative, AS-O/A-SO, e.g. Yucatec, Yukulta, Päri.
(e)	All accusative, part ergative: AS-O/A-S-O, e.g. Pitta-Pitta (Blake 1979a).
(f)	All ergative, part accusative: A-S-O/A-SO, e.g. Chorti.

Splits conditioned by the verb fall into just two types, split-S and fluid-S (there is no example where a special marking is used just for some S and not for A or O, for instance). Splits conditioned by main/subordinate clause should also, potentially, show types (a)–(g) but most languages with this sort of split combine it with a split of some other sort and for some of these it is difficult to separate out the parameters (see §§4.4–5).

5 The category of 'subject'

Turning our attention now to syntax, we can first of all note the confusion concerning the identity of the 'subject' in ergative languages. This confusion results simply from the fact that linguistic theory evolved in the context of the better-known languages of Europe, which have a predominantly accusative character at every level. For languages of this type, certain semantic and grammatical properties coincide to give a two-sided definition of subject. The 'subject' of a sentence is that NP whose referent *could be* the 'agent' that initiates and controls an activity; the subject NP is normally obligatory in a sentence, receives the unmarked case, may be cross-referenced in the verb, and is the pivot for operations of coordination and subordination.

For ergative languages, these semantic and grammatical criteria for 'subject' do not coincide;[1] to employ the notion of subject in such languages, one must decide, in effect, which of the two kinds of criteria should take precedence. Some linguists emphasise semantic criteria, but encounter severe difficulties in explaining all types of grammatical processes in terms of semantically defined 'subject' for ergative languages. (In the Appendix, I describe difficulties which Relational Grammar has had in accounting for antipassive derivations.) Other linguists take syntactic/morphological criteria as basic; this facilitates statements of

---

[1] There is an indirect analogy to the unit 'word'. Every language has a unit '(grammatical) word', with considerable psychological reality for the speaker (see Sapir 1921: 33–5); and grammatical criteria can always be given to define this unit, although the nature of the criteria differ from language to language. It appears also to be the case that every language has a phonological unit larger than the syllable, which can be called '(phonological) word'; and phonological criteria, usually involving considerations of stress etc., can always be given to define this unit. Now in many languages, 'grammatical word' and 'phonological word' coincide; but this is not so in *every* language. To mention just two examples, from my own field work: in Yidin^y a grammatical word consists of one or more phonological words (Dixon 1977a, b); in Fijian the units of grammatical and phonological word can coincide, or a grammatical word may comprise more than one phonological word; or a phonological word may comprise more than one grammatical word, or a phonological word may constitute the whole of one and part of another grammatical word (see Dixon 1988a: 21–4; 1988b).

grammatical derivation, but is bound to complicate any attempt to provide semantic interpretation for the grammar. Trubetzkoy (1939) said that if O received the same case marking as S, then it must be subject; Keenan (1976) followed a similar line of argumentation in taking 'absolute NP' as subject for Dyirbal – it bears unmarked case, is obligatory, is the pivot for most syntactic operations, etc. But this 'subject' relates to S and O, not S and A functions. (The Appendix discusses Marantz's 1984 proposal, along similar lines.)

Although all languages have reasonably complex grammars, with comparable sets of parts of speech etc., the details of syntactic and morphological patterning do show wide variation. Classes of 'noun' and 'verb' can, it seems, be recognised in every language on internal grammatical criteria. However, these criteria differ a good deal from language to language. In English, 'noun' can be defined as a word that can follow an article and need not itself be followed by any other item; in Latin, the criterion for 'noun' is a word that inflects for case and number but not gender. Note that English has no case system on nouns, while Latin has no articles and shows free constituent order. The word classes in these two languages are given the same label, 'noun', on semantic criteria – they are the classes which include words referring to concrete objects. The full semantic scopes of 'noun' classes in Latin and English are not identical (that is, not every noun in Latin would be translatable by a noun in English, and vice versa) but they have the same semantic core.

Any linguistic investigation should begin by describing the grammars of individual languages, in terms of structural criteria appropriate to each language, and then looking at the semantic content of the classes and categories established. As a next step, some of these classes and categories may be identifiable between languages, on semantic grounds. Every attempt to establish true typological universals must surely be semantically based. 'Subject' is most likely to be establishable as a universal category, playing a part in the grammar of each language, if viewed from a semantic angle.

I will show that 'subject' is a universal category, having a vital role in the grammar of every language that employs syntactically based marking, be it 'accusative', 'ergative' or any mixture of the two. But – and this is a vital point – it is not the *most* fundamental category. 'Subject' links functions from intransitive and transitive clause types; it effectively involves a grouping of S and A, out of the basic semantic–syntactic relations, S, A and O – a grouping that is made entirely on semantic grounds.

A basic thesis of this book is that A, S and O are the universal core categories, and that syntactic rules in every grammar are framed in terms of them. There is, as a further stage, a universal grouping of A and S as 'subject' – a category that plays an important role in the grammar of every language with a prototypical profile (i.e. with syntactically based marking of core constituents). Some types of syntactic processes will always be statable in terms of 'subject', in every language of this type. Other types of process may relate to 'subject' in some languages, but in other languages they may involve some other combination of the core functions.

Schieffelin (1979, 1985) provides important support for my suggestion that it is S, A and O – rather than 'subject' and 'object' – that are the basic universal syntactic relations. She studied how children learn Kaluli, a Papuan language. The basic constituent orders are OAV and SV. Nouns are marked for case – ergative -ε on A and absolutive -ɔ on S and O. An alternative constituent order, AOV, is used to put the O NP into 'focus'; here both A and O are generally in absolutive case unless they are both proper names or kin terms, in which case A must take the ergative ending.

Kaluli children go through three stages when they start producing transitive sentences. First, A NPs receive no marking. Then all A NPs (in OAV and in AOV clauses) are accorded ergative marking. Finally, the system described above is followed. The interesting point is that although Kaluli children wrongly generalise the ergative case suffix -ε to apply to A NPs in AOV clauses, they *never* generalise this ending also to apply to an S NP. Schieffelin concludes that Kaluli children operate in terms of a basic syntactic category A, and *not* in terms of a basic category of subject (which would be the concatenation of A and S).

In §5.1 I discuss the universal semantic bases of A and O (expanding on the preliminary account in §1.1) and suggest a universal definition of 'subject', covering all languages which employ syntactically based marking for core arguments (the first, prototypical, scheme from Chapter 2).

5.1   Universal definition of 'subject'

People observe events, of many different sorts, happening in the world; the participant roles show a great deal of diversity, and the effects of the activities on the participants vary a great deal. Yet all human languages classify actions into two basic types: those involving one obligatory participant, which are described by intransitive clauses, and those involving two or more obligatory participants, which are dealt with by transitive clauses.[2] As mentioned in §1.1, in some languages verbs are fairly strictly divided into intransitive and transitive subclasses, with little or no overlap between them. In contrast, Fijian allows almost every verb to function either transitively or intransitively, although there is an explicit morphological indicator – when a verb is used in a transitive clause it bears a transitive suffix, when used in an intransitive clause there is no suffix. In other languages a fair number of verbs may be used either transitively or intransitively (in some instances with $S = O$, in others with $S = A$) although there will still be a fair number of verbs that belong unambiguously either to the transitive or to the intransitive set. In each language, there is explicit grammatical marking of the transitivity type of a clause – in terms of case-marking on nouns and pronouns, occurrence of particles, pronominal affixes on verbs, inflectional allomorphs on verbs, and so on. The details of grammatical marking vary from language to language, but the *same types* of criteria recur.

Thus all languages treat 'cut' and 'give', 'rub' and 'carry', 'take' and 'cook' as transitive verbs. In addition, very nearly every language classifies 'see' and 'hear' (and many also treat 'like' and 'hate') in the same way. This is really a surprising fact, since these verbs refer to totally different kinds of events; but they all involve two basic participants, and are dealt with by verbs belonging to the semantic–syntactic class 'transitive' in all types of language. What is even more surprising is that all languages consistently identify participant roles between these different verbs. In §1.1 I described the varied semantic types that are associated with the verb class, each having its own semantic roles – Agent, Manip and Target for the AFFECT type; Donor, Gift and Recipient for GIVING; Speaker, Addressee and Message for SPEAKING; Perceiver and Impression for ATTENTION; and so on – and noted that the same semantic roles are mapped onto the basic syntactic relation A in just about every language. That is, the participant who makes the incision (for 'cut') is equated with the person who transfers possession of something he has had (for 'give'), with the participant who imparts some information (for 'tell'), with the participant who receives a sense impression (for 'see'), and so on. The A NPs for 'cut', 'give', 'tell'

---

[2] Activities involving more than two core participants are dealt with in the same way as those involving just two core participants (that is, ditransitives are always a subtype of transitives), i.e. the subject of a verb like 'give' or 'show' or 'tell' is always dealt with in the same way as the subject of 'take' or 'know' (whereas the subject of an intransitive verb such as 'run' or 'fall' or 'laugh' may be treated quite differently).

and 'see', etc. are consistently treated in exactly the same way, in all aspects of morphology and syntax, across every type of human language. For those transitive activities involving two core roles, that which is not identified as A is also treated in the same way between different semantic types;[3] for this I use the functional label 'O'. It is these facts which lead me to suggest that the syntactic–semantic functions A and O are universal linguistic primitives.

On a priori grounds, the various participants that occur with different transitive verbs would be classified in quite diverse ways. Fillmore's (1968) original suggestion that 'kill' involves NPs in Agentive and Dative cases, whereas 'see' requires Dative and Objective (and Dative is used to describe 'who is killed', but 'who does the seeing') has strong appeal, as a semantically based description. Why is it that no language (or, at least, none of the many tongues investigated by me, or by colleagues I have asked about this) treats the NPs associated with 'kill' and 'see' in this manner? There are in fact languages which treat 'kill' and 'see' differently but they do not support Fillmore's position. For instance, languages from the North-east Caucasian family typically use ergative case for 'who kills' but locative or dative case (depending on the language) for 'who sees'. Note, though, that 'who is killed' and 'what is seen' are both marked by absolutive case, realising the O relation. The fact that, in at least some of these languages, 'who kills' and 'who sees' are cross-referenced on the verb in the same way indicates that both are in A relation. There is overwhelming evidence that A and O NPs are consistently identified between 'kill', 'see', 'give', 'tell', 'carry', etc. over languages of every typological variety.

The basic reason for this identification appears to lie in the idea of 'agency' or 'control'. For most multi-participant events, there is just one participant who potentially initiates or controls the activity. It is the NP referring to this participant that is identified as being in A function. In *Mary hit John*, it is Mary (if anyone) who controls what is happening. It may be that Mary hit John accidentally, so that no one can be identified as the controller, for some particular token of this sentence; but it is clear that John can never be taken as 'agent'.

Some activities require the cooperation of two participants: both are, in a sense 'agents'. It is generally possible to focus on either participant (as

---

[3] Where there are more than two core roles, some languages have alternative construction types available, allowing each of the non-A core roles to be in O function. This is discussed below.

the A NP), either through employing two different but semantically related verbs (e.g. *Mary sold it to John, John bought it from Mary*) or through a single verb that effectively allows interchange of A and O NPs (*Mary shook hands with John, John shook hands with Mary*).[4] In such an event, it is often the case that one participant does play a leading role in initiating the transaction/salutation; this can be indicated by assigning it to A function. But where double agency is required by the nature of the event, either participant could conceivably be shown in A function; which is chosen will depend upon who the speaker wishes to focus on as being, in terms of his total discourse, 'the protagonist ... at the center of events' (Schachter 1977: 283).

Some languages have a single lexeme covering 'see, look at' and one covering 'hear, listen to'. Other languages are like English in having distinct lexemes 'see', 'hear' and 'look at', 'listen to'; these pairs of verbs have quite different syntactic properties. 'See' and 'hear' do not describe actions; indeed they cannot – except in quite marked circumstances – be used in imperative form. They contrast with 'look at' and 'listen to', which more clearly involve the idea of volition and effort on the part of the observer, and which can appear in imperative constructions (like almost every other transitive verb). But all verbs that involve some further specification – hyponyms of 'see' such as 'watch', 'observe', 'scan', 'ogle' – plainly involve the referents of the A NPs initiating or controlling the event (they also occur as imperatives). 'See' and 'hear' themselves, as the most neutral verbs describing visual and aural reception, scarcely accord with our criterion for why one particular participant is, in almost every language, marked as A, on a par grammatically with the A NPs for 'cut', 'give', etc. But with all other more specific verbs of seeing and hearing, the referent of one NP does initiate or control the event, satisfying the criterion for recognition of this NP as being in A function; 'see' and 'hear' are treated in the same way as their hyponyms, 'the one who sees' being assigned the same grammatical marking as 'the one who (purposefully) watches'.[5] *Mary saw John* can describe an event where John just came into

---

[4] Verbs of this kind can be symmetrical – like 'marry', 'meet', 'shake hands' and 'kiss' – or directional; compare *Mary rented the house to John, John rented the house from Mary* with the *buy/sell* example.

[5] Support for this line of argument comes from those languages which have a single verb covering both 'see' and 'look at', and another for 'hear' and 'listen to'. That is, a single lexical root is employed to describe chance or involuntary perception, and also for purposeful direction of attention; in the latter sense, these verbs can of course be used in imperative form. Almost all Australian languages, and many from other parts of the world, show this pattern (see Dixon 1972: 41 and see the examples in §6.2.2).

Mary's field of view, and no agency was involved; but there is the potentiality that Mary looked for and sought out John – then Mary, but not John, could be something like an 'agent'. (If John *tried* to be seen, then some other verb like 'show (oneself)', would be appropriate.)

We begin with our perception of the world: we see many activities, of many different kinds. Then a grammatical classification is imposed on these events: they are divided into those described by intransitive and those described by transitive clauses. The grammatical requirement is that an intransitive clause has a verb and one core NP, whereas a transitive clause has a verb and two obligatory NPs.[6] There is then a semantic identification of one transitive NP as being in A function – this is consistent across languages, for transitive verbs of all semantic types – and complementary identification of the other transitive core NP as in O function. This A NP refers to the actual or potential 'agent', who could (if anything could) initiate and control the activity. Note that, in some languages, the A NP must be animate (e.g. Jacaltec – Craig 1976: 108–9);[7] it is then likely that, for every transitive clause, the A NP could be agent. Most languages have some transitive verbs whose major occurrence is with an animate agent, but which can also be used in an extended sense with an inanimate noun in the agent slot, e.g., *The wind closed the door, Sorrow is eating at my heart.*[8] The central meanings of *close* and *eat* require animate agency; but the physical action of the wind can create the same impression as an animate agent, so that *the wind* is clearly regarded as an A NP in *The wind closed the door.* And a language-particular metaphorical extension views the effects

---

[6] Certain NPs are termed 'obligatory' not because they must necessarily occur in the surface structure of every clause involving a certain verb, but because the speaker and hearer must have some understanding of them if the clause is to form a conceptual whole, with the potentiality of referring to some actual, possible or habitual event.

   I refer to 'intransitive verb and S NP' or 'transitive verb plus A and O NPs' as the 'core' of a clause. Any core may of course be augmented by peripheral components: locational or temporal qualifiers, adverbial specifications, NPs in dative case, etc. Peripheral components can, as a rule, occur with a core of either transitivity.

[7] Craig notes that, corresponding to 'He closed the door', Jacaltec cannot have 'The wind closed the door', involving the same transitive verb *speba* 'close'; instead, a sentence translatable as 'The door closed by the wind' must be used, involving *xpehi* 'closed' and with 'wind' expressed through an agentive prepositional phrase.

[8] Note here the inclusion of *at* (cf. *He is eating the meat* and *He is eating at the meat.*) We could alternatively have *Sorrow is eating my heart out*, but scarcely **Sorrow is eating my heart.* This illustrates typical grammatical restrictions on metaphorical extensions of common verbs.

   I am grateful to W. S. Allen for drawing my attention to Homer's description (*Iliad* 6: 202) of Bellerophon 'eating his heart' (*hòn thumòn katédōn*) with sorrow; it may be significant that he here uses the verb (with *kata* 'down') which is elsewhere generally translatable as 'devour, eat up' rather than just 'eat'.

of sorrow as akin to 'eating' with respect to the institutionalised symbol 'heart'. (Note that this is a fairly general metaphorical extension, applying over a wide semantic field in English: e.g. *I am consumed by sorrow/with envy, She was devoured by anxiety*, etc.)

Certain transitive verbs occur in all languages: 'cut', 'carry', 'throw', 'give', 'eat' and a few score more. All these describe actions controllable by a human or animate agent. But individual languages allow different types of semantic extensions from the recurring 'central meaning'. Some extensions may retain the idea of animate agency, but enlarge the class of actions the verb can refer to (e.g. *We cut our losses*); other extensions may apply the verb to events that do not have a controlling agent, when there is some culturally perceived similarity to the central reference of the verb (e.g. *That interruption threw me off track, Rock music gives me a headache*). Metaphorical uses of these verbs are always outnumbered by occurrences in the 'central meaning', where there is a human or other animate agent who could (and most often does) control the activity.

Beyond this universal set of transitive verbs (and their more precise articulations and hyponyms),[9] individual languages include further verbs in the transitive class which have more-or-less idiosyncratic and language-particular meanings. Most of these will again demand an animate 'agent' in their central use. But for some, no core NP need be animate (e.g. *attract* in *A magnet will attract iron, Wealth attracts robbers* – Lyons 1968: 359); here one NP is recognised to be in A function, through a perceived similarity of this event to activities that are controllable (e.g. *pull*).

I am suggesting that all languages have a class of 'transitive verbs' whose semantic effect is defined in terms of the universally occurring 'controllable' verbs like 'cut' and 'carry'. But verbs describing other activities may then also be included in this class, with a participant recognised as being in A function because of culturally perceived similarities to some variety of controllable event. Typically, meteorological

---

[9] Of course some languages lack a single verb 'cut' or 'carry'. In Dyirbal one must choose between *nudi-l* 'cut right through, sever' and *gunba-l* 'cut partway through, cut a piece out'; and in Indonesian one would normally specify *pikul* 'carry on the shoulder', *jinjing* 'carry by the tips of the fingers', *kepit* 'carry under one's arms', *galas* 'carry with a carrying pole', *genggam* 'carry in fist or claws', or *junjung* 'carry on the head', etc. This in no way affects my argumentation. The point is that each language has one *or more* verbs 'cut', 'carry', etc.; the Dyirbal and Indonesian data could be taken to indicate a gap where a general verb would be expected, cultural reasons dictating more detailed specification by use of a hyponym. In fact, the Dyirbal 'mother-in-law' speech style does just have one verb *jalŋga-l*, whose central meaning exactly corresponds to that of English *cut*; see Dixon (1982: 66–7). And Indonesian does have a generic verb *bawa* 'carry', although use of a specific verb is always preferable.

and celestial phenomena such as 'wind', 'storm' and 'sun' (and the related 'fire') may function as A for certain verbs, e.g. *The storm broke our mast* and *The midday sun melted her ice-cream quicker than she could eat it*. Such natural phenomena are sometimes personified; they may, for instance, be assigned to a gender class normally reserved for humans (this happens in Dyirbal). We can, as foreshadowed in §1.1, provide a more general specification for 'what is A' as 'that which is most likely to be relevant to the success of the activity'. However, in the vast majority of cases the role mapped onto A will have human reference and 'most relevant to the success of the activity' does then reduce to 'could initiate or control the activity'.

Extensions of the transitive class to essentially non-controllable events differ from language to language (and could perhaps be taken as evidence for difference in Whorfian world-view). Some languages have 'like' as a transitive verb (as in 'I like tea'); others must use an intransitive or adjectival construction (something like 'Tea is likeable to me'). English has *annoy* and *endure* as transitive verbs.[10] These can take an animate A NP, but the referent could not be said to control the activity in the way that a 'cutter' or a 'carry-er' does. Note, though, that someone *can* purposely annoy, and that endurance implies a measure of will-power; the A NPs for these verbs do *not* initiate or control the activity, but the role they play can be *likened* to that of an agent. Verbs of this nature tend to be language-specific,[11] and should be regarded as idiosyncratic extensions to the

[10] Schachter (1976, 1977) mentions the Tagalog verb *-tiis* 'endure' as evidence that an actor nominal (the A NP for *-tiis*) is not necessarily the 'perceived instigator of the action' (this is Fillmore's 1968: 24 criterion for 'agent'). It appears, however, that the arguments from this section do apply to Tagalog: *most* members of the class of transitive verbs will have an animate actor that satisfies Fillmore's criterion for 'agent' (which is a part of my criterion for A function). Thus *-tiis* is just an extensional member of the transitive class in Tagalog, as *endure* is in English (and as the examples in note 11 are for Yidinʸ).

Note that the definition of an A NP in terms of a participant who 'initiates and/or controls the activity' is not vitiated by odd verbs like *endure*; the test of any such generalisation is whether it describes the majority pattern of a language. Idiosyncratic verbs in any language can be dealt with as institutionalised extensions to the universal definition, or they can be dealt with simply as 'exceptions' that have to be learnt by heart. (Exceptions are recognised as a valid category in phonology and morphology; the idea is also applicable within syntax and even within semantics.)

[11] I have recorded about 350 verbs for Yidinʸ, about 215 of them transitive. All but five occur predominantly with animate core NPs (although many have metaphorical extensions, e.g. 'The fever is eating my body'). The five exceptions – which are the only transitive verbs that cannot occur in imperative form – are *wigi-L* '(something, e.g. rich food) makes (a person: O) feel sick'; *manja-N* '(something, e.g. food or tiredness) fills up (a part of a person's body: O)'; *jaja-L* '(sacred water) rises up against (someone who has broken a taboo: O)'; *yama-L* '(something) makes (a person: O) cold' and *guba-N* 'burn', whose

universally occurring set of controllable verbs that make up the core of the class of transitive verbs in every language.[12]

The canonical transitive verb has just two core roles, and that NP which is not mapped onto A will be put into O syntactic relation. However, most (or perhaps all) languages have a subset of transitive verbs – which can be called 'extended transitive' or 'ditransitive' – that involve three core roles, e.g. 'give', 'show', 'tell'. Different languages show different strategies for dealing with such verbs. There are three basic possibilities: (1) the gift/message/thing-shown[13] is placed in O relation, with recipient/ addressee/person-to-whom-it-is-shown being marked by a peripheral case or preposition etc.; (2) the recipient/addressee/person-shown is in O function with the gift/message/thing-shown accorded peripheral marking; (3) two syntactic constructions are available, corresponding to both of the possibilities just mentioned.[14]

In languages of type (3) (which include English and Dyirbal), that NP which is most saliently affected by the activity is likely to be placed in O function. In §1.1 we mentioned the verb *hit* in English – this involves an Agent role (coded as A) moving or manipulating something (the Manip role) so that it comes into contact with some thing or person (the Target role). Generally, it is the Target that is most saliently affected by this impact, and is then placed in O syntactic function, e.g. *John hit the vase with a stick*; but, sometimes, the Manip may be more affected and an alternative construction is then used in which this is in O function, e.g. *John hit the vase*

A NP must be 'fire', 'sun' or something burning (there is another verb *waju-L* 'burn, cook' which must have a human A NP). See Dixon (1991b: 260, 273–4; 1977a: 257–8).

[12] Some putative counter-examples to the definition of the A function in terms of potential agency demand a different explanation. Consider *John underwent torture/an operation/an examination* (see Lakoff and Ross 1976: 161). Here the underlying semantic representation could be taken as (*Someone*) *tortured/operated on/examined John*, from which the sentence with *underwent* can be derived by a passive-like operation (but note that, unlike passive, this *does* change meaning). It appears that, in most instances of use, the 'object' of *undergo* is a deverbal nominal, as in the examples here.

[13] It is unusual to find a language that does not treat 'give', 'tell' and 'show' in a parallel manner for object identification, but there are occasional instances. In Gilbertese (or Kiribati), from the Austronesian family, the recipient of 'give' and the addressee of 'tell' are O, but the thing shown is in O function for 'show'. This is related to the fact that *kaota* 'to show' is the causative of *oti* 'be revealed, clear'. (Information from S. P. Harrison.)

[14] Languages of type (1) include Russian, Polish, Hindi, Telugu, Abkhaz, Burmese and Thai as well as Austronesian languages such as Acehnese, Fijian and Paamese and Australian languages such as Warlpiri and Kalkatungu. Those of type (2) include the Uto-Aztecan language Huichol (see Comrie 1989: 68–70, 1982a), the Austronesian language Tawala and the Australian language Nakkara. Others of type (3) include Banjarese and Buru, from the Austronesian family, and a number of Bantu languages, such as Kinyarwanda. There is discussion of all this – and references, etc. – in Dixon (1989); see also Dryer (1986) and Kuipers (1968).

against the doorframe. (Note that in the first construction – with Target as O – the Manip NP is marked with preposition *with*, and in the second one – with Manip as O – the Target is marked with a different preposition, *against* or *on*.) See also the discussion in note 13 to Chapter 3. There can be a further factor determining which construction type to use in such cases – the need to satisfy a syntactic constraint on a 'pivot' for inter-clausal linking; we return to this in §6.2.

Most languages use a single case marking for A and another for O. But there are some languages that employ variant cases for A, or else for O, often depending on the semantic type of the verb. In Icelandic there are verbs, such as 'think', that have the A NP in dative rather than in nominative case. Such a 'dative subject' does share the properties of A NPs in nominative case, e.g. it controls reflexivisation (Zaenen, Maling and Thráinsson, 1985).

I mentioned earlier that languages from the North-east Caucasian family, which are basically ergative, have varying case marking on A NPs. In Avar, the two verbs in the LIKING semantic type ('love/want' and 'like') have a dative A, while verbs of perception (my ATTENTION type – see §1.1) have locative A; other transitive verbs have the A NP in ergative case. In Ingush, verbs of LIKING and of ATTENTION both have dative A with other transitive verbs again showing ergative A. A number of languages, including Andi, have a special 'affective' case just for the A of verbs of LIKING and ATTENTION, but use ergative for A of other verbs. In these languages A can be recognised as a unitary category; A NPs with all transitive verbs – whatever their case marking – share certain grammatical properties (e.g. in the way they are or are not marked on the verb).[15]

A different kind of variation is found in the Australian language Yawuru (Hosokawa 1991: 242–3). Here the A NP of a transitive clause is always marked with ergative case and for most verbs the O NP is marked with absolutive (the case used for S in an intransitive clause). However, there is a smallish set of transitive verbs which mark O with dative case – this includes LIKING verbs such as 'hate/dislike' and 'want/like', ATTENTION verbs such as 'look for', and also 'wait (for)', 'approach', 'support', 'scold' and 'call'. For the North-east Caucasian languages there is consistent marking for O across all transitive verbs, but the marking on A varies; in Yawuru it is A that is treated consistently and the marking on O varies. Obviously, different sorts of principles are in operation in the two

---

[15] See, among other sources, Černý (1971), Hewitt (1980), Charachidzé (1981), Paris (1985) Comrie (1981a), Nichols (1982, forthcoming).

kinds of grammars (note how some of the verbs which mark O as dative in Yawuru correspond to English verbs that take *for*). But it is notable that in each system ATTENTION and LIKING verbs receive the variant marking.

I also mentioned before that in some languages one verbal form may cover both 'see' and 'look (at)' while another covers both 'hear' and 'listen (to)'. This is so for Lezgian, from the North-east Caucasian family, but here *akun* 'see/look at' and *van akun* 'hear/listen to' may occur in two syntactic frames – ergative(A)/absolutive(O) and dative(A)/absolutive(O). In fact they can be translated 'look at' and 'listen to' in the first construction and 'see' and 'hear' in the second. That is, the A NP is marked by ergative case when it refers to a controller, and by dative when it does not.[16]

In a most important study, Hopper and Thompson (1980) identify a number of parameters affecting the 'transitivity' of a clause. These include: whether the O is 'affected', the 'potency' of the agent, and whether an action is 'transferred' from A to O. Verbs in the ATTENTION and LIKING semantic types are certainly low on the transitivity scale and it is this which is signalled by using a variant on the normal transitive case marking. Note, though, that the verbs are still classed as grammatically transitive in languages such as Avar, Yawuru and Lezgian, i.e. they do have A and O NPs.[17]

We mentioned that a canonical transitive verb has just two core roles, but that most (or all) languages also have a subset of 'extended transitive' verbs with three core roles. All transitive verbs have two roles mapped onto syntactic relations A and O; for extended transitives the third role will be marked in some other way, e.g. by dative case. Now a canonical intransitive verb has one core role mapped onto S syntactic relation. There may also be a subset of the intransitive class, which we can call 'extended

---

[16] This information on Lezgian was supplied by David Kilby from Mejlanova (1960).

[17] Dravidian languages (which are basically accusative) normally have A and S marked by nominative case but some verbs (e.g. the intransitive 'tremble' and the transitive 'forget') allow dative in place of nominative when the activity is unintentional (Bhat 1988: 98; 1991: 41).

What is sometimes referred to as 'dative subject' in German (e.g. *mir* 'to me' in *Es ist mir kalt* or *Mir ist kalt* 'I am cold', literally 'it is cold to me') in fact have none of the properties of subjects. But, as mentioned above, in another Germanic language, Icelandic, some NPs that can be shown to be subjects do have dative marking (Zaenen, Maling and Thráinsson 1985); these appear to be found with verbs that are low on Hopper and Thompson's transitivity scale.

Masica (1991: 339–56) has an excellent discussion of dative subject in modern Indic languages, showing that it generally shares some, but not all, of the properties of a nominative subject.

intransitive', that involves two core roles – one is mapped onto S relation and the other is marked in some other way, e.g. by dative case. A fair number of languages show an 'extended intransitive' subclass, although many fewer than show an 'extended transitive' subclass. For example, Tongan (and other languages from the Polynesian subgroup of Austronesian) have all verbs from the LIKING and ATTENTION types as extended intransitives with the Perceiver role in S function and Impression role marked as an obligatory indirect object. For a verb like 'hit' the A is ergative and the O absolute; for 'go' the S is absolutive; for 'see', 'like' and similar verbs 'who sees' and 'who likes' are absolutive – there are syntactic tests, including coordination constraints, showing that these are in S function – while 'what is seen' and 'what is liked' receive locative/dative marking (Churchward 1953). Here we get two-argument verbs, which are low on Hopper and Thompson's transitivity scale, being classed as a rather special type of intransitive.

A similar situation holds in Trumai, a language isolate from the Upper Xingu River, Brazil. The transitive verb class includes canonical transitives, with two core roles, such as 'kill', 'cut' and 'pull' and also 'extended transitives', with three core roles, such as 'give'. The intransitive class mostly consists of canonical intransitives, with one core role, e.g. 'sit', 'speak', 'fall', but there is also an 'extended intransitive' subset, including 'see', 'smell', 'talk with' and 'eat'. Both canonical transitives and extended transitives have an A NP (marked by ergative case ending $-k \sim -ek$) and an O NP with zero marking. Both canonical and extended intransitives have an S NP, with zero marking. Extended transitives and extended intransitives include an additional NP marked by dative case $-tl$ (with various other allomorphs); this can, in fact, be omitted. (Data from Guirardello, 1992.) Similar systems are reported for Tibetan (Chang and Chang 1980: 29) and Newari (Givón 1985), which are – like Tongan and Trumai – ergative languages, and also for accusative languages such as Maká, from the Mataguayo family, spoken in Paraguay (Gerzenstein 1991).

An important point to note here is that these 'extended' subclasses are always relatively minor. Most transitive verbs are canonically transitive, with two core roles; only a small number will be extended transitive (or ditransitive) with an additional role. Similarly, most intransitive verbs will be canonically intransitive, with one core role; the extended intransitives, with an extra role, are always relatively few in number. There is in fact a semantic basis to the assignment of verbs to these classes and subclasses. For example, a verb like 'see' is much lower on Hopper and Thompson's transitivity scale than 'cut' or 'carry'. We saw that some languages treat 'see' as a transitive verb (with A and O arguments), but with a variation on the normal transitive marking. Other languages such as Tongan, Trumai and Lhasa Tibetan treat 'see' as an extended intransitive (with an S argument).

Canonical intransitive verbs take a single obligatory NP, which is in S function. With some verbs (e.g. 'run', 'jump'), the referent of the S NP will be unequivocal agent, controlling or initiating the activity (what I have called S_a). For other verbs (e.g. 'yawn', 'die') the S NP is unlikely to be able to exercise any measure of control (this is S_o). In §4.1.1 we discussed split-S systems, where S is marked like A for some verbs and like O for others. This division of S always has a semantic basis but is never perfectly semantically determined; there are generally a few 'volitional' verbs in the S_o set and a few 'non-volitionals' in S_a. In most (or all) split-S languages, the category S (the concatenation of S_a and S_o) does have a unitary syntactic role (see §4.1.1).

We then recognise S as the third basic relation, defined simply as the sole core NP in a canonical intransitive clause. (In some languages S may, as a later step, be subdivided into S_a and S_o.)

It will be seen that the universal syntactic–semantic functions A, S and O are defined on rather different principles: the only obligatory role in a canonical intransitive clause for S; the role in a transitive clause which is *most relevant to the success* of the activity (normally human, and this then equates with: *could initiate or control* the activity) for A; and for O either the *other core* role or – if there are more than one non-A core roles – that role which is *most saliently affected* by the activity. These functions appear to be valid for all natural languages and to be the basis for all grammatical operations. In Chapter 4 we surveyed the attested splits and variations in intra-clausal marking of syntactic functions; these can all be explained in terms of A, S and O, sometimes referring also to the semantic content of the verb, or of the NPs, or to the tense, aspect or mood of the clause.

We can now define a further universal category, 'subject'. A and S functions are grouped together as 'subject'.[18] These are the NPs which

---

[18] The status of A, S and O as universal primitives, having priority over the recognition of 'subject', is vital to the thesis of this book. Some linguists use symbolisations like S_t and S_i or TS and IS in place of A and S. But this suggests that 'subject' is the *first* category to be recognised, and that it can then be subclassified into transitive and intransitive varieties according to the clause type it occurs in. This is the traditional view, when the horizons of linguistics were defined by accusative-type languages. Now that many ergative languages have been described the use of such symbolisms has misleading implications. The symbols A, S and O used here (the choice of letters is immaterial – the main point is to choose

refer to functions that can be the initiating/controlling agents. There is a difference: an A NP almost always has the potentiality of exercising control for any transitive verb (the 'almost' may be omittable for languages like Jacaltec which limit A NPs to animates); and the referent of an S NP could conceivably exercise control only for certain verbs. (Interestingly, the fact languages like Tongan classify verbs such as 'like' and 'see' as an aberrant variety of intransitive makes no difference to the class of 'subjects'. It is just that these low-transitivity verbs, which are treated as having A-type subjects in other languages, here have S-type subjects.)[19]

The discussion thus far in this chapter relates to languages with syntactically based marking – those for which the basic syntactic relations A, S and O mediate between semantics and grammatical marking, and are the basis for valency-changing and clause-linking syntactic operations. For the second type of language described in Chapter 2, where morphological marking directly mirrors the semantics of a particular situation, a different definition of subject may be appropriate. I mentioned, in §4.1.2, that there are also languages that use syntactically based marking for transitive verbs but semantically based marking as far as intransitive verbs are concerned, and called these 'fluid-S'.

In the fluid-S language Acehnese, verbs are fairly strictly classified as transitive or intransitive so that we can recognise an S category in the normal way, as the sole core NP for an intransitive verb. But Durie (1987, 1988) maintains that a unitary S category plays no role in the grammar of Acehnese. In fact, he uses just two 'principal grammatical relations', Actor (corresponding to my A and S_a) and Undergoer (my O and S_o) and says that clauses demand both Actor and Undergoer, or just Actor (my S_a) or just Undergoer (my S_o). It may be that for Acehnese the only viable definition of 'subject' is his Actor (the concatenation of A and S_a, in my terms) which is in fact defined grammatically, in terms of its cross-referencing properties, but is a grammatical category with a relatively

different symbols for different primitive functions) emphasise the syntactic and semantic *differences* among these three functions; once these are established, A and S can as a next step be grouped into the category 'subject' on the basis of *partial similarities*.

[19] The discussion thus far has focussed on sentences containing a lexical verb. Of course, there are also sentences involving 'have' and 'be' (for languages that have a copula) and, in many languages, minor sentences that involve no verb at all but just, say, a noun as topic and an adjective as comment. Now it is a fact that a concept which is dealt with through a verb in one language may be rendered by an adjective in another; this suggests that, in any universal categorisation, the function S should be extended to apply to the topic of adjectival comment sentences and to the 'subjects' of 'to be' and 'to have'. I mentioned in note 18 to Chapter 3 that it is always the S form of a nominal or pronominal which is used in minor sentence types like these.

simple and unusually consistent semantic characterisation. Kibrik (1985) discusses the North-east Caucasian language Tabassaran, which is also of the fluid-S type. Here, it seems, a unitary S category (the concatenation of S_a and S_o) does have a grammatical role, in terms of conditions on clause chaining. Presumably, the category of subject defined as A-plus-S would be both valid and useful in Tabassaran.

Detailed work is needed on the grammars of a selection of other fluid-S languages, and of languages which more fully use semantically based marking, before we can make any definite pronouncements on the extent to which the discussion of 'subject' given above might apply to them, or else what alternative treatment would be appropriate.

Throughout this chapter – and indeed this book – I have referred to 'underlying' structures and relations. This refers to the construction a verb occurs in when in its most basic or underived form, lacking any causative, passive, antipassive, reflexive or other marking. In Dyirbal, for instance, the root *balga-l* 'hit (with a long rigid implement, held on to)' has derived forms which include antipassive *balgal-ŋa-y* (for which underlying A becomes S, and underlying O is marked by instrumental or dative case, or can be omitted), reflexive *balga-yirri-y* (where underlying A and O are coreferential, and are here mapped onto S), and instrumentive *balgal-ma-l* (where the underlying instrumental NP becomes O, and the underlying O receives dative marking – see §6.2.2). The underlying construction involves just *balga-l* with appropriate inflectional specification (for tense, etc.) but with no derivations having applied – the Agent role is in A function (marked by ergative case if a noun, nominative if a pronoun – see Table 1.1 in §1.2), the Target is in O function (absolutive case if a noun, accusative if a pronoun) and the Manip, if specified, is in instrumental case. Some languages, such as English, have a sparser morphology and may show syntactic derivation just by constituent order, and/or the addition or omission of a constituent. Speakers have clear and consistent intuitions as to which is the underlying function of an ambitransitive verb, e.g. that *walk* is basically intransitive, as in *The dog walked around the park*, with a derived causative, *I walked the dog around the park*; and that *cook* is basically transitive, although the O NP can be omitted in appropriate circumstances, *Mary is cooking (dinner)*. This notion of 'underlying' (or 'deep') structures does of course have some similarity to Chomsky's original idea of 'deep structure' or the more recent Government–Binding (GB) level of 'D-structure', but it is not dependent on these or on any other theoretical models.

Thus, I have defined 'subject' as a universal category at the level of underlying structure. Some linguists have also used the notion 'derived subject'; e.g. they may say that the passive derivation places 'underlying object' in 'derived subject' function. I shall show in §6.2 that, while 'derived subject' may be definable for some languages, it is by no means a workable universal category. It is useful and valid to speak of 'derived A/S/O' functional slots, but not in the same way of 'derived subject'. As a universal semantic–syntactic category, 'subject' must be defined at the underlying structure level, and always related to that level.

Every language could be said to have a degree of 'accusativity' at the level of underlying structure, in that the universal category of 'subject' – a grouping together of A and S – plays some role in its syntax; this is discussed in §5.3. I mentioned, in §3.3, that there are a number of properties shared by S and O in languages of all structural types. But it really makes little sense to attempt to characterise an individual language as 'accusative' or 'ergative' at this level. Underlying structure deals with the way in which syntax codes the semantic description of events. There are three basic syntactic–semantic categories, A, S and O; these are true universals, being applicable to every type of clause in every language. Then, A and S are grouped together as 'subject', an underlying-structure category by virtue of which certain universal syntactic phenomena follow. It is only in terms of 'derived structure', after syntactic derivations like passive and anti-passive have applied, that languages differ in the way they group syntactic functions. In Chapter 6 I will discuss a typological classification of languages in terms of the different sorts of syntactic constraints they place on clause-combining operations of coordination and subordination. It is at this level that languages can usefully be described as syntactically 'accusative' or 'ergative'.

5.2   Keenan's discussion of 'subject'

In a seminal paper, Keenan (1976) sought to 'provide a definition of the notion "subject of" which will enable us to identify the subject phrase(s), if any, of any sentence in any language'. A major motivation for this attempt was the reliance on 'subject' in a number of theoretical enquiries, e.g. Relational Grammar, and the Accessibility Hierarchy of Keenan and Comrie. A category 'subject' is still being referred to by people putting forward theoretical models and Keenan's discussion still has relevance and interest.

His procedure seems to be to survey the properties of what have been recognised as 'subjects' in a wide selection of languages. If the linguists working on a language have not used the term 'subject', then Keenan brings to bear his own criteria, which tend to emphasise surface grammatical factors. He presents a list of thirty-odd properties characteristically possessed by subjects. Almost all the properties are qualified by 'usually', 'normally', or 'in general'; there is no attempt at a universal 'definition' (in the logical sense of 'Every A which shows X is a subject'); rather, 'what is subject' is based on a statistical assessment of which NP satisfies the largest number of the thirty-odd properties. Keenan gives a miscellany of syntactic and semantic 'properties' with no priority among them (so that the whole argument runs the risk of being circular). Some are characteristics of derived structures; some involve morphological marking conventions; and some follow from universal semantic arrangements.

He does include, among his thirty-odd properties, that 'Subjects normally express the agent of the action, if there is one'; this is the universal defining criterion which I adopted for 'subject' above (but note Keenan's use of 'normally'). In Keenan's presentation, this semantic criterion follows a number of surface grammatical properties with which it appears to be accorded equal weighting: the subject is usually indispensable (i.e. non-deletable); the subject is usually the leftmost NP; if anything has zero marking, it will be the subject of an intransitive verb; and so on.

In §3.4, I showed the variety of types of case marking that occur. That NP which is in the unmarked syntactic case is the most likely candidate to be 'indispensable' – but the unmarked case can be (a) absolutive, covering S and O functions; or (b) nominative, covering S and A functions; or (c) accusative, with just O function. The property that 'Subject is usually indispensable' follows from the facts that the majority of languages are of type (b), and that the NP in unmarked nominative case is not normally deletable. The property that 'If anything has zero case marking, it will be intransitive subject' follows from the facts that the great majority of languages are of types (a) or (b), and that the unmarked case is likely to have zero realisation, if anything does. (Note that this last property says nothing about the category of 'subject', but just about S – one of the two basic functions grouped together to form 'subject' under my definition.)

I have already mentioned that 'subject' has been used by linguists in a variety of ways. It is illegitimate to compare the properties of 'subjects' without first considering the criteria used for recognising 'subject' in each grammar. Plainly, there is no uniquely correct notion of 'subject'; the category has to be carefully defined in any universal or language-particular enquiry. In the last section, I took A, S and O as universal functions, in terms of which all grammatical phenomena may be described; I then *defined* subject as the class {A, S}: thus every clause will have a subject. For transitive clauses, A is distinguished from O in terms of potential agency, the criterion that is later taken to underlie 'subject'. Intransitive clauses have only one obligatory NP (which I label as in S function), and so this is linked with A as 'subject', whether or not it could be 'agent' for any particular verb.

Certain of Keenan's properties automatically follow from my definition of subject. He notes that 'Subjects normally express the addressee phrase of imperatives'; if subject is defined as (potential) agent, the addressee phrase of an imperative *must* always be subject.[20] The 'normally' in 'subject = agent' and the 'normally' in 'subject = addressee of imperative' are linked (although this is not noted by Keenan) in that we must have 'addressee of imperative = agent'.

Most of Keenan's criteria effectively define the derived-structure category 'pivot' which was introduced in §1.2 and will be discussed in more detail in §6.2. 'Pivot' is a language-particular category: in some languages it links (derived) S and A, in others S and O; and there are languages which employ both types. But Keenan also includes some criteria that relate to 'underlying subject', the universal category {S, A}. There can be serious conflict between 'subject' and 'pivot' in the most ergative languages. For Dyirbal, the S and O NPs (marked by absolutive case, on nominals) show more of the thirty-odd properties – e.g. indispensable, leftmost, zero marking, syntactic pivot – than do S and A; thus Keenan takes {S, O} to be 'subject'[21] letting grammatical criteria override semantic considerations. He has effectively recognised that S/O is the derived-structure pivot in Dyirbal syntax. But with this definition of 'subject', Dyirbal must be noted as an exception to 'subject = agent', and it is also an exception to 'subject = addressee of imperative'.

[20] Keenan's reference to Maori and Malagasy as counter-examples indicates confusion between 'underlying subject' and 'derived subject' – see §5.3.1.

[21] Postal (1977: 278) mentions 'an analysis of ergativity phenomena which takes 'patient' nominals to be initial subjects of transitive clauses ... the analysis of Dyirbal in Dixon (1972: 128–30) is of this type'. In fact, 'subject' is used in a semantic sense throughout the grammar of Dyirbal, never in the 'grammatical' sense suggested by Postal. Tree structures of an 'ergative type' are used, but they do not imply that the notion of 'subject' is different in Dyirbal from any other language. The tree structures make syntactic, not semantic, claims. The notion of 'subject' is effectively defined through the feature [+actor] (Dixon 1972: 199–205); this is needed to deal with the 'accusative' syntactic properties of Dyirbal (see §5.3 below).

As Blake (1976) has shown, there can be even more serious difficulties attached to defining 'subject' on purely grammatical criteria. Pronouns in Dyirbal show a nominative–accusative paradigm, and it is the 'nominative' which is leftmost and unmarked (though it is not the syntactic pivot; see §1.2). So the label 'subject' should, on this type of criteria, be applied to a pronoun in S or A function, and also to a noun in S or O function. A sentence with pronominal A and nominal O, like (1) (cf. §1.2) would have two subjects, whereas a sentence with nominal A and pronominal O, like (2), would have none!

(1)   *ŋana   ŋuma   bura-n*
       we + NOM father + ABS see-NONFUT
       we saw father

(2)   *ŋana-na ŋuma-ŋgu bura-n*
       we-ACC father-ERG see-NONFUT
       father saw us

Further difficulties with this type of approach are discussed by Blake (1976).

Keenan and Comrie (1977) attempted to explain the ways in which languages relativise in terms of an 'accessibility hierarchy': 'NPs at the upper end of the hierarchy are universally easier to relativise than those at the lower end.' Now in Dyirbal a relative clause must have an S or O NP in common with an NP in the main clause (see §6.2.2). If S and A are taken as subject for Dyirbal, this language is an exception to Keenan and Comrie's generalisation. Taking S and O to comprise 'subject' allows Dyirbal to fit into the hierarchy; but this leads to a good many difficulties in other areas.

In fact, relativisation is a 'pivot' (not a 'subject') property, relating to the grammatical constraints on clause combining in a given language. As emphasised at the beginning of this chapter, one should clearly distinguish semantic criteria (e.g. agency) and grammatical criteria (e.g. conditions on subordination and coordination). Here I use basically semantic criteria to define 'subject' (which is relevant to the underlying level of structure) and grammatical criteria to define 'pivot' (a derived structure category). These two kinds of criteria happen to give the same results for some fully accusative languages, but more generally they do not do so.

5.3 Universal syntactic phenomena dependent on 'subject'

Classifying a language as 'ergative' in terms of morphological marking is a relatively straightforward matter when compared with making a decision between 'ergativity' (S treated in the same way as O) and 'accusativity' (S treated like A) at the syntactic level. Different kinds of syntactic evidence can be brought to bear, and these by no means all give the same result. It is, in fact, necessary to distinguish among (a) universal syntactic behaviour, which recurs in all languages – or which has the same form in every language in which it does occur; (b) syntactic operations needed to place an NP in 'pivot function' – usually corresponding to unmarked case – for a variety of syntactic and discourse purposes; and (c) language-particular clause-linking operations that provide genuine evidence for syntactic 'ergativity'. Possibilities (b) and (c) are interrelated and are discussed in Chapter 6.

Many of the syntactic properties that involve the same identification among A, S and O – in every language in which they occur – as in (a) above, are corollaries of the universal category of subject. I will now give three examples of such properties, and then discuss causatives, which have a universal basis that is dependent on A, not on {A, S}.

5.3.1 Imperatives

In an imperative sentence, the speaker requests the addressee to do something – to act as agent in initiating/controlling some activity. Imperatives in every language have a second person pronoun as (stated or understood) S or A NP.[22] This is a universal property; thus the fact that S and A have the same possibilities of reference for the imperative constructions of some particular language (and the fact that, say, either can be deleted from surface structure) is no evidence at all for the placement of that language on a continuum of syntactic 'ergativity' vs. 'accusativity'. Even the most ergative language will treat S and A NPs of imperatives the same. This follows from the meaning of imperatives (addressee is told to be agent) and the definition of 'subject' (the NP whose referent can be agent, if anything can).[23]

---

[22] Most languages restrict the subjects of imperatives to second person pronouns. In a few languages, there is extension to first or even to third person subjects (although these are always greatly outnumbered by second person subjects). The discussion here can naturally be extended to these additional cases (e.g. first/third person possibilities always apply equally to A and to S structural slots).

[23] Generally, an imperative will have a second person pronoun as the S or A NP in both underlying and derived structure; this condition is fully satisfied in reflexives. Passives

Whether any particular verb can occur in imperative form (marked by special inflection in many languages, and almost always characterised by distinctive intonation) depends upon its semantic type – whether it describes a state or activity that is controllable. Almost all (though – in most languages – not quite all) transitive verbs are controllable, but only some intransitive verbs fall into this category. Grammars of split-S languages sometimes state that only intransitive verbs from the S_a subclass (not those from S_o) may take imperative inflection – e.g. Gregores and Suárez (1967) on Guaraní, reported in §4.1.1.

Most languages do not, in their grammars, distinguish between controlled and non-controlled varieties of S, and all types of S are linked with A as being *potentially* the addressee of an imperative. Imperatives prototypically involve verbs that demand a fair level of control, but the grammatical construction can be extended to verbs where the level of control is minimal or non-existent. We can conceive of *Endure it for a few weeks longer* (*and then I'll arrange a transfer*)! or a whispered malevolent wish *Slip down there and break your leg!* Negative imperatives are more plausible with barely controllable verbs – *Don't yawn!* – though even here the limits of possibility can be crossed, e.g. *Don't die!* A similar extension applies to copular sentences, some of which do refer to something that is controllable and can legitimately be in the imperative, e.g. *Be on time!*, *Don't be different from other people!* Most adjectives refer to states that are scarcely controllable, yet the grammatical marking of imperatives is occasionally extended to *be*-plus-adjective, producing something that is in effect a metaphoric-type contraction, e.g. *Be thin!* ('Pull your stomach in and look thin'), *Be hungry!* ('Act as if you were hungry!'). Since some A and S NPs function naturally as addressees of imperatives, this property is potentially extendable to all members of the grammatical classes covered by A and S.

The natural linkage between S and A in imperatives is shown by the fact that in some languages there is a mood-based ergativity split: an accusative

cannot normally occur in imperative form. It is possible to devise examples of the type (a) *Come to Palm Court and be entertained by Joe Loss and his Orchestra!* and (b) *Be impressed by his stamp collection if you want him to like you!* But note that, for these to be acceptable, the passive must be linked to another clause with which it shares a subject NP. The acceptability of these sentences appears to stem from formal analogy to imperative copular sentences (e.g. *Be good when grandma calls!*). It is noteworthy that example (a) is recognisable as a compelling advertising slogan; most speakers would prefer to use *Come to Palm Court and let Joe Loss entertain you!* (the addressee has no control over whether he is entertained or not, only in whether he allows Joe Loss to try to entertain him). Example (b) is felt to be an elliptical version of *Try to be impressed ...!* or *Appear to be impressed ...!*

pattern appears in the imperative and an ergative pattern elsewhere (see §4.3).

It is of course possible that, *in addition to* this universal S/A linkage, imperatives in particular languages may also in some way treat S and O alike. There are languages that have one verbal affix cross-referencing S or O and another cross-referencing A. For some languages of this type the A affix can be omitted – for instance, when it would be second person, in an imperative – but the S/O affix is obligatory. This applies in two related dialects from British Columbia, Nass-Gitksan (Rigsby 1975) and Tsimshian (Mulder 1989b). Thus, A can be left unspecified in an imperative but not S. The opposite situation is found in Nadëb from Brazil – here the S/O pronoun is obligatorily absent and the A pronominal proclitic obligatorily present for a second person imperative (Helen Weir, personal communication). Such languages simply have a grammatical constraint (that there must be S/O cross-referencing, or that there must be an A pronominal clitic) which overrides the universal tendency to omit specification of A or S from an imperative when it is second person. They are in no way exceptions to the universal.[24]

Sometimes an obligatory operation must apply to an imperative. Keenan (1976: 321) gives, as an exception to his property that 'Subjects normally express the addressee phrase of imperatives', the fact that 'in many Malayo-Polynesian languages, e.g. Maori and Malagasy, imperatives are frequently in non-active forms, and the addressee phrase, if present, appears as a passive (or other type of non-active) agent phrase'. Keenan is here noting the non-application of a semantic criterion, which is valid for underlying subjects, to derived 'surface subjects' (on this, see §6.2 below). Maori and Malagasy conform perfectly to the universal pattern; it is just that the passive derivation which is optional for other construction types, is obligatory or nearly so for imperatives,[25] so that the underlying subject of an imperative is always realised with oblique marking.[26]

---

[24] Non-omittability of (information about) second person S and/or A in an imperative is only likely when this is coded through some obligatory morphological element. Where A and S are shown only through NPs, a second person imperative subject is likely always to be omittable.

[25] For cultural reasons of 'politeness' etc. (see Keenan and Keenan 1979).

[26] Malagasy, Maori and English all satisfy the universal requirement that 'underlying subject' of an imperative is second person. They differ in that English also requires this NP to come through into derived structure in S or A function (*Mary be watched by you* is unacceptable), whereas Malagasy and Maori do not impose this extra condition. In an ergative language like Dyirbal, the same universal requirement holds. But here an imperative can, optionally, be antipassivised (cf. §1.2):

5.3.2   *'Can', 'try', 'begin', 'want' and similar verbs*

Verbs in any language can be divided into two broad classes – Primary and Secondary. Primary verbs may constitute a complete sentence with NPs filling core functional slots. Some – such as 'jump', 'cut' and 'eat' – may just take NPs in subject and (if transitive) object slots; others may take either NPs or complement clauses, e.g. 'see', 'believe', 'describe', 'tell'. Secondary verbs – which often include 'can', 'begin', 'try' and 'not' – cannot stand alone, accompanied just by NPs with concrete reference, but must relate to some other verb.[27]

We can, more generally, say that there is a set of Secondary concepts, most of which are expressed in some way in each language – they include 'can', 'should', 'might', 'not', 'begin', 'finish', 'try', 'want', 'need' and 'hope'. Different languages have varying ways of expressing these concepts. They can be non-inflecting particles, or derivational affixes to lexical verbs, or they can be realised as independent lexemes, Secondary verbs. 'Not', for instance, is a non-inflecting particle in English, a derivational affix to the verb in some languages (e.g. Swahili), but a lexical verb in Fijian, taking a complement clause (*I'm not going* is translated into Fijian as *e sega niu lako*, literally 'It is not the case that I am going').

When Secondary concepts are expressed by verbs they show one of two major kinds of syntactic behaviour. One is for the Secondary verb to appear in the same verb phrase as the Primary verb it modifies, agreeing with it in inflection. This is what happens with a class of what I call 'adverbals' in Dyirbal. There are several dozen adverbals – including *jayŋu-l* 'finish doing' and *ŋuyma-l* 'do properly' – and they show exactly the same morphological possibilities as Primary verbs. Alongside *yara-ŋgu mija wamba-n* ('man-ERG house + ABS build-NONFUT') 'the man built the house' we can have *yara-ŋgu mija wamba-n jayŋu-n* 'the man finished building the house' and *yara-ŋgu mija wamba-n ŋuyma-n* 'the man built the

(*nʸurra*) *yabu bura* 'You look at mother!' (plain transitive)
(*nʸurra*) *bural-ŋa yabu-gu* 'You look at mother!' (antipassive)
It is impossible to decide whether Dyirbal should be classified with Malagasy and Maori or with English. Whereas a passive places an underlying O NP in derived S function, the antipassive places an underlying A in derived S function. Since A and S are subject functions, an antipassive imperative will, on almost any definition of 'subject', *necessarily* still have the addressee phrase in subject function.

27   There is fuller discussion of this, with especial reference to English, in Dixon (1991a: 90–1, 172–82). I there give arguments in favour of the position that a sentence such as *He began the book* has an underlying Primary verb (e.g. *reading, writing, binding*) and specify the conditions under which such underlying verbs can be omitted.

house properly'. Here the verb phrases *wamba-n jayŋu-n* and *wamba-n ŋuyma-n* each contain a verb and an adverbal, agreeing in transitivity (here, both are transitive) and inflection (non-future tense).[28]

The alternative is for a Secondary verb to have the syntactic properties of a main verb, taking a complement clause which includes the verb that it is semantically modifying. Thus, in *The man began to build the house*, *begin* is the main clause verb with *build* being syntactically subordinate to it as the verb of a complement clause filling object slot in the main clause; but, semantically, the sentence refers to an act of building, with *begin* providing aspectual modification. In a fair number of languages 'begin' is realised as a derivational affix to a primary verb, e.g. *-yarra-y* in Dyirbal; in this language one would say *yara-ŋgu mija wamba-yarra-nyu* 'the man began to build the house'.

There are several varieties of Secondary verb. The first includes items like 'can', 'might', 'not', 'begin', 'finish', 'continue' and 'try', where the Secondary verb adds no semantic roles to those of the verb it occurs with. Thus 'I began/finished/tried building the house' has exactly the same roles as 'I built the house'. Some of these concepts are realised in English as modals, which are syntactic modifiers to a main verb, and others (*begin, finish, continue, try*) as main verbs taking object complement clauses. The important point is that the subject of the main verb must be identical with the subject of the complement clause. This is a universal, relating to the universal category of subject. Whenever Secondary concepts of the first variety are realised as lexical verbs, taking an object complement clause construction which involves another verb, the two verbs must have the same subject (S or A) irrespective of whether the language is accusative or ergative at morphological and/or syntactic levels.[29]

Another variety of Secondary concepts includes 'want', 'need' and 'hope'. Once again these are realised as derivational affixes to verbs in some languages, and as independent verbs, taking complement clauses, in

[28] Each adverbal has fixed transitivity (as does every verb). Syntactic derivations which increase or decrease valency must be applied to ensure that verb and adverbal, within a verb phrase, agree in transitivity.

[29] There is a further possibility, that the Secondary verb take a complement clause in subject slot, e.g. in Fijian one translates *I can go* by *e rawa ni-u lako*, literally 'it is possible that I go' (Dixon 1988a: 279–85). *Rawa* 'can, be able to' in Fijian is thus an intransitive verb, taking a subject complement clause, whereas *begin, try*, etc. in English are transitive verbs taking an object complement clause. In each case the secondary verb adds no semantic role to those of the verb it is linked with. In English, the secondary verb has a stated subject identical with the underlying (but omitted subject) of the lexical verb. In Fijian the secondary verb has in subject slot just a clause containing the lexical verb together with its arguments.

others. In some languages the subject of a verb like 'want' must be coreferential with the subject of the verb to which it is linked (Dyirbal is of this type[30]). In other languages the subjects can differ (e.g. English *I want John to go*) although even here the subjects most often are identical and the complement clause token is then generally omitted (*I want to go* – note that *I want me/myself to go* is possible, but is only likely to be encountered in special circumstances, e.g. under discourse contrast). English is unusual in having the same syntactic construction available for both same-subject and different-subject with verbs like 'want'; most languages have different syntactic possibilities. In Swahili, for instance, an infinitival complement would be used for same-subject but a subjunctive complement when the subjects of 'want' and its linked verb are not the same (Vitale 1981). (There is further discussion and more examples in Dixon, forthcoming.)

Thus, where Secondary concepts of the varieties discussed are realised as lexical verbs they are always likely to have the same subject (A or S) as the verb to which they are linked. This universal property should not be taken as evidence of 'syntactic accusativity'. Discussing the North-east Caucasian language Archi, Kibrik (1979a: 68) mentions that a verb normally agrees with S or O, in keeping with the ergative character of the language, but that there are four auxiliary-type verbs ('with the aspectual meanings durative/terminative and the tense meanings present/ past and the additional tense/aspect meaning of continualis "begin and continue"') which agree with the A NP, rather than with O. This is what one would have predicted, and should not be taken as evidence of accusative marking in an otherwise ergative language. Discussing complement clauses in the Mayan language Chontal, Quizar and Knowles-Berry (1988) mention that an accusative pattern is found in constructions involving the main clause verbs 'begin' and 'finish', whereas other subordinate clauses show either ergative or tripartite marking. Again, this is a universal feature, found in every kind of language.[31]

---

[30] Dyirbal has a number of verbs that roughly correspond to part of the meaning of *want* in English: *walŋgarra-y* 'want to do, choose to do', *garrgi-y* 'want to go to a certain place', *nyurrŋi-y* 'be anxious/get ready to do something'. Interestingly, all are intransitive. They are linked with another verb in a purposive construction (see Dixon, forthcoming). Dyirbal has a thorough-going ergative syntax (see §§1.2, 6.2.2) and demands that two verbs linked in a purposive construction should have coreferential S or O NPs. There is also the universal expectation that 'want' should have the same subject as a verb to which it is linked. Both conditions are satisfied by having the 'want' verbs intransitive – their subject is S, and the verb is linked to another verb with coreferential S (if this second verb is transitive it must be antipassivised, with underlying A then becoming derived S).

[31] Kibrik (1987) presents information about sentences involving 'must', 'can', 'begin', 'want' and 'fear' in twenty Dagestanian languages. He shows that there are many types

Woodbury (1975: 66–70) mentions that Eskimo has constructions of the form NP_1 V_1 $[\Sigma_2]$, where V_1 is one of a restricted class of verbs that includes 'can', 'must', 'begin' and 'want'. Sentences of this form have a syntactic constraint that NP_1 must be coreferential with the A or S NP of the embedded clause Σ_2; equi-NP deletion then takes place. But 'can', 'must' and 'begin' always behave in this way, and 'want' almost always does. This syntactic constraint is a natural consequence of the meanings of these verbs and the universal category of subject; it provides no evidence concerning the syntactic typology of Eskimo.[32]

Chung (1978) has argued for an 'accusative' syntax in modern Polynesian languages, mostly on the basis of a handful of verbs – 'can', 'begin', 'must' – whose subject must coincide with the subject of the complement clause, triggering a 'raising rule' which applies only for these verbs (see also Anderson 1976: 13). This is insufficient basis for typological classification of the syntax of Polynesian languages, let alone as a major step in the argument that proto-Polynesian had accusative morphology and syntax (see §7.1).

I shall show in the next chapter that there are syntactic operations whose identifications within the set A, S, O do vary from language to language; these operations enable us to place languages along a typological continuum ranging from 'syntactically ergative' to 'syntactically accusative'. But we must be careful to distinguish them from universal syntactic phenomena of the type described here – which equate S and A – as a consequence of the universal category of 'subject' and its semantic implications.

of construction, some of which relate to syntactic relations and coreference restrictions and others to semantic factors. Kibrik concludes that the generalisations in this section (or the earlier version in Dixon 1979a) are not confirmed by his Dagestanian data. But it is not clear to me that they are disconfirmed. More work is needed on the syntax and semantics of the 'secondary concept' forms in each of these languages, with a full analysis of the grammar of each language, for their relevance to be fully apparent.

[32] Woodbury (1975: 118–19, 131) recognises that 'the accusativity of EQUI can be best explained in terms of the semantic class of EQUI type verbs, a subclass of which requires the 'like-subject' constraint discussed in Perlmutter (1971), which limits certain verbs and their complement clauses to coreferential subjects, e.g. English *begin, try, can* etc.'. Recognising that coreferentiality and deletion in Dyirbal depend on the S/O pivot, Woodbury then mentions that 'it would be interesting to see whether there are verbs in Dyirbal to which the like-subject constraint applies'. As already indicated, secondary concepts in Dyirbal are realised by non-inflecting particles ('not', 'might'), by verbal affixes ('begin'), by adverbals which are placed in apposition with a verb, or by intransitive verbs (note 30) whose S NP both satisfies the universal {S,A} subject condition, and the language-particular S/O pivot constraint.

5.3.3   Control in reflexives

Almost every language[33] has some grammatical mechanism which marks
the fact that underlying A and O for a transitive verb are coreferential.
There are two major ways of achieving this. The first is for there to be a
derivational affix which when added to a transitive verb root forms an
intransitive stem that has reflexive meaning – the S NP of this derived
intransitive then maps underlying A = O. This second method involves
maintaining transitivity, and for a 'reflexive pronoun' to be placed in O
slot, either the slot of an O NP in clause structure or the cross-referencing
slot of an O bound pronominal affix in verb structure. The first type of
reflexive is usually limited to marking A = O, but the second type is often
also used to mark other kinds of coreferentiality, e.g. an indirect object or
other peripheral constituent being coreferential with A ('they gave presents
to each other'); a peripheral constituent being coreferential with the O NP
('music takes me out of myself'); the modifier within an A NP being
coreferential with some other constituent (a sentence literally translatable
as 'John's mother hid himself', i.e. she hid the child); or the S NP of an
intransitive verb being coreferential with some other constituent ('he
laughed at himself').

The important point is that, in reflexives of the second type, if one of the
coreferential constituents is A or S then this will be the antecedent
(maintaining its normal form), while the other constituent goes into
reflexive form.[34] (In reflexives of the first type, where the S of a derived
intransitive codes coreferential A = O, there is of course no antecedent.)

Some of the most ergative languages (Dyirbal and Macushi, for instance)
have a reflexive construction of the first type. But many others (Burushaski,
Abaza and Basque, for instance) have constructions of the second type. In

---

[33] There are some languages that have no reflexive mechanism – one must just say 'I cut me'
and 'He cut him' (then, for third person, there is ambiguity as to whether or not the 'he'
and 'him' are coreferential). Examples include Pirahã, from Brazil (Everett 1986: 216) and
Fijian (Dixon 1988a: 255–6).

[34] This generalisation appears always to apply in the case of verbs such as 'cut', 'hit', 'hide',
'give' and 'see'. I have come across a handful of exceptions and they each involve a verb
referring to a mental process. For Basque, Saltarelli (1988: 113) mentions that O can be
antecedent and A reflexive and gives as one example 'Himself enchants my brother'; for
Modern Greek, Joseph and Philippaki-Warburton (1987: 80) mention the same possibility
and give as example 'Myself tortures me'. A. E. Kibrik (personal communication)
mentions that, in the Dagestanian language Dargwa, either A or O can be antecedent for
a verb such as 'praise' (he suggests that the controller of a reflexivisation is the focus of
empathy, which in fact appears to relate to word order). It seems that in all three languages
the normal situation is to have A as antecedent and O as reflexive.

every ergative language, as in every accusative language, the 'antecedent', i.e. the controller of reflexivity is A (or S, where it is extended to intransitives). This appears to be a universal and is related to the universal category of subject – that role which semantically controls the activity is also the grammatical controller in a reflexive construction of the second type.

5.3.4   Causatives

One of Keenan's (1976: 321) properties is that 'Subjects normally exhibit the same position, case-marking and verb agreement as does the causer NP in the most basic type of causative sentence.' Now a construction type is recognised as 'causative' partly on the semantic grounds that the referent of the 'causer NP' *makes the event happen.* We have shown that all languages assign one syntactic–semantic function (that which we are calling A) to that NP in a transitive clause which could initiate or control the activity. The causer must plainly be the A NP (one of the two basic functions covered by 'subject').

Many languages have one or more productive mechanisms for deriving a transitive causative verb from an intransitive verb (*The balloon burst →I burst the balloon*), or from an adjective (*The road is wide → I widened the road*). In addition, there are often a number of pairs of lexical roots which show a similar relation (e.g. in English *fell = make fall, kill = make dead*[35]). Here the S NP of the intransitive sentence (*The tree is falling*) corresponds to the O NP of the corresponding causative (*The woodman is felling the tree*). (As stressed in §1.3, this can in no way be taken as evidence of 'ergative syntax', as the term ergative is interpreted throughout this book.)

Keenan's comment relates not to 'subject' but to A function: the causer NP in a causative construction is in A function. If the underlying sentence is intransitive then S becomes O and a new role is introduced as causer, in A function; if the underlying sentence is transitive then – in the majority of cases – O remains as it is, underlying A is demoted to the nearest empty

---

[35] Sapir (1917: 84) suggested that *kill* be related to *cause to die*, and this has been repeated many times since. In fact *cause* is a quite uncommon verb in English, with fairly restricted meaning; causatives are more revealingly dealt with in terms of the very common verb *make. Make* takes an adjectival or participial complement, not just a *to* clause, and analyses such as *blacken = make black, kill = make dead* are a considerable improvement on *cause to become black* and *cause to die* (or *cause to become dead*). For instance, none of Fodor's (1970) arguments against a derivation of *kill* from *cause to die* apply against *make dead.*

syntactic slot (see Comrie 1975b, 1989: 165–84) and again a 'causer' enters as the new A. This does not relate to the universal category of subject (defined as a class consisting of the primitives A and S), nor to accusativity/ergativity.

I mentioned, in §1.3, that many languages have a number of verbs that can be used either transitively or intransitively; some are of type S = O (e.g. *trip*) and others of type S = A (e.g. *win*). In some languages these two lexical patterns can be reflected in morphological derivation. The productive process of forming transitive stems from intransitive roots (with some explicit derivational marking) is syntactically homogeneous in many languages, corresponding to the causative S = O type just discussed – e.g. Swahili (Loogman 1965: 104ff.) and Turkish (Lewis 1953: 106ff.). But in other languages the transitivising process may be of type S = O for some intransitive verbs, but S = A for others: in Yidin^y, *wanda-n* is 'fall down' and *wanda-ŋa-l* is 'make fall over (e.g. by pushing)', whereas *badi-n* is 'cry' and *badi-ŋa-l* is 'cry over (e.g. a lost child)'.[36] The derivational suffix *-ŋa-l* always signals a transitive verb; but in some cases it is genuinely causative (S = O), and in other cases it signals that the intransitive S NP has become A, and that an originally oblique NP (in, say, dative case) from the intransitive clause has moved into O function in the derived transitive clause (Dixon 1977a: 302–22). A similar situation is reported for the North-east Caucasian language Avar (Simon Crisp, personal communication).

There is in fact a semantic basis to which verb behaves in which way. Almost all verbs of MOTION (with the notable exception of 'follow') and REST show lexical pairs of type S = O (e.g. 'walk', 'return', 'drop', 'stand', 'float') as do verbs from the AFFECT semantic type which refer to changing the constitution of some object ('stretch', 'melt', 'break', 'burst'), a number of CORPOREAL verbs ('wake(n)', 'grow', 'hurt') and one or two other verbs such as 'work' and 'race'. S = A pairs are found in other semantic areas (e.g. 'eat', 'knit', 'watch', 'know'). If a derivational affix has varying effect it will most frequently be of type S = O for verbs from some or most of the semantic fields just specified and of type S = A elsewhere.

Rembarnga, a non-Pama-Nyungan language from Australia, shows an interesting rationalisation of this tendency: here the derivational suffix *-wa-* derives S = A transitives from intransitive roots of conjugations 1–2

---

[36] 'Make cry' can only be rendered by a two-clause sentence, normally specifying what was done to bring on the tears – e.g. 'The man teased me and I cried' (Dixon 1977a: 313–14).

(*kaḷuk* 'play', *kaḷuk-wa* 'play with'; *wak* 'laugh', *wak-wa* 'laugh at' etc.), but causative S=O forms from roots of conjugations 4–6 (*pariɲanə* 'be hanging up', *pariɲan-ʔ-wa* 'hang-up' etc.).[37] The important point is that most (but not quite all) of the intransitive verbs in conjugations 4–6 are concerned with motion or rest; but in fact *-wa-* has causative sense even with those verbs from these conjugations that belong to another semantic domain (e.g. 'yawn' → 'make yawn'). Which kind of syntactic effect the derivational affix *-wa-* has with any verb may have originally been semantically conditioned in Rembarnga, as in Yidin[y]; but this process has been grammaticalised in terms of the predominant semantic field associated with each conjugation, so that it is now conjugationally determined. (Rembarnga data from McKay 1975 and personal communication.)

The point of these examples is to stress that 'causative' can be one sense of a more general transitivising process, and that whether it is S = A or S = O can be, at least in part,[38] semantically conditioned. This is surely reminiscent of the semantic conditioning of morphological splits – especially split-S systems – discussed in Chapter 4. Languages with a transitivising process that is always causative in nature could be said to have generalised from one semantic type to all intransitive verbs (as Rembarnga appears to have generalised, in a more restrictive way, to all intransitive verbs in conjugations 4–6).

5.3.5 Summary

We have seen that certain constructions – imperatives, reflexives, verbs like 'can' and 'begin' – must involve identification of S and A at the underlying syntactic level, purely because of their semantic content and the semantic nature of A and S functions (it is these semantic factors that lead to the grouping of S and A as the universal category 'subject').

In §3.3 I mentioned universal properties that link together S and O. Most of these are lexical, e.g. if a verb has multiple senses these may relate to the nature of S or O, not of A; if a verb has variant forms depending on the singularity/plurality of one core participant this will be S or O, never A. Noun incorporation typically involves S or O, seldom A (but it also prefers

---

[37] There are no intransitive roots in conjugations 3 and 7.

[38] There is generally partial semantic explanation for this grammatical split, just as there was in split-S systems (§4.1.1). Once a phenomenon that was originally semantic becomes grammaticised, the semantic basis is likely gradually to contract. (As already mentioned, this is well attested in the case of noun/gender classes.)

S_o over S_a, in some split-S languages – see Rice 1991). There do not appear to be universal syntactic phenomena linking S and O, in the way that there are for S and A.

'Subject' is an important category. In some languages it appears to be the basis for many kinds of syntactic operation. But there are languages which require 'subject' only for the kinds of syntactic phenomena discussed in §§5.3.1–3. In other areas, they may work in terms of S and O, rather than S and A. This is a major topic of the next chapter.

6 Inter-clausal or syntactic ergativity

Chapters 3 and 4 dealt with intra-clausal or morphological ergativity, relating to ways in which S and O are marked in the same manner, and A in a different manner, within a single clause. It is now time to consider what happens when two clauses are linked together in a coordinate or subordinate construction. In some languages there are syntactic constraints on clause combination, or on the omission of coreferential constituents in clause combinations. If these constraints treat S and O in the same way and A differently, then the language is said to be 'syntactically ergative', with an S/O pivot; if they treat S and A in the same way and O differently, then it is said to be 'syntactically accusative', with an S/A pivot. (In some languages the syntactic pivot may have a further function, relating to syntactic processes within a clause, such as the questioning of an NP; this will be discussed in §6.3.)

Preliminary exemplification was given in §1.2 for Dyirbal, which is ergative at the inter-clausal syntactic level and works in terms of an S/O pivot. Two clauses may only be coordinated in Dyirbal if they have a common NP which is in S or O function in each clause; the occurrence of this NP in the second clause is then generally omitted. We also mentioned that English works in terms of an S/A pivot – if two clauses that are coordinated have a common NP this can only be omitted from the second clause if it is in S or A function in each of the clauses (we can say *Father returned and saw mother* but not **Father returned and mother saw*).

In many languages there are passive and antipassive syntactic operations, which derive an intransitive clause from an underlying transitive. Passive puts an underlying O NP into derived S function and demotes A (which will then often be omitted); antipassive puts an underlying A NP into derived S function and demotes O (which will then often be omitted). Passive and antipassive typically occur in a range of circumstances, with a variety of meanings (which sometimes include an aspectual sense). One use of passive or antipassive may be to 'feed' a syntactic pivot. If certain

143

constraints on clause linkage demand that appropriate NPs be in S or A function, then some syntactic mechanism may be needed to put an NP in underlying O relation into a pivot function – this can be passive, which puts underlying O into derived S function. Similarly, antipassive, which puts an NP that is in underlying A relation into derived S function, can feed an S/O pivot condition, which requires that NPs be in S or O function for a certain type of inter-clause linkage (and/or consequent NP omission) to occur.

Languages with an S/O pivot require an antipassive operation to 'feed' it and languages with an S/A pivot may have similar need of a passive operation. But it must be stressed that – in all the languages I have examined – this 'pivot feeding' is only one of the several functions of passive or antipassive. Languages that have no pivot, and thus no feeding requirement, may still use passive and/or antipassive derivations.

Only *some* languages work in terms of a pivot, and it is only *these* that can be characterised as 'accusative' or 'ergative' (or a mix of these) at the level of inter-clausal syntax. For others there are no constraints – dealing with the coreferentiality and status of NPs – on clause coordination, or, if there are, they do not relate to syntactic function. To illustrate the latter point first, Bhat (1988: 13, 128; 1991: 17) reports that for the Dravidian language Kannada basic syntactic relations are shown by cases, which allows constituent order to be rather free. In this language it is place in constituent order[1] that controls coreferential deletion. Consider:

(1) *ko:lu   maḍakege ta:gi   eraḍu tuṇḍu a:yitu*
     stick + NOM pot + DAT hit + PAST two   piece BECOME
     The stick hit the pot and (the stick) broke into two

(2) *maḍakege ko:lu   ta:gi   eraḍu tuṇḍu a:yitu*
     pot + DAT stick + NOM hit + PAST two   piece BECOME
     The stick hit the pot and (the pot) broke into two

Deletion of the intransitive subject NP in the second clause is here 'controlled' by whichever NP is placed in initial position in the first clause – 'the stick' (which is nominative) in (1) or 'the pot' (which is dative) in (2).

I mentioned in §2.2 that languages with semantically based marking – those for which morphological marking directly describes the semantics of each instance of use – do not assign a central syntactic role to S, A and O. Languages of this type tend to lack valency-reducing operations such as

---

[1] Initial position may relate to the 'topicality' of the NP (this is not something which Bhat mentions in his discussion).

passive and antipassive, and they also tend to lack pivot conditions on clause combining. Bhat (ms.) reports that in Manipuri, which has semantically based marking, there are no syntactic constraints on co-ordination, and the same appears to hold for fluid-S languages such as Acehnese (Durie 1985). This is one class of 'pivotless' languages.[2]

Only some languages with syntactically based marking – in which S, A and O are autonomous basic relations, mediating between semantics and morphological marking – do operate in terms of pivots. Whether or not a language has a pivot (or a mixture of pivots) appears to be a facet of its 'grammatical personality'. But this does correlate with one other typological parameter – languages with well-developed cross-referencing in the verb (that is, 'head-marking' languages at clause level, in the terminology of Nichols 1986, 1992) most often lack specific syntactic constraints on complex sentence formation and NP omission. It may be that there is so much information about nominal arguments encoded in the verb that NP omission may occur fairly freely with only a very limited chance of ambiguity resulting. Most of the languages with pivot conditions are 'dependent-marking', in which syntactic function is marked on NPs rather than in the verb.

This is only a tendency. There are some head-marking languages which do operate in terms of a pivot – in a group of Mayan languages, only NPs in S or O function can be questioned, relativised or focussed (and an antipassive syntactic operation is needed to bring an underlying A NP into derived S function for this purpose); see §6.3. And there are certainly a fair number of dependent-marking languages that appear to be pivotless. Nevertheless, there does appear to be a significant inverse correlation between degree of cross-referencing and syntactic constraints on clause combination and NP omission.

The next section discusses passive and antipassive, one of the functions of which is often to feed a pivot constraint. §6.2 discusses and exemplifies types of pivot and §6.3 surveys languages which are known to be wholly or partly 'ergative' at the syntactic level.

---

[2] Foley and Van Valin (1984: 120) mention that 'stative–active languages' (covering my split-S and fluid-S) 'seem to be pivotless'. Most or all of the languages they cite appear in fact to be fluid-S or with semantically based marking. There is no particular expectation – as I see things – why split-S languages should not operate with a pivot condition.

6.1   Passive and antipassive

Like 'ergative' and 'subject', the terms 'passive' and 'antipassive' have been used in a number of different ways, to describe a fair range of phenomena. Here, I shall put forward fairly strict criteria by which a syntactic derivation should be recognised as passive or antipassive.

Passive
(a)   applies to an underlyingly transitive clause and forms a derived intransitive;[3]
(b)   the underlying O NP becomes S of the passive;
(c)   the underlying A NP goes into a peripheral function, being marked by a non-core case, preposition, etc.; this NP can be omitted, although there is always the option of including it;
(d)   there is some explicit formal marking of a passive construction (generally, by a verbal affix or else by a periphrastic element in the verb phrase – such as English *be ... -en* – although it could be marked elsewhere in the clause).

Antipassive
(a)   applies to an underlying transitive clause and forms a derived intransitive;
(b)   the underlying A NP becomes S of the antipassive;
(c)   the underlying O NP goes into a peripheral function, being marked by a non-core case, preposition, etc.; this NP can be omitted, although there is always the option of including it;
(d)   there is some explicit formal marking of an antipassive construction (same preference and possibilities as for passive).

With such criteria, some of the constructions that have been referred to in the literature as 'passive' or 'antipassive' would not fall within the scope of these grammatical labels. (Whistler 1985 shows that what have been called 'passives' for Nootka are really integral parts of an inverse case-marking system, for instance.)[4]

---

[3] For all languages (with which I am acquainted) that have strict marking of transitivity, passives and antipassives are clearly intransitive; cf. Langacker and Munro (1975). For languages with more fluid transitivity (e.g. English), it has not been the custom to comment on the transitivity of passives. However, I do not believe that the treatment here is inconsistent with any properties of English passives (or with other treatments of them).

[4] Baker (1988) says that, in order to passivise, a verb must have an underlying subject (by which he means S or A) and an external theta role to assign. This would apply to a very wide range of construction types, so that what have traditionally been called passives (and

The label 'agentless passive' has sometimes been used for a construction where underlying O becomes S, and A is simply omitted, with there being no formal marking, i.e. (a) and (b) but not (c) or (d). Similarly, 'patientless antipassive' could refer to A becoming S, and O being omitted, with no formal marking – again (a) and (b) but not (c) or (d). Now I have mentioned that in accusative languages the S or A (nominative) NP is generally obligatory but that the O NP may be omittable in certain circumstances, e.g. English *He is drinking whiskey → He is drinking*. This might be taken as an instance of 'patientless antipassive'.[5] I also mentioned that in an ergative language the S or O (absolutive) NP is generally obligatory but that an A NP may be omitted in certain circumstances (this is always possible in Dyirbal, for instance). This might – under some analyses – be taken as an example of an 'agentless passive'. In fact, passives are typically found in accusative and antipassives in ergative languages. To introduce a further category of 'patientless antipassives' (found typically in accusative languages) and 'agentless passives' (found typically in ergative languages) would be unhelpful and confusing.[6]

I suggest that criterion (d) should always be maintained, so that an agentless passive only be recognised when there is some explicit formal marking; such constructions are found, for the most part, in accusative and also in split-S languages. Similarly, a patientless antipassive should also satisfy criteria (a), (b) and (d), with some formal marking.

A lexeme often has several related senses and, in a similar manner, so may both inflectional and derivational morphemes. In many languages a detransitivising verbal affix that marks passive or antipassive also has a reflexive or reciprocal meaning (or both).[7] And while the major function of

---

what are passives in terms of my criteria here) would comprise a small fraction of the class of Baker-passives.

[5] Sentences like this *were* described as a type of antipassive by Heath (1976: 203). Many of Heath's examples, and some of those in Postal (1977) fall outside the scope of 'antipassive' as the term is employed here.

[6] In some languages there are ambitransitive or 'labile' verbs which may be used either transitively or intransitively; some of these are S = A and others S = O. The intransitive use of S = A labile verbs has been called 'antipassive' but this is a mistaken application of the label, as Hewitt (1982) explains when discussing north Caucasian languages. (To be consistent, the S = O pairs should also be called 'passive', which would of course be equally mistaken.) Similar comments apply to the Tongan examples quoted in Hopper and Thompson (1980: 253). For Choctaw, Davies (1984, 1986) identifies an 'antipassive' that applies to just four verbs; it would probably be more appropriate to regard them as having 'alternate case frames' (see Dixon 1989).

[7] For instance, in the Australian language Anguthimri (Crowley 1981), the verbal derivational suffix *-pri* can signal an antipassive or a reciprocal (there is a different affix, *-thi*, for reflexive). In the Carib language Macushi (Abbott 1991) the detransitivising verbal

a passive derivation will be with transitive verbs, it may also – in limited circumstances – apply to some intransitive verbs, putting the object of a preposition into derived S slot and assigning oblique marking to the underlying S (for example *Henry VIII slept in this bed* → *This bed was slept in by Henry VIII*).[8] Rice (1991) describes how in the Northern Athapaskan language Slave, which has a split-S system, there is an agentless passive marked by derivational affix *-d-* that applies to transitive verbs and also to some intransitives of type S$_a$ (but to no S$_o$); e.g. from 'he worked' can be derived 'it is worked' meaning 'work was done'.

There are typically a range of syntactic and semantic circumstances in which passive or antipassive may be used; they differ from language to language but do show areas of commonality. As already stressed, one major function is often to feed a pivot constraint on clause combining – this can be a function of passive in a language with accusative syntax (S/A pivot) and of antipassive in one with ergative syntax (S/O pivot). But there are other circumstances in which it is appropriate to employ a passive or antipassive. In English, for instance, passive may be used to avoid mentioning the underlying A NP; to focus on O rather than A, especially when O is further to the left on the Nominal Hierarchy (shown in Figure 4.5 on page 85) and/or O is definite and A indefinite; to focus on the result of an activity; or to place a topic NP in S function (see Dixon 1991a: 298ff.; Thompson 1987). One use of antipassive in Dyirbal is to avoid mentioning the underlying O (recall that O and S are obligatory constituents). In Nez Perce, from the Sahaptian family, an antipassive construction is typically used when the underlying O is 'indefinite, non-referential or plural' (Givón 1984: 163; Rude 1982).

Passive and antipassive often also carry an aspectual meaning. In the Mayan language Tzutujil there is both a 'completive passive', which 'emphasises the result of the activity on the patient as well as the termination of the activity' and a 'simple passive' which simply 'defines and describes the activity' (Dayley 1985: 342; see also Dayley 1978).

---

prefix *at-/es-/e'-* marks reflexive, reciprocal and agentless passive. Dyirbal has verbal derivational suffixes *-rri-y* and *-nbarri-y* whose main functions are to mark reflexive and reciprocal respectively; but each can also function as a further antipassive marker. In Latin passive forms of the transitive verbs *moveo* 'move' and *verto* 'turn' (and their compounds) have a reflexive sense.

[8] Dixon (1991a: 315–20) discusses prepositional NPs becoming passive subjects in English. Note that this is only possible if there is no O NP in the underlying clause; from *Someone has drunk out of this glass* we can derive *This glass has been drunk out of*, but corresponding to *Someone has drunk whiskey out of this glass*, it is not legitimate to form **This glass has been drunk whiskey out of.*

Bittner (1987) states that the various antipassive suffixes in Eskimo are not suppletive variants (as had previously been thought) but carry semantic information, indicating 'imperfective', 'inceptive' etc. In the North-east Caucasian language Bezhta the antipassive carries a potential meaning – 'Brother boils the water' would be expressed by a regular transitive, with 'brother' in ergative and 'water' in absolutive case, but 'Brother can boil the water' requires an antipassive, with 'brother' in absolutive and 'water' in the oblique case, instrumental (Kibrik 1990: 27).

On the basis of the criteria given above it appears that – from a syntactic point of view – passive and antipassive[9] are parallel, with A and O interchanged. However, there is more to language than syntax – these two construction types have rather different semantic implications.[10] A passive typically focusses on the state which the referent of the underlying O NP is in, as a result of some action, e.g. *John was wounded/promoted*. An antipassive, in contrast, focusses on the fact that the referent of the underlying A is taking part in some activity that involves an object, while backgrounding the identity of the object, e.g. Dyirbal antipassive *Jani*(S) *gunyjalŋanⁿu* (*biya-gu*(DATIVE)) 'John is drinking (beer)', contrasting with active transitive *biya*(O) *Jani-ŋgu*(A) *gunyjan* 'John is drinking beer'.

Languages without a syntactic pivot can still show passive and/or antipassive (for instance, Kuku-Yalanji and Diyari, to be discussed soon). As already indicated, there can be several types of passive, or of antipassive, in a given language, with distinct semantic overtones. And a single language can include both passive(s) and antipassive(s). Mayan languages, which have considerable ergative characteristics, typically have both. Thus, in Mam there is an antipassive and at least four varieties of passive – one indicates that 'the agent has lost, or does not have, control of the action' (and may also be used in generic constructions of the form 'It is good/bad to do X'); another 'requires the use of a directional and includes motion or process in its meaning "X happened because someone went to do it"'; and so on (England 1983a: 110ff., 199ff.; 1988). Both passive and

---

[9] The term antipassive, while neat, is a little misleading in that it carries an implication of isomorphism. The label was coined, in late 1968, by Michael Silverstein, to describe the *-ŋa-y* derivation in Dyirbal (while he was attending a course I taught at Harvard on The Native Languages of Australia). At about the same time Jacobsen in a pioneering paper called 'The analog of the passive transformation in ergative-type languages' (conference paper 1969, published 1985), recognised the phenomenon of antipassive, which he called 'agentive'. Jacobsen also refuted the mistaken idea that ergative languages have no voice – the active/antipassive contrast in ergative languages is, in many ways, on a par with the active/passive contrast in accusative languages.

[10] See also the discussion in Lazard (1989, 1991: 34–9).

antipassive are also attested for Eskimo (Woodbury 1975: 26–7, 86; 1977: 322–5). Bollenbacher (1977) describes the passive in Basque, another language with morphological ergativity.[11]

There can be other syntactic uses of passive and antipassive. In a fascinating paper, Mondloch (1978)[12] describes how, in the Mayan language Quiché, a clause may be ambiguous if both S and O are third person and of the same number, in terms of cross-referencing on the verb. This can be exemplified in (3) and (4):

(3)   *š-Ø-u:-kuna-x*   *ri: ačih ri: išoq*
       COMPLETIVE-3sgO-3sgA-cure-ACTIVE THE man THE woman
       Either The woman cured the man *Or* The man cured the woman

(4)   *xačin š-Ø-u:-kuna-x ri: ačih?*
       WHO   THE man
       Either Who cured the man? *Or* Who did the man cure?

Constituent order appears not to be the mechanism used for disambiguation, but instead antipassive or one of the two passive voices is used – each of these ensures that underlying A and O are treated in distinct ways. Only one of these will be cross-referenced on the verb – underlying O for passive and underlying A for antipassive – with the other being accorded an oblique marking – the demoted A in a passive by prepositional -*umal* 'by', and the demoted O in an antipassive by *če:* 'for'. For instance, the inchoative passive version of (3), given in (3a), and the antipassive version of (4), in (4a) are both unambiguous:

(3a)   *š-Ø-kuna-š*   *ri: ačih r-umal*
       COMPLETIVE-3sgS-cure-INCHO.PASS THE man 3sg-BY
       ri: išoq
       THE woman
       The man was cured by the woman

(4a)   *xačin š-Ø-kuna-n*   *če:*   *ri: ačih*
       WHO COMPLETIVE-3sgS-cure-ANTIPASS FOR + HIM THE man
       Who cured (for) the man?

---

[11] On the basis of a wide-ranging typological survey, Nichols (1992: 158) suggests that languages with an antipassive but no passive are always ergative in type.
[12] Johnson (1980) discusses similar matters in Eskimo and has a most revealing discussion of the pragmatic function of antipassive.

Just occasionally, one finds a language in which a single derivational affix can have either passive or antipassive effect, depending on the circumstance.[13] Patz (1982: 241–59) describes the basic conditions for a transitive clause in Kuku-Yalanji, from north-east Queensland: (1) A and O must not be coreferential; (2) the described action must be intentional; (3) the A NP must be stated and should be the most prominent clause constituent; and (4) the described action must be discrete and performed on a specific object. If any of these conditions is not satisfied then the verb is marked by the derivational affix -*ji*-. When (1) is not satisfied and A and O are coreferential they are mapped onto S and here -*ji*- marks a reflexive or reciprocal construction. If something happens accidentally – contravening (2) – or if the underlying A is unknown or irrelevant or lower than O on the Nominal Hierarchy – contravening (3) – then underlying O becomes derived S and -*ji*- marks a passive-type construction (the underlying A NP may be included, in locative case). If condition (4) is broken, with the action or patient being 'generalised' (e.g. 'He is hitting all the children', 'He is throwing curses everywhere') then underlying A becomes S in an antipassive-type -*ji*- construction (with underlying O going into locative or perlative case).

In Diyari, from South Australia, there is a verbal derivational suffix -*ṭadi* that has reflexive, passive or antipassive sense[14] depending on the class of transitive verbs it is used with: reflexive with a root from class 2A (e.g. 'hit'); passive – where underlying A takes locative or instrumental case – with one from class 2D (e.g. 'lose'); and antipassive – where underlying O goes into locative case – with a root from class 2B (e.g. 'await') or class 2C (e.g. 'eat'). Passive tends to be used when the 'instigator' (underlying A) 'is inanimate or left unexpressed' while one use of antipassive is to mark non-volitionality on the part of the underlying A NP (Austin 1981a: 151–7). It is relevant to note that both Kuku-Yalanji and Diyari lack a syntactic pivot (Diyari has switch-reference marking – see §6.2). It may be

[13] Ayres (1983) describes the derivational suffix -$(o/u)n$ in the Mayan language Ixil. In underived clauses the A NP is cross-referenced on the verb by set A of bound pronominal affixes and S/O by set B. One function of -$(o/u)n$ is to form a normal antipassive, a derived intransitive clause in which underlying A is cross-referenced by set B and underlying O can optionally be included only as a peripheral constituent marked by *s* 'on'. But the derivational affix is used in another construction type in which O is still cross-referenced by set B and so is A, in a clause which appears still to be transitive.

[14] Austin (1981a: 156–7) mentions a fourth function of -*ṭadi* - it can mark durative aspect with verbs of all types (intransitive, transitive and ditransitive); this sense of the affix does not alter the transitivity of the verb to which it is attached, unlike the reflexive, passive and antipassive senses, which derive an intransitive from an underlying transitive. Compare with the information on Yidin^y given in note 26 to Chapter 3.

that a single affix would have both passive and antipassive senses only in a language in which there is no pivot (which needs to be 'fed' by an operation of this type). The derivational affix -:*ji-n* in Yidin^y (next language but one to the south of Kuku-Yalanji) is clearly cognate with Kuku-Yalanji -*ji-*; as described in §3.4.1, the Yidin^y affix marks reflexive, inanimate agent, and non-controlling human agent, but only antipassive, not passive. Yidin^y does have a syntactic pivot, which is fed by antipassive (see §6.2.4).

The function of passive and antipassive that most concerns us in this chapter is the feeding of pivots. And also their syntactic role in ensuring that each clause includes an NP of the type deemed obligatory by the grammar of that language. Eskimo is typical of ergative languages in that there must always be an S in an intransitive and an O NP in a transitive clause. Woodbury (1975) mentions that if, for some reason, the O NP is not to be stated then antipassive must be applied – the underlying A NP is now in derived S function (absolutive case) and the underlying O, taking instrumental inflection, can freely be omitted. Similarly for accusative languages, where S and A are generally obligatory, an underlying A NP may often only be omittable in the context of a passive construction. Kuryłowicz (1946) noted that there is no language with a passive derivation which does not then permit agent omission.

There can be other syntactic reasons for using passive or antipassive. In Dyirbal demonstratives exist only in absolutive case, for S and O functions. Thus, if any underlying A NP is to be qualified by 'this', it must be brought into derived S function, through antipassivisation.[15]

6.2   Syntactic pivots

I mentioned, towards the end of §5.1, that an 'underlying structure' involves a verb in its basic form, before any derivational processes have applied. A 'derived structure' is formed from an underlying structure by the application of one or more derivational processes, e.g. passive, antipassive, causative (or reflexive/reciprocal in languages where this involves a detransitivising derivation, rather than the use of reflexive pronouns in an underlying transitive structure). In most cases, underlying structures are unmarked, that is, they are used in unmarked circumstances; derived structures are only used when specific syntactic and/or semantic and/or pragmatic and/or discourse conditions are satisfied. Underlying

---

[15] See, for example, line 9 of text XXV in Dixon (1972: 388).

structures tend to be more frequent, on a text count, and they will be the first construction types taught by a teacher (whether in a formal classroom situation, or by an informant-teacher in a field work setting).

Each language has a morphological (or constituent order) marking convention that in most or all cases enables its speakers immediately to recognise which of the core functions (A, O or S) an NP is in within an underlying or derived structure. Referring back to Table 1.1 in §1.2, we see that in Dyirbal an S NP will be in absolutive case if a noun and nominative if a pronoun, an A NP will be in ergative case if a noun and in nominative if a pronoun, and an O NP will be in absolutive case if a noun and in accusative if a pronoun. In English an NP will be in O function if it immediately follows the verb, in A function if it precedes the verb and there is an O NP after the verb, and in S function if it precedes the verb and there is no following O. We can then tell that in *John hit Bill*, *John* is in A and *Bill* is in O function, and that in *Bill was hit by John*, *Bill* is in derived S function while John here bears no core syntactic function.

Syntactic operations of coordination and subordination, forming complex (i.e. multi-clausal) sentences always operate at the level of derived structure. That is, if operations such as passive and antipassive are applied they must be applied before any clause combining takes place. Of course, many clauses will not undergo syntactic derivations of this sort – we can say that they maintain the same syntactic configurations at the level of underlying structure and at the level of derived structure. Other clauses will have undergone derivation, sometimes partly to meet a syntactic condition on clause linking.

Languages have varying strategies for dealing with the syntax of clause combining:

(a) *Switch-reference marking.* For example, in the South Australian language Diyari there are two forms of verbal inflection for each type of subordinate clause – one indicating that the coreferential NPs are both in (derived) S/A function, and the other indicating that this is not the case.[16]

---

[16] The phenomenon of switch-reference marking has only been recognised and investigated quite recently (beginning with Jacobsen 1967) but there is already a considerable literature on it – see, for instance, Munro (1980), Haiman and Munro (1983), Keenan (1976: 315–16) and references therein.

It is noteworthy that all switch-reference systems reported thus far work in terms of 'same/different (derived) S/A'. Since there are well-attested instances of S/O pivots, as well as of S/A pivots (although the latter are much more common) we would expect, as more of the world's languages are provided with adequate grammatical descriptions, to encounter some instances of switch-reference systems that work in terms of 'same/different (derived) S/O' (although of course there is no guarantee that we will).

The second occurrence of the common NP can be freely omitted without any possibility of ambiguity or confusion. Languages with switch-reference marking typically lack passive and antipassive or – if they do include these – they do not have any pivot-feeding function (see comments in §6.1 on Diyari). It can be argued that there is no syntactic need of passive or antipassive, since it is not necessary to bring an underlying O or A NP into derived S function, to facilitate NP omission without any chance of ambiguity.

(b) *Pivot constraints.*   Many languages impose conditions on certain kinds of clause combining in terms of the syntactic functions (S or A or O) of coreferential NPs. Some of these constraints treat S and A as equivalent, while others treat S and O as equivalent. It is useful to have a label to describe such equivalence – the term *pivot* (first used in Dixon 1979a) is now quite widely employed (e.g. Foley and Van Valin 1984 among many other publications).

The category of pivot was introduced, with preliminary exemplification, in §1.2; it will now be discussed more exhaustively. We can recall that there are basically two varieties of pivot (some languages show just one type, others have a mixture of the two):

1.   S/A pivot – the coreferential NP must be in derived S or A function in each of the clauses being joined;

2.   S/O pivot – the coreferential NP must be in derived S or O function in each of the clauses being joined.

(c) *No syntactic mechanism* (neither switch-reference marking nor pivot constraints).   In languages of this sort any types of clauses may be joined in a coordinate or subordinate construction so long as this is semantically acceptable; an NP repeated between two clauses may be omitted not according to any syntactic rule (in terms of which it could be automatically retrieved by a hearer) but just according to the semantics of that bit of discourse. For instance, for a sentence from such a language translatable as 'Mary hit John and —— laughed', the omitted S NP for 'laugh' would probably be taken to be 'Mary', while for 'Mary hit John and —— cried', the S for 'cry' would probably be taken to be 'John'. In each case, the most plausible scenario is chosen – someone who is hit is likely to cry, and if

Austin (1981b) describes switch-reference systems as an areal phenomenon over a large area of west and central Australia; languages in this area typically have ergative morphology but accusative syntax. Ergative syntactic systems are found in languages along the east coast of Australia, and into western Queensland, a region that does not overlap with the switch-reference zone.

either of the two participants should laugh it is most likely – in unmarked circumstances – to be the hitter. Languages of this sort cannot be classified as either 'accusative' or 'ergative' at the syntactic level.

As already mentioned, languages with semantically-based marking, such as Manipuri, and fluid-S languages, such as Acehnese, have been reported to be pivotless. Among languages with syntactically-based marking, many in which the verb or predicate includes obligatory information about subject and object do not operate with a pivot, or else only in a very minor way.[17] Languages which have ergative characteristics at the morphological level but appear to be pivotless include Classical Tibetan (Andersen 1987: 306), Limbu (van Driem 1987), Samoan (Mosel and Hovdhaugen 1992: 704–17); Chechen-Ingush (Nichols 1980, 1983), Archi (Kibrik 1979a) and Lezgian (Haspelmath 1991).

In §1.2 the S/A and S/O pivots were contrasted in terms of sentences like (5) in English and (6) in Dyirbal:

(5) [*Mother*$_A$ *saw father*$_O$] *and* [$\emptyset_S$ *returned*]

(6) [*ŋuma*$_O$ *yabu-ŋgu*$_A$ *buran*][$\emptyset_S$ *banagan*^{y}*u*]
     father + ABS mother-ERG saw   returned
     Mother saw father and he returned

In each of (5) and (6) the subject of the intransitive verb, in the second clause of the coordination, has been omitted. Users of English work in terms of an S/A pivot – a speaker will omit the S NP for *returned* only when it is coreferential with the S/A NP of the preceding clause; a hearer operates in terms of the same grammatical rule and 'retrieves' this omitted NP, i.e. infers that *mother* is the subject of *returned*. If the speaker had wished to say that father returned he would have had to include at least a pronoun in the S slot, i.e. *Mary saw father and he returned*.

Users of Dyirbal work in terms of an S/O pivot. An S NP can only be

---

[17] I worked intensively on Fijian (living in a monolingual village for six months) but discovered no syntactic constraints on clause combining. (Note that Fijian is a cross-referencing language; the predicate has obligatory constituents referring to S/A and O.) Any two clauses can be combined together, subject to semantic plausibility; if there are coreferential NPs they can be in any function in each clause. I did, however, find two hints of pivots. (1) Where there is a main clause and a following 'when/because' clause, the unmarked expectation is that main clause O should be coreferential with S or A of the 'when/because' clause, e.g. the unmarked interpretation of 'John saw Mary when $\emptyset$ was laughing' is that the omitted S for 'was laughing' (shown here by $\emptyset$) should be 'Mary'. (2) When two clauses are linked by 'and' or 'if' the unmarked expectation is that S/A of one clause should be coreferential with S/A of the other, e.g. in 'John saw Mary and $\emptyset$ laughed', the unmarked interpretation would be that 'John' is S for 'laughed'. However, these pivot principles can be – and frequently are – overridden by explicit subject specification or simply by semantic expectations (Dixon 1988a: 299–301).

omitted – and then retrieved by a hearer – if it is coreferential with an NP in S or O function in the preceding clause. Thus the omission of the S NP from the second clause in (6) is only possible when it is identical to the O NP of the preceding transitive clause in the coordination, i.e. 'father returned'. If a speaker of Dyirbal wished to say 'Mother saw father and returned', he would have to use some syntactic device to get the occurrence of the common NP in the first clause, which is in underlying A function, into derived S or O function, to satisfy the pivot constraint; it could be achieved by antipassivising the first clause. This and other syntactic strategies in Dyirbal will be discussed in §6.2.2.

This exemplification should also help to demonstrate the difference between 'subject' and 'pivot'. S, A and O are taken as universal syntactic relations, which are applicable at both underlying and derived syntactic levels (indeed, a syntactic derivation is largely defined by the ways in which it reallocates syntactic relations). I use 'subject' for a universal category which links together underlying A and S; as noted in §5.3, this is applicable – in some ways – to the grammars of all languages. 'Pivot' is a language-particular category (and only *some* languages have one), with two possibilities: S/A and S/O.

When the syntactic pivot is exclusively (or almost exclusively) S/A, there is a temptation to use just one term. Linguists have often spoken of 'deep subject' (which does correspond to my universal category of subject) and of 'surface subject' (meaning pivot). If it is realised that 'deep subject' is essentially a semantic notion (determining universal conditions on imperatives, verbs like 'can' and 'begin', and the like), whereas 'surface subject' is a syntactic category (in terms of which the rules for coordination and subordination in any particular language may be described), then this terminology may be workable for languages with a consistently accusative profile.

But for a language that has a significant S/O pivot, the two terms must be kept apart. S and A will be related at the underlying structure level, but have quite different relevance at the level of derived structure: it would be pointless to group together 'derived S' and 'derived A' functions as 'surface subject' (and to take 'derived S' and 'derived O' as surface subject would be totally confusing). That is, for a language that is syntactically ergative, it is inappropriate to talk of 'surface subject', although the traditional category of 'subject' is applicable at the level of underlying structure.

Within a universal enquiry, it is best always to distinguish between underlying structure level *subject* and derived structure level *pivot*, even when discussing a language which has an S/A pivot. The terminology chosen for description of any individual language should be appropriate for the structural character of that language, and also appropriate for comparing that structure with the structures of other languages, of all types.

6.2.1 Basic framework for pivot investigation

As already stated, a pivot constraint may be invoked when two clauses are combined together to form a complex sentence; it will involve conditions on the syntactic functions of an NP that is common to the two clauses (that is, an NP in one clause that is coreferential with an NP in the other clause). Sometimes, as in Dyirbal, the pivot conditions must be satisfied for clauses to be combined. Other times, as in English, there is no pivot condition on clause combining, but there is on the omission of one occurrence of a common NP. Each language has a number of different processes of clause combining – pivot conditions may apply to only some of these, and different pivot conditions may apply to different kinds of clause combination, within a single language.

The basic core syntactic relations are S, A and O. When we have two clauses syntactically linked, each will be either intransitive (with S) or transitive (with A and O). We thus have nine basic possibilities for the syntactic functions of a common NP in the two clauses – any of S/O/A followed by any of S/A/O. There are two further possibilities, for when two transitive clauses have two core NPs in common.

These possibilities can be set out, with subscript $_1$ indicating that the common NP is in this function in the first clause, and $_2$ that it is in the specified function in the second clause.

> *Possible functions of a common NP in two syntactically linked clauses:*
> both clauses intransitive

(a) $S_1 = S_2$
> first clause intransitive, second transitive

(b) $S_1 = O_2$
(c) $S_1 = A_2$
> first clause transitive, second intransitive

(d) $O_1 = S_2$
(e) $A_1 = S_2$

both clauses transitive, one common NP

(f) $O_1 = O_2$
(g) $A_1 = A_2$
(h) $O_1 = A_2$
(i) $A_1 = O_2$

both clauses transitive, two common NPs

(j) $O_1 = O_2$ and $A_1 = A_2$
(k) $O_1 = A_2$ and $A_1 = O_2$

I mentioned just above that there is no pivot constraint on actual clause linking in English. In the case of coordination we can say (i) *John returned and saw Mary* (where $S_1 = A_1$) or (ii) *John returned and Mary saw him* (where $S_1 = O_1$). But there is a constraint on the omission of the second occurrence of a common NP – it must be in S or A function in each clause. Thus (i) satisfies this pivot condition and the occurrence of *John* from the second clause has been omitted; but (ii) does not satisfy it and here we had to retain the pronoun *him* in O slot. If we wished to fully omit mention of John from the second clause in (ii) then this must be passivised, putting underlying O into derived S function, and the pivot condition is now met, i.e. *John returned and was seen by Mary*. (English could be said to have a weak S/A pivot.)

The operation of the pivot condition on NP omission in English can be illustrated by constructing examples for each of (a)–(k):

Illustration of S/A pivot in English

(a) $S_1 = S_2$ *Bill entered and sat down*
(b) $S_1 = O_2$ *Bill entered and was seen by Fred*
(c) $S_1 = A_2$ *Bill entered and saw Fred*
(d) $O_1 = S_2$ *Bill was seen by Fred and laughed*
(e) $A_1 = S_2$ *Fred saw Bill and laughed*
(f) $O_1 = O_2$ *Bill was kicked by Tom and punched by Bob* (or *Tom kicked and Bob punched Bill*)
(g) $A_1 = A_2$ *Bob kicked Jim and punched Bill*
(h) $O_1 = A_2$ *Bob was kicked by Tom and punched Bill*
(i) $A_1 = O_2$ *Bob punched Bill and was kicked by Tom*
(j) $O_1 = O_2$ $A_1 = A_2$ *Fred punched and kicked Bill*
(k) $O_1 = A_2$ $A_1 = O_2$ *Fred punched Bill and was kicked by him* (or *Fred punched and was kicked by Bill*)

Omission is straightforward – with no syntactic derivations required – when the common NP is in S or A function in each clause, in (a), (c), (e),

(g) and (j). But when the common NP is in O function in one clause then that clause must be passivised for NP omission to be allowed; this applies to (b), (d), (f), (h), (i) and (k). In (f) it was necessary to passivise both clauses. English has a further clause-linking strategy – if two clauses differ only in their verbs, the verbs can simply be coordinated. Thus, from *Fred punched Bill* and *Fred kicked Bill* we can get *Fred punched and kicked Bill* in (j) in which both *Fred* and *Bill* are stated only once (*Fred punched Bill and kicked him* is a possible alternative). In (k), as an alternative to *Fred punched Bill and was kicked by him*, some (but not all) native speakers are happy with *Fred punched and was kicked by Bill*. There is also the possibility of combining A-NP-plus-verb from two clauses which have the same O NP so that, as an alternative to *Bill was kicked by Tom and punched by Bob* in (f), it is also possible to say *Tom kicked and Bob punched Bill* (although, again, not all native speakers are happy with this).

It must be stressed that this scheme only provides a basic framework for the investigation of whether a language has a pivot and, if so, what it is. The framework may need to be refined according to the grammatical organisation of each specific language; for instance, a pivot condition might also relate to indirect object (marked by dative case etc.) or to other types of clause constituent, in particular circumstances. A fuller set of possibilities would need to be set out and tested for a split-S or fluid-S language. And so on.

Other factors may also play a role. The syntactic condition on functions allowed to a common NP may vary according to the semantic/syntactic nature of the head of the NP: whether it is a pronoun or a noun, or whether – if a noun – it has human reference, and so on. (This will be exemplified in §6.2.4.)

And, as mentioned before, different pivots may apply – or a given pivot may apply in varying ways – for different kinds of clause combining. In English there is no pivot constraint on relativisation, for instance – any two clauses can be combined in a relative clause construction (one as main and the other as relative clause) so long as they have an NP in common; the NP can be in any (core or peripheral) function in each clause.

We have said that not all languages operate in terms of a pivot. For those with a switch-reference system, (a), (c), (e), (g) and (j) would receive the marking for 'same S/A' and (b), (d), (f), (h), (i), (k) would be marked for 'different S/A' (this marking generally goes onto the verb of the second clause). The second occurrence of the common NP can then be omitted, and will be retrievable by hearers.

Table 6.1. *Sample case inflections of nouns and pronouns in Dyirbal*

ROOT	*yabu* 'mother'	*ŋuma* 'father'	*ŋana* 'we all'	*nʸurra* 'you all'
A function	*yabu-ŋgu*	*ŋuma-ŋgu*	*ŋana*	*nʸurra*
S function	*yabu*	*ŋuma*		
O function			*ŋana-na*	*nʸurra-na*

For languages which lack both switch-reference marking and a pivot condition, any two clauses can be joined together to form a complex sentence – whether the clauses share a common NP or, if they do, whatever its function in either clause. Omission of the second occurrence of the common NP is conditioned not by any syntactic rule but by extragrammatical factors – whether the speaker considers that his potential hearers will, on the basis of the linguistic and extra-linguistic knowledge available to them, know what he is trying to say if he omits mention of a certain NP.

The next section looks at the operation of the S/O pivot in Dyirbal, a language that is decidedly ergative at the syntactic level. We then briefly look at languages that have ergative characteristics at the morphological level but employ an S/A pivot, i.e. are syntactically accusative. After this there is discussion of languages which use a combination of both kinds of pivot. The final section summarises available information on languages which do have (wholly or partly) ergative syntax.

6.2.2   The S/O pivot in Dyirbal

We can now return to the list of eleven possibilities, (a)–(k), and see how these would be expressed in Dyirbal, extending the discussion begun in §1.2. To save the reader having to refer back, some of the examples from §1.2 will be repeated here. It will also be useful to repeat Table 1.1, as Table 6.1, showing Dyirbal's split marking at the morphological level – with first and second person pronouns inflecting on a nominative–accusative pattern but all other types of NP constituent (nouns, adjectives, third person pronouns) showing an absolutive–ergative case system.

Sample one-clause sentences involving NPs with a noun as head are:

(7)   *ŋuma   banaga-nʸu*
       father + ABS_S return-NONFUT
       father returned

(8) *ŋuma   miyanda-n^{y}u*
  father-ABS$_S$ laugh-NONFUT
  father laughed

(9) *yabu   banaga-n^{y}u*
  mother + ABS$_S$ return-NONFUT
  mother returned

(10) *ŋuma   yabu-ŋgu   bura-n*
  father + ABS$_O$ mother-ERG$_A$ see-NONFUT
  mother saw father

(11) *yabu   ŋuma-ŋgu   bura-n*
  mother + ABS$_O$ father-ERG$_A$ see-NONFUT
  father saw mother

And sample one-clause sentences involving pronouns are:

(12) *ŋana   banaga-n^{y}u*
  we all + NOM$_S$ return-NONFUT
  we returned

(13) *ŋana   miyanda-n^{y}u*
  we all + NOM$_S$ laugh-NONFUT
  we laughed

(14) *n^{y}urra   banaga-n^{y}u*
  you all + NOM$_S$ return-NONFUT
  you all returned

(15) *n^{y}urra   ŋana-na   bura-n*
  you all + NOM$_A$ we all-ACC$_O$ see-NONFUT
  you all saw us

(16) *ŋana   n^{y}urra-na   bura-n*
  we-all + NOM$_A$ you all-ACC$_O$ see-NONFUT
  we saw you all

Recall that although Dyirbal has a split ergative--accusative system of morphological marking, it is entirely ergative at the syntactic level. That is, coordination and relativisation operate entirely in terms of an S/O pivot, whether nouns or pronouns are involved (or any mixture of the two).

Possibility (a), $S_1 = S_2$, can be exemplified by (17), a coordination of (7) and (8), and by (18), from (12) and (13):

(17) *ŋuma banaga-n^{y}u miyanda-n^{y}u*
  father returned and laughed

(18)   *ŋana banaga-n^{y}u miyanda-n^{y}u*
        we returned and laughed

As noted in §1.2, there is no overt coordinating particle in Dyirbal, similar to English *and*; coordination is recognised by the whole complex making up one intonation group and by the omission of the second occurrence of the NP in pivot function, i.e. the S NP for *miyanda-n^{y}u* 'laughed' in (17) and (18).

The other instances where coordination is straightforward, requiring no derivational processes, are (b), (d), (f) and (j), where the common NP is in a pivot function (S or O) in each clause. Thus (b), $S_1 = O_2$ is illustrated by (19) and (20):

(19)   *ŋuma banaga-n^{y}u yabu-ŋgu bura-n*
        father returned and mother saw him

(20)   *ŋana banaga-n^{y}u n^{y}urra bura-n*
        we returned and you all saw us

Possibility (d), $O_1 = S_2$ is illustrated by (21) and (22):

(21)   *ŋuma yabu-ŋgu bura-n banaga-n^{y}u*
        mother saw father and he returned

(22)   *n^{y}urra ŋana-na bura-n banaga-n^{y}u*
        you all saw us and we returned

In (19) and (21) the pivot NP has the same form, *ŋuma* 'father', in each of the underlying clauses, (7) and (10), being a noun in S function in the one clause and in O function in the other. But for (20) and (22) the pivot NP has the form *ŋana* in the intransitive clause, (12), and *ŋana-na* in the transitive clause, (15). Coordination operates on an ergative basis, with an S/O pivot, and this applies equally to nouns (which have ergative morphology) and to pronouns (with accusative morphology). In each case, the occurrence of the pivot NP in the second clause of the conjunction is omitted. Thus in (20) *ŋana* is retained in the first clause while *ŋana-na* is omitted from the second and in (22) *ŋana-na* is retained and *ŋana* omitted.

Possibility (f), $O_1 = O_2$ can be illustrated by conjoining (10) with (23), giving (24):

(23)   *ŋuma*   *jaja-ŋgu*   *ŋamba-n*
        father + ABS_O child-ERG_A hear-NONFUT
        the child heard father

(24)   *ŋuma yabu-ŋgu bura-n jaja-ŋgu ŋamba-n*
       mother saw father and the child heard him

and, for a pronominal pivot, by conjoining (15) with (25), giving (26):

(25)   *ŋana-na   jaja-ŋgu   ŋamba-n*
       we all-ACC_O child-ERG_A hear-NONFUT
       the child heard us

(26)   *n^{y}urra ŋana-na bura-n jaja-ŋgu ŋamba-n*
       you all saw us and the child heard us

Possibility (j) involves both $O_1 = O_2$ and $A_1 = A_2$. From (10) and (27) we obtain (28) and from (15) and (29) there is (30):

(27)   *ŋuma yabu-ŋgu ŋamba-n*
       mother heard father

(28)   *ŋuma yabu-ŋgu bura-n (yabu-ŋgu) ŋamba-n*
       mother saw and heard father

(29)   *n^{y}urra ŋana-na ŋamba-n*
       you all heard us

(30)   *n^{y}urra ŋana-na bura-n (n^{y}urra) ŋamba-n*
       you all saw and heard us

Note that the critical factor in (28) and (30) is $O_1 = O_2$. The second occurrences of this pivot NP will be omitted. We also have $A_1 = A_2$ and this second occurrence can also be omitted. If no A NP is stated for the second clause in (28) and (30), it would be understood – in unmarked circumstances – to be identical to the A NP of the first clause. (Recall that an S/O NP is normally obligatory in each Dyirbal sentence; it can be omitted from the second clause of a conjunction under the pivot condition. In contrast, an A NP is always omittable.)

When the common NP is in S or O function in the first clause but in A for the second – in (c), (h) and (k) – then the second clause must be antipassivised to bring this underlying A NP into derived S function and thus satisfy the pivot constraint. I mentioned, in §1.2, that in an antipassive derivation underlying A becomes S of the antipassive, underlying O goes into dative case (which is *-gu* with nouns and *-ngu* with pronouns), and the verb bears an antipassive derivational suffix *-ŋa-y*, between root and inflection, i.e.

(31)   NP^1 NP^2 V + tense
      A   O

⇒ NP^1 NP^2 V + *ŋa-y* + tense
      S   DAT

The antipassive version of (11) is then (32), and of (16) is (33):

(32)   *ŋuma   bural-ŋa-n^{y}u   yabu-gu*
      father + ABS$_S$ see-ANTIPASS-NONFUT mother-DAT
      father saw mother

(33)   *ŋana   bural-ŋa-n^{y}u n^{y}urra-ngu*
      we all + NOM$_S$ see-ANTIPASS you all-DAT
      we saw you all

For (c), $S_1 = A_2$, we can coordinate together (7) and (32), the antipassive version of (11), giving (34), and (12) and (33), the antipassive version of (16), giving (35).

(34)   *ŋuma banaga-n^{y}u bural-ŋa-n^{y}u yabu-gu*
      father returned and saw mother

(35)   *ŋana banagu-n^{y}u bural-ŋa-n^{y}u n^{y}urra-ngu*
      we returned and saw you all

Similarly for (h), $O_1 = A_2$, we can coordinate (23) and (32), giving (36), and (25) and (33), giving (37):

(36)   *ŋuma jaja-ŋgu ŋamba-n bural-ŋa-n^{y}u yabu-gu*
      the child heard father and he (father) saw mother

(37)   *ŋana-na jaja-ŋgu ŋamba-n bural-ŋa-n^{y}u n^{y}urra-ngu*
      the child heard us and we saw you all

For possibility (k), $O_1 = A_2$ and $A_1 = O_2$, it is the $O_1 = A_2$ NP which functions as pivot. Suppose we wanted to coordinate

(38)   *ŋuma yabu-ŋgu ŋamba-n*
      mother heard father

with (11) 'father saw mother'. The second clause must first be antipassivised, as (32); we then get

(39)   *ŋuma yabu-ŋgu ŋamba-n bural-ŋa-n^{y}u yabu-gu*
      mother heard father and he saw her

Similarly, from (40) and (33), the antipassive version of (16), we get (41).

(40) *n^yurra ŋana-na ŋamba-n*
you all heard us

(41) *ŋ^yurra ŋana-na ŋamba-n bural-ŋa-n^yu n^yurra-ngu*
you all heard us and we saw you all

Note that in (39) and (41) the final dative NPs, *yabu-gu* and *n^yurra-ngu*, could not be omitted.

Turning now to (e), $A_1 = S_2$, and (i), $A_1 = O_2$, we find that the common NP is in pivot function for the second clause but not for the first. As mentioned in §1.2, we could simply antipassivise the first clause, putting the underlying A NP into derived S function and then coordinate. This strategy can be illustrated for (e), where $A_1 = S_2$, by coordinating the antipassive (32) with (7), giving (42), and antipassive (33) with (12), giving (43):

(42) *ŋuma bural-ŋa-n^yu yabu-gu banaga-n^yu*
father saw mother and returned

(43) *ŋana bural-ŋa-n^yu n^yurra-ngu banaga-n^yu*
we saw you all and returned

Similarly for (i), where $A_1 = O_2$, we can coordinate (32) and (23), and (33) and (25), giving

(44) *ŋuma bural-ŋa-n^yu yabu-gu jaja-ŋgu ŋamba-n*
father saw mother and the child heard him

(45) *ŋana bural-ŋa-n^yu n^yurra-ngu jaja-ŋgu ŋamba-n*
we saw you all and the child heard us

It will be noted that this strategy involves a certain amount of planning ahead – a speaker has to have decided what the second clause is to be before he states the first one, in order to know how to process the first one so that the pivot condition is satisfied.

Dyirbal does have an alternative construction available, which involves no forward planning. There is a verbal inflection *-ŋurra* which conveys two pieces of information, one semantic and the other syntactic. It indicates that the event referred to by its verb follows immediately after the event described by the previous clause, with nothing else intervening. And it marks that the S or O NP of its clause (which can be omitted) is identical to the A NP of the preceding clause. Thus, (11) and (7) can be linked together as (42), in which (11) is first antipassivised, or through a *-ŋurra* construction:

(46) *yabu   ŋuma-ŋgu bura-n   (ŋuma)   banaga-ŋurra*
      mother + ABS_O father-ERG_A see-NONFUT father-ABS_S return-*ŋurra*
      father saw mother and then he immediately returned

Note that (46) may only be used if the activity of father returning immediately followed his being seen by mother; if any other event intervened then (46) would not be appropriate. Similarly, clauses involving pronouns, (16) and (12), can be combined as (43), with the first clause antipassivised, or else through a -*ŋurra* construction:

(47) *ŋana   nʸurra-na   bura-n*
      we all + NOM_A you all-ACC_O see-NONFUT
      (ŋana)   banaga-ŋurra
      we all + NOM_S return-*ŋurra*
      we saw you all and we immediately returned

Similarly, as alternatives to (44) and (45) for possibility (i), $A_1 = O_2$, we can have -*ŋurra* constructions:

(48) *yabu   ŋuma-ŋgu   bura-n*
      mother + ABS_O father-ERG_A see-NONFUT
      (ŋuma)   jaja-ŋgu   ŋamba-ŋurra
      father + ABS_O child-ERG_A hear-*ŋurra*
      father saw mother and the child immediately heard him

(49) *ŋana   nʸurra-na   bura-n*
      we all + NOM_A you all-ACC_O see-NONFUT
      (ŋana-na)   jaja-ŋgu   ŋamba-ŋurra
      we all-ACC_O child-ERG_A hear-*ŋurra*
      we saw you all and the child immediately heard us

Note that in -*ŋurra* constructions the occurrence of the common NP in the second clause can be either included or omitted; hence the parentheses around *ŋuma* in (46) and (48), *ŋana* in (47) and *ŋana-na* in (49).

The final possibility is (g), $A_1 = A_2$, which would involve linking (11) 'father saw mother' and (50), or (16) 'we saw you all' and (51).

(50) *jaja   ŋuma-ŋgu   ŋamba-n*
      child + ABS_O father-ERG_A hear-NONFUT
      father heard the child

(51) *ŋana   jaja   ŋamba-n*
      we all + NOM_A child + ABS_O hear-NONFUT
      we heard the child

There are again two possibilities. Both clauses can be antipassivised so that both A_1 and A_2 are placed in derived function to satisfy the pivot condition. This would yield

(52) *ŋuma bural-ŋa-ŋʸu yabu-gu ŋambal-ŋa-nʸu jaja-gu*
      father saw mother and he heard the child

(53) *ŋana bural-ŋa-nʸu nʸurra-ngu ŋambal-ŋa-nʸu jaja-gu*
      we saw you all and we heard the child

Or just the second clauses can be antipassivized, so that we have $A_1 =$ (derived) S_2, and the *-ŋurra* construction used:

(54) *yabu*   *ŋuma-ŋgu*   *bura-n*
      mother + ABS$_O$ father-ERG$_A$ see-NONFUT

      (*ŋuma*)   *ŋambal-ŋa-ŋurra*   *jaja-gu*
      father + ABS$_S$ hear-ANTIPASS-*ŋurra* child-DAT
      father saw mother and he immediately heard the child

(55) *ŋana*   *nʸurra-na*   *bura-n*
      we all + NOM$_A$ you all-ACC$_O$ see-NONFUT

      (*ŋana*)   *ŋambal-ŋa-ŋurra*   *jaja-gu*
      we all + ABS$_S$ hear-ANTIPASS-*ŋurra* child-DAT
      we saw you all and we immediately heard the child

We have now surveyed how each of the eleven possible functions of a common NP in coordinated clauses, (a)–(k), is dealt with in Dyirbal. This has been followed through in detail to illustrate the sorts of questions that every field worker must investigate if they are to properly study the syntax of a language. In Dyirbal each of (a)–(k) had to be checked out for nouns and for pronouns. Other languages may require further parameters to be included. (One would not, of course, simply *ask* an informant about each of (a)–(k). The only sound technique is to assemble a fair body of texts and look for instances of coreferentiality. As a final step one could check the generalisations made, and fill in gaps, by asking putative sentences made up in the language under study – *not* by asking sentences in English or some other lingua franca.)

The *-ŋurra* construction in Dyirbal is used relatively sparingly; it comes up once in perhaps every three or four pages of text. It looks a little like the S/O equivalent of a switch-reference marker, but there are significant differences. A switch-reference system always has a system of two markers, one for $S_1/A_1 = S_2/A_2$ and the other for $S_1/A_1 \neq S_2/A_2$. Dyirbal has a single marker, for $A_1 = S_2/O_2$ (note that it does *not* mark $S_1/O_1 \neq S_2/O_2$).

Discourse in Dyirbal tends to be organised about 'pivot chains'.[18] An
NP may be stated once, in S or O function, and then function as pivot for
a longish sequence of clauses, some in underlying and some in derived form
(the derivations applying so that the pivot condition is always met). The
verbal ending *-ŋurra* effectively provides a syntactic means of linking
together two pivot chains. For example (11) might have been the last
member of a chain of clauses all having 'mother' as pivot, and (7) or (50)
might be the first member of a chain of clauses having 'father' as pivot;
combining these – through (46) or (54), respectively – syntactically coheres
the two chains.

It must be noted that in Dyirbal two clauses cannot be coordinated to
form a complex sentence construction (which is marked by intonation, and
freedom of the order of words within the complex sentence) *unless* they
have a common NP and the pivot condition is satisfied. (It will be seen that
the S/O pivot in Dyirbal is far stronger than the S/A pivot in English.) We
have thus far discussed 'and'-type coordination. The same syntactic
conditions apply to purposive-type coordination, in which the tense or
other inflection on the verb of the second clause is replaced by the
purposive inflection *-ygu* ∼ *-li* 'in order to, as a result of'. Compare (19)
and (34) with (56) and (57) respectively:

(56)   *ŋuma   banaga-n^{y}u   yabu-ŋgu   bura-li*
       father + ABS$_S$ return-NONFUT mother-ERG$_A$ see-PURP
       father returned in order for mother to see him; *or* father returned
           and as a result mother saw him

(57)   *ŋuma   banaga-n^{y}u   bural-ŋa-ygu*
       father + ABS$_S$ return-NONFUT see-ANTIPASS-PURP
       yabu-gu
       mother-DAT
       father returned in order to see mother; *or* father returned and as
           a result saw mother

I mentioned in §4.4 that for a purposive construction one would expect
S and A to be treated in the same way within the purposive clause. This
does not happen in Dyirbal (and it is an indication of the strength of
syntactic ergativity in that language that it doesn't) – the main and

---

[18] In Dixon (1972) I used the label 'topic' for what is now called 'pivot', and 'topic-chain'
in place of 'pivot-chain'. Between 1972 and 1979 the term 'topic' came into general use
with a quite different sense and because of this I introduced 'pivot' in Dixon (1979a).
There are examples of pivot-chains in Dyirbal in Dixon (1972: 72, 369–97).

purposive clauses must have a common NP and these must be in S or O function in each clause. Consider constructions involving the verb *giga-l* 'tell to do' in the main clause: we get $O_1 = S_2$ in (58) and $O_1 = O_2$ in (59):[19]

(58) *yabu   ŋuma-ŋgu   giga-n   banaga-ygu*
      mother + ABS$_O$ father-ERG$_A$ tell to do-NONFUT return-PURP
      father told mother to return

(59) *yabu ŋuma-ŋgu giga-n gubi-ŋgu   mawa-li*
                          doctor-ERG$_A$ examine-PURP
      father told mother to be examined by the doctor

If $O_1 = A_2$ then the purposive clause must be antipassivised, bringing A_2 into derived S function to meet the pivot condition, e.g.

(60) *yabu ŋuma-ŋgu giga-n bural-ŋa-ygu   jaja-gu*
                          see-ANTIPASS-PURP child-DAT
      father told mother to look at the child

The S/O pivot also plays a role in relativisation. There must be an NP common to main and relative clauses; this can be in almost[20] any function in the main clause, but it must be in S or O function within the relative clause. The verb in a relative clause bears the suffix *-ŋu*, followed by a case inflection agreeing with the case of the common NP in the main clause. Thus, from (10) as main clause and (7) as relative clause can be formed:

(61) *ŋuma   [banaga-ŋu]   yabu-ŋgu   bura-n*
      father + ABS$_O$ return-REL + ABS mother-ERG$_A$ see-NONFUT
      mother saw father who was returning

The common NP 'father' is in S function in the relative clause and is then omitted; the relative clause verb has ending *-ŋu* followed by absolutive $\emptyset$,

---

[19] I made a serious error when stating in Dixon (1979a: 128) that the O NP of *giga-l* 'tell to do' has to be coreferential with the underlying A or S NP of its purposive clause, i.e. in effectively saying that a construction like (59) was impossible. In late 1979 I was sitting in on one of Bernard Comrie's lectures when he retailed what I had said in print. Just from my knowledge of Dyirbal I realised that this wasn't right and spoke up. 'But I'm quoting you', he insisted. I told him that I must have suffered some sort of lapse (maybe letting my theoretical ideas overwhelm my knowledge of the data, something not unknown among linguists!). At the next field opportunity, in 1980, I checked that constructions such as (59) are perfectly acceptable (as I knew they were). Nothing concerning the structure of Dyirbal should be inferred from this error, e.g. that constructions such as (59) must be marginal or rare since I at one time denied their existence – this is not true.

[20] The common NP in the main clause can be in S, O or A function or in a peripheral function marked by dative, locative or instrumental case; it cannot be marked by allative or ablative case.

agreeing with the $\emptyset$ ending on the common NP, in O function, in the main clause. From (10) and (9) we can form:

(62)   *ŋuma*   *yabu-ŋgu*   [*banaga-ŋu-rru*] *bura-n*
        father + ABS$_O$ mother-ERG$_A$ return-REL-ERG see-NONFUT
        mother, who was returning, saw father

Here the relative clause bears relative ending *-ŋu* followed by ergative case (shown by allomorph *-rru*) to agree with the ergative inflection on the occurrence of the common NP 'mother' in the main clause.

Let us now take (9) as the main clause and (10) as relative clause. There is a common NP, 'mother', but it is in A relation in the relative clause and does not meet the pivot condition on relativisation. Antipassive must then be applied before relativisation, putting this underlying A NP into derived S function; we can then form:

(63)   *yabu*   [*bural-ŋa-ŋu*   *ŋuma-gu*]
        mother + ABS$_S$ see-ANTIPASS-REL + ABS father-DAT
        banaga-n^{y}u
        return-NONFUT
        mother, who saw father, was returning.

There is one other syntactic derivation that feeds the S/O pivot in Dyirbal.[21] Suppose that we wished to coordinate:

(64)   *yugu*   *ŋuma-ŋgu*   *maŋga-n*
        stick + ABS$_O$ father-ERG$_A$ pick up-NONFUT
        father picked up a stick

(65)   *yabu*   *ŋuma-ŋgu*   *balga-n*   *yugu-ŋgu*
        mother + ABS$_O$ father-ERG$_A$ hit-NONFUT stick-INST
        father hit mother with a stick

These two clauses have two NPs in common, 'father', which is in A function in each, and 'stick', which is O for (64) and in a peripheral function marked by instrumental case[22] in (65). Now Dyirbal has a

---

[21] Blake (1987a: 67–76) provides other examples of the 'advancement' of a peripheral NP to derived O function, in Australian languages.

[22] Ergative and instrumental cases have identical realisation but rather different syntactic behaviour: the antipassive derivation affects an A NP in ergative inflection (putting it into derived S function) but leaves an instrumental NP unchanged; the instrumentive derivation affects an instrumental NP (putting it into derived O function) but leaves an A NP, in ergative case, untouched. It is in view of this that I recognise two distinct cases, with homonymous form.

derivation – which we can call 'instrumentive' – that places an underlying instrumental NP into derived O function, demoting the underlying O into dative case, leaving A as is, and marking the verb with the suffix *-ma-l* (which, like antipassive *-ŋa-y*, comes between verb root and final inflection). Thus, from (65) is derived:

(66) *yugu   ŋuma-ŋgu   balgal-ma-n   yabu-gu*
      stick$_O$ father-ERG$_A$ hit-INSTV-NONFUT mother-DAT
      father used a stick to hit mother

Since (64) and (66) now show a common NP which is in O function in each clause they can be coordinated, either with the verb of the second clause tensed 'Father picked up a stick and hit mother with it', or with the second verb in purposive inflection:

(67) *yugu ŋuma-ŋgu maŋga-n balgal-ma-li yabu-gu*
      father picked up a stick to hit mother with

The instrumentive derivation can also be used to feed the S/O pivot condition on relative clauses. If one wanted to say 'The child saw the stick that father hit mother with', then (65) would be recast as (66) before being embedded as a relative clause, giving

(68) *yugu   [ŋuma-ŋgu balgal-ma-ŋu   yabu-gu]*
      stick + ABS father-ERG hit-INSTV-REL + ABS mother-DAT
      jaja-ŋgu   bura-n
      child-ERG see-NONFUT
      the child saw the stick that was used by father to hit mother

It was mentioned in §5.1 that in some languages ditransitive verbs have alternative syntactic frames, so that each non-A core role may be mapped into O function. This applies in Dyirbal; for verbs of GIVING there are three alternatives (Dixon 1972: 300):

	Donor	Gift	Recipient
1	A	Instrumental case	O
2	A	O	dative case
3	A	O	genitive marking

(Note that the basic form of the verb, without any derivational appendage, is used in each construction.) There are likely to be a number of interrelating factors determining which construction is used in any particular instance – semantic, pragmatic and also syntactic. One factor is pivot feeding. If one wanted to say 'I saw the dog that you gave to mother' then construction 2 or 3 would be chosen for the relative clause, whereas if one wanted to say 'I saw the dog that you gave the bone to' then construction 1 would have to be chosen – in each case the occurrence of the common NP in the relative clause is placed in O, which is a pivot function.

Dyirbal grammar does group together S and A in some ways, but these are all universal features – of the kind described in §5.3 – that are found in languages of every type. For instance, S and A of an imperative are treated in the same way – they are most likely to be second person, and are generally omitted when they are. In almost every aspect of its syntax which is language-particular, rather than language-universal, Dyirbal exhibits an ergative nature, shown most powerfully through the operation of the S/O pivot.[23]

6.2.3   *Languages with morphological ergativity and an S/A pivot*

I said, at the beginning of Chapter 1, that some sort of intra-clausal or morphological ergativity is found in perhaps one quarter of the languages in the world. Only a small proportion of these also show syntactic ergativity, in terms of an S/O pivot. (No language is known that is ergative at the syntactic but not at the morphological level.) Some morphologically ergative languages use no pivot, others have a switch-reference system. And there are a considerable number which show an S/A pivot.

The latter combination can be exemplified from another Australian language, Walmatjari (data from Joyce Hudson 1976a, b, 1978 and personal communication). It is a close genetic relative of Warlpiri (discussed in §4.2.1). As in Warlpiri, nouns and free-form pronouns show an absolutive/ergative paradigm of case inflection:

> absolutive (S and O functions): $\emptyset$
> ergative (A function): -*ŋu* ~ -*lu* etc.

Each sentence involves an 'auxiliary', usually as second word. The auxiliary begins with a modal root (the three possibilities are indicative *pa-*, interrogative *ŋa-*, or imperative/hortative $\emptyset$) and then four orders of

---

[23] Heath (1979) in a paper called 'Is Dyirbal ergative?' provided a negative answer to his question. However, Heath's main thesis appeared to be that *no* language could be categorised as ergative or accusative. In addition, his conclusions concerning Dyirbal depend on assigning great importance to a couple of odd examples I recorded (and noted in small print, for the sake of completeness) while ignoring the regular construction types of which I recorded several thousand examples. There are many other errors and misunderstandings – for a full rebuttal see Dixon (1979b).

person/number markers.[24] The first- and fourth-order suffixes cross-reference (derived) S or A NPs. Second- and third-order suffixes cross-reference an 'accessory NP' if there is one (e.g. 'you' in 'The boys were talking with you', or 'The boys sat with you', or 'I blew the grass out of your eye'); otherwise they refer to 'dative NP' if there is one (e.g. 'them' in 'I told them about my dream', 'I work for them'). If the sentence involves neither accessory nor dative NPs, then a surface O NP will be cross-referenced by second- and third-order suffixes (see note 27 to Chapter 4).[25] First- and second-order suffixes essentially indicate person of subject and accessory/dative/object, while third- and fourth-order suffixes show their number.

Thus, at the morphological level, case marking on NPs is ergative, but cross-referencing suffixes in the auxiliary are quite accusative. It is noteworthy that, despite its ergative case-marking conventions, Walmatjari does not have any antipassive derivation. As in all languages, imperatives operate on an S/A principle at the underlying-structure level. S or A must be second person. The auxiliary root is ∅, and the first-order suffix (marking person of S or A) is absent; note, though, that the fourth-order suffix (showing number of S or A) is retained. Suffixes of orders two to four are removed from the domination of the auxiliary and attached to the verb.

Hudson (1976a: 9–12) describes three syntactic operations, each of which links two clauses to form a complex sentence. In the first, -*ula* '-ing' is added as a suffix to the verb of the subordinate clause:

(69) [*ṭikiřyan-uḷa*] *ma-ṇa-∅-nja-lu*   *mana-waṇṭi-∅ patjani*
     return-*uḷa*   INDIC-1(EXCL)-3-PL-PL tree-PL-ABS   chopped
     having returned, we chopped trees.

An -*uḷa* construction describes the activity of the subordinate clause as completed before that referred to by the main clause is begun.

In the second syntactic operation, the addition of -*u* 'in order to' to the subordinate verb indicates that the action of the main clause was performed so that the subordinate clause activity would be possible:

---

[24] Some details have been omitted here; they do not affect the point under discussion. Complete information is in Hudson (1978).

[25] Accessory and dative NPs can occur in transitive and in intransitive clauses. Note that the auxiliary will always cross-reference two NPs for a transitive sentence (there will always be an O NP, which gets cross-referenced if accessory and dative are lacking). A single NP is cross-referenced only in an intransitive sentence that involves no accessory or dative NP.

(70)   *payintaři-ŋuřa-∅*   *pa-∅-lu*   *yanku pikipiki-wu*
       Bieundurry-friends-ABS INDIC-3-PL will go pig-DAT
       pa-∅-∅-ḷa-lu   *mu:puŋ-u*
       INDIC-3-3-SG-PL search-*u*
       Bieundurry and his friends will go to look for pigs

In the third, simple coordination is shown by the addition of *-tja*: 'and' to the last word of the first of two coordinate clauses (the clauses must have the same mood and tense):

(71)   *ŋanpayi-∅ pa-∅-∅*   *papatjani-njiřa-tja:*
       man-ABS   INDIC-3-SG cry out-ALWAYS-*tja:*
       tjuŋani ma-∅-∅-njanu   *pamař-tjaṭi-ḷu*
       cut   INDIC-3-SG-REFL stone-WITH-ERG
       the man was always calling out and cutting himself with stones

There is a syntactic condition common to *-uḷa, -u* and *-tja*: constructions: there must be an NP common to the clauses, and it must be in derived S or A function in each clause. That is, S/A is the syntactic pivot for Walmatjari. On the data presented by Hudson, the language has an entirely accusative syntax, despite the split ergative–accusative morphology. This might have been predicted from the lack of an antipassive derivation. Any language that works with a fully fledged S/O pivot surely requires an antipassive derivation to place an underlying A NP into the pivot function S.

But Walmatjari not only lacks antipassive, there is also no trace of a passive derivation. Surely – one might ask – if antipassive is needed to feed an S/O pivot, passive should be needed to feed an S/A pivot. This is an important question, to which we return in §8.1. The brief answer is 'no'. There is lesser need for a passive to feed an S/A pivot in a language with accusative syntax than there is for an antipassive to feed an S/O pivot in a language with ergative syntax. This is due to the fact that, in every language, discourse is organised about a series of 'topics', which are most often human, and controllers of actions, and thus most likely to be in underlying A or S function; an S/A pivot condition accords with this while an S/O pivot is at odds with it. A language with thoroughgoing ergative syntax *must* have an antipassive derivation, to feed its S/O pivot, otherwise it could not operate. In languages with an S/A pivot it is desirable, but by no means absolutely necessary, that there should be a passive derivation to feed this pivot.

The split-ergative system of morphological marking in Kuikúro was described in §4.5, and its ergative constituent order was mentioned in §3.2. Like Walmatjari, this language is accusative at the syntactic level. Franchetto (1990 and personal communication) reports that an NP in A function may be omitted under coreferential identity, but never one in S or O function. If we have a sequence of clauses $O_1V_1A_1$, $O_2V_2A_2$ or S_1V_1, $O_2V_2A_2$ then A_2 may optionally be omitted if $A_1 = A_2$ or if $S_1 = A_2$ (but not if $O_1 = A_2$).

Other languages with some ergative morphology but an entirely accusative syntax include Hindi (Kachru 1987: 224–5 and further references therein), Basque (Ortiz de Urbina 1989),[26] North-east Caucasian languages such as Avar (Simon Crisp, ms.) and Papuan languages such as Enga (Van Valin 1981).

6.2.4   *Languages with mixed pivots*

Some languages combine S/A and S/O pivots; this can be illustrated from a further Australian language, Yidinʸ. It will be recalled that Yidinʸ is like Dyirbal in having a morphological split conditioned by the semantic nature of NPs – this was set out in Table 4.3 of §4.2. Basically, nouns inflect on an ergative pattern and (first and second person) pronouns on an accusative one, with tripartite marking applying to items from a central portion of the Nominal Hierarchy. There are no bound cross-referencing forms.

In Yidinʸ, rules for coordination precisely reflect the case marking – there is an S/A pivot for joining together two clauses which have a common NP that is pronominal, and an S/O pivot for linking clauses whose common NP is non-pronominal. That is, clauses translated by 'let us(S) sneak up' and 'let us(A) have a look at them(O)' may be coordinated, and the second occurrence of 'us' omitted; and clauses translated by 'the mother(A) bore two children(O)' and 'the grandmother(A) covered up the two children(O) in this crib' can also be coordinated, with the second occurrence of 'the children' omitted.

But relative clauses in Yidinʸ work strictly in terms of an S/O pivot. There is generally an NP common to main and relative clauses and it must be in S or O function in *each* clause. If a common NP is in underlying A function then it must be placed in derived S function through the antipassive derivation. This applies to all kinds of NP, whether non-

---

[26] But see Brettschneider (1979) and Bossong (1984) for a different view, that Basque is pivotless.

pronominal or pronominal. Thus 'I(A) saw the mouse(O)' and 'an eaglehawk(A) was eating the mouse(O)' can be straightforwardly combined in a relative clause construction 'I(A) saw the mouse(O) being eaten by the eaglehawk(A)'. But for 'I(A) saw the eaglehawk(O)' and 'the eaglehawk(A) was eating the mouse(O)', the second clause must be recast as an antipassive, in which 'the eaglehawk' goes into derived S function (absolutive case) and 'the mouse' is in dative or locative case, before the second clause can be embedded within the first, as a relative clause. Other types of subordinate clause construction – including purposive (or infinitive) clauses – also operate with an entirely S/O pivot. (For full details and exemplification, see Dixon 1977a: 388–92, 323–7, 334–7.)

Thus, Yidin^y has an S/O pivot for all types of relativisation and one kind of coordination, but an S/A pivot for another kind of coordination. It has an antipassive derivation (see §3.4.1), as every language with an S/O pivot should have, to feed this pivot. However, there is no passive derivation. We mentioned above that passive is less necessary in a language with accusative syntax than antipassive is in one with ergative syntax, and in Yidin^y the S/A pivot does play a relatively minor role.

There are other languages which appear to mix S/A and S/O pivots. In Chukchee, the negative participle can be used to relativise on S or O, not on A; but other syntactic processes work in terms of an S/A pivot (Comrie 1979; Nedjalkov 1979). Woodbury (1975, 1977) reports that in Greenlandic Eskimo most operations of subordination (e.g. 'because', 'when', 'that') employ an S/A pivot, as do infinitive constructions, but Thomas Payne (1982) documents an S/O pivot for coordination and nominalisation in Yupik Eskimo (spoken in Alaska). In Tongan (my own field work), clauses coordinated by *mo* 'and (simultaneously)' operate with an S/A pivot while those linked by *'o* 'as a result' use an S/O pivot. Thus, in (72) the unstated S argument for the verb *kata* 'laugh' is taken to be coreferential with the A NP of the previous transitive clause, while in (73) the unstated S NP of *kata* is taken to be coreferential with the O of the transitive clause:

(72) *na'e tā'i 'a Mele 'e Hina mo*   *kata*
      PAST hit ABS Mary ERG Hina and(simultaneously) laugh
      Hina hit Mary and Hina (simultaneously) laughed

(73) *na'e tā'i 'a Mele 'e Hina 'o*   *kata*
                         as a result
      Hina hit Mary and as a result Mary laughed

(See also note 17 on the very minor S/O and S/A pivots in Fijian.)

It would be nice if one could uncover a universal rationale for the occurrence of S/A and S/O pivots in a single language. Perhaps a hierarchy (similar to the Nominal Hierarchy) along which complex sentence construction types could be arranged, according to some syntactic and/or semantic principles, with an S/O pivot being used for constructions towards one end of the hierarchy, and an S/A pivot for those towards the other end. The limited data set out above, on languages with both kinds of pivot, do not immediately reveal any such rationale.

It may be that we need to look beyond syntax, to discourse structure. Towards the end of §8.2, I provide further discussion of the 'split syntax' of Yidin^y, and put forward an explanation for it in terms of a specific discourse strategy of that language.

There can be more complex coreferentiality conditions on clause combining than simple S/O and S/A pivots. Thomas Payne (1991) discusses what he calls 'medial clause operators' in the Carib language Panare, spoken in Venezuela. Each of these marks a type of subordination and is suffixed to the verb of the second clause. The first three suffixes 'all signify that the situation expressed by the verb they are attached to closely follows in temporal sequence the action expressed in the previous clause'. The fourth suffix *-pómën* 'indicates that the action described takes place prior to the action described in the previous clause'. There are coreferentiality constraints on the use of each of these affixes (subscripts refer to occurrences in first and second clauses, respectively):

-séjpe	'and then, in order to'	$S_1/A_1 = S_2/A_2$
-sé'ñape	'as a result'	$S_1/O_1 = O_2$
-ñépe	'and then/in order to'	$S_1/O_1 = S_2/A_2$
-pómën	'after/because'	$S_1/A_1 = S_2/A_2$

6.3 Languages with ergative inter-clausal syntax

Ergativity can be manifested in various ways. Any language that is syntactically ergative will also have some ergative characteristics at the morphological level. And there can be other ways in which S and O are grouped together within a grammar. For instance, Dyirbal has a verbal derivational affix *-ja-y* which does not affect transitivity but indicates that the activity of the verb refers to 'many of' the referent of the S NP (for an intransitive verb) or of the O NP (for a transitive), thus linking S and O. There is also a non-inflecting particle *warra* indicating that the reference of the S or O NP is inappropriate for that activity, e.g. 'he(A) *warra* cut the tree(O)' indicates that he cut the wrong tree and 'he(S) *warra* went' indicates that the wrong person went (see Dixon 1972: 249–50, 118).[27]

I have already referred to the ergative characteristics of Nadëb, spoken in Amazonia (a member of the small Maku family). Constituent order is SV and OAV with alternatives VS and AVO; this is ergative, since A must immediately precede V while S can either precede or follow V and O can either precede or follow AV (§3.2). Second and third person pronouns have one form for A and another for S/O (§4.2). Each clause – even an imperative – must include some reference to A, through a proclitic to the verb, but S or O need not be mentioned (§5.3.1). Nadëb also shows limited syntactic ergativity, with an S/O pivot in the third person for coordinate constructions: that is, two coordinated main clauses may show $S_1 = S_2$, $S_1 = O_2$, $O_1 = S_2$ or $O_1 = O_2$ with the occurrence of S or O from the second clause being omitted (Helen Weir, personal communication).

Languages in the Pama-Nyungan group of the Australian family almost all show ergative inflection on nouns and adjectives. Some of them are like Diyari in having a switch-reference mechanism and others are like Walmatjari in using an S/A pivot. But there are a fair number, in the eastern states, which are like Dyirbal and Yidin[y] in making use of an S/O pivot. For instance, Kalkatungu employs an S/O pivot for participle formation (Blake 1982) while Warrgamay uses an S/O pivot for subordination (Dixon 1981a, and see §7.2) as does Bandjalang (Crowley 1978: 111–15).

As already mentioned, languages from the Mayan family generally show an ergative pattern in the cross-referencing of core NPs – one series of bound pronominal forms (set A) coding A and another series (set B) coding S/O. Many Mayan languages work in terms of an S/O pivot for certain types of complex sentence formation: nominals may only be relativised, focussed, negated or questioned if in S or O function, so that an NP in underlying A function must be brought into derived S function through antipassivisation to undergo one of these operations (Larsen and Norman 1979; and England 1983a, b; Bricker 1979; Dayley 1978, 1985; Larsen 1981). This illustrates how a pivot may underlie not only syntactic

---

[27] The particle *warra* also occurs in Dyirbal's northerly neighbour Yidin[y] but with a slightly different meaning – it refers to an inappropriate place, or an inappropriate manner, or an inappropriate O (but *not* an inappropriate S). We saw in §6.2.2 and §6.2.4 that Dyirbal is more strongly ergative than Yidin[y]; it is quite in keeping with this that in Dyirbal *warra* should refer to inappropriate S or O (an ergative grouping) but in Yidin[y] just to inappropriate O.

derivations involving two clauses (coordination and relativisation) but also derivations within a single clause (focussing, negating and questioning).

Edmonson (1988) discusses Huastec, an isolate within the Mayan family which shows ergative cross-referencing and also ergative constituent order (§3.2). There is a little ergativity in the syntax of relativisation, where coreferentiality can encompass $A_1 = A_2$ and $O_1/S_1 = O_2/S_2$ but not $A_1 = O_2$ (here an antipassive must be used) although $A_1 = S_2$ and $S_1 = A_2$ are acceptable.

Kibrik (1979b) gives a brief account of syntactic ergativity in Alutor, from the Chukotko-Kamchatkan family – an S/O pivot is employed for relativisation and in conjunction reduction.[28]

Relatively few languages have been thoroughly studied at the syntactic level. Once the basic framework, set out in §6.2.1, is investigated for a fair range of languages that have some ergative features at the morphological level, more examples are likely to be uncovered of languages with a (strong or weak) S/O pivot. Work is needed on many languages – those still spoken,[29] of course, and also on the materials available for extinct

---

[28] Tagalog and other languages of the Philippines subgroup of Austronesian are not easily characterisable in terms of the accusative/ ergative parameter. Each clause has one NP in focus – this is cross-referenced on the verb and is itself marked by the focus 'preposition' *ang*, replacing its normal case preposition (actor, patient, locative or benefactive). Arguments have been given that the unmarked focus is O for a transitive and S for an intransitive clause, an ergative pattern at the level of intra-clausal marking. Fairly persuasive evidence has also been presented that Tagalog operates in terms of an S/O pivot, controlling 'equi' deletion, quantifier float and relativisation – Cena (1977, 1979), Kroeger (1991a, b), Blake (1988).

[29] One must always exercise great care when working on a language that has ceased to be actively spoken. During the 1970s I worked with the last three old people who knew Warrgamay, a language that had not been used in daily life for some decades. One of the speakers also knew the Girramay dialect of Dyirbal, a language that was still actively spoken, and tended to muddle together Warrgamay and Girramay. I managed to disentangle the languages by asking him – for almost every word and sentence – how to 'say this' in Warrgamay and also in Girramay, forcing him to concentrate on the differences between the languages. Fortunately, the other two speakers knew no Dyirbal and the data they gave confirmed the Warrgamay I was able to infer from the first speaker.
  In 1964 and 1967 I worked with Alf Palmer, an old Warungu man who knew that language (which had also not been spoken for decades) in addition to Warrgamay and the Girramay and Jirrbal dialects of Dyirbal (both still actively used in Aboriginal speech communities). I elicited several hundred words and sentences in each of four languages/ dialects – Warungu, Warrgamay, Girramay and Jirrbal – in order to minimise the chance that I was being given a mixture of languages. During the early 1970s Tasaku Tsunoda worked with Palmer, ostensibly on Warungu but – since Tsunoda did not follow the same sort of procedure as I had – the material he obtained mingled together Warungu, Dyirbal and Warrgamay. This is clear in the manuscript vocabulary he assembled, and in his grammatical work. Tsunoda has not yet published his 'grammar of Warungu' (submitted as an MA thesis, 1974) but he has made much reference in print to the 'antipassive in

tongues. Analysing materials on the extinct South American tongue Kipeá Kirirí, for instance, Larsen (1984) suggests that an S/O pivot underlay subordination strategies.

Appendix: Chamalal

Kibrik (1990: 32–3) gives a fascinating partial account of coordination in the North-east Caucasian language Chamalal. It appears that if an intransitive clause is coordinated with a transitive one, then coreferential omission is possible for either $S_1 = O_2$ or for $S_1 = A_2$; from the case marking on the NP that is retained in the transitive clause, one can infer what the case marking would have been on the omitted NP, which is taken to be coreferential with the S of the previous intransitive clause. Thus ['brother-ABS came'] ['∅ sister-ABS hit'], in (74), must be 'brother came and hit sister', with $S_1 = A_2$, while ['sister-ABS came'] ['brother-ERG ∅ hit'] in (75) must be 'sister came and brother hit her', with $S_1 = O_2$.

(74)   [*wac*   *w-i'a*]   [∅ *jač*   *č'in*]
        brother + ABS_S 1 + come + PAST A sister + ABS_O hit + PAST
        brother came and he hit sister

(75)   [*jac*   *n-i'a*]   [*wac-ud*   ∅ *č'in*]
        sister + ABS_S 2 + come + PAST brother-ERG_A O hit + PAST
        sister came and brother hit her

Note that the different initial consonants of the verb 'come' in (74) and (75) are due to concord with the noun class of the head noun of the S NP – class 1 and class 2 respectively.

One would imagine difficulty arising when a transitive clause was followed by an intransitive one – with $[A_1O_1V][∅ \ V]$ how could one tell whether the omitted S NP of the second clause were coreferential with A_1 or with O_1? Kibrik explains that Chamalal deals with this by moving S_2 to the beginning of the sentence so that this is the occurrence of the common NP which is stated, with the coreferential O_1 or A_1 (as the case may be) being omitted. Thus, one gets $S_2[∅ \ O_1 \ V_{tr}]V_{intr}$, in (76), from which one infers that $A_1 = S_2$ (e.g. 'brother hit sister and he went') and $S_2[A_1 \ ∅ \ V_{tr}]V_{intr}$, in (77), from which one infers that $O_1 = S_2$ (e.g. 'brother hit sister and she went').

Warungu'; this is entirely based on material from Palmer, who was heavily influenced by Dyirbal. Tsunoda's comments on the syntactic ergativity of Warungu – e.g. 'it would thus seem that Warungu possesses the strongest syntactic ergativity among the world's languages' (Tsunoda 1988: 642) – are even more dubious since they are based on 'texts' given by Palmer, many of which are conversations in Warungu between him and Tsunoda.

(76)   *wac*   [∅ *jac-la*   *č'in*]
       brother + ABS$_S$ A sister + ABS-EMPHATIC$_O$ hit + PAST
       w-exa w-una
       1 + go + PAST
       brother hit sister and he went

(77)   *jac*   [*wac-ud-la*   ∅ *č'in*] *j-exa j-ina*
       sister + ABS$_S$ brother-ERG-EMPHATIC$_A$ O hit   2 + go + PAST

       brother hit sister and she went

This is neat, as far as it goes, showing that in this type of clause combination one occurrence of a common NP can be omitted without this being restricted by any syntactic rule (e.g. an S/O or S/A pivot). But Kibrik does not discuss the coordination of two transitive clauses. That is, he deals with (a)–(e) from §6.2.1 but ignores (f)–(k). (Kibrik states, personal communication, that his consultants experienced difficulties in translating into Chamalal sentences that involved two transitive clauses, essentially avoiding them and trying to find some other construction. This is what one might expect; it would be fascinating to know exactly what grammatical strategies they might employ for (f)–(k) from §6.2.1.)

7 Language change

Particular linguistic changes generally proceed in a single direction. For example, a preposition or postposition may develop into an affix, and a velar or labial stop may lenite to the semi-vowel *w* (changes in the opposite directions are either unknown or extraordinarily rare). Through a combination of specific changes a language can shift from one typological profile to another. There is nothing unidirectional about changes at this level (see Croft 1990: 229). Any type of language – in terms of any typological parameter – can change into another type, and back again. (If this were not the case all languages would be inexorably moving in a single direction, towards some 'ultimate' language typé)

We have written records going back at the most five thousand years (and then for very few languages). For a number of language families, scholars have reconstructed aspects of a proto-language and suggested an approximate date for this – all of these dates are within the last ten thousand years. Yet language is presumed to have been spoken by *Homo sapiens* during many tens (perhaps hundreds) of millennia. We thus have available for study only a fraction of the history of human language. It is, however, enough to perceive a clearly cyclic pattern of change.

Consider the somewhat simplistic typological parameter dealing with the morphological make-up of a language. This recognises three basic types: *isolating*, where most words consist of a single morpheme (e.g. Vietnamese, Classical Chinese); *agglutinative*, where a word typically consists of several morphemes but these have clear boundaries, i.e. the word can be neatly segmented into its morphological components (e.g. Turkish, Swahili); and *fusional* (previously, and misleadingly, called *inflectional*), where a word involves several morphemes, some or all of which are fused into 'portmanteau' forms (e.g. Latin).

There is in fact a cycle of change,[1] by which a fusional language can

---

[1] Note that Jespersen (1922: 421–5), for instance, denied this, and stated that the general direction of linguistic change is unilinear, from 'flexional' to 'flexionless'. Jespersen had

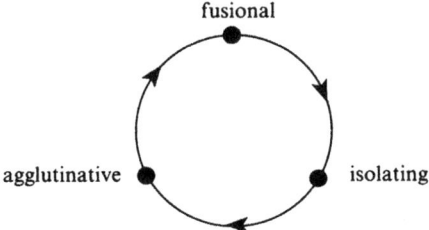

Figure 7.1 The cycle of change

develop into one of the isolating type, an isolating language can become agglutinative, an agglutinative language may move towards a fusional profile, and so on. This is illustrated in Figure 7.1.

Languages change in a number of different ways. These include: (1) *phonological change*, which is predominantly simplifying and reducing, e.g. consonant clusters may be simplified, unstressed vowels may be omitted (which may give rise to newly complex consonant clusters that will in turn be simplified over time), and so on. This leads to and interrelates with (2) *morphological simplification* where, for instance, inflectional markers may be omitted from the end of a word. These two kinds of change are illustrated in the development from Old English to Modern English: first, final *m* and *n* fell together, then final nasals were dropped, then *a*, *o*, *u* and *e* in inflectional endings were neutralised as a central vowel (Baugh 1959: 190ff.). These changes were largely responsible for the loss of all case endings on nominals (save for genitive) and of almost all of the portmanteau inflections on verbs that combined information on tense with specification of the person and number of the subject. We also get (3) *morphological amalgamation* – separate roots being put together to form complex stems – and *augmentation* – what were distinct words being 'grammaticalised' as new affixes, e.g. postpositions becoming cases. (At the same time, of course, there is also *semantic change*, the shift of meaning of roots, affixes and construction types; this does not play so direct a role in moving a language round the cycle of change.)

A language with an isolating profile will tend to become more and more agglutinative through the operation of (3), morphological amalgamation and augmentation; what were syntactic modifiers or relators will develop

put forward this idea in his doctoral dissertation (in 1891) but one of the examiners, Hermann Møller disagreed, arguing that language history moves in spirals, not along a line of constant 'progress' (see Juul and Nielson 1989: 71).

into bound morphological elements. Then, from an agglutinative profile, the operation of (1), phonological change, will effectively preserve the same morphological elements but fuse their realisations – here omitting a vowel, then blending two adjacent segments into one (e.g. *ai > e, md > n*). Through the further application of (1), interrelating with (2), morphological simplification, a fusional language will tend to lose its truncated inflectional and derivational impedimenta, and develop into the isolating type.

For every language family that has been studied in detail, a clear progression around some part of this cycle is evident. We can refer to the fusional type as the twelve o'clock position, to isolating as four o'clock and to agglutinative as eight o'clock. Proto-Indo-European was at about twelve o'clock but modern branches of the family have moved, at different rates, towards a more isolating profile (some to one or two o'clock, others towards three o'clock). Early Chinese is thought to have been at about three o'clock, Classical Chinese was a fairly pure isolating type at four o'clock, while Modern Chinese dialects are acquiring a mildly agglutinative structure, towards five o'clock. Proto-Dravidian was on the isolating side of agglutinative, at about seven o'clock, and modern Dravidian languages have moved around the cycle towards nine o'clock. Proto-Australian can be placed at about seven o'clock; modern languages from the Pama-Nyungan group have become more agglutinative, at eight or nine o'clock, while the non-Pama-Nyungan groups have moved more radically, towards ten or eleven o'clock. Proto-Finno-Ugric may have been at around nine o'clock, with modern languages moving to ten or eleven o'clock. And so on. For Egyptian, which has a long recorded history, Hodge (1970) documents a complete turn around the cycle; Old Egyptian (about 3000 BC) had a complex verb structure which included reference to person; most of these affixes were lost by Late Egyptian (about 1000 BC), which used periphrastic constructions involving auxiliaries; by the time of Coptic (AD 200 onwards) a new complex verb structure had evolved, using quite different forms from those of Old Egyptian. DeLancey (1985) provides striking exemplification of cyclic changes affecting the verbal category 'directive' in Tibeto-Burman languages.

The cycle given in Figure 7.1 is schematic and should not be taken to imply that every language changes in exactly the same way. Corners can be cut – for instance, it would be possible to move from an agglutinative to an isolating type without going through a thoroughly fusional stage. But it does indicate the general way in which languages shift, from one morphological type to another.

It is fascinating to ask how long it takes to complete the cycle. There is great variation – under normal conditions of change, probably anything from two or three thousand years to fifty thousand or more. But, in special circumstances, the cycle can be turned in just three generations. This involves the establishment of a pidgin, which then develops into a creole. Nida and Fehderau (1970) describe the creole Kituba, spoken by one and a half million people in the Lower Congo, which is related to the Bantu language Kimanianaga but has a drastically simplified morphology: aspect–tense prefixes were greatly reduced; subject prefixes to the verb were dropped and replaced by independent pronouns; the number of noun classes was reduced from six to four; and tonal contrasts were simplified. But what is a language of predominantly isolating profile, for older speakers, is developing an agglutinative structure in the mouths of younger speakers, probably under diffusional pressure from the other agglutinative languages in the region. The older generation (as at 1970) would say *munu imene kwenda* for 'I have gone', the middle generation said *munu me-kwenda*, while younger speakers used *mu-me-kwenda*.

For every typological dimension the same story can be told – a language may move from one profile to another, and then back to the first. Tonal contrasts may develop, and may then be lost (a few centuries or – more likely – a few millennia later). A simple phonotactic template, with a CV syllable pattern, may develop into a complex structure (e.g. (C)(C)(C)V(V)(C)(C)(C)(C) as in English). Syntactic constructions which involve nominal classifiers used with specific nouns can develop into a morphological system of noun class or gender marking; this may in time be lost, and then generic nouns may develop into classifiers, to recommence that cycle. A language which marks reflexives by a special verbal derivation that forms an intransitive stem may replace this by a reflexive construction in which transitivity is maintained, with a reflexive pronoun filling the O slot. A language may switch from dependent marking to head marking, and vice versa.

A language which shows accusative properties at some grammatical level may replace these by an ergative or partly ergative profile, and vice versa. There is no directionality involved;[2] either method of grouping syntactic relations can be replaced by the other, as shown in Figure 7.2.

---

[2] Klimov (1973) recognises three linguistic types – accusative, ergative and 'active' (my fluid-S). He suggests (pp. 232ff.) a unilinear direction of change: active > ergative > accusative (what he actually says is, in rough translation 'the ergative system is a stage in the transformation of the active system into the nominative'). As evidence he quotes relics

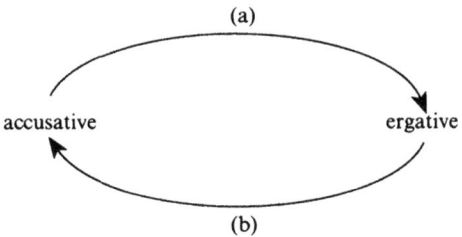

Figure 7.2

What is interesting is the ways in which a language moves (a) from accusative to ergative, or (b) from ergative to accusative. There are several kinds of diachronic mechanism that may be involved: the reinterpretation of a passive or antipassive as the unmarked transitive construction type; the development of a new periphrastic system of tense and/or aspect marking based on participial forms; the creation of a new case or the extension in meaning of an existing one; generalisation of the marking on one syntactic relation to another; generalisation from one kind of NP constituent to others; generalisation from one tense–aspect to another; shift in constituent order and topicalisation; and so on.

Path (a), from accusative to ergative, is by no means the mirror-image of (b), from ergative to accusative. It is true that one way of achieving (a) is through reinterpretation of a passive, and of (b) by reinterpretation of an antipassive. But I emphasised, in §6.1, that although passive and antipassive appear to be syntactically parallel, with A and O interchanged, in fact they are semantically quite different. As a result, the circumstances in which passive reinterpretation can trigger (a) are quite different from those in which antipassive interpretation can trigger (b).

We will document some of the reported examples of diachronic change (a), and then of (b). These concern morphological ergativity and accusativity, but we shall see that the syntactic profile and demands of a language can play an important role in motivating the changes.

One preliminary remark is in order. Although we have information on ergativity in a fair number of modern languages, for only a limited number of languages is there attested historical data. Where reconstruction has been attempted, in some instances almost all scholars are in agreement and

of an active system in ergative languages, e.g. ambitransitive or labile verbs. However, his sample of ergative languages was limited. Many Australian languages, which are among the most ergative known, have few or no verbs that can have either transitivity value.

we can confidently talk of change in to or out of an ergative pattern; in other cases there is disagreement (as in the case of Polynesian and Carib, mentioned below). And in the survey that follows I will mention some theoretical possibilities for which no example is yet to hand; as more work is done on these questions, relevant examples may turn up.

7.1   Accusative to ergative

In Chapter 4 the different kinds of ergativity split were listed. Each of these is likely to have different possible paths of evolution. A split-S system (§4.1.1), for instance, may arise through 'grammaticisation' of a fluid-S system. From a position where each intransitive verb had the possibility of marking its S like A or like O, majority choices could harden into grammatical restrictions. A verb that most often took S_a marking would – through this change – only be allowed S_a marking; and so on. Or, alternatively, a split-S system might develop from an accusative model. Some transitive verbs could allow the A NP to be omitted; from 'man(A) plate(O) break' we might just get 'plate(O) break'. This could be reinterpreted as an intransitive clause with its S marked like O, i.e. S_o; the transitive sense of the verb might be lost (another lexeme being employed for transitive 'break'). The pattern of S_o marking could be extended to some other intransitive verbs describing 'states resulting from actions' and perhaps to some just describing states, yielding a split-S pattern of marking. Indeed, it could eventually be extended to all intransitive verbs, then yielding a fully ergative system. A split-S system could equally well develop from ergative beginnings. Some transitive verbs could omit their O NPs; from 'the man(A) followed the woman(O)' we could just get 'the man(A) followed'. This could be reinterpreted as an intransitive clause with S_a marking, and this marking could be extended to the subjects of other intransitive verbs describing 'controlled actions'. And so on.

Turning now to languages that have an ergativity split conditioned by the semantic nature of NPs (§4.2), Garrett (1990) makes a strong case for Hittite having had an ergative case which was used just with nouns of neuter gender, which are predominantly inanimate; his examples include 'the bindings (ERG) clasp the head (ACC)'. This accords with the Nominal Hierarchy in Figure 4.5 – accusative marking extends across all types of NP constituent while ergative is only found on the right-hand side, with inanimates. Rejecting earlier suggestions that the ergative marker (singular *-anza*, plural *-anteš*) comes from a derivational 'animatizing' suffix, Garrett relates it to the ablative inflection -*anza*, which could also have an instrumental sense. He draws attention to English sentences such as *John opened the door with the key* and *The key opened the door*. The first of these would be translatable into Hittite with 'John' in nominative case, 'the door' in accusative, and with instrumental/ablative marking on 'the key'. Now if the human agent were not stated, 'the key', with -*anza* inflection could be interpreted as transitive subject; -*anza* would now have an ergative sense, in addition to its ablative and instrumental uses. (We noted in §3.4 that ergative case is sometimes confined to marking A function but often has other syntactic functions, instrumental being one of the most common.). Garrett presents evidence that an inanimate noun, marked by -*anza*, in a transitive clause without a human noun in nominative case, is indeed a realisation of the category A.[3]

In §§3.2 and 4.4 we mentioned the Western Nilotic language Päri, which is ergative in morphological marking and in constituent order (OVA, SV) in independent indicative clauses, although imperatives and some types of subordinate clause have the A marker extended also to cover S, effecting a nominative–accusative system. Andersen (1988) states that in Eastern and Southern branches of Nilotic there is nominative–accusative case marking, generally expressed not by affixation but by tones. However, the accusative form is unmarked morphologically and is used in citation, making this appear to be a 'marked nominative' system – see §3.4.3. In Turkana the basic constituent order is VAO/VS, with A and S having nominative and O accusative marking. But A can be fronted (to AVO) in order to mark it as topic, and then receives the unmarked accusative inflection, like O. Andersen suggests that the ergative system in Päri may have developed from such a schema, through O and S being habitually fronted from VAO and VS structures, yielding OVA and SV, with the S having its nominative marking replaced by the unmarked accusative when it was fronted. This would naturally yield the present system, in which S and O are marked alike (by absolutive, with zero realisation) and A differently (by ergative -*ì* ~ -*ì* ~ -*è* ~ -*ɛ̀*, which under this hypothesis would be the original nominative). He also quotes data from Murle, belonging to another branch of the same family, which has a nominative (marking S and A) that

---

[3] A related idea has been put forward by Rude (1991), concerning the Sahaptian language Nez Perce. He emphasises that Nez Perce is not strictly an ergative language (in which S is treated in the same way as O and in a different way to A). In fact it has different marking for all of A, O and S (S receiving zero marking) on nouns. What is relevant to this section is Rude's hypothesis that A and O marking have their genesis in the peripheral cases cislocative 'hither' and translocative 'thither' respectively.

is -*i* or -*ε* in the singular. These nominative suffixes in Murle may be cognate with ergative suffixes in Päri (this is not certain; the phonetic similarity may be a coincidence – Torben Andersen, personal communication); if they are, it would provide support for the hypothesis. It thus appears that the original accusative marking is preserved in Päri in imperatives – which typically preserve archaic patterns (e.g. Whitney 1889: 215; Watkins 1963, 1970; Kuryłowicz 1964: 137 and see the discussion in §7.2) – and in subordinate clauses, which also tend to be syntactically conservative (e.g. Givón 1979: 83ff.).

Towards the end of the last century, linguists like Schuchardt (1896) learnt of ergative marking in Caucasian languages and decided that it must be a kind of passive (see Seely 1977: 197–9 for a full bibliographic survey). This is a classic case of reinterpreting novel data to fit an accepted theory (rather than revising the theory to account for the data). A linguist brought up on a fare of ergative languages might respond in similar fashion, when first shown an accusative system, by saying that it seemed to be a kind of antipassive. In fact both passive and antipassive are derived intransitive construction types, with explicit morphological marking, and are used in specifiable syntactic/semantic/pragmatic circumstances; they cannot be equated with the unmarked transitive construction in an ergative language, and in an accusative language, respectively.

There are very few people who would, today, seriously promote the view that ergative constructions are 'really passives'. But we do still encounter scholars who insist that there is a necessary diachronic connection, e.g. Estival and Myhill (1988: 445): 'we propose here the hypothesis that in fact all ergative constructions have developed from passives'. The Hittite and Päri examples just quoted should provide adequate counter-examples; see also the discussion of Carib languages at the end of this section.

It is certainly the case that *some* ergative systems have arisen through reinterpretation of a passive. Note, though, that there are considerable differences between a passive construction in an accusative language and the unmarked transitive construction in an ergative language. The passive is a (derived) intransitive, with underlying O in derived S function; the underlying A NP, while it may be included, with oblique marking, is most often omitted; a passive is used only in syntactically/semantically/pragmatically marked circumstances (§6.1).

Thus, a number of significant syntactic changes must be implemented in any passive-to-ergative reinterpretation. First, the passive construction must come to normally include the underlying A NP, in its oblique marking. Next, the use of the passive must be extended so that it is the normal (or unmarked) construction involving a transitive verb, in certain syntactic environments (e.g. those motivating one of the types of split mentioned in Chapter 4), with the original active construction dropping out of use in those environments. It must now be treated as a basic construction, not a derived one; O will receive the same marking as S in a plain intransitive and the original oblique marker on A is reinterpreted as the ergative marker, the normal indicator on A in a transitive clause. What was the derived passive form of the verb is taken to be the basic stem form.[4]

We must now enquire as to what might condition such an interpretation. It is useful to recall (from §6.1) a typical semantic property of passives: they tend to focus on the state which the referent of the underlying O NP is in, as a result of some action. As Anderson (1977: 336) puts it 'passive constructions are semantically close to perfect in that they generally present a state resulting from a completed action' (see also Comrie 1976: 85–6; Hopper and Thompson 1980: 271). We might thus expect a split-ergative system conditioned by aspect or tense (§4.3), where the ergative is found in perfect aspect or past tense, to be likely to have a passive origin.

This is precisely what happened in the Indic and Iranian branches of Indo-European (for which we do have written records and can be fairly certain about what happened, although different scholars have suggested diverse interpretations). Sanskrit and other ancient languages of the Indic branch were entirely accusative. Then the inflectional perfect was lost and replaced by a periphrastic construction based on a passive participle. In the imperfect S and A were marked in the same way and O differently, but in the perfect O was marked in the same way as S, while an erstwhile instrumental inflection, which had also been used to mark the demoted A in a passive construction, took on ergative function, to mark A (Bloch 1965; Anderson 1977; Lahiri 1986; Masica 1991: 339–46; but see Klaiman 1978, 1987 for a different interpretation). This explains the split-ergative system in modern languages from the western group of Indic – Hindi, Punjabi, Rājāsthānī, Gujarathi, Marathi and Sindhi. For example, in Hindi, clauses in imperfective tenses have zero marking for S and A but accusative *-ko* for O (if definite and animate) and the verb agreeing in gender and number with S or A; in perfective tenses S and O have zero

---

[4] There is a useful discussion of all this in Estival and Myhill (1988: 466–7). However, they include as a final step, that 'syntactic subject properties' (i.e. my pivot properties) be transferred from O to A. This would apply for a language that was morphologically ergative but had an S/A pivot; it would not apply if there was an S/O pivot (see §6.2).

marking while A shows ergative -*ne* and the verb agrees in gender and number with S or O (Allen 1951; Anderson 1977).

Similar changes have taken place in languages of the Iranian branch. Some scholars argue that it was a possessive construction which was reanalysed as ergative in past tenses, explaining why genitive case came also to take on ergative function (Benveniste 1952; Anderson 1977). However, others maintain that the past-tense ergative came from a passive, in which the demoted A was marked by genitive case (see Cardona 1970; Pirejko 1979; John Payne 1980; Bynon 1980). There is, in any case, a pervasive connection between possession and perfect in languages from many parts of the world, e.g. in English *have* is a possessive verb and also part of the perfect auxiliary, *have ... -en* (for a full discussion see Allen 1964 and Benveniste 1952). The story of Iranian will be continued in §7.2.

Polynesian languages form a coherent subgroup within the large Austronesian family. Some of these – e.g. Tongan and Samoan – have ergative constructions while others show an accusative system. Maori is noteworthy in that it is accusative, with a passive construction which is extensively used – it may be more frequent than the active. This suggests that proto-Polynesian may have been accusative, with Maori demonstrating the first stage in a passive-to-ergative shift that has been completed in Tongan and Samoan. Indeed, the passive in Maori is marked by a verbal suffix -*Cia* (where *C* is a consonant), that can optionally be included or omitted from transitive verbs in the ergative languages. This is exactly what we would expect – as a passive became reinterpreted as the unmarked transitive construction, the erstwhile passive marker would become redundant and might be dropped (its optional presence, with no apparent semantic effect, could be the first step in this process).

There are, however, difficulties with this scenario. Polynesian languages have several alternative syntactic constructions for transitive verbs, whose use is not fully understood; and there are verbal affixes -*Ci* and -*a* in addition to -*Cia*, which are also not well understood. In Fijian, which is closely related to proto-Polynesian (and has an entirely accusative grammar), -*Ci* marks a standard transitive verb, with a following -*a* marking third person singular object; it is not clear how this can be reconciled with the hypothesis that -*Cia* was a passive marker in proto-Polynesian. Hale (1968) and Hohepa (1969) first suggested that proto-Polynesian had an accusative structure. Then Clark (1973, 1976) and Foley (1976) argued against this, suggesting instead that proto-Polynesian was ergative. Chung (1977, 1978) and Seiter (1979) then put forward a new case for the accusative alternative. Unlike in the case of Indic and Iranian languages, we have no written records and so must wait for a plausible reconstruction that is plainly superior to any competitor (and is accepted by almost all scholars working in the field). It seems to me that neither side in this debate has so far proved its case; the matter requires further study.

Languages of the Carib family, from the northern part of South America, show both accusative and ergative construction types. In the accusative construction, transitive verbs have a fused A + O prefix and intransitive verbs an S prefix; there is no case marking on NPs; constituent order is generally either OVA and VS or AOV and SV with, in each type, O being closely linked to the verb and S and A somewhat detached. The ergative construction has a verbal proclitic marking S and O while an enclitic (which is the S/O form plus an ergative increment) cross-references A; S and O NPs lack case inflection while an A NP takes an ergative ending; constituent order is typically OVA and SV, with S and O placed before the verb and A after it.

In all Carib languages, subordinate clauses (which generally have the status of nominalisations) show the ergative pattern. In many languages, main clauses are exclusively accusative, in some they are exclusively ergative, and in a handful they can be accusative or ergative, depending on tense choice (see §4.3 and note 25 there). Just looking at these facts in broad outline, it would appear most plausible that proto-Carib was basically ergative, with an accusative pattern having been innovated into main clauses in some languages (Franchetto 1990; Derbyshire 1991); changes in syntactic alignment generally apply first to main clauses and, at a later stage, filter through to subordinate clauses, so that subordinate clauses typically preserve archaic features.

Gildea (1992) has undertaken a thorough and insightful study of this problem and comes to the opposite conclusion. Languages with accusative main clauses are found in almost all branches of the family, while those with ergative main clauses occur in just two subgroups. The A + O prefix can be traced back to proto-Carib verbs, whereas the S/O proclitic had a nominal origin in the proto-language. In view of this, he suggests that the proto-language had an accusative syntax for main clauses and ergative for subordinate clauses; and he then suggests mechanisms by which a number of modern languages have extended ergative marking into some or all main clauses. This appears a likely proposal, although more work is needed fully to validate it (firstly, on description of modern Carib languages, so that these can be fed into the comparison).

7.2   *Ergative to accusative*

There appears to be a general consensus of opinion that proto-Mayan, proto-Tibeto-Burman and proto-Australian were substantially ergative in their intra-clausal marking. Most modern descendants of these proto-languages retain ergative characteristics but some have moved towards a more accusative system. In this section we survey some of the ways in which this shift has taken – or is taking – place, in these families, and also in South Caucasian and Iranian.

Just as one (but not the only) route of development for an ergative system is from a passive construction in an accusative language, so one (but certainly not the only) route of development for an accusative system is from an antipassive in an ergative language. But, as emphasised in §6.1, passive and antipassive have rather different meanings. As a consequence of this, antipassive-to-accusative is likely to be conditioned by quite different sorts of factors from those relevant for passive-to-ergative.

This can be demonstrated for Warrgamay, the southern neighbour of Dyirbal, and with very similar grammatical structure. We can reconstruct that at an earlier stage Warrgamay had – as Dyirbal and many other Pama-Nyungan languages still have – a strict division of verbs into transitive and intransitive, and also two verbal conjugations that correlated with (but did not coincide with) conjugation classes. That is, most verbs in the -*y* conjugation would have been intransitive and most of those in the -*l* conjugation transitive, but with a fair number of exceptions (something of the order of 20 per cent). We also hypothesise that the earlier stage of Warrgamay was like modern Dyirbal in having an S/O pivot (at least for subordinate constructions) and – partly to feed the pivot constraint – an antipassive derivation, marked by the verbal derivational affix -*la*-.

Warrgamay is like many other Australian languages in having a split-case-marking system. Non-singular first and second person pronouns have an accusative pattern with the base form used for S and A and an accusative suffix -*nya* marking O function. Singular first and second person pronouns show a tripartite system, with different forms for each of A, S and O. Nouns and adjectives follow an ergative paradigm, with the plain stem used for S and O and ergative inflection -*ŋgu* ~ -*du* (the allomorphs being phonologically conditioned) added for A. This is set out in Table 7.1.

Table 7.1. *Case marking in Warrgamay*

A	*nʸubula*	*ŋaja*	*ŋinda*	*-ŋgu ~ -du*
S		*ŋayba*	*ŋinba*	*∅*
O	*nʸubula-nʸa*	*ŋanʸa*	*ŋina*	
	non-singular pronouns, e.g. *nʸubula* second person dual	first person singular pronoun	second person singular pronoun	nouns and adjectives

The first historical change was that conjugational classes came to coincide exactly with transitivity: the few intransitive roots in the *-l* class were transferred to the *-y* class and the few transitive roots in the *-y* class were moved to the *-l* class. Thus *bungi-l* 'to lie down' in Dyirbal corresponds to *bungi-* in Warrgamay, used only with allomorphs from the intransitive conjugation. (Evidence that such a change has taken place comes from the Biyay dialect of Warrgamay where just a few exceptions remain, e.g. in Biyay *bungi-*, although an intransitive verb, takes inflectional allomorphs normally reserved for transitive verbs.)

There was still at this stage a productive antipassive derivation; each transitive verb could take *-l* conjugation allomorphs and function in a transitive clause, with A and O NPs, or an intransitive stem could be derived by the addition of *-la-*, and this would then take *-y* conjugation allomorphs and function in an intransitive sentence with the underlying A NP being in derived S function and underlying O taking dative or instrumental case. The suffixes added to verb roots would at this stage have been, for three sample inflections:

(1)

	intransitive root	derived antipassive stem	transitive root
future	*-ma*	*-la-ma*	*-lma*
purposive	*-gu*	*-la-gu*	*-gu*
imperative	*-ga*	*-la-ga*	*-ya ~ ∅*

Then a further change occurred; just one set of additions to the verb root in an intransitive clause developed, effectively through merger of the first and second columns in (1). That is, the modern language allows:

(2)

	intransitive root in intransitive construction	transitive root in	
		intransitive construction	transitive construction
future	*-ma-*		*-lma*
purposive	*-lagu*		*-gu*
imperative	*-ga*		*-ya* ~ ∅

In present-day Warrgamay an intransitive root can only occur in an intransitive clause, and must take inflections from the left-hand column. Transitive roots most commonly appear in transitive clauses – with A and O NPs – and must then take inflections from the right-hand column; but almost all of them can also occur in intransitive constructions – with just one core NP, in S function – and then take inflectional forms from the left-hand column. The A NP in a transitive construction corresponds to the S NP of an intransitive clause containing a transitive root; the transitive O NP is placed in either instrumental–ergative or dative case in the intransitive clause (normally instrumental–ergative, but dative if the verb of the clause shows purposive inflection) or it may be omitted.

There appear to be three main circumstances under which a basically transitive verb may occur in an intransitive construction. One is when the speaker does not want to specify the underlying O NP. The second is to mark reflexive, when underlying A and O coincide – they are mapped onto the S of the intransitive. The third is to satisfy the S/O pivot condition; in relative clause and in purposive constructions there must be an NP common to main and subordinate clauses which is in S or O function in each clause (its second occurrence is then generally omitted). If a common NP is in underlying A function in one clause then this must be recast as an intransitive, putting it into S function.

To illustrate how this system works, consider examples (3–7). Intransitive verbs such as *gaga-* 'go' and *wirga-* 'bathe' can only occur in intransitive constructions, such as (3–5). A transitive verb, such as *n^yuunja-* 'kiss' can be used in a transitive clause such as (6) and, under appropriate syntactic conditions, in an intransitive construction such as (7):

(3) *muyma$_s$ gaga-ma*, the boy will go
(4) *gajiya$_s$ gaga-ma*, the girl will go
(5) *muyma$_s$ wirga-ma*, the boy will bathe

(6)   *muyma$_O$ gajiya-ngu$_A$ nʸuunja-lma*, the girl will kiss the boy

(7)   *gajiya$_S$ nʸuunja-ma (muyma-ngu$_{INST}$)*, the girl will kiss (the boy)

(Note that the functional identity of the NPs in these sentences can be verified by substitution possibilities from the same row in Table 7.1. For instance, replacing 'the girl' by 'I', we would use *nayba* in (4) and (7), and *naja* in (6). Replacing 'the boy' by 'you' we would use *ninba* in (3) and (5), and *nina* in (6).)

Now (3) and (5) share an NP which is in S function in each, meeting the pivot conditions. They can be combined in a purposive construction, with purposive inflection, *-lagu*, on the second verb, and the second occurrence of the common NP omitted:

(8)   *muyma gaga-ma wirga-lagu*, the boy will go to bathe

Similarly, (3) and (6) show a common NP which is in S function in the first and in O in the second, again satisfying the pivot condition. They can be combined in a purposive construction, with the transitive purposive inflection, *-gu*, on the second verb:

(9)   *muyma gaga-ma gajiya-ngu nʸuunja-gu*, the boy will go for the girl
        to kiss him

When we look at (4) and (6) they are seen to have a common NP, *gajiya* 'girl', which is in S function in the first but in A in the second, not satisfying the pivot constraint. We must, therefore, recast (6) into intransitive form, as (7), where *gajiya* assumes S function, and *muyma* 'the boy' is in a peripheral case; (7) can now be combined with (4), the verb taking intransitive allomorph of purposive, *-lagu*, instead of the transitive allomorph, *-gu*, which it took in (9):

(10)   *gajiya gaga-ma nʸuunja-lagu muyma-gu$_{DAT}$*, the girl will go to kiss
         the boy.

Let us now consider the inflectional forms in (2), and their development from those in (1). It will be seen that the left-hand column in (2) takes purposive from the middle column in (1) but future and imperative come from the left-hand column. The main function of purposive is to mark the second verb in a purposive construction (e.g. 'I went to spear the wallaby'); transitive roots occur more frequently than intransitives in this slot and so *-lagu* would have been more common than *-gu* in intransitive clauses. For the other inflections the straightforward intransitive forms (*-ma* and *-ga*) would have been more common than the derived intransitives -*la-ma* and -*la-ga*, and have replaced them. The new intransitive allomorph of purposive -*lagu* involves the old antipassive -*la*-, and the old intransitive suffix -*gu*; note that -*lagu* is not analysable within modern Warrgamay (-*la* does not now occur outside this form).[5]

It is not hard to see how an entirely accusative morphology could arise from the present Warrgamay system. Currently, although nearly all transitive verbs can occur in intransitive clauses, they do so only sparingly. Transitive verbs would have to be used more and more in intransitive constructions, like (7), until eventually the original transitive construction type, illustrated in (6), ceased to be used; transitive allomorphs, from the right-hand column of (2), would simply be lost.

Transitive roots would now only occur with their subject (A) NP in what we have been calling absolutive case – this is also used for the subject (S) of an intransitive verb – and their object (O) NP in ergative–instrumental case (or in dative case, just in a purposive construction). But this is simply a nominative–accusative system, and it would surely be appropriate to rename absolutive as nominative, and ergative–instrumental as accusative–instrumental.

The most interesting feature of this sequence of changes is that it began with an S/O pivot, the indicator of ergative syntax, and an antipassive operation to feed this. By eventual reinterpretation of what was originally an antipassive construction as the unmarked construction type for transitive verbs, we would arrive at a language which is firmly accusative, both in morphological marking and also in its syntax – the S/O pivot would naturally have been replaced by an S/A pivot. (Full details on Warrgamay are in Dixon 1981a, b.)

In §6.1 I described the major semantic effect of an antipassive, to focus on the fact that the underlying A is taking part in some activity that involves an object, while backgrounding the identity of the object. In the plain transitive sentence (6) *muyma* 'boy' (O) and *gajiya* 'girl' (A) are both

---

[5] There is a nearby language with similar syntactic phenomena to Warrgamay. In Kala Lagaw Ya (spoken on the Western Torres Strait islands) each transitive verb can occur in a regular transitive construction with ergative marking on A and absolutive on O NP; or it can occur in an intransitive construction with the underlying A NP taking on derived S function and with underlying O NP in ergative inflection. As in Warrgamay, there are distinct allomorphs of verbal inflections for intransitive and for transitive clauses. There is, however, a semantic difference from Warrgamay: in the Western Torres Strait language an intransitive construction involving a transitive verb indicates, roughly, that the action was done to *all* of a set of objects (e.g. 'I cut down all of these trees'). (See Bani and Klokeid 1976.)

core constituents, but in the intransitive (7) – which is historically derived from an antipassive – *gajiya* (underlying A, derived S) is the only core NP, with *muyma* either being omitted or included with a peripheral case marking. The semantic function of the antipassive, to focus on the role of the underlying A, ties in well with a purposive construction in which, typically, someone does something in order to be able to achieve something else. It was undoubtedly the frequent use of a transitive verb in antipassive form within a purposive construction, in early Warrgamay, that triggered the generalisations involved in fully collapsing the two left-hand columns in (1), yielding (2), through which transitive verbs can be used in intransitive constructions without any overt derivational marking.

Thus, just as a passive is suited to perfective aspect or past tense – and is sometimes the genesis of an ergative system that is found only in perfect or past – so antipassive relates to tenses/aspects/moods in which the subject is likely to control the activity (e.g. purposive) or where the possibility of an activity happening depends on the propensity of the subject (e.g. future possibility or irrealis).

In §4.5 I described the split-ergative system in Yukulta, from the Tangkic subgroup within the Australian family. Construction (a) is a plain transitive, with A marked by ergative, and O by absolutive case, while the verb takes transitive suffixes. Construction (b) has A marked by absolutive and O by dative case, with the verb taking intransitive suffixes; it is, effectively, an intransitive construction involving a transitive verb, as in Warrgamay. Here, (a) is used with statements of past fact and future intention and (b) in all other cases, e.g. negative sentences in past tense ('He didn't do it') and future irrealis (e.g. wishing). Construction (b) may well stem from an old antipassive; it relates to activities that depend, or depended, on a propensity of the referent of the underlying A NP. Blake has described two Pama-Nyungan languages spoken to the south of Yukulta – in Pitta-Pitta a transitive verb is used in an intransitive-type construction just when reference is being made to the future (Blake 1979a), and in Kalkatungu to focus on the underlying A's 'indulgence in an activity, rather than to express what happened to the patient' (it tends to be used for uncompleted, continuing activity and when the O is indefinite and non-specific) (Blake 1979b: 28, 1978).

There is one geographically compact group of Pama-Nyungan languages that have an entirely accusative grammar – they are Panyjima, Ngarluma, Yinyjiparnti and Martuthunira, from the Ngayarda subgroup in the north-west of Western Australia (see Dench 1987, 1991; O'Grady, Voegelin and

Voegelin 1966). Interestingly, the other three Ngayarda languages – Ngarla, Nhuwala and Nyamal – have ergative case marking (and the ergative case form *-ŋgu* ~ *-du*, is the same as that in Warrgamay, Dyirbal and many other Pama-Nyungan languages). In the accusative Ngayarda languages, nominative (with zero realisation) is used for S and A, and accusative, *-gu*, for O. This accusative *-gu* is plainly related to *-gu* which functions as dative case in many Australian languages, including the Ngayarda group. Here it covers accusative, dative and benefactive; thus, the ditransitive verb 'give' has both gift and recipient marked by case inflection *-gu*. It is tempting to suggest that the process of language change observed in its early stages for Warrgamay has been carried to completion for the four accusative languages of the Ngayarda group – there was an antipassive syntactic derivation, one of whose purposes was to feed an S/O pivot, and then this antipassive construction became generalised as the only construction for transitive verbs.

Dench (1982) has pointed to real difficulties with this scenario. All instances of an S/O pivot come from languages in the eastern part of Australia. The Pama-Nyungan languages of Western Australia – including the non-accusative members of the Ngayarda subgroup – are like Walmatjari (see §6.2.3) in employing an exclusively S/A pivot, and in lacking any antipassive derivation. Proto-Ngayarda would have been like Walmatjari in having morphological marking on nouns that was out of step with the S/A pivot, S being marked by absolutive and A by ergative. It may be that the ergative-to-accusative shift happened to bring case marking into line with pivot identification. The fact that O is now marked by *-gu*, the previous (and present) dative, does suggest that the shift essentially involved transitive verbs being used in intransitive constructions, although without the intermediate mechanism of an antipassive derivation.

Interestingly, the accusative Ngayarda languages have a productive passive derivation, which can help feed the S/A pivot; it is marked by derivational suffix *-ɲuli* to the verb, O goes into derived S function (with zero inflection) and underlying A is marked by *-ŋgu*, which is ergative–instrumental inflection in the non-accusative Ngayarda languages (as in Dyirbal and many other Pama-Nyungan languages). (In the accusative Ngayarda languages, instruments are marked by a quite different suffix.) The passive marker *-ɲuli* appears to be cognate with an inchoative derivational suffix *-ɲuli*, which forms intransitive verbs from nominals in both accusative and non-accusative Ngayarda languages. It may be that inchoative -*ŋuli* was generalised to form passive-like intransitive constructions from something like participial clauses which do preserve the original ergative inflectional system. (Or there may be some other explanation. The changes that have led to syntactic realignment in the four Ngayarda languages are not yet fully understood.)

There is another group of Australian case-marked languages that follow an accusative system – Lardil and Kayardild from the small Tangkic subgroup, spoken in the Gulf country of north-west Queensland. They are closely related to Yukulta which, as mentioned in §4.5 and just above, has both an ergative and an intransitive-like construction associated with transitive verbs. In fact, the accusative inflection in Lardil, -*n* ~ -*in*, can be shown to be cognate with dative, -*ntha*, in Yukulta, suggesting that an original antipassive construction, which was used in certain aspects in Yukulta, has been generalised as the only construction for transitive verbs in Lardil. There is in Lardil a passive derivation marked by the verbal suffix -*yi*, which is cognate with the reflexive verbal derivation in other languages; it is likely that the function of this affix was extended from reflexive to passive after the ergative-to-accusative change took place.[6] (A single verbal derivation is used for both reflexive and passive, or else both reflexive and antipassive, in languages from all parts of the world; some examples were mentioned in §6.1. Note that all three are detransitivising derivations.)

The accusative languages of the Tangkic and Ngayarda groups show one relic of an original ergative system – the O NP in an imperative bears zero (nominative) inflection, rather than the expected accusative.[7] In ergative languages like Dyirbal imperatives can, potentially, be in antipassive form but seldom are; thus, an antipassive-based reorientation of the grammar might not apply to imperatives. The A NP in a transitive imperative must be second person, and any non-second-person NP could only be understood as being in O function, so that this 'irregularity' would

---

[6] Hale (1970) suggested that proto-Tangkic (and also proto-Australian – see Dixon 1972: 135–7 on this) was accusative, and that ergative constructions in modern languages came from an original passive, such as that in Lardil. Hale did not have access to information on Kayardild. In fact, underlying A has different marking in the Lardil passive and in the Kayardild passive, suggesting that it is a recent innovation, after these languages underwent the ergative-to-accusative shift.

A full account of the Tangkic evidence and argumentation will be found in Klokeid (1978), McConvell (1981) and Evans (1987). Note that Klokeid and McConvell put forward some lines of argumentation (concerning loss of case endings due to phonological change) that are disputed by Evans, and others (concerning an original non-ergative syntax of subordinate clauses) that I do not find convincing and thus do not include here.

[7] As noted in §4.2, accusative is marked just on first person O in an imperative clause in Lardil (an exception to the exception).

not lead to misunderstanding. (As mentioned in §7.1, imperatives typically preserve archaic grammatical patterns; and note the lack of accusative marking on an O NP in an imperative construction in Finnish, mentioned in §3.4.2.)

Languages from the Pama-Nyungan and Tangkic groups of Australian are dependent-marking, showing syntactic function by case inflection on NPs. It is likely that proto-Australian showed the same typology (Blake 1987b). However, languages in other subgroups of this family – all spoken within a smallish area in the central north – have developed complex verb structures with extensive cross-referencing and have lost almost all case marking on core NPs. Proto-Australian most probably had accusative inflection on pronouns and ergative on nouns (see Blake 1987a: 189–90). As bound cross-referencing forms developed from free pronouns they would be expected to be – as they are – accusative. Once cross-referencing took over the major role of indicating syntactic function, case markers would naturally have been lost, and with them the ergative character of the languages. This demonstrates another route by which a language could shift from a partly ergative to a wholly accusative character.

Syntactic function is shown by verbal cross-referencing in Mayan languages (and, it is believed, in the proto-language) with typically set A of affixes marking A function and set B marking S and O functions. However, some modern languages have moved towards a partly accusative profile. This can be traced to a tendency to extend the scope of set A, which has happened in different ways in different Mayan languages (see note 29 to Chapter 4). In Mocho, set A is extended to S just for first and second person pronouns; in Mopan and two other languages, set A also covers S just in progressive aspect; in Jacaltec, the extension applies only in aspectless subordinate clauses. Larsen and Norman (1979) state that tense and aspect splits which trigger the use of set A for S function always involve an auxiliary verb, and may be traced to subordinate clause constructions; they may in turn relate to nominalisations, in which A and S are treated in the same way. (See also Bricker 1981 on Yucatec Maya.)

Current opinion has it that proto-Tibeto-Burman showed an absolutive-ergative system of case marking on nominals and third person pronouns (with absolutive marked by zero and ergative by a suffix), but no case marking on first and second person pronouns. This system is in accord with the Nominal Hierarchy, in Figure 4.5. There was cross-referencing on the verb, in terms of a hierarchy 1st > 2nd > 3rd, or 1st = 2nd > 3rd (DeLancey 1987; Kepping 1979; Bauman 1979; Bhat 1988, 1991).

Some modern languages (e.g. Kiranti, Gyarong) retain what is essentially the original split case-marking system. Others (e.g. Gurung) have eliminated the split by generalising ergative marking to apply to all free pronouns. In Newari, an aspect-conditioned split has developed – ergative marking (which applies to all NP constituents) is obligatory in perfect/past and future/irrealis but optional in durative/progressive (see §4.3 – Givón 1985; Genetti 1988; Malla 1985). A further group, including most Lolo-Burmese languages, has lost ergative marking altogether (perhaps partly through general loss of affixes in adopting a more isolating profile).

Comrie (1981a: 224) describes how, among the languages of the South Caucasian family, Georgian and Svan have an ergative construction just in the aorist series. In Mingrelian, the original ergative marker has been extended to cover S as well as A in the aorist, making a nominative-accusative system. But in the closely related Laz (or Chan), the range of ergative has been extended so that it marks all A, regardless of tense. Thus, from an original split-ergative system, Mingrelian has developed into a more fully accusative and Laz into a more fully ergative one, by different sorts of generalisation.

Among the most interesting languages – in terms of development in to and out of ergativity – are members of the Iranian branch of Indo-European. The proto-language appears to have been fully accusative but, as mentioned in §7.1, an ergative construction developed in the past tense, probably from a passive-like participle; S and O were marked by direct case, a continuation of the Old Iranian nominative, and A by an oblique case, which is a historical continuation of the original genitive. Some modern languages maintain this pattern while others – including those of the south-eastern or Pamir subgroup – have undergone varied changes. As described in §2.2, Wakhi has moved to semantically based marking, but other languages have retained a syntactically based system.

Proto-Pamir had just two cases, direct and oblique, used in quite different ways in present and past tenses:

	Direct	Oblique
Present	S, A	O
Past	S, O	A

This is a simple split system, with the interesting feature that marking of A and O is reversed between the tenses; S is the only constant, being always shown by the direct case. In the modern language Yazgulyam a new accusative prefix has developed (from prepositions) to mark O in both tenses. In the past there is now tripartite marking – oblique case for A, direct for S, and the newly formed accusative for O.

In Rushan, the oblique marking on O in the present was generalised to apply also in the past, so that A and O now receive identical marking in past tense – surely an unstable system (since one of the major functions of case marking is to distinguish A from O). Among younger speakers, two changes are in progress. First, there is a tendency to use direct in place of oblique on A in the past (presumably again generalising from present tense); and second, the preposition *az* 'from' is sometimes used before the O NP, in both tenses. In the closely related language Bartang, A is always marked like S, by the direct case, and the preposition *az* has become grammaticised as an accusative case prefix *a-*. Here, the cycle of change from Figure 7.2 is complete. An original accusative system developed into a split-ergative system by passive-to-ergative reinterpretation in the periphrastic past tense. Then – a thousand or two years later – this was replaced by a fully accusative paradigm, by generalisation from one tense to the other, and by the formation of a new accusative case. (See Comrie 1981a: 164–79; John Payne 1979, 1980; Bynon 1980.)

7.3   General comments

In Chapter 4 I described the types of factor that condition ergativity splits – the semantics of the verb, of NPs, and of tense, aspect or mood (which also relate to splits between main and subordinate clauses). In each case there appears to be a natural division between accusative and ergative systems – ergative is more likely to be found with verbs that refer to some non-controlled activity, with inanimate NPs (which typically do not control an activity), in perfect aspect or past tense or in relative clauses (which typically just describe what happened, without focussing on any propensity of the agent).

Ergative-to-accusative and accusative-to-ergative changes tend to produce a split system that fits within these semantic parameters, or else move a split system towards a more homogeneous accusative or ergative arrangement. We saw that in Hittite instrumental inflection developed into an ergative case just for inanimates, at the right of the Nominal Hierarchy. Under the hypothesis that proto-Australian had ergative marking on nouns but not on pronouns, the development from dependent marking to head marking in some non-Pama-Nyungan groups led to the loss of core case marking on nouns, and thus of the part-ergative character of the languages.

We saw that a passive-to-ergative change tends to operate within perfective aspect or past tense, the expected location of ergativity within this kind of split (since perfective and past tend to focus on what happened to the O, rather than on what the A did). And an antipassive-to-accusative change tends to begin in purposive constructions and other aspects, tenses or moods within which the agent's control is critical.[8]

Where there is a split it may be shifted or eliminated through generalisations of one sort or another. A certain pattern of marking may be generalised to apply to all kinds of NP constituent, as in the Tibeto-Burman language Gurung, where the ergative marking on nouns and third person pronouns was extended also to cover first and second person forms. (And see the discussion of Warlpiri in §4.2.1.) A type of marking that applies in one tense or aspect may be generalised to apply in some (or all) other tenses/aspects, as described for Mayan, South Caucasian and Iranian.

A further type of generalisation is when the marking on one syntactic function is extended also to apply to another function. There are two main possibilities here – A extended to cover S, and O extended to S. There are a fair number of examples of the first possibility. In §3.4.3 we discussed languages from the Cushitic, Omotic, Nilotic and Yuman families with 'marked nominative'; some of these systems probably resulted from the generalisation of A also to cover S. The ergativity changes described above for Mayan and South Caucasian included the same generalisation. Generalisation of O also to cover S is much rarer, although not unknown. Australian languages often have accusative suffix -n^ya on pronouns and proper names, and ergative -ηgu on all varieties of noun (including names). However, in the Western Desert language, -n^ya marks both O and S functions with proper names (Dixon 1980: 308). This may be a case of O marking being generalised to S just for those NP constituents – from the middle of the Nominal Hierarchy – which originally showed tripartite

---

[8] Note that these alternatives are not precisely complementary. Ergativity-from-passive may focus on perfect aspect or past tense, say, with accusative taking over the rest of the semantic space (e.g. present and all kinds of future). Accusativity-from-antipassive may occur in purposive or in a desiderative future mood, with ergativity filling the remainder of the semantic space (e.g. present and past). Thus, present tense might be in the 'remainder' space in both scenarios (and would show an accusative construction in the first instance, an ergative one in the second).

marking (*-ŋgu* for A, zero for S, *-nʸa* for O), and serves to give them a straightforward absolutive–ergative paradigm, like other kinds of noun.

The examples presented in §§7.1 and 7.2 were of shifts relating to intra-clausal or morphological ergativity. Little is known about how languages gain or lose different kinds of syntactic pivots, marking syntactic ergativity or accusativity.[9] But we have seen that pivot properties can motivate morphological change. An earlier stage of Warrgamay is believed to have had an antipassive derivation to feed its S/O pivot. This led to a series of changes which, if followed through to an eventual conclusion, would make the language accusative at both morphological and syntactic levels. In the case of the Ngayarda languages the shift from ergative to accusative may have been motivated by a wish to make morphological marking correspond to the pivot grouping of S and A.

This short survey has provided a sample of the sorts of mechanisms of change that can operate, and their conditioning factors. We understand little about how languages change in to or out of split-S systems (not to mention fluid-S systems and languages with more thorough-going semantically based marking).[10] There are doubtless many other kinds of factor. For instance, in discussing Iranian languages mention was made of the evolution of a new accusative case from prepositions. As a language loses or gains morphological material, in slowly moving around the cycle

---

[9] I stated, in the last chapter, that no language is known that has syntactic ergativity (an S/O pivot) but shows no ergativity at the morphological level. Schmidt (1985) describes the 'language death' situation in which younger speakers of Dyirbal switched from an ergative case-marking system to an accusative constituent-order system (similar to English). The examples Schmidt gives suggest that the original S/O syntactic pivot was replaced by an S/A pivot for these younger speakers.

In traditional Dyirbal, two clauses in a purposive construction that had a common NP in S function in the first and in A function in the second (e.g. 'The policeman came to take Lillian') would require the antipassive derivational suffix *-l(ŋ)a-* before purposive inflection *-ygu* on the second verb. This is found in Schmidt's materials but *-laygu* also occurs on intransitive verbs (which it never did in the traditional language). The data is compatible with a reanalysis involving (a) innovation by younger speakers of an S/A pivot; and (b) purposive inflection always having the form *-laygu* (historically, but not synchronically, derived from antipassive *-la-* plus the original purposive *-ygu*).

It would be instructive to study similar change in a non-language-death situation. If a language with some degree of S/O pivot lost, say, its ergative case marking, could the S/O pivot survive?

[10] By examination of the syntaxes of related languages we can suggest that Tsova-Tush developed a fluid-S pattern from an original ergative pattern (which is preserved in other languages of the Nakh subgroup of North-east Caucasian) and that Acehnese developed its fluid-S system from an original accusative pattern (as in related Austronesian languages). I mentioned, in Chapter 2 that Sinhalese appears to be shifting from syntactically based to semantically based marking. However, in none of these cases has the mechanism of change yet been studied.

of change set out in Figure 7.1, it is highly likely that its ergative/accusative character will shift.

Even phonological change can assist grammatical shift. The original marking system for languages of the Pama-Nyungan group, within the Australian family, can be reconstructed with accusative inflection on non-singular pronouns, ergative inflection on nouns, and with all of A, S and O shown differently for singular first and second person pronouns (Dixon 1980: 339–46):

	A	S	O
First person singular	*ŋaju	*ŋay	*ŋanᵛa
Second person singular	*ŋindu	*ŋin	*ŋina

The proto-language allowed monosyllabic words but in many modern languages there has developed a convention that every word should consist of at least two syllables. Languages appear to have dealt with the need to replace monosyllabic S forms for the singular pronouns in two different ways. Some have added a meaningless syllable -ba to the S form, creating *ŋayba* and *ŋinba* (see the Warrgamay paradigm in Table 7.1), maintaining separate forms for S. Others simply generalised the A forms, *ŋaju* and *ŋindu*, also to cover S, giving singular pronouns a nominative–accusative paradigm alongside that already in existence for non-singular pronouns. This further example of A marking being extended to cover S was here motivated by phonological factors.

There may of course sometimes be competing factors. I mentioned in §4.3 that, if there is a split conditioned by mood, then imperative is likely to be accusative since this must focus on the agent's control. But grammatical changes tend to begin in indicative main clauses, with both subordinate clauses and imperative constructions maintaining earlier grammatical patterns. Thus, in a shift from ergative to accusative, imperative may retain ergative characteristics while indicative main clauses show nominative–accusative marking (as was noted above for some languages from the Ngayarda and Tangkic subgroups), even though this is at odds with semantic expectations.

And there can be factors which go beyond the confines of syntax or semantics. Andersen (1988) suggests that ergativity in Päri may be due to the fronting of O and S – presumably for pragmatic reasons, to make them discourse topic. This opens up another dimension that we have not so far considered – the structure of discourse. It will be taken up in the next chapter.

8   The rationale for ergativity

In this final Chapter I first examine the role of the universal syntactic relations S, A and O in discourse structure, perceiving that S and A are linked in one respect and S and O in another. This helps to explain why there are more examples of morphological ergativity than there are of syntactic ergativity. It also adds to the explanations given earlier for types of ergativity split.

I then focus on what it means for a language to be ergative – whether this carries any implications about the intellectual status or world-view of its speakers (I argue that it does not), or any implications concerning other grammatical parameters. The reasons why some languages are more ergative than others may relate to such things as narrative style, and accidents of historical development. §8.3 summarises some of the main conclusions of this work, and then §8.4 asks what lessons can be drawn, from this survey of ergativity, for our understanding of how language works, and what a linguistic theory should include.

8.1   The discourse basis

Categories like 'ergative' and 'accusative' belong to grammar, that aspect of language which involves definite structures and rules. Recently, attention has been paid to the organisation of discourse. This is a field in which statistical tendencies can be noticed, and quantified, but in which there are no definite constraints. We would not expect labels such as 'ergative' and 'accusative' (which were first used to describe specific conventions of morphological marking and can – for some languages – also be extended to describe specific constraints on complex sentence formation and/or on subsequent NP omission) to be applicable in the field of discourse; nor do they appear to be. However, study of the organisation of discourse can provide important clues to the pragmatic basis and rationale for accusative and ergative systems in grammar.

A number of sentences that describe some connected series of actions and/or states can be strung together to form a discourse. There must be a thread connecting successive sentences. Typically, they will deal with a series of actions that members of the language community perceive to make up a familiar unit – or set of related units – of habitual behaviour. A man may rouse himself, pick up a weapon, bid farewell to his wife, walk some considerable distance, spot the tracks of an animal, stalk and eventually kill it, make sure it is dead, fetch it home, where his wife will prepare the carcass, put it in an oven, after a time check to see whether it is fully cooked, then cut up the meat and distribute pieces to her husband, herself and other members of the family to eat. Such a discourse has coherence through the series of connected activities and states described (by verbs and adjectives) and also through the participants who occur in consecutive sentences, or who recur at a later stage (the hunter, his wife, the animal tracks, the animal, the oven, their family members).

A discourse will typically begin with a single piece of information, e.g. 'it was a cold snowy day in the Alps' or 'a brave hunter lived in the African jungle'. Further bits of information will generally be provided one at a time – 'there was starvation in the valleys' or 'he picked up his bow and arrow'. Two of the most important things to study concerning the organisation of discourse, are (a) the ways in which sentences are linked – by a common participant and/or by connected actions/states; and (b) the ways in which new information is introduced (either new participants, or new kinds of actions/states).[1] Discourse study is a relatively new and under-developed field within linguistics; most progress has been made in studying participants – their roles in linking sentences, and the techniques used for introducing new participants into the discourse.

In two insightful and influential studies, Du Bois (1987a, b) has noted a number of traits in the way participants function in a discourse. These appear to be universal tendencies – which apply to a greater or lesser extent in every sort of language, whatever its morphological and syntactic profile. He mentions that the theme or topic of a part of a discourse tends to be an NP which is in underlying S or A function. This is in line with my comments in Chapter 5 on the universality of the subject category, which comprises underlying S and A.[2] It emphasises the importance of having an

---

[1] Care must be taken to distinguish between the main thrust of a discourse, and subsidiary parenthetic-type sections that provide background information. Different patterns concerning S, A and O may apply in the two kinds of passage.

[2] Cooreman, Fox and Givón (1984) have shown, by counting, that 'agent' tends to have a high 'topic persistence' ('the number of contiguous subsequent clauses in which the

antipassive derivation in a language that shows an S/O syntactic pivot. A discourse theme is likely often to be in S function in one clause and in A in the next, e.g. 'the man got up, and picked up his weapon'; when the language operates with an S/O pivot, the second clause must be cast into antipassive form to satisfy this grammatical condition.[3]

Du Bois's second major insight – and one which is of vital interest for the study of ergativity – is that a new participant tends to be introduced through an NP in S or O function, and only fairly seldom through one in A function. Like all other generalisations in the field of discourse, this is a tendency, not any sort of definite rule. But it is a most recurrent tendency.

In some languages there is a special type of verbless 'presentational' construction (similar to 'there is an X' or 'there's this X' in English) typically used for the introduction of new participants (see Herring 1989 on Tamil). Leaving this aside (from languages in which it occurs) it is the case that less (often, considerably less) than 10 per cent of new participants enter in the form of an NP in A function. For instance in a study of the syntactic function of introduction for 139 new participants in narrative discourse from Jarawara, an Amazonian language, I found 57 in S function, 67 in O, 6 in A and 9 in a peripheral NP. That is, 89.2 per cent were in S or O and only 4.3 per cent in A function. Similar figures have been reported for Sacapultec Maya (Du Bois's first language of study – see §3.1.3 above); Mam (another Mayan language which is, like Sacapultec Maya, ergative at the morphological level – see also England 1988); Chamorro and Malay (from the Austronesian family – Chamorro being predominantly accusative and Malay arguably ergative); and Quechua, Modern Hebrew, German and Japanese (all accusative) (references are in Du Bois 1987a: 837–9). Similar results apply to Dyirbal and Yidin^y (my own counts) and to the head-marking non-Pama-Nyungan language Ngan'giwumirri (counted by Nicholas Reid). For the fluid-S language Acehnese (from the Austronesian family), Durie (1988: 18–19) reports that most new mentions are in O or S_o function, not in A or in S_a. The coding

---

participant NP remains a semantic argument of the verb') in a number of languages (I would predict this to be a property of all languages) but then imagine that this gives evidence for whether a language is ergative or accusative at the 'discourse level'. This is a nonce use of 'ergative', not obviously related to the way the term is used in this book. They do *not* show that S and O behave in the same way, and A in a different way, which is the standard criterion for ergativity.

[3] Cooreman (1988) is a partial study of discourse organisation in Dyirbal, showing that topic or theme tends to be in terms of underlying S and A in this language (as, I would guess, probably in all others). Pace Cooreman, this does not relate to ergativity, which is a grammatical category. (See also Dryer 1990 for comments on Cooreman's effort.)

of information concerning new participants in various styles of English was investigated by members of a typology class at the Australian National University in 1989 – less than 10 per cent of the occurrences were in A function for conversations, novels, magazines and magazine-type articles in newspapers.[4] (However, for news reports in newspapers the use of A increased dramatically, to 20–25 per cent of all instances of new information. I would predict that the percentage would be even higher in the language of telegrams. The reason for this is that news reports and telegrams are not properly narrative discourse, introducing a theme and then developing and commenting on it. The functions of these genres is to get several bits of information across in a succinct way; many readers just read the first few sentences of a news item to get the gist of what has happened, something that is not normally possible for a novel or conversation.)

It has already been mentioned (§6.1) that in Dyirbal demonstratives only exist in absolutive form, for S or O function; demonstratives are of course typically used for introducing new information which is most often in S or O function (in some languages demonstratives have an additional, anaphoric, function, but not in Dyirbal). Dyirbal also has a particle *anyja* which is only used to mark new information – a new participant (more precisely, an NP in S or O function which is different from the S or O of the previous sentence), a new kind of action (referred to by a verb) or a new state (shown by an adjective). The critical point is that *anyja* can be used with a noun in absolutive case (derived S or O function), never with one in ergative case (A function) (Dixon 1972: 117). Larsen (1981) reports that in the Mayan language Aguacatec new information is often introduced by means of the existential predicate *at* 'there is/are', whose argument is always cross-referenced by set B (i.e. S/O) suffixes to the verb. (Interestingly, Aguacatec also has a particle *tz* marking theme, which is generally A or S. It thus has particles corresponding to both of Du Bois's discourse groupings.)[5]

In a perceptive study of oral narratives in Brazilian Portuguese, Dutra (1987) states that constituent order for transitive sentences is AVO and for

---

[4] O'Dowd (1990) demonstrates similar patterning in discourse during a medical training session.
[5] Diffloth (1976) mentions that in Jah-hut (from the Temiar group of the Mon-Khmer branch of Austroasiatic), spoken in Malaysia, an A or S NP will generally precede the verb and an O NP follow it. New information appears to be most commonly introduced by O. But S or A may be used for new information, and when this happens they are likely to be placed after the verb, in the position that appears to be earmarked for new information.

intransitives either SV or VS. The intransitive subject NP tends to follow the verb when it is indefinite and introducing new information (here showing similarities with O) and to precede the verb when definite and continuing an established theme (properties typical of A).

Yagua (no extant relatives) and Pajonal Campa (Arawak family) are two languages from the same part of lowland Peru, although they are not genetically related. Each has what looks like a kind of fluid-S system, but one quite different from those described in §4.1.2. Most intransitive verbs mark S like A but there is a small set of verbs, all referring to 'active movement' (e.g. 'run out', 'fall') which can have S marked either like A or like O. The unusual feature is that the choice between these alternatives is motivated not by whether or not the activity is controlled but by discourse factors. S_a is the unmarked coding, with S_o tending to be used to mark a change of state, a change of location, or a point of episodic climax. That is, S is marked like O to highlight some new information (but not a new participant). (See Thomas Payne 1985; Heitzman 1982; Doris Payne and Thomas Payne 1990: 257.)[6]

These examples, from Dyirbal, Aguacatec, Jah-hut, Brazilian Portuguese, Yagua and Pajonal Campa add further support to Du Bois's claim that S and O are typically associated with the introduction of new information. Note how this correlates with an ergative pattern of intraclausal marking; in a case-marked language, for instance, a new participant will typically be introduced by an NP in absolutive case (S or O function). The continuation of a theme provides the other critical factor in building a discourse, and it is useful to have constant grammatical marking for the grammatical relations (S and A) that play the most prominent role here; this is consistent with nominative–accusative grammatical marking.

Most of the ergativity splits described in Chapter 4 can be explained in discourse terms. A discourse theme is most often associated with control of activities and is more likely to be the S of an intransitive verb that refers to a controlled activity than of one which does not; this explains the basis for split-S grammatical systems. First and second person pronouns, from the left of the Nominal Hierarchy in Figure 4.5, are most likely to function as

---

[6] Judith Payne and David Payne (1991) remark that most Maipuran Arawak languages show a normal split-S system (as in §4.1.1) and that this may be 'an old pattern in the language family'. From it has developed the discourse-oriented way of using S_a and S_o described by Thomas Payne for Pajonal Campa, and also a rather different discourse-oriented scheme found in Asheninca, in which a form marked as S_o tends to be 'more foregrounded and topically continuous' than one marked as S_a (this is *not* what we would have expected, from the studies of Du Bois and others).

theme, and there is thus most reason to identify S and A in the same way for these constituents. Note that this is essentially another way of stating the rationale presented in §4.2 – that first and second person pronouns are prototypical agents, and will be unmarked when in this role. (For all languages 'agency' correlates with 'theme'.) Non-humans, and especially inanimates, are more likely, after being introduced, not to assume a major thematic role; this provides further explanation for the grammatical identification of S and O, at the right-hand end of the Nominal Hierarchy. (We explained in §4.2.1 how, if there is a bound/free split, the bound forms are likely to be accusative, since they relate to pronouns, from the left-hand end of the hierarchy.)

There is a further interrelating parameter. When a new participant is introduced it is likely to be indefinite (e.g. 'a tall man came into the room') whereas at subsequent mentions, when functioning as theme, it will be accorded definite marking (in a language which shows this grammatical distinction), e.g. 'the tall man ate an orange'. We mentioned in §4.2 that indefiniteness tends to be associated more with the right-hand end of the Nominal Hierarchy and definiteness more with the left-hand end. There is thus a correlation between (a) indefinite status and new information, most often introduced in S or O function; S and O being identified at the right-hand side of the Nominal Hierarchy; and indefiniteness being associated with this end of the hierarchy; (b) definite status and old information, which can be thematic; the theme typically being in S or A function; S and A being identified at the left-hand end of the hierarchy; and definiteness being associated with this end of the hierarchy.

If there is a split involving clause types, then main clauses and purposive constructions – involved in the development of a theme – are likely to have accusative grammar (treating S and A in the same way) while relative clauses, providing incidental or background information, often relating to some new participant which plays a minor role in the discourse, will assume the ergative side of the split (treating S and O in the same way). Perfect aspect (and past tense) may provide participial/adjectival-type information about the result of an activity, which often has a passive-type slant in an accusative language (linking S and O). This is less likely to be related to the development of a theme than is imperfective aspect (or present and future tenses), and is thus likely to be on the ergative side in any split conditioned by aspect or tense.

I have several times remarked that ergativity is commoner at the intra-clausal or morphological than at the inter-clausal or syntactic level. Du

Bois's insights concerning discourse organisation provide a clue as to why this should be. The introduction of a new participant – where S and O are associated – is something that happens within one clause, and relates to intra-clausal grammatical marking; here an ergative system is most useful. But a discourse theme – typically in A or S function – links together a sequence of clauses through inter-clausal grammatical conventions; here an accusative system (that is, an S/A pivot) will be particularly useful. Of course, not all languages show morphological ergativity, and not all are syntactically accusative; there are other factors involved, including a preference for congruence between morphological and syntactic grammatical orientations. But the discourse bases provide an explanation for the statistical patterns observed in the occurrence of accusativity and ergativity at different grammatical levels.

Languages with an S/A pivot do sometimes lack a passive derivation. In §6.2.3 I described Walmatjari, a language which has split ergativity at the morphological level but a pivot – underlying certain types of complex sentence construction – which is entirely S/A. This pivot accords with the prevailing S/A functions for a discourse theme, which is why Walmatjari can get by with no passive. In contrast, a language with a thorough-going S/O pivot, such as Dyirbal, *must* have an antipassive derivation (which puts an underlying A NP into derived S function, to feed the pivot) simply because the pivot relations here differ from the typical relations for a discourse theme. Dyirbal syntax has its basis in the new-participant-as-S-or-O discourse trait. This is a perfectly workable grammatical system (not at all hard to learn or to use), but it does require a well-developed grammatical apparatus with an antipassive derivation. Interestingly, antipassive clauses are almost never used at the beginning of a discourse, but just to continue it, putting an underlying A NP into pivot relation within one of a series of coordinated clauses (for instance, sentence (34) in §6.2.2).

In summary, consideration of two basic principles of discourse organisation provides a pragmatic basis for ergativity and for accusativity at the grammatical level, and helps explain the general circumstances in which these alternative groupings of basic syntactic relations are found. Languages differ in the particular ways they organise discourse, and study of these ways can provide more particular explanations for the syntactic profiles (ergative or accusative, etc.) which different languages adopt. This will be exemplified, for Yidin^y and Dyirbal, at the end of the next section.

8.2   What it means for a language to be ergative

All human groups have a tendency to consider the unfamiliar to be inferior. When European linguists first noticed the ergative construction type their judgement extended to the peoples who used such languages. They were held to have not only a different mentality from people who use accusative languages, but an inferior one. This opinion was assisted by the fact that most ergative languages then known were spoken by small communities outside the mainstream of European culture (even the Basques were characterised in this way).

Several eminent scholars suggested that to 'primitive man', speaking an ergative language, 'the actual agent is a hidden power'; that 'savage man apparently feels that most events are not due to his own volition'; and that in any action 'what for us is a true cause is for primitive man merely an event involving mystical forces'. (These quotations are taken from Seely 1977: 196, who provides full references. See also Klimov 1973: 206ff.; Fillmore 1968: 60.)

A moment's reflection should be enough to confound the reader. Consider a few typical transitive sentences: 'the hunter picked up a weapon', 'his wife cut up the meat', 'I punched John in the stomach', 'Do eat the cake!' Could any human being imagine that mystical forces are involved here, that such actions are not due to the agent's own volition? There are a small number of transitive verbs that relate to natural forces and events – wind, fire, lightning – but mysterious agencies tend to be invoked for these in all kinds of societies (we refer to them as 'acts of God!').

An argument could in fact be constructed that only speakers of ergative languages have a true notion of agency, since only they have a special grammatical marking for a participant who controls or initiates an activity that affects some other participant. Speakers of accusative languages have the same case marking or cross-referencing for 'John' in all of 'John killed the snake', 'John ran home' and 'John fell down', covering both controlled and uncontrolled events. They must thus be assumed to be unaware of the nature of control. This is, of course, not a valid argument; it is simply put forward to show that this kind of (specious) reasoning can be applied in favour of either side. In fact, there is no one-to-one correspondence between grammatical marking and mental view of the world.

Many other ideas have been expressed about people who use ergative languages – that they see themselves as people to whom things happen, rather than as people who do things. These ideas are connected with the assumption that an ergative construction is really a sort of passive (and might indeed have some validity if the assumption were true). Van Ginneken (1939: 91–2) went so far as to say that the 'passive' nature of ergative languages is characteristic of feminine-oriented or matriarchal societies (he appears to have been generalising from Basque, which is matrilineal, and Indo-European societies, which are patrilineal).

Consider the seven languages belonging to the Ngayarda subgroup in Western Australia (discussed in §7.2); three of them retain ergative case marking while the other four have adopted an accusative system. Have the accusative-language speakers experienced an increase in mental status, or acquired a different world-view? Not at all. I have spent nearly thirty years working fairly steadily with speakers of Dyirbal and other ergative languages; we do have differences in world-view, but none of these can be attributed to the accusativity/ergativity of our languages. The ergative or accusative profile of a language is simply a choice between typological alternatives, just like the choice of which constituent order (AVO, AOV, VOA, etc.) to employ. Neither of these types of choice correlates in any way with the economic basis or cultural organisation of a community, or with the way in which the speakers of a language view the world and their place in it. As stated in the last chapter, all kinds of change from one linguistic typological profile to another are cyclic. A language can move from accusative to partly ergative (e.g. some modern Indic languages), or vice versa (some modern Tibeto-Burman languages); there is no necessary accompanying shift in world-view.

There are a number of pragmatic and semantic pressures on a language to identify S and A in the same way, and also a number of pragmatic and semantic pressures to identify S and O in the same way. These have been discussed in preceding chapters and will be summarised in the next section (note that they are essentially the same for every language). Whether a language adopts an accusative or an ergative grammar, or whatever sort of mixture of the two, depends on the type of grammatical compromise it evolves to deal with these competing pressures.

It is now time to consider some of the suggestions that have been made concerning the linguistic properties of languages that show some degree of ergativity. First, the totally erroneous idea which we have already mentioned several times, that an ergative construction is a 'kind of passive'. There is in fact a considerable syntactic difference between the unmarked construction type in an ergative language – two core NPs, in A and O function – and a passive construction in an accusative (or in an ergative) language – one core NP in derived S (underlying O) function, specific passive marking on the verb, an underlying A NP that is most often omitted but can be included with peripheral marking (and is never cross-referenced on the verb). There are also important semantic differences: a passive tends to focus on the state which the referent of the underlying O NP is in, as a result of some activity, whereas the unmarked transitive construction in an ergative language focusses on the activity and the role of the agent.

Associated with the idea that 'ergative is really passive' is the suggestion that ergative languages have no system of voice (see, for example, Entwistle 1953: 215; Martinet 1962: 72; and the critical discussion in Jacobsen 1985). This is also unfounded – there is typically an active/antipassive voice contrast in an ergative language, corresponding to the active/passive contrast in accusative languages. Indeed, we have seen that languages which are syntactically ergative, with an S/O pivot, should have an antipassive derivation, while only some of those languages that are syntactically accusative employ a passive. Thus a voice system is more important for an ergative language than for one which is accusative (at the syntactic level). (And I also mentioned, in §6.1, that languages can have one or several passives and/or antipassives.)

Many other suggestions have been made concerning the typological profiles that correlate with ergativity. One is that there is no class of adjectives in ergative languages (Klimov 1973: 171, quoting Holz 1953). There is in fact no connection whatsoever between ergativity/ accusativity and whether a language has a distinct adjective class or, if it does, the size of the class. Dyirbal, for instance, has an open adjective class with many hundreds of members.

It has been suggested by a number of people (including the present writer – Dixon 1981a: 87) that ergative languages have greater need than accusative ones of a strict categorisation of each verb as either transitive or intransitive. This idea is also mistaken. We noted, in §1.3 and §5.3.4, that when a language has verbs that are used either transitively or intransitively (what are often called 'labile' verbs), some are likely to be of type S = O (e.g. 'break', 'move', 'cool') and others of type S = A (e.g. 'eat', 'watch', 'sew'). The two varieties of ambitransitive verbs pose different sorts of problems for accusative and for ergative languages.

Consider English, as an example of an accusative language. Ambitransitive verbs of the type S = A pose no problems – *Mary is sewing* and

Mary is sewing a shirt. It appears to be the case that an O NP can be omitted from some (but not all) transitive verbs in appropriate circumstances. In fact it is hard to decide whether to recognise two senses of verbs such as *eat, watch* and *sew* – one transitive and one intransitive – or simply to say that these are transitive verbs whose O NPs can be fairly freely omitted. In the case of S = O ambitransitive verbs, though, English has to be much more careful. Consider *march*; this is generally considered to be a verb which is basically intransitive but can also be used transitively with a causative sense – *The soldiers marched around the square* and *The officer marched the soldiers around the square.* For the transitive use of such a verb, the O NP may not be omitted; if it were, the verb would be understood in its intransitive sense, and the meaning would be quite different – *The officer marched around the square* (here the officer did the marching whereas in the transitive sentence the soldiers did the marching, and the officer might well have remained stationary, shouting out orders from the centre of the square).

The same arguments apply the other way round in ergative languages. Ambitransitive verbs of type S = O pose no problems, e.g. 'the man (ERG) the cup (ABS) broke' and 'the cup (ABS) broke' are understood in much the same way as *Mary is sewing* and *Mary is sewing a shirt* are in English. It may be hard to decide whether this is a verb that has both transitive and intransitive senses, or a transitive verb for which the A NP can be omitted. However, ambitransitive S = A verbs have to be treated just as carefully in ergative languages as the S = O variety must be in accusative languages. Suppose there were a verb 'eat' that could be used in a transitive construction – 'the man (ERG) the crocodile (ABS) ate' – and also in an intransitive construction – 'the man (ABS) ate' – both describing the same event, a man having a feed of crocodile meat. If the ergative NP were omitted from the transitive clause, the verb would be interpreted as being used in its intransitive sense – 'the crocodile (ABS) ate' describes the crocodile doing the eating, not being eaten (as in the transitive alternative). Thus, if an ergative language has S = A ambitransitives it would have to incorporate a rule blocking the omission of the A NP from their transitive use.

The existence of a set of labile verbs has been mentioned by some writers (e.g. Klimov 1973) as a characteristic of ergative languages, but they have been scholars most familiar with Caucasian languages; the ambitransitives quoted have all (or very nearly all) been of the type S = O (see also Koshal 1979: 183–4 on Ladakhi, an ergative language from the Tibeto-Burman family). Most of the ergative languages in Australia – and perhaps most of those in other parts of the world – freely allow the A NP to be omitted from any transitive clause. It is in keeping with this that they have very few ambitransitives, certainly few or none of the type S = A. (If English always allowed an O NP to be omitted, from any transitive clause, it could not operate with labile verbs like *break, move* and *cool* as it does at present; there would have to be something like a verbal affix marking the transitive/causative sense, in order to avoid ambiguity.)

In §7.2 we saw that Warrgamay has begun to move towards an accusative profile by allowing all transitive verbs also to function in intransitive constructions, always with S = A. In this language the transitivity of a clause is shown by the inflectional allomorphs used (see (2) in §7.2). Thus, following on from the examples of §7.2, *muyma n^{v}uunja-lma* means 'the boy will be kissed' – here *muyma* is O in a transitive clause (it is simply (6) with the A NP omitted) involving the transitive allomorph -*lma* of future. In contrast, *muyma n^{v}uunja-ma* is 'the boy will kiss' – here *muyma* is S in an intransitive clause marked by intransitive allomorph -*ma*. Warrgamay is still basically ergative and so needs this inflectional-allomorphic identification of transitivity in order to deal with S = A ambitransitives. But if, in time, the present basic transitive construction type – exemplified by (6) in §7.2 – should drop out of use, to be replaced by the antipassive-derived construction type – exemplified by (7) – then the language would have taken on accusative case marking. There would no longer be any need for marking of transitivity to deal with ambitransitives of type S = A (and then, the two columns from (2) of §7.2 could safely merge into one). Evans (1989) quotes examples of ambitransitive verbs in accusative languages from the Ngayarda and Tangkic subgroups of the Australian family; all the verbs he quotes appear to be of the S = A type, as one would have predicted.

In summary, there is no necessary correlation between ergativity/accusativity and whether the transitivity of a verb is fixed or more fluid. The points at issue are that an accusative language can naturally handle ambitransitives of type S = A and an ergative language those of type S = O. For the other type there must in each case be some grammatical restriction (against the omission of an O NP for an accusative and an A NP for an ergative language), or else some explicit marking of each clause type as transitive or intransitive, or something else that achieves the same ends.

The discussion so far in this section has been entirely dismissive. All the suggestions made about a connection between ergativity and type of society or manner of thinking were rejected. Those about typological characteristics of ergative languages (that they have no adjectives, or require strict transitivity) were likewise shown to be without foundation. I would suggest that there is no necessary connection between ergative characteristics and any other linguistic feature. There are, of course, likely to be statistical correlations. For instance, Nichol's (1992) global typological survey has suggested that ergativity is more common in dependent-marked than in head-marked languages. This might have been predicted. In a head-marking language the verb includes pronominal information concerning clause arguments, and pronouns are at the accusative end of the Nominal Hierarchy; in a dependent-marking language, case or other marking goes onto NPs, which span the whole breadth of the hierarchy.[7]

What then does it mean for a language to be ergative? Exactly what we said in the first paragraph of Chapter 1 – that S is treated in the same way as O and differently from A in some part or parts of the grammar. Nothing else necessarily accompanies this.

Why then do languages vary? Why are some totally accusative, others partly ergative – and these can be ergative in all sorts of different ways. Just as different people each evolve a mode of living to cope with the pressures of life, so individual languages develop a grammatical strategy to deal with semantic and pragmatic (discourse structure) demands.

One reason for grammatical variation is that these pressures and demands are not quite the same for each language. The most important task for future work on 'why some languages are ergative in a certain way and others are not' is to investigate the semantic and discourse-pragmatic

---

[7] A head-marking language will generally have two cross-referencing series of affixes in the verb (one for SA and one for O in an accusative language; one for SO and one for A in an ergative language), and often also a pronominal affix to a noun, indicating 'possessor'. Quite frequently, the possessive series has the same or similar form to one of the verbal affix series. It has been suggested (see Hofling 1990 and references therein) that in head-marking ergative languages the possessor series on nouns is likely to be related to the A series on verbs. Allen (1964) gives a number of examples along these lines; for instance, prefixes from the A series for Abaza (given in part at (15) in §3.1.3 above) are used to mark possession; he also gives examples of connections between SA affixes and possessors in accusative languages such as Hungarian. But there are examples of SO marking on verbs in an ergative language being similar to possessive markers on nouns – in Kamaiurá from the Tupí-Guaraní family (Seki 1990) and in Jabutí, an isolate spoken in Brazil (Pires 1992). And there are accusative languages in which the O series on verbs also marks possession with nouns, e.g. this applies for all except first person singular in Hebrew (see Aikhenvald 1990: 58; Cohen and Zafrani 1968: 205–7; Glinert 1989: 51–2). (And see note 2 to Chapter 4, on Tunica.) It thus seems that all possibilities are attested for identity between possessive marking on nouns and a cross-referencing pronominal series on verbs. This is a matter that would repay detailed study: there may be some statistical correlation; but it is certain that there is no implicational connection.

make-up of each of a sample of languages, and study the way in which this determines (or partly determines) its grammatical profile.

An illustration of the sort of thing I mean can be given by comparing Dyirbal and Yidin^y, neighbouring languages from north-east Queensland on which I have worked intensively. Both have split-ergative morphology with, roughly, first and second person pronouns inflecting in an accusative and nouns inflecting in an ergative system. At the syntactic level, Dyirbal has a straightforward S/O pivot for coordination and for relativisation (see §§1.2, 6.2.2). Yidin^y, in contrast, has an S/A pivot for coordination involving a first or second person pronoun and an S/O pivot for coordination involving a noun (§6.2.4). Why this difference between the languages in the syntax of coordination? For relativisation, Yidin^y uses an S/O pivot, whether the relative clause is founded on a noun or on a pronoun. Why this difference between coordination and subordination in Yidin^y? If it employs a split pivot in the first case, why not carry this over into relativisation (making the syntactic pivot always iconic with case marking)?

There are explanations. The first concerns a matter seldom attended to by grammarians, that of discourse style. Dyirbal narrative style is quite close to that of English – a narrator sets the scene and refers to the characters in the third person, being sure to quote exactly any significant dialogue between them. (I have never encountered a Dyirbal story – as opposed to a reminiscence – in which the narrator assumes the role of a/the central character.)

In contrast, Yidin^y stories typically involve the principal character serving as narrator, with the whole tale being given a 'first person' slant. There may be a few sentences at the beginning told in the third person – these set the scene and introduce the main character, who thereafter takes over the narrative. If the central character changes, the narrator will shift (still remaining in the first person); the first narrator will introduce the arrival of the second character and then silently relinquish his meta-role to him. This can be exemplified by an extract from a text published in full in Dixon (1991b: 44–8; the line numbers of the full text are retained; note that each line is a 'pivot chain' recognised in intonational criteria). The story is about the time when speakers of Yidin^y first came into their present-day territory. The narrator began by taking on the identity of Gulmbira, an old Yidin^y man who travelled around the country naming places. Half-way through the text he gets sick, and then dies:

(37) *ŋayu gali-in^y ŋayu wula-an^y*
I+S go-PAST I+S die-PAST
I've gone, I'm dead

(38) *gindaja-ŋgu   ŋan^{y}an^y buji-in^y 'n^{y}undu gali-n, wula-n'*
cassowary-ERG I+O   tell-PAST you+S go-IMP die-IMP
The Cassowary told me: 'You go! Die!'

(39) *gindaaja   gali-in^y*
cassowary+ABS go-PAST
The Cassowary went

(40) *baŋgilan-n^{y}a wawa-ali-n^{y}u wala   gali-in^y*
Name-ACC   SEE-GO-PAST   FINISHED   go-PAST
[He] went to look for Banggilan [but couldn't see him since Banggilan had] already gone

(41) *ŋayu yiŋgu guya   wuja-ana,   ŋayu*
I+S HERE ACROSS cross-PURPOSIVE I+S
   gana waŋgi bayi-ili-na,   ŋayu gali+in^y
   TRY UP   emerge-GO-PURP I+S go+PAST
   gaŋgu+juŋga-an^y
   take short cut-PAST
I must try to cross over the river here. I must try to come out uphill. I went, and took a short-cut.

Sentence (38) is the last one in which the narrator assumes the role of Gulmbira. This sentence introduces Gindaja, the Cassowary (another ancestral character). Lines (39) and (40) are told in the third person (there is no A NP stated for (40) but it is understood to be the Cassowary). Then, from (41) until the end of the story, the narrator takes on the identity of the Cassowary. This style of first person narrative is common to all the Yidin^y storytellers I recorded (and note that the two major consultants belonged to different branches of the tribe, and had never had any contact with each other).

As a result, first person (and second person) pronouns are extraordinarily frequent in Yidin^y texts, occurring two to four times as often as first and second person pronouns in Dyirbal texts. This is certainly a reason why coordination in Yidin^y depends upon identification of S = A for pronouns (following their morphological form) but of S = O for nouns (also following their morphological form), whereas Dyirbal employs an

S/O pivot for all kinds of coordination (this accords with the morphological form of nouns, but is out of step with that of pronouns).

Turning now to relativisation, we can note that a main function is to restrict the reference of a head noun (e.g. 'the man who lives next door'). Singular pronouns are fully specified and cannot take a restrictive relative clause. Relative clauses are always rare with singular pronouns. They do occur in Yidin[y] and in Dyirbal (one can say, literally, 'I, who was laughing, sat down'); they are not found at all in many languages, including English (one would instead have to say something like *I sat down while I was laughing*, employing a temporal clause). This was mentioned, in §4.4, as part of the explanation for why relative clauses generally have ergative grammar when there is a split between clause types. It helps to explain why Yidin[y] has a simple S/O pivot for relativisation (where the common NP is only rarely a pronoun) but a split pivot for coordination (where the common NP is very often a pronoun).

Investigation of why the grammar of a particular language shows a certain sort of ergativity will have to pay attention to matters such as discourse style, and probably to other aspects of the way in which the language is used within its society. These are likely to provide some motivation for grammatical orientation, in addition to the fairly universal pragmatic, semantic and syntactic factors that will be recapitulated in the next section.

Future work should also pay attention to more subtle matters, such as when a speaker of an ergative language will employ a transitive construction, with ergative marking on the A NP, and when he may prefer to use an alternative construction type. Duranti (1990) has conducted an illuminating study of this question in the context of formal meetings on Samoa. He finds that transitive clauses, with the A NP marked by ergative particle *e*, are typically used when the referent of the A NP is 'being held or made accountable for some act of doing something' (they are typically used of the Christian God). When a speaker wishes to moderate an accusation, for instance, he may instead use a nominalised clause (in which the A NP is marked as genitive) or else a 'from' marker, e.g. 'the petition from Savea has been filed' rather than 'Savea (ERGATIVE) has filed the petition.'

Duranti shows how the frequency of use of ergative agents indicates the political weight of various members of the local council, i.e. the extent to which each member is prepared to make unequivocal statements of agency relates to his political status in the community. He notes that the most powerful leader in the community uses more ergative agents than anyone else. As Duranti points out 'language does not simply reflect the world, it also shapes it, fashions it'. More studies of this kind, in communities using accusative as well as ergative languages, are needed if we are to understand the full pragmatic significance of different types of grammatical alignment, and how these may develop and change.

8.3   Summary

I began, in Chapter 2, by drawing attention to the existence of languages where grammatical marking directly describes the semantics of a particular situation. Case labels such as nominative, accusative, absolutive and ergative are not properly applicable to such languages, and they do not fall within the scope of this study. The notions of ergativity and accusativity apply only to familiar languages, with what I call syntactically based marking, where case affixes, cross-referencing, etc. relate to the roles of NPs in the prototypical instance of use of a verb.

My basic assumption is that there are three universal syntactic–semantic primitives, S, A and O, that apply to verbal clauses in all languages. (There are of course alternative assumptions that other grammarians have employed. I know of none that could state or explain the facts for the wide range of languages that are reported in this book, in the way that the S–A–O approach can.)

An underlying structure involves the simple root form of a verb, to which no derivational processes have applied (these are typically marked by a derivational affix or other morphological process to the root, or some periphrastic element, or a shift in constituent order); an active construction in an accusative language is an example of an underlying structure. Derivations can then apply – passive, antipassive, causative and so on – forming derived structures; they change the assignment of syntactic functions to NPs.

An underlying canonical intransitive clause will have one core NP which is allocated to S syntactic function. In an underlying transitive clause there are two or more core NPs, one of which is assigned to A and another to O function. There is a semantic basis to this assignment of functions. That NP which is most relevant to the success of the activity is placed in A function; most frequently, this NP has human reference, and the condition can then be stated more specifically as 'could initiate or control the activity'. If there are just two core NPs then the one not assigned to A will be placed in O function. If there are more than two, that one most saliently affected by the activity will go into O. (Some languages have alternative construction types for ditransitive verbs, allowing each non-A argument to be in O slot, with different semantic emphases, e.g. English *load the wagon with timber* and *load timber into the wagon*).

A main task of the grammar of each language is to distinguish between A and O. This can be achieved by case marking, use of adpositions or particles, cross-referencing on the verb (or on some other clause constituent), contrastive constituent order, or by a combination of these means. There will be some marking for each of A, O and S. All of these functions may be marked differently – the 'tripartite' system – but this is in fact rare. Generally, S is marked either like A or like O. If case marking is employed, 'nominative' is the name for the case covering S and A and 'accusative' for that covering O, or 'absolutive' for the case covering S and O and 'ergative' for that covering A. When other mechanisms of marking are used, what were originally case labels can be extended to them, e.g. a verbal prefix cross-referencing S on an intransitive and A on a transitive can be called the nominative series, and a prefix cross-referencing O the accusative series; and so on. If one case has unmarked realisation it is always absolutive in an absolutive–ergative system and usually (but not invariably) nominative in a nominative– accusative system. For brevity, we can talk of 'accusative' and 'ergative' systems, and describe a language showing one of these systems as having 'accusativity' or 'ergativity'.

Some languages are fully accusative but many (perhaps about one quarter of the languages in the world) show some ergative characteristics. No language has so far been reported that is fully ergative; that is, having an exclusively ergative system of intra-causal marking on core arguments, and also an exclusively S/O pivot for inter-clausal operations such as coordination and subordination.

There are various ways in which ergativity splits are conditioned. They all relate to the fact that an NP in A function refers to a participant who initiates or controls the activity, and the NP in O function to a non-controller. For some intransitive verbs the S NP is always the controller, for some never the controller, and for others sometimes the controller. An accusative system emphasises the fact that S is sometimes a controller, and links S with A; an ergative system emphasises that S is not always the controller and links S with O.

An ergativity split can be conditioned by the semantics of any clause constituent or category. It can be according to the semantics of the verb – those intransitive verbs whose S is always or usually the controller have the S marked like A, and those whose S is seldom or never the controller have their S marked like O (a split-S system). Note, however, that although there is always an original semantic basis to the split, it has in each case been grammaticised, and there are thus some semantic exceptions. (Where this is not the case we have a rather different kind of language, with a fluid-S system, involving semantically based marking just with intransitive verbs.) Similar comments about 'exceptions' apply for the other varieties of split.

Another important type of split is according to the semantics of NPs: those most likely to be controllers (pronouns, nouns with human reference) are most likely to show accusative grammar, and those less likely to be controllers (non-human, and especially inanimate, nouns) are more likely to show an ergative grammatical system. A Nominal Hierarchy explains most splits of this kind, when taken together with the observation that sometimes more grammatical distinctions are made in singular than in non-singular numbers (almost never the reverse).

There can also be a split according to tense, aspect or mood. The matter of control is generally looked upon as most relevant for action in progress, or predicted for the future, or ordered to be done (this yields an accusative profile) and less relevant for actions which are completed, in the past (an ergative scheme). A split may also be conditioned by the grammatical status of clauses – a relative clause is likely to describe something that has happened, and which relates to a noun (not a pronoun); this engenders an ergative grammar. A purposive ('in order to') or an imperative construction relates to the agent's control, and is likely to show accusative grammar.

All of these splits provide stable grammatical systems, each having its own strengths with respect to the role of the grammar in reflecting the semantics of a situation. There can be splits based on any combination of these factors (i.e. relating simultaneously to the semantics of several clause constituents). What we would not expect to be stable would be a grammatical system in which A and O are marked in the same way and S in some different way; such a system has been reported for the Iranian language Rushan (§7.2) but it is – as would be expected – in process of change.

All languages have some means of marking S, A and O within a clause and can thus be characterised in terms of the accusative/ergative typological parameter at the intra-clausal level. Some – but not all – languages have syntactic conditions on (some or all) types of complex sentence constructions, involving coordination and subordination. There may be conditions on what syntactic function a certain NP is in within each clause of the construction, either to enable the construction to be formed or else to allow the omission of one occurrence of a repeated NP. Some languages that show such constraints on inter-clausal linking treat S and O in the same way (an S/O syntactic pivot), others treat S and A in the same way (an S/A pivot), while others employ both kinds of pivot, in a split system. All languages with an S/O pivot – they can be termed syntactically ergative – also show some ergativity at the morphological or intra-clausal level. But many languages that show morphological ergativity are syntactically accusative, with an entirely S/A pivot.

The term subject, as traditionally used for languages of the accusative type, involves a combination of semantic and syntactic criteria. The traditional term cannot be unambiguously applied to ergative languages since the two kinds of criteria yield different results. Some scholars define 'subject' for an ergative language on syntactic grounds (and it is then semantically quite different from the subject in an accusative language) while others give precedence to semantic criteria (with a consequent lack of syntactic correspondence to subject in an accusative language). The terms 'underlying (or deep) subject' and 'surface subject' have also been used. These will relate to comparable sets of functions in accusative languages but to quite different ones in a language with ergative syntax.

It is in view of this – and to avoid possible ambiguity and confusion – that in this book I reserve 'subject' as a cover label for underlying A and S, having noted that there are universal semantic links between these two syntactic–semantic primitives. And I employ the term 'pivot', at the level of derived structure, in place of 'surface subject'.

There are a number of universal grammatical features that relate to my category of subject: in an imperative, S or A is likely to be second person; verbs like 'can' and 'try' require the same subject as the verb they relate to; in a reflexive construction it is always the subject that can be grammatical controller. A section of a discourse will be organised around a nominal or pronominal 'theme', which is typically in S or A function in each clause. This property of discourse theme, and the universal category of subject, both relate to the same basic notion of 'controller'.

There are also ways in which S and O naturally group together. New information is most likely to be introduced into a discourse in S or O function. Verbs may have varying senses depending on the identity of an S or O (but not an A) NP. In some languages verbs have different forms depending on whether the S or O (but never the A) NP is singular or plural. Nouns which are incorporated into a verb generally come from O or S function.

There are thus some ways in which S is like A, and others in which it is like O. At the lexical level, where a language has ambitransitive (or labile) verbs, some are likely to be of the type S = O (e.g. 'trip') and others of the type S = A (e.g. 'win'). There is thus pragmatic and semantic pressure for a grammar to treat S and A in the same way (an accusative system) and also for it to treat S and O in the same way (an ergative system), or to combine these possibilities. It is surely in view of these pressures that there are so few tripartite systems, where all of S, A and O are treated differently.

A language in daily use is always changing in some way or other; change in one area can engender changes in some other part of the language. A phonological change could bring into being an ergative arrangement, as it were by accident (see note 2 to Chapter 1), or else might require some change that could shift the grammatical profile. We remarked in §7.2 that the ancestor of modern Pama-Nyungan languages, in Australia, is reconstructed to have had monosyllabic forms for first and second person pronouns in S function. When some of its descendants adopted the convention that each word should consist of at least two syllables, two alternatives were followed (each by a different group of languages). Either a dummy syllable was added to the original monosyllabic form, retaining the tripartite system for singular pronouns; or the disyllabic A forms were generalised also to cover S, providing an accusative paradigm for singular pronouns, in accord with that already in existence for non-singular pronouns. And we saw in §7.1 that a discourse strategy – fronting S and O NPs – is believed to have brought into being an ergative system in some Nilotic languages.

The various types of split system (and the pure accusative one) are all viable and stable. But each can change into one of the other types. Past participles are typically passive in orientation and as a language loses inflections (in moving around the cycle of change) it is likely to innovate periphrastic constructions; those for perfect aspect or past tense are likely to be based on a passive-type participle and may be the genesis for an ergative system in this aspect/tense.

A passive derivation can feed an S/A pivot and is thus typically found in languages with accusative syntax; an antipassive derivation can feed an

S/O pivot and is thus typically found in languages with ergative syntax. But there are other functions of passive and antipassive so that these derivations do occur in languages with no syntactic pivot; both of them (sometimes several varieties of both) can occur in one language, of any linguistic type. Since a discourse theme is typically in S or A function, a language with an S/O pivot should have an antipassive; there is not the same absolute necessity for a passive in a language with an S/A pivot.

In §7.2 we showed how, in a language with ergative case marking (on nouns) and an S/O pivot, the antipassive construction can – over time – come to be adopted as the basic construction for transitive verbs; this would yield a fully accusative morphology, and also accusative syntax, with an S/A pivot. Thus, an antipassive can give rise to an accusative system, but in a quite different way from that in which a passive gives rise to an ergative system.

Much grammatical change is analogical. There is always a tendency to align morphology and syntax, by making changes at either level. We suggested that in Yidin^y the split pivot for coordination may have evolved to mirror the split morphological marking, while in languages of the Ngayarda group accusative morphology may have been innovated to mirror the accusative syntax. Other generalisations that affect accusativity/ergativity can be from one tense or aspect to others; from one type of NP constituent to others; or for the marking on one syntactic function to be extended to another (A to S or, less frequently, O to S). We saw, in §7.1, that the Hittite ergative is believed to have come about through the reinterpretation of a peripheral case as a core one.

Languages also show a tendency to become more like their neighbours in the same geographical region. Some of the ergative characteristics of modern Indic languages (from the Indo-European family) in northern India may have developed under diffusional pressure from neighbouring Tibeto-Burman languages which have an ergative profile (see Zakharyin 1979).

At the simplest level, accusative and ergative structures differ grammatically in that A and O play opposite roles – in an accusative system A is treated like S, and O differently; while in an ergative system O is treated like S, and A differently. But, as the examples and discussion in this book have shown, these systems are far from being exact complements. They each have fairly individual grammatical and semantic properties. I have described the pragmatic, semantic and syntactic links between S and A, and the rather different links between S and O. We might infer that the S/A links must be stronger and more important from the fact that there are many languages with no trace of ergativity, whereas no language lacks a degree of accusativity. But the S/O links are significant and are accorded a role in that fair-sized minority of languages that show some ergative characteristics in their grammar.

8.4   *Envoi*

Finally, we can ask what lessons are to be learnt, from this study of ergativity, for our understanding of what language is, how a language works, and what a linguistic theory of language should include.

The most important point is that a language can only profitably be studied as a whole. One must recognise and distinguish different levels of structural organisation – phonological, morphological, syntactic, semantic, discourse and pragmatic – but each of these continuously interrelates with the others. Someone who specialises in just one or two of these levels will never achieve revealing linguistic description or explanation. All of the levels must be considered, together with the ways in which they interrelate. A phonological change may set off a morphological realignment, which affects the ways in which core syntactic relations are marked, and the consequences of this – in certain semantic circumstances and for particular kinds of discourse – may lead to syntactic realignment. The inter-dependencies between the components of a full linguistic description have been exemplified at many points in this book. At the present time, linguistics has little need for further theories, just of syntax, or just of discourse organisation, or just of semantics. Rather the future development of the discipline requires the development of an integrated theory of language, viewed as a holistic phenomenon.

We then need informed descriptions of particular languages within such a theory. There are several thousand languages still spoken in the world, belonging to perhaps 200 distinct language families. The majority of languages are endangered – only a few hundred are likely to be still spoken in a hundred years' time. Good and adequate grammars are available for perhaps a few score languages; grammars of at least mediocre quality have been provided for less than half of the languages currently spoken. If every person who called themself a linguist settled down to provide a full description of a single previously undescribed language, then he or she would justify the title. This is not an easy task. It invariably demands extended field work, often in difficult circumstances; but it is – as I and others have found – the most satisfying and rewarding of tasks.

Description of the full range of human languages is needed if we are to achieve a complete understanding of the nature of human language. For instance, my 1979 paper 'Ergativity' included a number of generalisations based on structural patterns found in the languages of Europe, Asia, Oceania, Africa and North America. At that time little had been published on patterns of ergativity in the numerous languages of South America. I have now learned a fair amount about languages from that continent with the result that my generalisations and conclusions have been thoroughly revised and extended. (However, much more work is still needed on the languages of South America, of Papua New Guinea and of Africa, in particular.)

More specific lessons to be learnt from this book include the need to draw a clear distinction between different levels of linguistic organisation. For instance, syntax and semantics must be distinguished; one should provide syntactic criteria for setting up syntactic categories and structures, and semantic criteria for semantic constructs. There is a correlation between levels, but this can only properly be studied and appreciated if the levels have been clearly identified.

As pointed out in Chapter 2, one must first distinguish between languages in which the marking of core arguments of a verb is semantically based and those in which it is syntactically based. Within syntax, the most vital step is the identification of basic grammatical relations S, A and O, and their role and realisation in a given language. Failure to do this can result in unclarity and vagueness. For instance, some writers of grammars mention a class of ambitransitive or labile verbs, each of which can be used both intransitively and transitively. However, there are two quite different kinds of ambitransitive verb, those for which S = A (e.g. English *win*) and those for which S = O (e.g. *break*). Most writers fail to say whether their ambitransitives are of type S = A or of type S = O or a mixture of the types (and, in the last case, to go on to investigate the semantic basis of the division).

In every language (even those that are highly accusative), the recognition of basic relations S, A and O leads to the uncovering of important generalisations that would not otherwise have come to notice. Each individual grammar should be cast in terms of universally-applicable categories (such as S, A and O) so that its structure can readily be compared with those of other languages. This will assist us in establishing genetic relationships between languages (for which comparison of grammatical categories and their realisations is of great importance) and in the reconstruction of proto-languages. It will also assist in the most important task of all, the inductive formulation of a typological theory of what language is, how it functions, and how and why it changes.

Appendix: *A note on theoretical models*

There has been a vogue during recent decades for the formulation of theoretical models in linguistics. These are sometimes suggested on the basis of data in a very limited set of languages, but are then put forth as general accounts of how all human languages operate. When unexpected data from new languages come to notice there can be a number of reactions: ignore it; reinterpret the data so that it fits the theory; revise the theory so that it does explain the data; acknowledge that the theory cannot explain the data and as a consequence abandon it.

In this short Appendix I shall comment on some of the ways in which some theoretical models have approached ergativity. My treatment is partial and selective; a full discussion of this topic would require a book in itself.

Foley and Van Valin's (1984) Role and Reference Grammar (RRG) is one of the few theoretical models to have been formulated with full knowledge of a range of ergative phenomena. Their discussion of syntactic ergativity, pivots, passives and antipassives is informed and useful. My one reservation is that they do not always make a sufficiently clear distinction between syntax and semantics, sometimes talking about syntactic operations applying to semantic categories (I prefer to specify that syntactic operations apply to syntactic categories and then to discuss the semantic correlates of both the categories and the operations.) Lexical Functional Grammar (LFG) has also paid some attention to the various kinds of ergativity; see, for instance Kroeger (1991a, b) for an LFG treatment of ergativity in Tagalog.

Early work by Chomsky and his followers paid only a little attention to ergative patterns in grammar. De Rijk (1966) did propose a perceptive analysis of Basque, suggesting that the first constituent split for a clause in that language be into Verb Phrase and an NP in S or O function, with a transitive Verb Phrase then including, as a constituent, the A

NP.¹ However, De Rijk's ideas were not at the time integrated into Chomskian theory.

More recently, Marantz (1984) noted the parallelism between the assignment of S and A to nominative and O to accusative (in a nominative–accusative language) and the assignment of S and O to absolutive and A to ergative (in an absolutive–ergative system), and built this into his 'ergativity hypothesis', in the context of Chomsky's Government–Binding (GB) framework. At the D-structure level (this is reminiscent of 'deep structure' in Chomsky 1965) he defines:

	In a syntactically accusative language	*In a syntactically ergative language*
D-subject	S and A	S and O
D-object	O	A

Then, passive in a syntactically accusative language and antipassive in a syntactically ergative language will coincide.

This effectively assumes that all languages have either an S/O or an S/A pivot, and that passive occurs only if there is an S/A pivot and antipassive only if there is an S/O pivot. It also assumes that a language with an S/O pivot identifies S and O for all grammatical purposes. In fact, we saw that the universal category of subject – involving underlying S and A – plays a role in the grammar of every language. This could not be acknowledged within Marantz's framework which, for a language like Dyirbal, illicitly projects a derived-structure pivot linking (of S and O) onto underlying structure.

Terminological sleight-of-hand of this sort may help fit some of the data into the framework of a particular grammatical theory; it can only obscure the real differences – discussed throughout this book – between ergative and accusative systems. For instance, the fact that there is more need for an antipassive in a language with S/O pivot than for a passive in one that employs an S/A pivot (since the preferred functions for discourse theme are S and A). It would also be difficult to account – within Marantz's model – for languages that have a 'split syntax', combining both kinds of

---

¹ Seely (1977:192) suggests that de Rijk's paper was an attempt 'to save Chomsky's standard theory'. Dixon (1972: 137ff.) argued for a similar type of constituent structure in the case of Dyirbal. Strong arguments can also be given that Nadëb should be treated in this way (e.g. constituent order is SV or VS and OAV or AVO, where A must immediately precede the verb, but S and O can vary in position – see §3.2). Working in terms of a GB framework, Larsen (1987) suggests that for the Mayan language Quiché both S and O NPs should be dominated by the VP node in S-structure, while the A NP would be dominated by the sentence node.

pivot for different varieties of complex sentence formation (§6.2.4), or for languages that show one or more passive operations and one or more antipassives (§6.1).

Keenan and Comrie (1977) suggested a hierarchy of grammatical relations which describes and explains relativisation strategies across all types of natural language. The only way the facts of a syntactically ergative language like Dyirbal could be accommodated was to take S and O as the underlying 'subject'.[2] This was dealt with in §5.2, as part of my discussion of Keenan's treatment of 'subject' – under this approach, some clauses might have two subjects and some none (see Blake 1976).

In the early 1970s, Postal and Perlmutter put forward a function-based theory called Relational Grammar (RG) – see Perlmutter (1983), Perlmutter and Rosen (1984). This recognises a hierarchy of 'grammatical relations', which they view as primitives:

1. Subject (this corresponds to my S and A)
2. Object (my O)
3. Indirect object...

There are a number of 'laws'. The Relational Annihilation Law states that if NP_i assumes the grammatical relation borne by NP_j, then NP_j ceases to bear any grammatical relation at all (it is said to be a chômeur or en chômage). The Motivated Chômage Law states that chômeurs can arise only as a result of the Relational Annihilation Law. The Reranking Law states that an NP can only be moved up the hierarchy.

This scheme works perfectly for most phenomena in accusative languages (where the sole syntactic pivot is S/A). Thus the passive rule puts the original 1 (A NP) into chômage and raises the original 2 (O NP) to 1 (it is now in S function, since there is now no O and the sentence is intransitive).[3]

However, substantial difficulties arise with ergative languages and antipassives. The antipassive derivation involves underlying A becoming derived S, and O going into chômage. RG cannot handle this in terms of the hierarchy given above. O cannot go into chômage unless something replaces it, and only something from below can replace it. Obviously, some law must be dropped. The simplest change would be to relax the 'motivated

---

[2] Fox (1987) has an illuminating discussion of this issue, showing that relative clauses are more common to O or S NPs than to A NPs.

[3] Comments in parentheses are added by me. In their early writings on this theory, Postal and Perlmutter made no mention of transitivity, nor did they perceive any distinction between A and S.

chômage' requirement; if O is allowed to go spontaneously into limbo, as it were, the absence of a term 2 would lead automatically to the underlying A NP being interpreted as derived S (still remaining 1) in what is now a derived intransitive antipassive construction.[4]

The difficulty with the RG hierarchy is that it conflates semantic 'subject' with syntactic 'pivot'. Although it is set up to explain syntactic relations (which relate to pivot, not subject), Perlmutter and Postal require term 1 always to be subject (i.e. {S, A}) – thus imposing a valid universal category at the level of underlying structure onto *every* syntactic level. A more appropriate course would be to explain syntactic phenomena in syntactic terms, and to recognise two distinct types of hierarchy:

Hierarchy A	Hierarchy B
1. Pivot (S, A)	1. Pivot (S, O)
2. Non-pivot core NP (O)	2. Non-pivot core NP (A) ...

Now antipassive works in terms of B as neatly as passive does in terms of A, and does conform to Postal and Perlmutter's three laws.[5]

Somewhat later, Perlmutter (1978) considered intransitive verbs and their relationship to transitives, employing the terms 'unaccusative' (this implies there is a 2, i.e. object, but no 1, i.e. subject) and 'unergative' (here there is a 1 but no 2). These labels are used to describe a wide range of phenomena including ambitransitive verbs (the S = O type is said to be 'unaccusative' and the S = A type 'unergative') and also the marking on S in split-S languages. In connection with Dakota, for instance, 'unergative' is used for what I call S_a and 'unaccusative' for S_o (see §4.1.1).

[4] There appears to be no a priori semantic or syntactic motivation for any of the three laws. They have been put forward as putative components of a hypothetical 'grammatical theory' (in much the same way that mathematicians define a new system in terms of a set of axioms), and appear to work well for some languages. Attempts have then been made to fit the facts of other languages into this (in essence, arbitrary and unmotivated) framework.

Postal (1977) suggested a different derivation for 'antipassive'. Preferring apparently to relax the Reranking Law and retain the Motivated Chômage Law (although no reason is given as to why Motivated Chômage should be considered more important than Reranking), he suggests that the A NP replace O, pushing it en chômage; since term 1 is then vacant, the term 2 NP (underlying A) ascends to it. This implies a derivation A → O → S; there is no justification of any sort for the intermediate step. (But see Davies and Sam-Colop 1990.)

Davies (1984, 1986) discusses what he calls 'antipassive' in Choctaw. However, this only applies to four verbs and is surely better regarded as an alternative case frame than as a productive grammatical derivation.

[5] The two-hierarchy approach was suggested by Johnson (1974), but appears to have been abandoned by him in 1976. Woodbury (1977) shows the most sophisticated approach to dealing with ergative phenomena in RG terms; his detailed discussion, with particular reference to Eskimo, has considerable similarities to the approach suggested here.

Perlmutter then suggests that since, by another 'law', every clause must have a final 1, we need to require that 'every clause with an unaccusative stratum involves an advancement to 1'. This treats S_o like O at one level, but like A and S_a at another, and does allow explanation of the unitary functions of S (the sum of S_a and S_o) when these are held in common with A (as Harris 1982 demonstrates for Georgian). But there is no mechanism for treating properties of $S_a + S_o$ which group with O, rather than with A, or which differ from properties of A and of O.

Some theorists shy away from any mention of ergativity. Others provide a mechanism for dealing with some of the more superficial aspects of ergative systems. There have been few serious attempts to modify an existing theory to account for the full panoply of facts concerning ergativity (as described in this book), or to devise a theory which will cover accusative and ergative languages with equal facility and plausibility. Any such theory would have to recognise that there are three basic syntactic–semantic primitives (A, S and O) rather than just two ('subject' and 'object' – however these are defined), and it would have to distinguish between the universal underlying-structure grouping of S and A (which underlies part of the grammar of every language) and language-particular pivots, S/A and S/O; and so on.

References

The following abbreviations are used:

AJL	*Australian Journal of Linguistics*
BLS	*Proceedings of the Annual Meetings of the Berkeley Linguistics Society*
BSOAS	*Bulletin of the School of Oriental and African Studies, University of London*
CLS	*Papers from the Regional Meetings of the Chicago Linguistic Society*
IJAL	*International Journal of American Linguistics*
JL	*Journal of Linguistics*
JML	*Journal of Mayan Linguistics*
JPS	*Journal of the Polynesian Society*
Lg	*Language*
LI	*Linguistic Inquiry*
LLM	*Language and Linguistics in Melanesia* (formerly *Kivung*)
OL	*Oceanic Linguistics*
SAL	*Studies in African Linguistics*
SL	*Studies in Language*
TPS	*Transactions of the Philological Society*

Abbott, M. 1991. 'Macushi', pp. 23–160 of Derbyshire and Pullum, 1991.

Adelaar, K. A. Forthcoming. 'The classification of the Tamanic languages (West Kalimantan)', to appear in *Contact-induced language change in the Austronesian-speaking area*, edited by T. Dutton and D. Tryon. Berlin: Mouton de Gruyter.

Aikhenvald, A. Y. 1986. 'On the reconstruction of syntactic system in Berber-Lybic', *Zeitschrift für Phonetik, Sprachwissenschaft und Kommunikationsforschung*, 39.527–39.

1990. *Sovremennyj Ivrit* (Modern Hebrew). Moscow: Nauka.

Aikhenvald-Angenot, A. Y. and Angenot, J.-P. 1991. 'Problemas de ergatividade em Arawák', *Anais de V Eucontro Nacional da ANPOLL* (Recife, Brazil), 140–53.

Allen, W. S. 1951. 'A study in the analysis of Hindi sentence structure', *Acta Linguistica Hafniensa*, 6.68–86.

1956. 'Structure and system in the Abaza verbal complex', *TPS*, 127–76.

1960. 'Notes on the Rājāsthanī verb', *Indian Linguistics*, 21.1–10.

1964. 'Transitivity and possession', *Lg*, 40.337–43.

237

Andersen, P. K. 1987. 'Zero-anaphora and related phenomena in Classical Tibetan', *SL*, 11.279–312.

Andersen, T. 1988. 'Ergativity in Päri, a Nilotic OVS language', *Lingua*, 75.289–324.

Anderson, J. M. 1968. 'Ergative and nominative in English', *JL*, 4.1–32.

Anderson, N. and Wade, M. 1988. 'Ergativity and control in Folopa', *LLM*, 19.1–16.

Anderson, S. R. 1976. 'On the notion of subject in ergative languages', pp. 1–23 of Li, 1976.

1977. 'On mechanisms by which languages become ergative', pp. 317–63 of Li, 1977.

Arlotto, A. 1972. *Introduction to historical linguistics*. Boston: Houghton Mifflin.

Austin, P. 1981a. *A grammar of Diyari, South Australia*. Cambridge: Cambridge University Press.

1981b. 'Switch-reference in Australia', *Lg*, 57.309–34.

1981c. 'Case marking in southern Pilbara languages', *AJL*, 1.211–26.

Ayers, G. 1983. 'The antipassive "voice" in Ixil', *IJAL*, 49.20–45.

Baker, M. C. 1988. *Incorporation, a theory of grammatical function changing*. Chicago: University of Chicago Press.

Bani, E. and Klokeid, T. J. 1976. 'Ergative switching in Kala Lagau Langgus', pp. 269–83 of Sutton, 1976.

Bashir, E. 1986. 'Beyond split-ergativity: subject marking in Wakhi', *CLS*, 22.14–35.

Baugh, A. C. 1959. *A history of the English language*, 2nd edn. London: Routledge and Kegan Paul.

Bauman, J. J. 1979. 'An historical perspective on ergativity in Tibeto-Burman', pp. 419–34 of Plank, 1979.

Bender, M. L. 1976. *The non-Semitic languages of Ethiopia*. East Lansing: Michigan State University.

Bennett, D., Bynon, T. and Hewitt, G. (eds.) Forthcoming. *Essays on voice and ergativity*.

Benveniste, E. 1952. 'La construction passive du parfait transitif', *Bulletin de la Société de Linguistique*, 48.52–62. (Translated in his *Problems in general linguistics*, pp. 153–61. Coral Gables: University of Miami Press, 1971.)

Bhat, D. N. S. 1988. *Grammatical relations in Indian languages*. Mysore: Central Institute of Indian Languages.

1991. *Grammatical relations: the evidence against their necessity and universality*. London: Routledge.

ms. Core functions in Manipuri.

Bhat, D. N. S. and Ningomba, M. S. ms. 'Case marking'. (Chapter 4 of draft Manipuri grammar.)

Bittner, M. 1987. 'On the semantics of the Greenlandic antipassive and related constructions', *IJAL*, 53.194–231.

Blake, B. J. 1976. 'On ergativity and the notion of subject: some Australian cases', *Lingua*, 39.281–300.

1978. 'From semantic to syntactic antipassive in Kalkatungu', *OL*, 17.163–9.

1979a. 'Pitta-pitta', pp. 183–242 of Dixon and Blake, 1979.

1979b. *A Kalkatungu grammar*. Canberra: Pacific Linguistics.

1982. 'The absolutive: its scope in English and Kalkatungu', pp. 71–94 of Hopper and Thompson, 1982.

1987a. *Australian Aboriginal grammar*. London: Croom Helm.

1987b. 'The grammatical development of Australian languages', *Lingua*, 71.179–201 (= Dixon, 1987).

1988. 'Tagalog and the Manila – Mount Isa axis', *La Trobe Working Papers in Linguistics*, 1.77–90.

Bloch, J. 1965. *Indo-Aryan* (English edition by A. Master). Paris: Maisonneuve.

Boas, F. 1911. 'Tsimshian', pp. 283–422 of *Handbook of American Indian Languages*, Part 1, edited by F. Boas. Washington: Smithsonian Institution.

Boas, F. and Deloria, E. 1939. *Dakota grammar* (Memoirs of the National Academy of Science, 23). Washington: Government Printing Office.

Boelaars, J. H. M. C. 1950. *The linguistic position of south-western New Guinea*. Leiden: E. J. Brill.

Bollenbacher, J. 1977. 'The Basque passive', pp. 181–92 of *Anglo-American contributions to Basque studies*, edited by W. A. Douglass et al. Reno: University of Nevada Desert Research Institute.

Borgman, D. M. 1990. 'Sanuma', pp. 15–248 of Derbyshire and Pullum, 1990.

Bossong, G. 1984. 'Ergativity in Basque', *Linguistics*, 22.341–92.

Breen, J. G. 1976. 'Ergative, locative and instrumental case inflections – Wangkumara', pp. 336–9 of Dixon, 1976.

Brettschneider, G. 1979. 'Typological characteristics of Basque', pp. 371–84 of Plank, 1979.

Bricker, V. R. 1978. 'Antipassive constructions in Yucatec Maya', pp. 3–24 of *Papers in Mayan Linguistics* (University of Missouri Miscellaneous Publications in Anthropology No. 6, Studies in Mayan Linguistics No. 2), edited by N. C. England. Columbia, Missouri.

1979. 'WH-questions, relativisation and clefting in Yucatec Maya', pp. 107–36 of *Papers in Mayan linguistics*, edited by L. Martin. Columbia, Missouri: Lucas Brothers.

1981. 'The source of the ergative split in Yucatec Maya', *JML*, 2.83–127.

1986. *A grammar of Mayan hieroglyphs*. Tulane University, New Orleans: Middle American Research Institute.

Bromley, H. M. 1981. *A grammar of Lower Grand Valley Dani*. Canberra: Pacific Linguistics.

Bull, W. E. 1960. *Time, tense and the verb: a study in theoretical and applied linguistics, with particular attention to Spanish.* (University of California Publications in Linguistics, 19). Berkeley and Los Angeles: University of California Press.

Burrow, T. and Bhattacharya, S. 1970. *The Pengo language*. Oxford: Clarendon Press.

Burzio, L. 1981. 'Intransitive verbs and Italian auxiliaries', PhD dissertation, MIT.

Buth, R. 1981. 'Ergative word order – Luwo is OVS', *Occasional Papers in the Study of Sudanese Languages*, 1.74–90. (Juba: SIL.)

Byington, C. 1870. 'Grammar of the Choctaw language', *Proceedings of the American Philosophical Society*, 11.317–67.

Bynon, T. 1980. 'From passive to ergative in Kurdish via the ergative construction', pp. 151–61 of *Papers from the 4th International Conference on Historical Linguistics*, edited by E. C. Traugott, R. Labrum and S. Shepherd. Amsterdam: John Benjamins.

Camp, E. L. 1985. 'Split ergativity in Cavineña', *IJAL*, 51.38–58.

Campbell, L. and Mithun, M. (eds.) 1979. *The languages of Native America: a historical and comparative assessment*. Austin: University of Texas Press.

Capell, A. 1962. *Some linguistic types in Australia* (Oceanic Linguistic Monographs, 7). Sydney: Oceania Publications.

  1969. *A survey of New Guinea languages*. Sydney: University of Sydney Press.

Cardona, G. 1970. 'The Indo-Iranian construction *mana* (*mama*) kṛtam', *Lg*, 46.1–12.

Cena, R. M. 1977. 'Patient primacy in Tagalog', paper presented to LSA Annual Meeting, Chicago.

  1979. 'Tagalog counterexamples to the accessibility hierarchy', *Studies in Philippine Linguistics*, 3.119–24.

Černý, V. 1971. 'Some remarks on syntax and morphology of verb in Avar', *Archiv Orientální*, 39.46–56.

Chafe, W. L. 1970. *A semantically based sketch of Onondaga* (Indiana University Publications in Anthropology and Linguistics, Memoir 25). Bloomington, Indiana.

Chaker, S. 1988. 'Annexion (état d') (linguistique)', pp. 686–95 of *Encyclopédie berbère*, V. Aix-en-Provence.

Chang, B. S. and Chang, K. 1980. 'Ergativity in spoken Tibetan', *Bulletin of the Institute of History and Philology, Academia Sinica*, 51.15–32.

Chapman, S. and Derbyshire, D. C. 1991. 'Paumarí', pp. 161–352 of Derbyshire and Pullum, 1991.

Chappell, H. 1980. 'Is the *get*-passive adversative?', *Papers in Linguistics*, 13.411–52.

Charachidzé, G. 1981. *Grammaire de la langue Avar* (*langue de Caucase Nord-Est*) (Document de linguistique quantitative, No. 38). Editions Jean-Favard.

Chomsky, N. 1965. *Aspects of the theory of syntax*. Cambridge, Mass.: MIT Press.

Chung, S. 1977. 'On the gradual nature of linguistic change', pp. 3–55 of Li, 1977.

  1978. *Case marking and grammatical relations in Polynesian*. Austin: University of Texas Press.

Churchward, C. M. 1953. *Tongan grammar*. Oxford: Oxford University Press.

Clark, R. 1973. 'Transitivity and case in eastern Oceanic languages', *OL*, 12.559–605.

  1976. *Aspects of proto-Polynesian syntax* (Te Reo Monographs). Auckland: Linguistic Society of New Zealand.

Cohen, D. and Zafrani, H. 1968. *Grammaire de l'hébreu vivant*. Paris: Presses Universitaires de France.

Cole, P. and Sadock, J. M. (eds.) 1977. *Grammatical relations* (Syntax and Semantics, 8). New York: Academic Press.

Collinder, B. 1965. *An introduction to the Uralic languages*. Berkeley and Los Angeles: University of California Press.

Comrie, B. 1975a. 'The antiergative: Finland's answer to Basque', *CLS*, 11.112–21.

1975b. 'Causatives and universal grammar', *TPS for* 1974, 1–32.

1976. *Aspect*. Cambridge: Cambridge University Press.

1978. 'Ergativity', pp. 329–74 of *Syntactic typology: studies in the phenomenology of language*, edited by W. P. Lehmann. Austin: University of Texas Press.

1979. 'Degrees of ergativity: some Chukchee evidence', pp. 219–40 of Plank, 1979.

1981a. *The languages of the Soviet Union*. Cambridge: Cambridge University Press.

1981b. 'Ergativity and grammatical relations in Kalaw Lagaw Ya (Saibai dialect)', *AJL*, 1.1–42.

1982a. 'Grammatical relations in Huichol', pp. 95–115 of Hopper and Thompson, 1982.

1982b. 'Verb agreement in Ket', *Folia Slavica*, 5.115–27.

1989. *Language universals and linguistic typology*, 2nd edn. Oxford: Blackwell.

Constenla, A. 1982. 'Sobre la construcción ergativa en la lengua Guatusa', *Revista de Filología y Lingüística de la Universidad de Costa Rica*, 8.97–101.

Cooreman, A. 1988. 'Ergativity in Dyirbal discourse', *Linguistics*, 26.717–46.

Cooreman, A., Fox, B. and Givón, T. 1984. 'The discourse definition of ergativity', *SL*, 8.1–34.

Craig, C. 1976. 'Properties of basic and derived subjects in Jacaltec', pp. 99–123 of Li, 1976.

1977. *The structure of Jacaltec*. Austin: University of Texas Press.

Creider, C. A. 1975. 'The semantic basis of noun classes in proto-Bantu', *Anthropological Linguistics*, 17.127–38.

Crisp, S. ms. 'Subject marking in some languages of Daghestan'.

Croft, W. 1990. *Typology and universals*. Cambridge: Cambridge University Press.

Crowley, T. 1978. *The middle Clarence dialects of Bandjalang*. Canberra: Australian Institute of Aboriginal Studies.

1981. 'The Mpakwithi dialect of Anguthimri', pp. 146–94 of Dixon and Blake, 1981.

Crystal, D. 1991. *A dictionary of linguistics and phonetics*, 3rd edn. Oxford: Blackwell.

Cumming, S. and Wouk, F. 1987. 'Is there "discourse ergativity" in Austronesian languages?', *Lingua*, 71.271–96. (= Dixon, 1987.)

Dahlstrom, A. 1983. 'Agent–patient languages and split case marking systems', *BLS*, 9.37–46.

Davies, W. D. 1984. 'Antipassive: Choctaw evidence for a universal characterisation', pp. 331–76 of Perlmutter and Rosen, 1984.

1986. *Choctaw verb agreement and universal grammar*. Dordrecht: Reidel.

Davies, W. D. and Sam-Colop, L. E. 1990. 'K'iche' and the structure of antipassive', *Lg*, 66.522–49.

Dayley, J. P. 1978. 'Voice in Tzutujil', *JML*, 1.20–52; a later version appeared as pp. 192–226 of Nichols and Woodbury, 1985.

1985. *Tzutujil grammar* (University of California Publications in Linguistics, 107). Berkeley and Los Angeles: University of California Press.

De Guzman, V. P. 1988. 'Ergative analysis for Philippine languages: an analysis', pp. 323–45 of McGinn, 1988.

Deibler, E. W. 1966. *Semantic relationships of Gahuku verbs.* SIL and Norman: University of Oklahoma.

DeLancey, S. 1981. 'An interpretation of split ergativity and related patterns', *Lg.* 57.626–57.

1985. 'The analysis-synthesis cycle in Tibeto-Burman: a case study in motivated change'. pp. 367–90 of *Iconicity in syntax*, edited by J. Haiman. Amsterdam: John Benjamins.

1987. 'Sino-Tibetan languages', pp. 797–810 of *The world's major languages*, edited by B. Comrie. London: Croom Helm.

1989. 'Verb agreement in proto-Tibeto-Burman', *BSOAS*, 52.315–33.

Dench, A. 1982. 'The development of an accusative case marking pattern in the Ngayarda languages of Western Australia', *AJL*, 2.43–59.

1987. 'Martuthunira: a language of the Pilbara region of Western Australia', PhD thesis. Australian National University (to be published by Pacific Linguistics).

1991. 'Panyjima', pp. 124–243 of Dixon and Blake, 1991.

Denny, J. P. and Creider, C. A. 1976. 'The semantics of noun classes in proto-Bantu', *SAL*, 7.1–30.

Derbyshire, D. C. 1986. 'Comparative survey of morphology and syntax in Brazilian Arawakan', pp. 469–566 of Derbyshire and Pullum 1986.

1987. 'Morphosyntactic areal characteristics of Amazonian languages', *IJAL* 53.311–26.

1991. 'Are Cariban languages moving away from or towards ergative systems?', pp. 1–30 of 1991 *Work Papers of the Summer Institute of Linguistics, North Dakota Session*, Vol. XXXV, edited by R. A. Dooley and S. Quackenbush. Dallas: SIL.

Derbyshire, D. C. and Pullum, G. K. (eds). 1986. *Handbook of Amazonian languages*, Vol. I. Berlin: Mouton de Gruyter.

1990. *Handbook of Amazonian languages*, Vol. II. Berlin: Mouton de Gruyter.

1991. *Handbook of Amazonian languages*, Vol. III. Berlin: Mouton de Gruyter.

De Rijk, R. P. G. 1966. 'Redefining the ergative', unpublished paper, MIT.

Dešeriev, Ju. D. 1953. *Bacbijskij jazyk* (The Batsbi language). Moscow: Nauka.

Diakonoff, I. M. 1988. *Afrasian languages.* Moscow: Nauka.

Diffloth, G. 1976. 'Jah-hut, an Austroasiatic language of Malaysia', pp. 73–118 of *South-east Asian linguistic studies*, edited by N. D. Liem. Canberra: Pacific Linguistics.

Dimmendaal, G. J. 1985. 'Prominence hierarchies and Turkana syntax', pp. 127–48 of *Current approaches to African linguistics*, Vol. III, edited by G. J. Dimmendaal. Dordrecht: Foris.

Dirr, A. 1912. 'Rutulskij jazyk (The Rutul language)', *Sbornik Materialov dlya Opisaniya Plemen Kavkaza* (Tbilisi), 42:3.1–204.

1928. *Einführung in das Studium der kaukasischen Sprachen.* Leipzig: Verlag der Asia Major.

Dixon, R. M. W. 1968. 'The Dyirbal language of North Queensland', PhD thesis, University of London.

1972. *The Dyirbal language of North Queensland.* Cambridge: Cambridge University Press.

(ed.) 1976. *Grammatical categories in Australian languages.* Canberra: Australian Institute of Aboriginal Studies, and New Jersey: Humanities Press.

1977a. *A grammar of Yidiɲ.* Cambridge: Cambridge University Press.

1977b. 'Some phonological rules in Yidinʸ, *LI*, 8.1–34.

1977c. 'The syntactic development of Australian languages', pp. 365–415 of Li, 1977.

1979a. 'Ergativity', *Lg*, 55.59–138.

1979b. 'Comments and corrections concerning Heath's "Is Dyirbal ergative?"', *Linguistics*, 17.1003–15.

1980. *The languages of Australia.* Cambridge: Cambridge University Press.

1981a. 'Wargamay', pp. 1–144 of Dixon and Blake, 1981.

1981b. 'Grammatical reanalysis: an example of linguistic change from Warrgamay (North Queensland)', *AJL*, 1.91–112.

1982. *Where have all the adjectives gone? and other essays in semantics and syntax.* Berlin: Mouton.

(ed.) 1987. *Studies in ergativity.* Amsterdam: North-Holland. (Reissue of *Lingua*, 71.)

1988a. *A grammar of Boumaa Fijian.* Chicago: University of Chicago Press.

1988b. '"Words" in Fijian', pp. 65–71 of *Lexicographical and linguistic studies: essays in honour of G. W. Turner*, edited by T. L. Burton and Jill Burton. Cambridge: D. S. Brewer.

1989. 'Subject and object in universal grammar', pp. 91–118 of *Essays on grammatical theory and universal grammar*, edited by D. Arnold, M. Atkinson, J. Durand, C. Grover and L. Sadler. Oxford: Clarendon Press.

1991a. *A new approach to English grammar, on semantic priniciples.* Oxford: Clarendon Press.

1991b. *Words of our country: stories, place names and vocabulary in Yidiny, the Aboriginal language of the Cairns-Yarrabah region.* St Lucia: University of Queensland Press.

Forthcoming. 'Complement clauses and complementation strategies', Cambridge.

Dixon, R. M. W. and Blake, B. J. (eds.) 1979. *Handbook of Australian languages*, Vol. I. Canberra: ANU Press, and Amsterdam: John Benjamins.

1981. *Handbook of Australian languages*, Vol. II. Canberra: ANU Press, and Amsterdam: John Benjamins.

1983. *Handbook of Australian languages*, Vol. III. Canberra: ANU Press, and Amsterdam: John Benjamins.

1991. *Handbook of Australian languages*, Vol. IV. Melbourne: Oxford University Press.

Donaldson, T. 1980. *Ngiyambaa, the language of the Wangaaybuwan of New South Wales*, Cambridge: Cambridge University Press.

Dryer, M. S. 1986. 'Primary objects, secondary objects, and antidative', *Language* 62.808–45.

1990. 'What determines antipassive in Dyirbal?', pp. 90–101 of *Proceedings of the Seventh Eastern States Conference on Linguistics*, edited by Y. No and M. Libucha. Columbus: Ohio State University.

Du Bois, J. 1987a. 'The discourse basis of ergativity', *Lg*, 63.805–55.

1987b. 'Absolutive zero: paradigm adaptivity in Sacapultec Maya', *Lingua*, 71.203–22 (= Dixon, 1987).

Duranti, A. 1990. 'Politics and grammar: agency in Samoan political discourse', *American Ethnologist*, 17.646–66.

Durie, M. 1985. *A grammar of Acehnese, on the basis of a dialect of North Aceh*. Dordrecht: Foris.

1986. 'The grammaticization of number as a verbal category', *BLS*, 12.355–70.

1987. 'Grammatical relations in Acehnese', *SL* 11.365–99.

1988. 'Preferred argument structure in an active language: arguments against the category "intransitive subject"', *Lingua*, 74.1–25.

Dutra, R. 1987. 'The hybrid S-category in Brazilian Portuguese: some implications for word order', *SL*, 11.163–80.

Eades, D. 1979. 'Gumbaynggir', pp. 245–361 of Dixon and Blake, 1979.

Edmonson, B. 1988. 'A descriptive grammar of Huastec (Potosino dialect)', PhD thesis, Tulane University.

England, N. C. 1983a. *A grammar of Mam, a Mayan language*. Austin: University of Texas Press.

1983b. 'Ergativity in Mamean (Mayan) languages', *IJAL*, 49.1–19.

1988. 'Mam voice', pp. 525–45 of Shibatani, 1988.

Entwistle, W. J. 1953. *Aspects of language*. London: Faber and Faber.

Estival, D. and Myhill, J. 1988. 'Formal and functional aspects of the development from passive to ergative systems', pp. 441–91 of Shibatani, 1988.

Evans, N. 1987. 'Kayardild, the language of the Bentinck Islanders of north-west Queensland', PhD thesis, Australian National University (to be published by Mouton de Gruyter).

1989. 'Morphological ergativity and fixed-transitivity phenomena in Australian languages', paper given at a Conference on Non-standard Case, Tuscon, Arizona, July 1989.

Everett, D. L. 1986. 'Pirahã', pp. 200–325 of Derbyshire and Pullum, 1986.

Fabricius, O. 1801. *Forsøg til en forbedret grønlandsk grammatika*, 2nd edn. Cophenhagen: E. F. Sehnsart.

Farrell, T. Forthcoming, 'Fading ergativity?, a study of ergativity in Balochi', to appear in Bennett, Bynon and Hewitt.

Feltenius, L. 1977. *Intransitivizations in Latin* (Studia Latina Upsaliensia, 9). Upsala: Acta Universitatis Upsaliensis.

Fillmore, C. J. 1968. 'The case for case', pp. 1–88 of *Universals of linguistic theory*, edited by E. Bach and R. T. Harms. New York: Holt, Rinehart and Winston.

Fodor, J. A. 1970. 'Three reasons for not deriving "kill" from "cause to die"', *LI*, 1.429–38.

Foley, W. A. 1976. 'Comparative syntax in Austronesian', PhD dissertation, University of California at Berkeley.

1986. *The Papuan languages of New Guinea*. Cambridge: Cambridge University Press.

1991. *The Yimas language of New Guinea*. Stanford: Stanford University Press.

Foley, W. A. and Van Valin, R. D. 1984. *Functional syntax and universal grammar*. Cambridge: Cambridge University Press.

Fox, B. A. 1987. 'The Noun Phrase Accessibility Hierarchy revisited', *Lg*, 63.856–70.

Foxvog, D. A. 1975. 'The Sumerian ergative construction', *Orientalia Nova Series*, 44.395–425.

Frajzyngier, Z. 1984a. 'Ergative and nominative–accusative features in Mandara', *Journal of African Languages and Linguistics*, 6.35–45.

1984b. 'On the proto-Chadic syntactic pattern', pp. 139–59 of *Current progress in Afro-Asiatic linguistics, Papers of the third international Hamito-Semitic Congress*, edited by J. Bynon. Amsterdam: Benjamins.

Franchetto, B. 1990. 'Ergativity and nominativity in Kuikúro and other Carib languages', pp. 407–27 of Doris Payne, 1990.

Frank, P. 1990. *Ika syntax*. SIL and University of Texas at Arlington.

Friberg, B. 1991. 'Ergativity, focus and verb morphology in several South Sulawesi languages', pp. 103–30 of *VICAL 2, Western Austronesian and Contact Languages, Papers from the Fifth International Conference on Austronesian Linguistics*, edited by R. Harlow. Auckland: Linguistic Society of New Zealand.

Gair, J. W. 1970. *Colloquial Sinhalese clause structure*. The Hague: Mouton.

Garrett, A. 1990. 'The origin of NP split ergativity', *Lg*, 66.261–96.

Genetti, C. 1988. 'A syntactic correlate of topicality in Newari narrative', pp. 29–48 of *Clause combining in grammar and discourse*, edited by J. Haiman and S. A. Thompson. Amsterdam: John Benjamins.

Geniušienė, E. 1987. *The typology of reflexives*. Berlin: Mouton de Gruyter.

Gerdts, D. B. 1988. 'Antipassives and causatives in Ilokano: evidence for an ergative analysis', pp. 295–321 of McGinn, 1988.

Gerzenstein, A. 1991. 'Grados de transitividad en el verbo maká', pp. 39–56 of *Temas de lingüística aborigen*, edited by A. Gerzenstein. Universidad de Buenos Aires.

Gildea, S. L. O. 1992. 'Comparative Cariban morphosyntax: on the genesis of ergativity in independent clauses', PhD dissertation. University of Oregon.

Givón, T. 1970. 'Some historical changes in the noun-class system of Bantu, their possible causes and wider applications', pp. 33–54 of *Papers in African linguistics*, edited by C. W. Kim and H. Stahlke. Edmonton: Linguistic Research.

1972. *Studies in ChiBemba and Bantu grammar*. Supplement No. 3 to *SAL*.

1979. *On understanding grammar*. New York: Academic Press.

1984. *Syntax, a functional-typological introduction*, Vol. I. Amsterdam: John Benjamins.

1985. 'Ergative morphology and transitivity gradients in Newari', pp. 89–107 of Plank, 1985.

Glinert, L. 1989. *The grammar of Modern Hebrew*. Cambridge: Cambridge University Press.

Goddard, I. 1967. 'The Algonquian independent indicative', pp. 66–106 of *Contributions to anthropology: Linguistics*, 1. Ottawa: National Museum of Canada.

Grafstein, A. 1984. 'Argument structure and the syntax of non-configurational language', PhD thesis. McGill University.

Greenberg, J. H. 1963. 'Some universals of grammar with particular reference to the order of meaningful elements', pp. 73–113 of *Universals of language*, edited by J. H. Greenberg. Cambridge, Mass.: MIT Press.

Gregores, E. and Suárez, J. A. 1967. *A description of colloquial Guaraní*. The Hague: Mouton.

Grewendorf, G. 1989. *Ergativity in German*. Dordrecht: Foris.

Guirardello, R. 1992. 'Aspectos da morfossintaxe da língua Trumai (isolada) e de seu sistema de marcação de caso', MA thesis. Universidade Estadual de Campinas.

Haas, M. 1940. *Tunica*. New York: Augustin.

Haiman, J. 1980. *Hua, a Papuan language of the Eastern Highlands of New Guinea*. Amsterdam: John Benjamins.

Haiman, J. and Munro, P. (eds.) 1983. *Switch reference and universal grammar*. Amsterdam: John Benjamins.

Hale, K. L. 1968. Review of *A profile-generative grammar of Maori* by P. W. Hohepa, *JPS*, 77.83–99.

1970. 'The passive and ergative in language change: the Australian case', pp. 757–81 of *Pacific linguistics studies in honour of Arthur Capell*, edited by S. A. Wurm and D. C. Laycock. Canberra: Pacific Linguistics.

1973. 'Person marking in Walbiri', pp. 308–44 of *A Festschrift for Morris Halle*, edited by S. R. Anderson and P. Kiparsky. New York: Holt, Rinehart and Winston.

Halliday, M. A. K. 1967. 'Notes on transitivity and theme in English, part 1', *JL*, 3.37–81.

Hardman, M. J. 1966. *Jaqaru*. The Hague: Mouton.

Harris, A. C. 1981. *Georgian syntax: a study in relational grammar*. Cambridge: Cambridge University Press.

1982. 'Georgian and the unaccusative hypothesis', *Lg*, 58.290–306.

1990. 'Georgian: a language with active case marking. A reply to B. G. Hewitt', *Lingua*, 80.35–53.

Harrison, C. H. 1986. 'Verb prominence, verb initialness, ergativity and typological disharmony in Guajajara', pp. 407–39 of Derbyshire and Pullum, 1986.

Haspelmath, M. 1991. 'On the question of deep ergativity: the evidence from Lezgian', *Papiere zur Linguistik*, 44/5.5–27.

Hayward, R. J. 1990a. 'Notes on the Zayse language', pp. 210–355 of Hayward, 1990c.

1990b. 'Notes on the Aari language', pp. 425–93 of Hayward, 1990c.

(ed.) 1990c. *Omotic language studies*. London: School of Oriental and African Studies.

Heath, J. 1976. 'Antipassivization: a functional typology', *BLS*, 2.202–11.

1977. 'Choctaw cases', *BLS*, 3.204–13.

1979. 'Is Dyirbal ergative?', *Linguistics*, 17.401–63.

Heitzman. A. 1982. 'Some cohesive elements in Pajonal Campa narratives' (ms. SIL, Peru).

Hercus, L. A. Forthcoming. *A grammar of Arabana-Wangkangurru*. Canberra: Pacific Linguistics.

Herring, S. C. 1989. 'Verbless presentation and the discourse basis of ergativity', *BLS*, 25.123–37.

Hershberger, H. 1964. 'Case marking affixes in Gugu-Yalanji', pp. 73–82 of Pittman and Kerr, 1964.

Hershberger, R. 1964. 'Personal pronouns in Gugu-Yalanji', pp. 55–68 of Pittman and Kerr, 1964.

Hetzron, R. 1976. *The Agaw languages* (*Afroasiatic Linguistics*, 3:3). Malibu: Undena.

1990. 'Dialectal variation in Proto-Afroasiatic', pp. 577–97 of *Linguistic change and reconstruction methodology*, edited by P. Baldi. Berlin: Mouton de Gruyter.

Hewitt, B. G. 1980. 'The causative: Daghestanian variations on a theme', *International Review of Slavic Linguistics* 5:173–204. Reprinted in *Papers in Linguistics*, 16 (1983).171–202.

1982. '"Anti-passive" and "labile" constructions in North Caucasian', *General Linguistics*, 22.158–71.

1987. 'Georgian: active or ergative', *Lingua*, 71.319–40 (= Dixon, 1987).

Hinnebusch, T. J. 1989. 'Bantu', pp. 450–73 of *The Niger-Congo languages*, edited by J. Bendor-Samuel. Lanham, Md.: University Press of America.

Hinton, L. and Langdon, M. 1976. 'Object–subject pronominal prefixes in La Huerta Diegueño', pp. 113–28 of *Hokan studies*, edited by M. Langdon and S. Silver. The Hague: Mouton.

Hodge, C. T. 1970. 'The linguistic cycle', *Language Sciences*, 13.1–7.

Hofling, C. A. 1984. 'Irrealis subordinate clauses and related constructions in Itza Maya', *BLS*, 10.596–608.

1990. 'Possession and ergativity in Itzá Maya', *IJAL*, 56.542–60.

Hohepa, P. W. 1969. 'The accusative-to-ergative drift in Polynesian languages', *JPS*, 78.297–329.

Hoijer, H. 1933. 'Tonkawa, an Indian language of Texas' pp. 1–148 of *Handbook of American Indian languages*, Vol. III, edited by F. Boas. New York: Columbia University Press.

Holisky, D. A. 1987. 'The case of the intransitive subject in Tsova-Tush (Batsbi)', *Lingua*, 71.103–32 (= Dixon, 1987).

1991. 'A grammatical sketch of Laz', pp. 395–472 of *Indigenous languages of the Caucasus*, Vol. I, *The Kartvelian languages* edited by A. Harris. Delmore, N.Y.: Caravan Books.

Holz, H. H. 1953. *Sprache und Welt, Probleme der Sprachphilosophie*. Frankfurt/ Main.

Hook, P. E. 1985. 'The super-anti-absolutive in Kashmiri', pp. 142–51 of *Proceedings of the First Annual Meeting of the Pacific Linguistics Conference*, edited by S. DeLancey and R. S. Tomlin. Eugene: University of Oregon.

Hopper, P. J. and Thompson, S. A. 1980. 'Transitivity in grammar and discourse', *Lg*, 56.251–99.

(eds.) 1982. *Studies in transitivity* (*Syntax and semantics*, Volume XV). New York: Academic Press.

Hosokawa, K. 1991. 'The Yawuru language of West Kimberley: a meaning-based description', PhD thesis, Australian National University.

Howard, C. 1986. 'Formulário dos vocabulários padrões, Mawayana', ms. held in Museu Nacional, Rio de Janeiro.

Hudson, J. 1976a. 'Walmatjari: nominative–ergative or nominative–accusative', pp. 1–30 of *Papers in Australian linguistics*, No. 9. Canberra: Pacific Linguistics.

1976b. 'Simple and compound verbs: conjugation by auxiliaries in Australian verbal systems – Walmatjari', pp. 653–7 of Dixon, 1976.

1978. *The core of Walmatjari grammar*. Canberra: Australian Institute of Aboriginal Studies.

Hymes, D. 1975. 'From space to time in tenses in Kiksht', *IJAL*, 41.313–29.

Jacobsen, W. H. 1967. 'Switch-reference in Hokan-Coahuiltecan', pp. 238–63 of *Studies in south-western ethnolinguistics*, edited by D. Hymes and W. Bittle. The Hague: Mouton.

1985. 'The analog of the passive transformation in ergative-type languages', pp. 176–91 of Nichols and Woodbury, 1985.

Jelinek, E. Forthcoming. 'Ergativity and argument type', to appear in *MIT Working Papers in Linguistics*.

Jelinek, E. and Demers, R. A. 1983. 'The agent hierarchy and voice in some Coast Salish languages', *IJAL*, 49.167–85.

Jensen, C. 1990. 'Cross-referencing changes in some Tupí-Guaraní languages', pp. 117–58 of Doris Payne, 1990.

Jespersen, O. 1922. *Language, its nature, development and origin*. London: Allen and Unwin.

1933. *Selected writings of Otto Jespersen*. London: Allen and Unwin.

Job, M. 1985. 'Ergativity in Lezgian', pp. 159–73 of Plank, 1985.

Johnson, D. 1974. 'On the role of grammatical relations in linguistic theory', *CLS*, 10.269–83.

1976. 'Ergativity in Relational Grammar' (mimeo).

Johnson, M. 1980. *Ergativity in Inuktitut (Eskimo), in Montague Grammar, and in Relational Grammar*. Bloomington, Ind.: Indiana University Linguistics Club.

Jones, L. W. 1986. 'The question of ergativity in Yawa, a Papuan language', *AJL*, 6.1–36.

Joseph, B. D. and Philippaki-Warburton, I. 1987. *Modern Greek* (Croom Helm Descriptive Grammar Series). London: Routledge.

Juul, A. and Nielson, H. F. 1989. *Otto Jespersen: facets of his life and work*. Amsterdam: John Benjamins.

Kachru, Y. 1965. 'A transformational treatment of Hindi verbal syntax', PhD thesis, University of London.

1987. 'Ergativity, subjecthood and topicality in Hindi-Urdu', *Lingua*, 71.223–38 (= Dixon, 1987).

Kaschube, D. V. 1967. *Structural elements in the language of the Crow Indians of Montana*. Boulder: University of Colorado Press.

Keen, S. 1983. 'Yukulta', pp. 190–304 of Dixon and Blake, 1983.

Keenan, E. L. 1976. 'Towards a universal definition of "subject"', pp. 303–33 of Li, 1976. (Reprinted in Keenan 1987: 89–120.)

1984. 'Semantic correlates of the ergative/absolutive distinction', *Linguistics*, 22.197–223. (Reprinted in Keenan 1987: 166–94.)

1987. *Universal grammar: fifteen essays*. London: Croom Helm.

Keenan, E. L. and Comrie, B. 1977. 'Noun phrase accessibility and universal grammar', *LI*, 8.63–100. (Reprinted in Keenan 1987: 3–45.)

Keenan, E. L. and Keenan, E. O. 1979. 'Becoming a competent speaker of Malagasy', pp. 113–58 of *Languages and their speakers*, edited by T. A. Shopen. Cambridge, Mass.: Winthrop.

Kennard, E. 1936. 'Mandan grammar', *IJAL*, 9.1–43.

Kennedy, B. H. 1962. *The revised Latin primer*, new edition. London: Longmans.

Kepping, K. B. 1979. 'Elements of ergativity and nominativity in Tangut', pp. 263–77 of Plank, 1979.

Kibrik, A. E. 1979a. 'Canonical ergativity and Daghestan languages', pp. 61–77 of Plank, 1979.

1979b, 'Unikal'ny li sintaksičeski èrgativnye jazyki?' (Are the syntactically ergative languages unique?), pp. 261–3 of *Tezisy dokladov XIV Tixookeanskogo naučnogo kongressa* (Xabarovsk). Moscow.

1985. 'Towards a typology of ergativity', pp. 268–323 of Nichols and Woodbury, 1985.

1987. 'Constructions with clause actants in Daghestanian languages', *Lingua* 71.133–78 (= Dixon, 1987).

1990. 'As línguas semanticamente ergativas na perspectiva da tipologia sintática geral', *Cadernos de estudos lingüísticos* (Universidade Estadual de Campinas), 18.15–36.

Kimball, G. 1991. 'Koasati fluid-S (and split-A) marking', paper given to AAA meeting, Tulane University, 23 November.

Klaiman, M. H. 1978. 'Arguments against a passive origin of the IA ergative', *CLS*, 14.204–16.

1987. 'Mechanisms of ergativity in South Asia', *Lingua*, 71.61–102 (= Dixon, 1987).

Klimov, G. A. 1973. *Očerk obščej teorii ergativnosti* (Outline of a general theory of ergativity). Moscow: Nauka.

Klokeid, T. J. 1976. 'Topics in Lardil grammar', PhD dissertation, MIT.

1978. 'Nominal inflection in Pama Nyungan, a case study in relational grammar', pp. 577–615 of *Valence, semantic case and grammatical relations*, edited by W. Abraham. Amsterdam: John Benjamins.

Koshal, S. 1979. *Ladakhi grammar*, Delhi: Motilal Banarsidass.

Koul, O. N. 1977. *Linguistic studies in Kashmiri*. Chandigarh: Bahri.

Krishnamurti, Bh. 1969. *Koṇḍa or Kūbi, a Dravidian language*. Hyderabad: Tribal Cultural Research and Training Institute.

Krishnamurti, Bh. and Gwynn, J. P. L. 1985. *A grammar of Modern Telugu*. Delhi: Oxford University Press.

Kroeger, P. R. 1991a. 'Phrase structure and grammatical relations in Tagalog', PhD dissertation, Stanford University.

1991b. 'Non-subject controllers in Tagalog', paper presented to the LSA annual meeting.

Kuipers, A. H. 1968. 'The categories verb–noun and transitive–intransitive in English and Squamish', *Lingua*, 21.610–26.

Kuno, S. 1973. *The structure of the Japanese language*. Cambridge, Mass.: MIT Press.

1976. 'Subject, theme and the speaker's empathy – a reexamination of relativisation phenomena', pp. 417–44 of Li, 1976.

Kuryłowicz, J. 1946. 'Ergativnost' i stadial'nost' v jazyke', *Isvestija Akademii Nauk Sojuza SSR, Fak. Lit i. Jaz.*, 5.387–93. (Reprinted as pp. 95–103 of his *Esquisses linguistiques*, Wrokław-Krakow: PAN, 1960. English translation by P. Culicover 'Ergativeness and the stadial theory of linguistic development', *The Study of Man* (University of California, Irvine), 2 (1973).1–21.)

1964. *The inflectional categories of Indo-European*. Heidelberg: Winter.

Lahiri, U. 1986. 'The ergative construction in (Modern) Western Indo-Aryan and its absence in (Modern) Eastern Indo-Aryan', paper given at the Annual Meeting of the LSA.

Lakoff, G. and Ross, J. R. 1976. 'Is deep structure necessary?', pp. 159–64 of *Notes from the linguistic underground* (*Syntax and Semantics*, 7), edited by J. D. McCawley. New York: Academic Press.

Langacker, R. W. and Munro, P. 1975. 'Passives and their meaning', *Lg*, 51.789–830.

Larsen, T. W. 1981. 'Functional correlates of ergativity in Aguacatec', *BLS*, 7.136–53.

1984. 'Case marking and subjecthood in Kipeá Kirirí', *BLS*, 10.189–205.

1987. 'The syntactic status of ergativity in Quiche', *Lingua*, 71.33–59 (= Dixon, 1987).

Larsen, T. W. and Norman, W. M. 1979. 'Correlates of ergativity in Mayan grammar', pp. 347–70 of Plank, 1979.

Lashkarbekov, B. 1982. 'K istoriji vaxanskoj kosvennoj konstruktsij', ('Towards a history of the oblique construction in the Wakhi language'), pp. 1–4 of *Acta Iranica: Monumentum George Morgenstierne*, Vol. II, 2nd series (Hommages et Opera Minora, 18). Leiden: E. J. Brill.

1985. 'Stanovlenie sistemy vaxanskogo glagola na trex stadijax jazykovogo razvitija (The emergence of the Wakhi verb system in three stages of language development)', *Voprosy Jazykoznanija*, 1.97–108.

Lazard, G. 1986. 'Le type linguistique di "actif": reflexions sur une typologie globale', *Folia Linguistica*, 20.87–108.

1989. 'Transitivity and markedness: the antipassive in accusative languages', pp. 309–31 of *Markedness in synchrony and diachrony*, edited by O. M. Tomić. Berlin: Mouton de Gruyter.

1991. 'Researches on actancy', *Actances*, 6.3–58.

Legendre, G. and Rood, D. S. 1992. 'On the interaction of grammar components in Lakhóta: evidence from split intransitivity', *BLS* 18.

Lewis, G. L. 1953. *Teach yourself Turkish*, London: English Universities Press.

Li, C. (ed.) 1976. *Subject and topic*, New York: Academic Press.

1977. *Mechanisms of syntactic change*. Austin: University of Texas Press.

Li, C. and Lang, R. 1979. 'The syntactic irrelevance of an ergative case in Enga and other Papuan languages', pp. 307–24 of Plank, 1979.

Li, C., Thompson, S. A., and Sawyer, J. O. 1977. 'Subject and word order in Wappo', *IJAL*, 43.85–100.

Lister-Turner, R. and Clark, J. B. 1930. *Revised Motu grammar and vocabulary*. Port Moresby.

Loogman, A. 1965. *Swahili grammar and syntax*. Pittsburgh: Duquesne University Press.

Lorimer, D. L. R. 1935. *The Burushaski language*, Vol. I: *introduction and grammar*. Oslo: Aschehoug.

Lyons, J. 1968. *Introduction to theoretical linguistics*. Cambridge: Cambridge University Press.

McAlpin, D. W. 1974. 'Towards proto-Elamo-Dravidian', *Lg*, 50.89–101.

McConvell, P. 1981. 'How Lardil became accusative', *Lingua*, 55.141–79.

McDonald, M. and Wurm, S. A. 1979. *Basic materials in Wankumara (Galali): grammar, sentences and vocabulary*. Canberra: Pacific Linguistics.

McGinn, R. (ed.) 1988. *Studies in Austronesian languages* (Monographs in International Studies, Southeast Asian Series, Number 76). Athens, Ohio: Ohio University Center for International Studies.

McGregor, W. 1989 'The discourse basis of ergative marking in Gooniyandi', *La Trobe Working Papers in Linguistics*, 2.127–58.

McKay, G. R. 1975. 'Rembarnga: a language of central Arnhem Land', PhD thesis, Australian National University.

1990. 'Agent and patient in Ndjebbana bound pronouns: a study in markedness' (ms.)

McLendon, S. 1978. 'Ergativity, case and transitivity in Eastern Pomo', *IJAL*, 44.1–9.

Malla, K. P. 1985. *The Newari language: a working outline*. Tokyo: Institute for the Study of Languages and Cultures of Asia and Africa.

Mallinson, G. and Blake, B. J. 1981. *Language typology: cross-cultural studies in syntax*. Amsterdam: North-Holland.

Marantz, A. 1984. *On the nature of grammatical relations*. Cambridge, Mass.: MIT Press.

Martinet, A. 1962. *A funçtional view of language*. London: Oxford University Press.

Masica, C. P. 1991. *The Indo-Aryan languages*. Cambridge: Cambridge University Press.

Meillet, A. 1917, *Caractères généraux des langues germaniques*. Paris: Hachette. (English translation, *General characteristics of the Germanic languages*. Coral Gables: University of Miami Press, 1970.)

Mejlanova, U. A. 1960. *Morfologičeskaja i sintaksičeskaja xarakteristika padežej lezginskogo jazyka* (Morphological and syntactic characteristics of Lezgian cases). Maxačkala: Dagestanskij Filial Akademii Nauk SSSR.

Mel'čuk, I. A. 1978. 'Toward a formal model of Alutor surface syntax: predicative and completive constructions', *Linguistics*, special issue, 5–39.

1983. 'Grammatical subject and the problem of the ergative constructions in Lezgian', *Proceedings of the second conference on the non-Slavic languages of the USSR*, edited by H. I. Aronson and B. J. Darden. *Folio Slavica*, 5.246–93.

Mercer, S. A. B. 1961. *Assyrian grammar*. New York: Frederik Ungar.

Merlan, F. 1985. 'Split intransitivity: functional oppositions in intransitive inflection', pp. 324–62 of Nichols and Woodbury, 1985.

Merlan, F. and Rumsey, A. 1990. *Ku Waru: language and segmentary politics in the Western Nebilyer Valley, Papua New Guinea*. Cambridge: Cambridge University Press.

Merrifield, W. R., Naish, C. N., Rensch, C. R. and Story, G. (eds.) 1965. *Laboratory manual for morphology and syntax*. Santa Ana: SIL.

Michalowski, P. 1980. 'Sumerian as an ergative language, I', *Journal of Cuneiform Studies*, 32.86–103.

Mithun, M. 1991a. 'Active/agentive case marking and its motivations', *Lg*, 67.510–46.

1991b. 'The role of motivation in the emergence of grammatical categories: the grammaticalization of subjects', pp. 159–84 of *Approaches to grammaticalization*, Vol. II: *Focus on types of grammatical markers*, edited by E. C. Traugott and B. Heine. Amsterdam: John Benjamins.

Forthcoming. 'The implications of ergativity for a Philippine voice system', to appear in *Grammatical voice: its form and function*, edited by P. Hopper. Amsterdam: John Benjamins.

Mock, C. 1979. 'Chocho transitivity', paper presented to Conference on American Indian Languages, AAA, 1979. Later published as 'Los casos morfosintácticos del chocho' in *Anales de Antropología*, edited by L. Gonzales, Mexico City: Instituto de Investigaciones Antropologicas, Universidad Nacional Autonoma de México, 1983.

Mondloch, J. L. 1978. 'Disambiguating subjects and objects in Quiche', *JML*, 1.3–19.

Monserrat, R. and Soares, M. F. 1983. 'Hierarquia referencial em línguas Tupí', *Ensaios de lingüística* (Faculdade de Letras de UFMG, Belo Horizonte, Brazil), 9.164–87.

Moore, D. 1984. 'Syntax of the language of the Gavião Indians of Rondônia, Brazil', PhD dissertation, CUNY.

Moravcsik, E. 1978. 'On the distribution of ergative and accusative patterns', *Lingua*, 45.233–79.

Moreau, J.-L. 1972. 'La corrélation du sujet et de l'objet en finnois', *Etudes Finno-Ougriennes*, 8.193–202.

Mosel, U. 1984. *Tolai syntax and its historical development*. Canberra: Pacific Linguistics.

Mosel, U. and Hovdhaugen, E. 1992. *Samoan reference grammar*. Oslo: Norwegian University Press.

Mulder, J. 1989a. 'The viability of the notion of subject in coast Tsimshian', *Canadian Journal of Linguistics*, 34.129–44.

    1989b. 'Syntactic ergativity in coast Tsimshian (Sm'algyax)', *SL*, 13.405–35.

Munro, P. (ed.) 1980. *Studies of switch-reference* (UCLA Papers in Syntax, No. 8). Los Angeles: UCLA.

Munro, P. and Gordon, L. 1982. 'Syntactic relations in Western Muskogean', *Lg*, 58.81–115.

N'Diaye, G. 1970. *Structure du dialecte basque de Maya*. The Hague: Mouton.

Nedjalkov, V. P. 1979. 'Degrees of ergativity in Chukchee', pp. 241–62 of Plank, 1979.

Nichols, J. 1980. 'Control and ergativity in Chechen', *CLS*, 16.259–68.

    1982. 'Ingush transitivization and detransitivization', *BLS*, 8.445–62.

    1983. 'Chechen verb forms in *-na* and *-ča*: switch reference and temporal deixis', *Studia Caucasica*, 5.17–44.

    1986. 'Head-marking and dependent-marking grammar', *Lg*, 62.56–119.

    1992. *Language diversity in space and time*. Chicago: University of Chicago Press.

    Forthcoming. 'Ingush, a grammatical sketch', to appear in *Indigenous Languages of the Caucasus*, Vol. III: *North-east Caucasian*, edited by R. Smeets and M. Job. Delmore, N. Y.: Caravan Books.

Nichols, J. and Woodbury, A. (eds.) 1985. *Grammar inside and outside the clause: some approaches to theory from the field*. Cambridge: Cambridge University Press.

Nida, E. A. and Fehderau, H. W. 1970. 'Indigenous pidgins and koinés', *IJAL*, 36.146–55.

Noda, K. 1983. 'Ergativity in Middle Persian', *Gengo Kenkyu*. 84.105–25.

O'Dowd, E. 1990. 'Discourse pressure, genre and grammatical alignment – after Du Bois', *SL*, 14.365–403.

O'Grady, G. N., Voegelin, C. F. and Voegelin, F. M. 1966. 'Languages of the world: Indo-Pacific fascicle Six', *Anthropological Linguistics*, 8:2.

Ortiz de Urbina, J. 1989. *Parameters in the grammar of Basque: a GB approach to Basque syntax*. Dordrecht: Foris.

Paris, C. 1985. 'Relations actancielles et valence verbale en avar: effacement d'actant et mise au jour du sens', *Actances*, 1.135–53.

Patz, E. 1982. 'A grammar of the Kuku Yalanji language of North Queensland', PhD thesis, Australian National University.

Payne, Doris. L. 1982. 'Chickasaw agreement morphology: a functional explanation', pp. 351–78 of Hopper and Thompson, 1982.

  (ed.) 1990. *Amazonian linguistics: studies in lowland South American languages.* Austin: University of Texas Press.

Payne, Doris, and Payne, Thomas E. 1990. 'Yagua', pp. 249–474 of Derbyshire and Pullum, 1990.

Payne, John R. 1979. 'Transitivity and intransitivity in the Iranian languages of the USSR', pp. 436–47 of *Papers from the Conference on non-Slavic languages of the USSR, CLS.*

  1980. 'The decay of ergativity in Pamir languages', *Lingua*, 51.147–86.

Payne, Judith and Payne, David. 1991. 'The pragmatics of split-intransitivity in Asheninca', paper presented to the 37th International Congress of Americanists, New Orleans.

Payne, Thomas E. 1982. 'Role and reference related subject properties and ergativity in Yup'ik Eskimo and Tagalog', *SL*, 6.75–106.

  1985. 'Some discourse motivation for S_o coding' (mimeo).

  1990. 'Transitivity and ergativity in Panare', pp. 429–53 of Doris Payne, 1990.

  1991. Review of *The body in the mind: the bodily basis of meaning, imagination and reason* by Mark Johnson, *IJAL*, 57.118–29.

Perlmutter, D. M. 1971. *Deep and surface structure constraints in syntax.* New York: Holt, Rinehart and Winston.

  1978. 'Impersonal passives and the unaccusative hypothesis', *BLS*, 4.157–89.

  (ed.) 1983. *Studies in relational grammar*, I. Chicago: University of Chicago Press.

Perlmutter, D. M. and Rosen, C. G. (eds.) 1984. *Studies in relational grammar*, II. Chicago: University of Chicago Press.

Perrot, J. 1986. 'Actance et diathèse en ostiak oriental', *Actances*, 2.135–50.

  1989. 'Nouvel examen des relations actancielles en vach', *Actances*, 4.13–32.

Pesetsky, D. 1982. 'Paths and categories', PhD dissertation, MIT.

Piper, N. 1989. 'A sketch grammar of Meryam Mir', MA thesis, Australian National University.

Pirejko, L. A. 1979. 'On the genesis of the ergative construction in Indo-Iranian', pp. 481–8 of Plank, 1979.

Pires, N. N. 1992. 'Estudo da gramática da língua Jeoromitxi (Jabuti), aspectos sintáticos das cláusulas matrizes', MA thesis, Universidade Estadual de Campinas.

Pittman, R. and Kerr, H. (eds.) 1964. *Papers on the languages of the Australian Aborigines.* Canberra: Australian Institute of Aboriginal Studies.

Plank, F. (ed.) 1979. *Ergativity: towards a theory of grammatical relations.* London: Academic Press.

  1985. *Relational typology.* Berlin: Mouton.

Polinskaja, M. S. and Nedjalkov, V. P. 1987. 'Contrasting the absolutive in Chukchee: syntax, semantics and pragmatics', *Lingua*, 71.239–69 (= Dixon, 1987).

Popjes, J. and Popjes, J. 1986. 'Canelo-Krahô', pp. 128–99 of Derbyshire and Pullum, 1986.

Postal, P. M. 1977. 'Antipassive in French', *Lingvisticae Investigationes*, 1.333–74.

Pullum, G. K. 1988. 'Topic ... comment: citation etiquette beyond thunderdome', *Natural language and linguistic theory*, 6.579–88.

Quizar, R. and Knowles-Berry, S. M. 1988. 'Ergativity in Cholan languages', *IJAL*, 54.73–95.

Regamey, C. 1954. 'A propos de la "construction ergative" en indo-aryen moderne', pp. 363–84 of *Sprachgeschichte und Wortbedeutung: Festschrift Albert Debrunner*. Bern: Francke.

Rice, K. 1991. 'Intransitives in Slave (Northern Athapaskan): arguments for unaccusatives', *IJAL*, 57.51–69.

Richards, J. 1977. 'Orações em Waurá', pp. 141–84 of *Série Lingüística*, No. 7, edited by L. I. Bridgeman. Brasilia: SIL.

Rigsby, B. 1975. 'Nass-Gitksan: an analytic ergative syntax', *IJAL*, 41.346–54.

Robinett, F. M. 1955. 'Hidatsa', *IJAL*, 21.1–7, 160–77, 210-16.

Rodrigues, A. D. 1953. 'Morfologia do Verbo Tupi', *Letras* (Curitiba, Brazil), 1.

Rood, D. S. 1971. 'Agent and object in Wichita', *Lingua*, 28.100–7.

Rude, N. 1982. 'Promotion and topicality of Nez Perce objects', *BLS*, 8.463–83.

1983. 'Ergativity and the active-stative typology in Loma', *SAL*, 14.265–83.

1991. 'On the origin of the Nez Perce ergative NP suffix', *IJAL*, 57.24–50.

Rumsey, A. 1980. 'Prologomena to a theory of Australian grammatical case systems', pp. 1–29 of *Contributions to Australian linguistics* (Papers in Australian linguistics, No. 13), edited by B. Rigsby and P. Sutton. Canberra: Pacific Linguistics.

1982. *An intra-sentence grammar of Ungarinyin, north Western Australia*. Canberra: Pacific Linguistics.

1987a. 'The chimera of proto-Indo-European ergativity', *Lingua*, 71.297–318 (= Dixon, 1987).

1987b. 'Was proto-Indo-European an ergative language?', *Journal of Indo-European Studies*, 15.19–37.

Saltarelli, M. 1988. *Basque* (Croom Helm Descriptive Grammars). London: Routledge.

Sapir, E. 1917. Review of 'Het passieve karakter van het verbum transitivum of van het verbum actionis in talen van Noord-Amerika' by C. C. Uhlenbeck, *IJAL*, 1.82–6. Reprinted as pp. 69–74 of *The collected works of Edward Sapir*, Vol. V (*American Indian Languages*, 1), volume editor William Bright. Berlin: Mouton de Gruyter, 1990.

1921. *Language*. New York: Harcourt Brace.

1929. 'Central and North American languages', *Encylopaedia Britannica*, Vol. V, pp. 138–41.

1930. *Southern Paiute, a Shoshonean language*. (*Proceedings of the American Academy for Arts and Science*, 65:1). Boston.

Sasse, H-J. 1984. 'Case in Cushitic, Semitic and Berber', pp. 111–26 of *Current progress in Afro-Asiatic linguistics: papers of the Third International Hamito-Semitic Congress*, edited by J. Bynon. Amsterdam: Benjamins.

Schachter, P. 1976. 'The subject in Philippine languages: topic, actor, actor–topic, or none of these', pp. 491–518 of Li, 1976.

1977. 'Reference related and role-related properties of subjects', pp. 279–306 of Cole and Sadock, 1977.

Schieffelin, B. 1979. 'How Kaluli children learn what to say, what to do, and how to feel', PhD dissertation, Columbia University.

1985. 'The acquisition of Kaluli', pp. 525–93 of *The cross-linguistic study of language acquisition*, Vol. I: *The data*, edited by D. I. Slobin. Hillsdale, N.J.: Lawrence Erlbaum.

Schiefner, F. A. von. 1859. 'Versuch über die Tusch-Sprache', *Mémoires de l'Académie Impériale des Sciences de Saint-Petersburg*, Sixth Series, 9.1–160.

Schmidt, A. 1985. *Young people's Dyirbal: an example of language death from Australia*. Cambridge: Cambridge University Press.

Schuchardt, H. 1896 'Über den passiven Charakter des Transitivs in den kaukasischen Sprachen', *Sitzungsberichte der philosophisch-historischen Classe der Akademie der Wissenschaften zu Wien*, 133.1–191.

Seely, J. 1977. 'An ergative historiography', *Historiographia Linguistica*, 4.191–206.

Seiter, W. J. 1979. 'Studies in Niuean syntax', PhD dissertation, University of California at San Diego.

Seki, L. 1990. 'Kamaiurá (Tupí-Guaraní) as an active–stative language', pp. 367–91 of Doris Payne, 1990.

Shibatani, M. (ed.) 1988. *Passive and voice*. Amsterdam: John Benjamins.

1990. *The languages of Japan*. Cambridge: Cambridge University Press.

Shipley, W. F. 1964. *Maidu grammar* (University of California Publications in Linguistics, 41). Berkeley and Los Angeles: University of California Press.

Silverstein, M. 1976. 'Hierarchy of features and ergativity', pp. 112–71 of Dixon, 1976; republished as pp. 163–232 of *Features and projections* (1986), edited by P. Muysken and H. van Riemsdijk. Dordrecht: Foris.

Speiser, E. A. 1941. *Introduction to Hurrian* (Annual of the American Schools of Oriental Research, 20). New Haven: American Schools of Oriental Research.

Steiner, G. 1979. 'The intransitive-passival conception of the verb in languages of the Ancient Near East', pp. 185–216 of Plank, 1979.

Sutton, P. (ed.) 1976. *Languages of Cape York*. Canberra: Australian Institute of Aboriginal Studies.

Sweet, H. 1875–6. 'Words, logic and grammar', *TPS*, pp. 470–503.

Taylor, A. J. 1970. 'Syntax and phonology of Motu (Papua): a transformational approach', PhD thesis, Australian National University.

Taylor, G. 1991. *Introdução à língua Baniwa do Içana*. Campinas, Brazil: Editora da Universidade Estadual de Campinas.

Tchekhoff, C. 1980. 'The economy of a voice-neutral verb: an example from Indonesian', pp. 71–81 of *Austronesian studies: papers from the Second Eastern Conference on Austronesian languages* (Michigan Papers on South and Southeast Asia, 15), edited by P. Naylor.

Thompson, S. A. 1987. 'The passive in English: a discourse perspective', pp. 497–511 of *In honor of Ilse Lehiste*, edited by R. Channon and L. Shockley. Dordrecht: Foris.

Thomsen, M.-L. 1984. *The Sumerian language* (Copenhagen Studies in Assyriology, 10). Copenhagen: Akademisk Forlag.

Tiffou, E. and Morin, Y.-C. 1982. 'A note on split ergativity in Burushaski', *BSOAS*, 45.88–94.

Timberlake, A. 1974. 'The nominative object in North Russian', pp. 219–43 of *Slavic transformational syntax*, edited by R. Brecht and C. Chvany. Ann Arbor: University of Michigan.

Trubetzkoy, N. S. 1939. 'Le rapport entre le déterminé, le déterminant et le défini', pp. 78–82 of *Mélanges de linguistique, offerts à Charles Bally*. Geneva: Georg. (Reprinted as pp. 133–8 of *Readings in Linguistics II*, edited by E. P. Hamp, F. W. Householder and R. Austerlitz. Chicago: University of Chicago Press, 1966.)

Tsunoda, T. 1974. 'A grammar of the Waruŋu language, North Queensland', MA thesis, Monash University.

1988. 'Antipassives in Warrungu and other Australian languages', pp. 595–649 of Shibatani, 1988.

Tucker, A. N. and Bryan, M. A. 1966. *Linguistic analyses: the non-Bantu languages of north-east Africa* (Handbook of African Languages, Part 5). London: Oxford University Press.

Uhlenbeck, C. C. 1901. 'Agens und Patiens im Kasussystem der idg. Sprachen', *Indogermanische Forschungen*, 12.170–1.

Urban, G. 1985. 'Ergativity and accusativity in Shokleng (Gê)', *IJAL*, 51.164–87.

Van der Meer, T. H. 1985. 'Case marking in Surui', pp. 208–30 of *Porto Velho workpapers*, edited by D. L. Fortune. Brasilia: SIL.

Van Driem, G. 1987. *A grammar of Limbu* (Mouton Grammar Library, 4). Berlin: Mouton.

Van Ginneken, J. 1939. 'Avoir et être du point de vue de la linguistique générale', pp. 83–92 of *Mélanges de linguistique offerts à Charles Bally*. Geneva: Georg.

Van Valin, R. D. 1977. 'Aspects of Lakhota syntax', PhD dissertation, University of California, Berkeley.

1981. 'Grammatical relations in ergative languages' *SL*, 5.361–94.

Velázquez-Castillo, M. 1991. 'The semantics of Guaraní agreement markers', *BLS*, 17.324–35.

Vitale, A. J. 1981. *Swahili syntax*. Dordrecht: Foris.

Vogel, A. R. 1989. 'Grammar and gender agreement in Jaruára (Arauan)', MA dissertation, University of Texas at Arlington.

Vogt, H. 1971. *Grammaire de la langue georgienne*. Oslo: Universitetsforlaget.

Wagner, H. 1978. 'The typological background of the ergative construction', *Proceedings of the Royal Irish Academy*, 78: C.37–74.

Walsh, M. 1976a. 'Ergative, locative and instrumental case inflections – Murinjpata', pp. 405–8 of Dixon, 1976.

1976b. 'The Murinypata language of north-west Australia', PhD thesis, Australian National University.

Watkins, C. 1963. 'Preliminaries to a historical and comparative analysis of the syntax of the Old Irish verb', *Celtica*, 6.1–49.

1970. *Indo-Germanische Grammatik*, Vol. III. Heidelberg: Winter.

Weisemann, U. 1986. 'The pronoun systems of some Jê and Macro-Jê languages', pp. 359–80 of *Pronominal systems*, edited by U. Wiesemann. Tübingen: Gunter Narr.

Whistler, K. W. 1985. 'Focus, perspective, and inverse marking in Nootka', pp. 227–65 of Nichols and Woodbury, 1985.

Whitehead, C. R. 1981–2. 'Subject, object and indirect object: towards a typology of Papuan languages', *LLM*, 13.32–63.

Whitman, W. 1947. 'Descriptive grammar of Ioway-Oto', *IJAL*, 13.233–48.

Whitney, W. D. 1889. *Sanskrit grammar*. Leipzig.

Wierzbicka, A. 1981. 'Case marking and human nature', *AJL*, 1.43–80.

Wijayawardhana, G., Wickramasinghe, D. and Bynon, T. Forthcoming. 'Passive-related constructions in Colloquial Sinhala', to appear in Bennett, Bynon and Hewitt.

Wilkins, D. 1989. 'Mparntwe Arrernte (Aranda): studies in the structure and semantics of grammar', PhD thesis, Australian National University.

Williams, K. 1989a. 'An alternative model of word order in proto-Chadic', pp. 111–20 of *Current progress in Chadic linguistics*, edited by Z. Frajzyngier. Amsterdam: John Benjamins.

1989b. 'Chadic historical syntax: reconstructing word order in proto-Chadic', PhD dissertation, Indiana University.

Woodbury, A. C. 1975. 'Ergativity of grammatical processes: a study of Greenlandic Eskimo', MA thesis, University of Chicago.

1977. 'Greenlandic Eskimo, ergativity and relational grammar', pp. 307–36 of Cole and Sadock, 1977.

Wurm, S. 1976. 'Accusative marking in Duungidjawu (Waga-Waga)', pp. 106–11 of Dixon 1976.

Zaenen, A., Maling, J. and Thráinsson, H. 1985. 'Case and grammatical functions: the Icelandic passive', *Natural Language and Linguistic Theory*, 3.441–83.

Zakharyin, B. 1979. 'On the formation of ergativity in Indo-Aryan and Dardic', *Osmania Papers in Linguistics* (Osmania University, Hyderabad, India), 5.50–71.

Index of authors

Abbott, M. 51, 147, 237
Adelaar, K. A. 4, 237
Aikhenvald, A. Y. 5, 73, 81, 105, 219, 237
Aikhenvald-Angenot, A. Y., *see*
 Aikhenvald, A. Y.
Allen, W. S. 3, 43, 100, 117, 190, 219, 237
Andersen, P. K. 57, 155, 238
Andersen, T. xv, 5, 44, 51, 64, 101, 103,
 188–9, 206, 238
Anderson, J. M. 20, 238
Anderson, N. 32, 238
Anderson, S. R. 68, 95, 137, 190–1
Andrews, A. 81
Angenot, J.-P. 5, 237
Arlotto, A. 44, 238
Austin, P. 41, 93, 151, 154, 238
Ayers, G. 151, 238

Baker, M. C. 146–7, 238
Bani, E. 197, 238
Bashir, E. 33–4, 238
Baugh, A. C. 183, 238
Bauman, J. J. 201, 238
Bender, M. L. 64, 238
Bennett, D. 238
Benveniste, E. 191, 238
Bhat, D. N. S. 30–3, 122, 144–5, 201, 238
Bhattacharya, S. 58, 239
Bittner, M. 149, 238
Blake, B. J. 4, 85, 91, 106, 110, 130, 170,
 178–9, 198, 205, 234, 238–9, 243, 251
Bloch, J. 190, 239
Boas, F. 5, 52, 73, 103, 239
Boelaars, J. H. M. C. 4, 239
Bollenbacher, J. 150, 239
Borgman, D. M. 52, 239
Bossong, G. 2, 175, 239
Breen, J. G. 41, 239
Brettschneider, G. 2, 175, 239
Bricker, V. R. 5, 100, 104, 178, 201, 239
Bromley, H. M. 58, 239
Bryan, M. A. 65, 257

Bull, W. E. xiv, 239
Burrow, T. 58, 239
Burzio, L. 20, 239
Buth, R. 51, 239
Byington, C. 35, 37, 240
Bynon, T. 27, 191, 203, 238, 240, 258

Camp, E. L. 5, 106, 240
Campbell, L. 5, 240
Capell, A. 41, 59, 240
Cardona, G. 191, 240
Cena, R. M. 4, 179, 240
Černý, V. 7, 44, 68, 121, 240
Chafe, W. L. 73, 240
Chaker, S. 64, 240
Chang, B. S. 57, 80, 123, 240
Chang, K. 80, 123, 240
Chapman, S. 47, 52, 240
Chappell, H. 28, 240
Charachidzé, G. 44, 121, 240
Chomsky, N. 126, 232–3, 240
Chung, S. 137, 191, 240
Churchward, C. M. 4, 7, 41, 123, 240
Clark, J. B. 41, 251
Clark, R. 191, 240
Cohen, D. 219, 240
Cole, P. 240
Collinder, B. 63, 241
Comrie, B. xiv, 3–4, 6, 57, 62, 67, 73, 88,
 92, 100, 120–1, 127, 130, 140, 169, 176,
 190, 203, 234, 241, 249
Constenla, A. 5, 241
Cooreman, A. 208–9, 241
Costa, R. 101
Craig, C. 103, 117, 241
Creider, C. A. 74, 241–2
Crisp, S. 95, 140, 175, 241
Croft, W. 182, 241
Cromack, R. E. 86
Crowley, T. 92, 147, 178, 241
Crystal, D. 19, 241
Cumming, S. 21, 241

259

Dahlstrom, A. 77, 241
Davies, W. D. 35–7, 147, 235, 241
Dayley, J. P. 148, 178, 241–2
De Guzman, V. P. 4, 242
Deibler, E. W. 96, 242
DeLancey, S. 4, 21, 88, 91, 184, 201, 242
Deloria, E. 73, 239
Demers, R. A. 88, 90, 248
Dench, A. 198, 242
Denny, J. P. 74, 242
Derbyshire, D. C. xv, 47, 52, 77, 88–9, 192, 240, 242
De Rijk, R. P. G. 232–3, 242
Dešeriev, Ju. D. 79, 242
Diakonoff, I. M. xvi, 242
Diffloth, G. 210, 242
Dimmendaal, G. J. 65, 242
Dirr, A. 3, 242–3
Donaldson, T. 85, 244
Dryer, M. S. 120, 209, 244
Du Bois, J. 44, 55, 208–13, 244
Durante, A. 222–3, 244
Durie, M. 55, 80, 82, 125, 145, 209, 244
Dutra, R. 210, 244
Dutton, T. 4, 48

Eades, D. 93, 244
Edmonson, B. 52, 179, 244
England, N. C. 27, 103, 149, 178, 209, 244
Entwistle, W. 216, 244
Estival, D. 189–90, 244
Evans, N. 63, 200, 218, 244
Everett, D. L. 138, 244

Fabricius, O. 5, 244
Farrell, T. 104, 244
Fehderau, H. W. 185, 253
Feltenius, L. 6, 244
Fillmore, C. J. 73, 115, 119, 214, 244
Fodor, J. A. 139, 245
Foley, W. A. 4, 32, 57–8, 89, 145, 154, 191, 232, 245
Fox, B. A. 208, 234, 241, 245
Foxvog, D. A. 3, 245
Frajzyngier, Z. 5, 42, 50, 245
Franchetto, B. 5, 51, 57, 105, 175, 192, 245
Frank, P. 73, 245
Friberg, B. 4, 245

Gair, J. W. 27, 245
Garrett, A. 3, 100, 187–8, 245
Genetti, C. 101, 202, 245
Geniušienė, E. 27, 245
Gerdts, D. B. 4, 245
Gerzenstein, A. 123, 245
Gildea, S. L. O. 99, 192, 245

Givón, T. 74, 101, 123, 148, 189, 202, 209, 241, 245–6
Glinert, L. 219, 246
Goddard, I. 91, 246
Gordon, L. 35–7, 253
Grafstein, A. 90, 246
Greenberg, J. H. 57, 246
Gregores, E. 73, 132, 246
Grewendorf, G. 30, 246
Grimes, C. E. 73, 90
Guirardello, R. 5, 123, 246
Gwynn, J. P. L. 62, 250

Haas, M. 57, 72–3, 246
Haiman, J. 4, 58, 153, 246
Hale, K. L. 96, 191, 200, 246
Halliday, M. A. K. xiii, 19–20, 246
Hardman, M. J. 63, 246
Harris, A. C. xvi, 106, 236, 246
Harrison, C. H. xv, 74, 107, 246
Harrison, S. P. 120
Haspelmath, M. 22, 155, 246
Hayward, R. J. 64, 91, 247
Heath, J. xiv, 35, 37, 147, 172, 247
Heitzman, A. 211, 247
Hercus, L. A. 91, 247
Herring, S. C. 209, 247
Hershberger, H. 85, 247
Hershberger, R. 85, 247
Hetzron, R. 57, 64, 88, 247
Hewitt, B. G. xiv, xvi, 121, 147, 238, 247
Hinnebusch, T. J. 74, 247
Hinton, L. 45, 247
Hodge, C. T. 184, 247
Hofling, C. A. 100, 103, 219, 247
Hohepa, P. W. 191, 247
Hoijer, H. 81, 247
Holisky, D. A. 76, 79–80, 82, 247–8
Holz, H. H. 216, 248
Hook, P. E. 100, 248
Hopper, P. J. 122–3, 147, 190, 248
Hosokawa, K. 121, 248
Hovdhaugen, E. 4, 155, 253
Howard, C. 105, 248
Hudson, J. 172–4, 248
Hudson, R. A. 64
Hymes, D. 97, 248

Jacobsen, W. H. 149, 153, 216, 248
Jelinek, E. 88, 90, 91, 248
Jensen, C. 5, 75, 89, 107, 248
Jespersen, O. 65–6, 182–3, 248
Job, M. 22, 248
Johnson, D. 235, 248
Johnson, M. 150, 248
Jones, L. W. 4, 76, 248

Joseph, B. D. 138, 249
Juul, A. 183, 249

Kachru, Y. 100, 175, 249
Kaschube, D. V. 81, 249
Keen, S. 105, 249
Keenan, E. L. 54–5, 112, 127–30, 133, 139, 153, 234, 249
Keenan, E. O. 133, 249
Kennard, E. 71–3, 249
Kennedy, B. H. 58, 249
Kepping, K. B. 201, 249
Kerr, H. 254
Kibrik, A. E. 35, 80, 83, 126, 136–8, 149, 155, 179–81, 249
Kilby, D. xiv, 122
Kimball, G. 38, 249
Klaiman, M. H. 3, 108, 190, 249
Klimov, G. A. 57, 77, 185–6, 214, 216–7, 249
Klokeid, T. J. 63, 90, 197, 200, 238, 249–50
Knowles-Berry, S. M. 45, 100, 136, 255
Koshal, S. 57, 217, 250
Koul, O. N. 83, 250
Krishnamurti, Bh. 58, 62, 250
Kroeger, P. L. 4, 179, 232, 250
Kuipers, A. H. 120, 250
Kuno, S. 41, 88, 250
Kuryłowicz, J. 44, 152, 189, 250

Lahiri, U. 190, 250
Lakoff, G. 120, 250
Lang, R. 4, 251
Langacker, R.W. 146, 250
Langdon, M. 45, 247
Larsen, T. W. 5, 100, 103, 178–80, 210, 233, 250
Lashkarbekov, B. 34, 250–1
Lazard, G. 6, 149, 251
Legendre, G. 73, 251
Lewis, G. L. 19, 140, 251
Li, C. 4, 65, 251
Lister-Turner, R. 41, 251
Loogman, A. 140, 251
Lorimer, D. L. R. 3, 100, 251
Lyons, J. xiii, 19, 53, 118, 251

McAlpin, D. W. 3, 251
McConvell, P. 109, 200, 251
McDonald, M. 41, 251
McGinn, R. 251
McGregor, W. 59, 251
McKay, G. R. 89, 100, 141, 251
McLendon, S. 81, 251
Maling, J. 121–2, 258
Malla, K. P. 202, 251
Mallinson, G. 91, 251

Marantz, A. 112, 233, 252
Martin, J. 37
Martinet, A. 216, 252
Masica, C. P. 122, 190, 252
Meillet, A. 66, 252
Mejlanova, U.A. 122, 252
Mel'čuk, I. 21, 57, 252
Mercer, S. A. B. 58, 252
Merlan, F. 4, 75, 106, 252
Merrifield, W. R. 86, 252
Michalowski, P. 3, 88, 101, 104, 252
Mithun, M. 4–5, 73–4, 77, 83, 240, 252
Mock, C. 73, 252
Møller, H. 183
Mondloch, J. L. 150, 252
Monserrat, R. 89, 252
Moore, D. 46, 55, 253
Moravcsik, E. 73, 253
Moreau, J.-L. 62, 253
Morin, Y.-C. 3, 99, 257
Mosel, U. 4, 76, 83, 155, 253
Mulder, J. 5, 133, 253
Munro, P. 35–7, 65, 146, 153, 247, 250, 253
Myhill, J. 188–9, 244

N'Diaye, G. 2, 253
Nedjalkov, V. P. 25, 89, 91, 93, 100, 176, 253–4
Nichols, J. 80, 121, 145, 150, 155, 219, 253
Nida, E. A. 185, 253
Nielson, H. F. 183, 249
Ningomba, M. S. 30–1, 238
Noda, K. 100, 253
Norman, W. M. 5, 100, 103, 178, 201, 250

O'Dowd, E. 210, 253
O'Grady, G. N. 63, 198, 253
Ortiz de Urbina, J. 2, 68, 175, 253

Paris, C. 121, 253
Patz, E. 85, 151, 253
Payne, David 211, 254
Payne, Doris L. 35–8, 211, 254
Payne, John R. xiv, 3, 34, 39–40, 100, 191, 203, 254
Payne, Judith 211, 254
Payne, Thomas E. 5, 83, 176–7, 211, 254
Perlmutter, D. M. 137, 234–6, 254
Perrot, J. 4, 254
Pesetsky, D. 20, 254
Philippaki-Warburton, I. 138, 249
Piper, N. 55, 254
Pirejko, L. A. 191, 254
Pires, N. N. 5, 219, 254
Pittman, R. 254
Plank, F. xiv, 254

Polinskaja, M. S. 25, 254
Popjes, Jack 44, 254
Popjes, Jo 44, 254
Popovich, H. 51, 55
Postal, P. M. 129, 147, 234–5, 255
Pullum, G. K. xv, 20, 242, 255

Quizar, R. 45, 100, 136, 255

Regamey, C. 4, 99, 255
Reid, N. 209
Rice, K. 75, 142, 148, 255
Richards, J. 77, 255
Rigsby, B. 5, 52, 133, 255
Robinett, F. M. 74, 255
Rodrigues, A. D. 83, 255
Rood, D. S. 73, 75, 251, 255
Rosen, C. G. 234, 254
Ross, J. R. 120, 250
Rude, N. 5–6, 105, 148, 188, 255
Rumsey, A. 3–4, 58, 68, 90, 100, 252, 255

Sadock, J. M. 240
Saltarelli, M. 138, 255
Sam-Colop, L. E. 235, 241
Sapir, E. 5, 55, 63, 73, 83, 111, 139, 255
Sasse, H.-J. 64, 255
Sawyer, J. O. 65, 251
Schachter, P. 116, 119, 255–6
Schieffelin, B. 4, 113, 256
Schiefner, F. A. von 79, 256
Schmidt, A. 205, 256
Schuchardt, H. 189, 256
Seely, J. 3, 5, 189, 214, 233, 256
Seiter, W. J. 191, 256
Seki, L. 5, 75, 89, 107, 219, 256
Shibatani, M. 41, 256
Shipley, W. F. 66, 256
Silverstein, M. xiii-xiv, 5, 88–91, 104, 149, 256
Soares, M. F. 89, 252
Speiser, E. A. 3, 256
Steiner, G. 3, 256
Suárez, J. A. 72, 132, 246
Sutton, P. xiv, 256
Sweet, H. 65, 256

Taylor, A. J. 41, 58, 256
Taylor, G. 81, 256
Tchekhoff, C. 21, 256

Testelec, Y. 90
Thompson, S. A. 3, 65, 122–3, 147–8, 190, 248, 251, 256
Thomsen, M.-L. 55, 88, 257
Thráinsson, H. 121–2, 258
Tiffou, E. 3, 99, 257
Timberlake, A. 63, 257
Trubetzkoy, N. S. 112, 257
Tsunoda, T. 180, 257
Tucker, A. N. 65, 257

Uhlenbeck, C. C. 3, 257
Urban, G. 5, 65, 103, 106, 257

Van der Meer, T. H. 46, 257
Van Driem, G. 57, 155, 257
Van Ginneken, J. 215, 257
Van Valin, R. D. 73, 100, 145, 154, 175, 232, 245, 257
Velázquez-Castillo, M. 83, 257
Vitale, A. J. 136, 257
Voegelin, C. F. 63, 198, 253
Voegelin, F. M. 63, 199, 253
Vogel, A. R. 48, 257
Vogt, H. 106, 257

Wade, M. 32, 238
Wagner, H. xiv, 257
Walsh, M. 59, 257
Watkins, C. 189, 257
Weir, H. xv, 5, 51, 55, 89, 133, 178
Weisemann, U. 55, 258
Whistler, K. W. 146, 258
Whitehead, C. R. 33, 258
Whitman, W. 73, 258
Whitney, W. D. 189, 258
Whorf, B. L. 119
Wickramasinghe, D. 27, 258
Wierzbicka, A. 88, 258
Wijayawardhana, G. 27, 258
Wilkins, D. 90, 258
Williams, K. 50, 258
Woodbury, A. C. 62, 137, 150, 152, 176, 235, 253, 258
Wouk, F. 21, 241
Wurm, S. A. 41, 86, 251, 258

Zaenen, A. 121–2, 258
Zafrani, H. 219, 240
Zakharyin, B. 228, 258

Index of languages and language families

For each language, the family to which it belongs is noted, and sometimes also the branch of the family. Most Indo-European languages are identified only by the branch, since these are so well known. For proto-X, see the entry under X.

Aari (Omotic, Afroasiatic) 91
Abaza (N-W Caucasian) 43–8, 138, 219
Abkhaz (N-W Caucasian) 120
Acehnese (Austronesian) 80–2, 120, 125–6, 145, 155, 205, 209
African languages 5, 230
Afroasiatic family xvi, 5, 64, 88
Aguacatec (Mayan) 103, 210–11
Algonquian family 90–1, 106
Alutor (Chukotko-Kamchatkan) 4, 57, 179
Amazonian languages 46
Amharic (Semitic, Afroasiatic) 73
Anatolian (branch of Indo-European) 3
Ancient Greek (Indo-European) 98
Andi (N-E Caucasian) 57, 121
Anguthimri (Pama-Nyungan, Australian) 147
Arabana (Pama-Nyungan, Australian) 92–3
Arawá family 47
Arawak family 5, 73, 89, 211
Archi (N-E Caucasian) 136, 155
Arikara (Caddoan) 75
Armenian (Indo-European) 3, 101, 110
Arrernte (Pama-Nyungan, Australian) 90
Asheninca (Arawak) 211
Assyrian (Semitic, Afroasiatic) 58
Australian family 4, 57, 67, 85, 90, 92, 96–7, 116, 120, 154, 170, 184, 186, 193, 200–1, 203–4
Austronesian family 4, 21, 120, 205
Avar (N-E Caucasian) 7, 44, 57, 68, 95, 121–2, 140, 175

Balochi (Iranian) 104
Balto-Finnic (Finno-Ugric, Uralic) 63

Bandjalang (Pama-Nyungan, Australian) 92, 178
Baniwa do Içana (Arawak) 81
Banjarese (Austronesian) 120
Bantu subgroup (Niger-Congo) 74, 120
Bartang (Pamir, Iranian) 203
Basque (isolate) 2, 57, 68, 138, 150, 175, 214–15, 232
Bats, Batsbi, see Tsova-Tush
Berber family (branch of Afroasiatic) 64–5, 73
Bezhta (N-E Caucasian) 149
Biu-Mandara (branch of Chadic, Afroasiatic) 50
Biyay dialect of Warrgamay (Pama-Nyungan, Australian) 194
Brazilian Portuguese (Italic) 210–11
Burmese (Tibeto-Burman) 120
Buru (Austronesian) 120
Burushaski (isolate) 3, 57, 99–100, 104, 109–10, 138

Caddo (Caddoan) 73
Caddoan family 73
Campa (Arawak), see Pajonal Campa
Canelo-Krahô (Jê) 44
Carib family xvi, 5, 89, 99, 187, 189, 192
Cariña (Carib) 99
Cashinawa (Panoan) 86, 109
Caucasian, see North-east, North-west, South
Cavineña (Tacanan) 89, 106–7
Chadic (branch of Afroasiatic) 5, 42, 50
Chamalal (N-E Caucasian) 180–1
Chamorro (Austronesian) 209
Chan (S Caucasian), see Laz
Chechen (N-E Caucasian) 80, 155
Cheyenne (Algonquian) 90
Chibchan family 5
Chickasaw, see Choctaw-Chickasaw
Chinese 182, 184
Chinook (Chinookan family) 5, 90

Choctaw-Chickasaw (Muskogean) 35–8, 147, 235
Chontal (Mayan) 136
Chorti (Mayan) 45, 100, 110
Chukchee (Chukotko-Kamchatkan family) 4–5, 25–8, 88–9, 93, 100, 176
Chukotko-Kamchatkan family 4, 57
Classical Armenian (Indo-European) 3, 100, 110
Classical Chinese 182, 184
Classical Tibetan (Tibeto-Burman) 57, 155
Coast Salish (Salish family) 88, 90
Cocho (Popolocan, Oto-Manguean) 73
Coptic (Semitic, Afroasiatic) 184
Creek (Muskogean) 57
Crow (Siouan) 81
Cushitic (branch of Afroasiatic) 64–6, 204
Cuzco Quechua (Quechuan) 68

Dagestanian (branch of N-E Caucasian) 2, 7, 136–7
Dakota (Siouan) 73–5, 236
Dalabon (Gunwinyguan, Australian) 59
Dani (Dani family, Papuan) 58
Dargwa (N-E Caucasian) 138
Dasenech (Cushitic, Afroasiatic) 64
Dhalanji (Pama-Nyungan, Australian) 41, 89
Diyari (Pama-Nyungan, Australian) 93, 149, 151, 153–4, 178
Dravidian family 3, 58, 122, 184
Dyirbal (Pama-Nyungan, Australian) 118, 179–80, 193–4, 215–6
  accusative inflection on pronouns 14–15, 160–1
  adverbials 134–5
  antipassive 13–16, 126, 133, 148–9, 152, 163–4, 200, 213
  avoidance speech style 18
  coordination, *see* S/O pivot
  demonstratives 152, 210
  discourse structure 209–11, 220–2
  ergative inflection on nouns 9–11, 40, 160–1
  ergative syntax, *see* S/O pivot
  free constituent order 10, 49
  gender classes 9, 119
  imperatives 133, 200
  instrumental case 57
  instrumentive constructions 126, 170–1
  language change 205
  markedness 56
  morphological split 85–6, 109
  -*ŋurra* suffix 165–7
  omission of ergative NP 62, 147
  purposive construction 136, 168–71
    reciprocals 148
    reflexives 126, 138, 148
    relative clauses 169–72, 222
    S/O pivot 12–16, 119, 136–7, 143, 155–7, 160–72, 178, 213, 220–2, 233
    secondary concepts 134–5, 137
    strict transitivity 6, 18, 193
    subject properties 112, 129–30, 234
    syntax of 'give' 120, 171–2
    young people's language 205

Eastern Pomo (Hokan) 81–2
Egyptian (Afroasiatic) 184
Elamite (isolate) 3
Enga (Engan family, Papuan) 4, 175
English (Germanic) 31, 37, 60, 112, 116, 118–19, 122, 187, 210, 224
  accusative morphology 21, 42, 68, 88
  accusative syntax, *see* S/A pivot
  ambitransitive verbs 6–7, 19, 54, 126, 216–18
  complement clauses 135–6
  constituent order 10, 39, 49, 126, 153
  coordination, *see* S/A pivot
  imperatives 131–3
  markedness 56, 65–7
  modals 98
  morphological change 183
  passive 12, 21, 23–4, 28, 131–2, 146–8
  preposition insertion 24
  presentational devices 209
  promotion to subject 20–1
  relative clauses 159, 222
  S/A pivot 11–13, 143, 155, 157–9, 168
  secondary verbs 134–6
  split marking 88
  syntactically based marking 23–8
  syntax of *give* 52–3, 120
Eskimo (Eskimo-Aleut) 5, 57, 62, 137, 149–50, 152, 176, 235
Eskimo-Aleut family 5

Fijian (Austronesian) 6, 18, 49, 111, 114, 120, 134–5, 138, 155, 176, 191
Finnish (Balto-Finnic) 24–5, 62, 73
Finno-Ugric (branch of Uralic) 184
Folopa (Teberan, Papuan) 32–4
French (Italic) 65–6

Gahuku (Gorokan family, Papuan) 96
Galali (Pama-Nyungan, Australian) 41
Gavião (Mondé family, Tupí stock) 46–8, 55
Georgian (S Caucasian) xvi, 106, 202, 236
German (Germanic) 20, 65–6, 122, 209
Germanic (branch of Indo-European) 65–7

Gilbertese (Kiribati)(Austronesian) 120
Greek (Indo-European) 98, 117, 138
Greenlandic Eskimo, *see* Eskimo
Guajajara (Tupí-Guaraní family, Tupí
  stock) 74
Guaraní (Tupí-Guaraní family, Tupí stock)
  72–5, 83, 132
Gujarathi (Indic) 190
Gumbaynggir (Pama-Nyungan, Australian)
  93
Guniyandi (South Kimberley, Australian)
  59
Gurinji (Pama-Nyungan, Australian) 109
Gurung (Tibeto-Burman) 202, 204
Gyarong (Tibeto-Burman) 202

Hattic (isolate) 3
Hebrew (Semitic, Afroasiatic) 209, 219
Hidatsa (Siouan) 74
Hindi (Indic) 100, 120, 175, 190
Hittite (Indo-European) 3, 187–9, 203, 228
Hua (Gorokan family, Papuan) 4, 58
Huastec (Mayan) 51–2, 179
Huichol (Uto-Aztecan) 120
Hungarian (Finno-Ugric, Uralic) 73, 219
Hurrian 3

Icelandic (Germanic) 121–2
Ikan (Chibchan) 73
Indic (branch of Indo-European) 3, 122,
  190–2, 215, 228
Indo-European family 44, 58, 65, 88, 184,
  215
  ergative characteristics 3, 58, 90
Indonesian (Austronesian) 118
Ingush (N-E Caucasian) 57, 80, 121, 155
Ioway-Oto (Siouan) 73
Iranian (branch of Indo-European) 3, 57,
  100, 190–3, 202–4
Iroquoian family 73
Ixil (Mayan) 151

Jabuti (isolate) 5, 219
Jacaltec (Mayan) 68, 103, 117, 125, 201
Jah-hut (Temiar, Mon-Khmer,
  Austroasiatic) 210–11
Japanese 41, 209
Jaqaru (Aymara) 63
Jarawara (Arawá) 46–8, 94, 209
Jê family 5, 89
Jur Luo (Nilotic) 51
Jyarong (Tibeto-Burman) 91

Kabardian (N-W Caucasian) 91
Kala(w) Lagaw Ya (associated with
  Australian) 92–3, 197

Kalkatungu (Pama-Nyungan, Australian)
  106, 120, 178, 198
Kaluli (Bosavi family, Papuan) 4, 113
Kamaiurá (Tupí-Guaraní) 75, 219
Kambata (Cushitic, Afroasiatic) 64
Kannada (Dravidian) 144
Kanum (Morehead and Upper Maro rivers
  family, Papuan) 4
Kartvelian, *see* South Caucasian
Kashmiri (Dardic, Indo-European) 83, 100
Kayardild (Tangkic, Australian) 63, 200
Kemant (Cushitic, Afroasiatic) 57
Ket (isolate) 73
Khanty (Finno-Ugric, Uralic) 4
Kimanianaga (Bantu, Niger-Congo) 185
Kinyarwanda (Bantu, Niger-Congo) 120
Kipeá Kiriri (Kiriri family) 180
Kiranti (Tibeto-Burman) 202
Kiribati (Gilbertese) (Austronesian) 120
Kituba (creole) 185
Koasati (Muskogean) 38
Koiari (Koiarian family, Papuan) 2, 48, 94
Koṇḍa (Dravidian) 58
Ku Wara (Papuan) 4
Kuikúro (Carib) 51, 57, 89, 101, 105, 174–5
Kuku-Yalanji (Pama-Nyungan, Australian)
  85, 109, 149, 151–2

Ladakhi (Tibeto-Burman) 57, 217
Lak (N-E Caucasian) 57
Lakhota (dialect of Dakota, Siouan) 73,
  100
Lardil (Tangkic, Australian) 63, 89–90,
  110, 200
Latin (Italic) 6, 9–11, 13, 40, 58, 62, 68, 95,
  109, 112, 148, 182
Laz (or Chan)(S Caucasian) 76, 202
Lezgian (N-E Caucasian) 22, 122, 155
Lhasa Tibetan, *see* Tibetan
Limbu (Tibeto-Burman) 57, 155
Lolo-Burmese (branch of Tibeto-Burman)
  202
Loma (Mande branch, Niger-Congo) 5–6,
  105

Macro-Jê stock 55
Macushi (Carib) 51, 138, 147
Maidu (Maiduan family, Californian
  Penutian) 66
Maipuran Arawak, *see* Arawak
Maká (Mataguayo) 123
Maku family 5
Malagasy (Austronesian) 129, 133–4
Malay (Austronesian) 209
Malayo-Polynesian (branch of
  Austronesian) 73, 133

Mam (Mayan) 27–8, 103, 149, 209
Mandan (Siouan) 71–4
Mandara (Chadic, Afroasiatic) 5
Manipuri (Tibeto-Burman) 29–34, 145, 155
Maori (Polynesian, Austronesian) 129,
    133–4, 191
Marathi (Indic) 190
Martuthunira (Pama-Nyungan, Australian)
    198
Marubo (Panoan) 101, 107, 110
Mawayana (Arawak) 104–5
Maxakalí (Macro-Jê) 51, 55
Mayan family 5, 17, 44, 100, 103, 145, 149,
    178, 193, 201, 204
Mayan hieroglyphs (Mayan) 5, 104
Meryam Mer (Eastern Trans-Fly family,
    Papuan) 55
Middle Persian (Iranian) 100
Mingrelian (S Caucasian) 202
Mocho (Mayan) 201
Modern Chinese 184
Modern Greek (Indo-European) 138
Modern Hebrew (Semitic, Afroasiatic) 209
Mohawk (Iroquoian) 73
Mojave (Yuman) 65
Mondé family (Tupí stock) 46
Mopan (Mayan) 201
Motu (Austronesian) 40–1, 58–9
Murinypata (Daly, Australian) 58–9, 95
Murle (Nilotic) 188
Muskogean family 35–8

Nadëb (Maku) 51, 55, 89, 134, 178, 233
Nakh (branch of N-E Caucasian) 2, 80,
    205
Nakkara (Gunwinyguan, Australian) 120
Nass-Gitksan (dialect of Tsimshian) 52,
    133
Ndjebbana (Gunwinyguan, Australian) 89
Newari (Tibeto-Burman) 101, 123, 202
Nez Perce (Sahaptian) 148, 189
Nganasan (Samoyedic, Uralic) 90
Ngan'giwumirri (Daly, Australian) 209
Ngarla (Pama-Nyungan, Australian) 199
Ngarluma (Pama-Nyungan, Australian) 63,
    198
Ngayarda subgroup (Pama-Nyungan,
    Australian) 198–200, 205–6, 215, 218,
    228
Ngiyambaa (Pama-Nyungan, Australian)
    85, 109
Nhuwala (Pama-Nyungan, Australian) 199
Niger-Congo family 5, 74
Nilotic family 5, 64–5, 188–9, 204, 227
Non-Pama-Nyungan (Australian) 4, 184,
    204

Nootka (Wakashan) 146
Norse, Runic (Germanic) 65
North-east Caucasian family 2–3, 57, 88,
    115, 121–2, 147, 175, 189
North-west Caucasian family 2–3, 88, 147,
    189
Nyamal (Pama-Nyungan, Australian) 199

Ojibwa (Algonquian) 90
Old English (Germanic) 183
Omotic family (branch of Afroasiatic)
    64–5, 204
Onondaga (Iroquoian) 73
Oromo (Cushitic, Afroasiatic) 64

Paamese (Austronesian) 120
Pajonal Campa (Arawak) 83, 211
Paleo-Siberian linguistic area 4
Pama-Nyungan typological group
    (Australian) 4, 178, 184, 198–201, 206,
    227
Pamir subgroup (Iranian) 33, 100, 202–5
Panare (Carib) 177
Panoan family 5, 89
Panyjima (Pama-Nyungan, Australian)
    198
Papuan linguistic area 4, 57–8, 175, 230
Päri (Nilotic) 5, 44, 50–1, 65–7, 101, 103,
    110, 188–9, 206
Paumarí (Arawá) 47, 52
Pengo (Dravidian) 58
Persian (Iranian) 100
Philippines (subgroup of Austronesian) xvi,
    4, 179
Pirahã (isolate) 138
Pitta-Pitta (Pama-Nyungan, Australian)
    106, 110, 198
Podopa, see Folopa
Polish (Slavic) 120
Polynesian (subgroup of Austronesian) xvi,
    4, 123, 137, 187, 191–2
Pomo, see Eastern Pomo
Portuguese (Italic) 210–11
Potawatomi (Algonquian) 91
Punjabi (Indic) 190

Quechua (Quechuan) 68, 209
Quiché (Mayan) 150, 233

Rājāsthanī (Indic) 100, 190
Rembarnga, (Gunwinyguan, Australian)
    100, 140–1
Runic Norse (Germanic) 65
Rushan (Pamir, Iranian) 39, 203, 225
Russian (Slavic) 63, 120
Rutul (N-E Caucasian) 3

Sacapultec Maya (Mayan) 45–8, 68, 209
Samoan (Polynesian, Austronesian) 4, 155, 191, 222–3
Sanskrit (Indic) 190
Sanuma (Yanomami) 50, 52
Shokleng (Jê) 65, 103, 106
Sindhi (Indic) 190
Sinhalese (Indic) 26–8, 205
Siouan family 73
Slave (Athapaskan) 75, 148
South American languages 5, 46, 230
South Asian languages 108
South Caucasian family 2–3, 88, 189, 193, 202, 204
South Suluwesi (subgroup of Austronesian) 4
Southern Paiute (Uto-Aztecan) 63
Spanish (Italic) 74
Sumerian (isolate) 3, 55, 88, 101, 104
Surui (Mondé, Tupí) 46
Svan (S Caucasian) 202
Swahili (Bantu, Niger-Congo) 42–8, 134, 136, 140, 182

Tabassaran (N-E Caucasian) 80–1, 126
Tacanan family 5, 89
Tagalog (Philippines, Austronesian) xvi, 4, 119, 179, 232
Tamanic subgroup (Austronesian) 4
Tamil (Dravidian) 209
Tangkic subgroup (Australian) 200–1, 206, 218
Tawala (Austronesian) 120
Telugu (Dravidian) 62, 120
Thai (Tai-Kadai) 120
Tibetan (Tibeto-Burman) 57, 80, 123–4, 155
Tibeto-Burman family 4, 88, 184, 193, 201–2, 204, 215, 228
Timbe (Teberan, Papuan) 33
Tolai (Austronesian) 50, 76, 83
Tongan (Polynesian, Austronesian) 4, 7, 41–2, 123–5, 147, 176, 191
Tonkawa (isolate) 81
Trumai (isolate) 5, 123–4
Tsimshian (isolate) 5, 52, 103, 106, 133
Tsova-Tush (Bats, Batsbi) (N-E Caucasian) 79–82, 205
Tunica (isolate) 72–3, 219
Tupí stock 89
Tupí-Guaraní family (Tupí stock) 5, 75, 107
Tupinambá (Tupí-Guaraní) 83
Turkana (Nilotic) 188
Turkish (Turkic) 19, 73, 140, 182
Tzutujil (Mayan) 148

Ungarinjin (North Kimberley, Australian) 68, 100
Uralic family 4
Urartian 3
Uto-Aztecan family 63

Vakh, dialect of Khanty (Finno-Ugric, Uralic) 4
Vietnamese (Mon-Khmer, Austroasiatic) 182

Waga-Waga (Pama-Nyungan, Australian) 86, 109
Wakhi (Waxi) (Pamir, Iranian) 33–4, 202
Walmatjari (Pama-Nyungan, Australian) 100, 172–5, 178, 199, 213
Wangkumara (Pama-Nyungan, Australian) 41
Wappo (Yukian) 65–7
Warlpiri (Pama-Nyungan, Australian) 96–7, 120, 172, 204
Warrgamay (Pama-Nyungan, Australian) 178–80, 193–9, 205–6, 218
Warungu (Pama-Nyungan, Australian) 180
Waurá (Arawak) 77
Western Desert language (Pama-Nyungan, Australian) 67, 204
Western Torres Strait language 93–4, 197
Wichita (Caddoan) 75–6

Yagua (Peba-Yanguan) 83, 211
Yanomami family 89
Yawa (isolate, Papuan) 4, 76
Yawuru (Dampier Land subgroup, Australian) 121–2
Yazgulyam (Pamir, Iranian) 40, 202
Yidiny (Pama-Nyungan, Australian) 25, 57, 178
  antipassive 60, 152
  discourse structure 209, 220–2
  mixed pivots, 175–8, 220–1, 228
  phonological and grammatical words 111
  reflexive 60, 152
  relative clauses 176, 222
  split morphological marking 87, 109
  split syntax, *see* mixed pivots
  transitivising derivation, 140–1
  verbal suffix - :*ji-n* 59–62, 82, 151–2
  verbs with inanimate A 119–20
Yimas (Lower Sepik family, Papuan) 4, 89, 93
Yinyjiparnti (Pama-Nyungan, Australian) 198
Yucatec Maya (Mayan) 100, 110, 201
Yukagir (isolate) 4, 67

Yukulta (Tangkic, Australian) 105–6, 110, 198, 200
Yuman family 65–6, 204

Yupik Eskimo, *see* Eskimo

Zayse (Omotic, Afroasiatic) 64

Subject index

A, universal syntatic–semantic primitive
6ff, 113ff
semantic basis 52, 115
absolutive, as unmarked case 58–62
Accessibility Hierarchy 127, 130, 234
accusative
case marking 8ff, 62–7
other functions 57–8
accusativity 16–17
morphological 8ff, 42ff
syntactic 11–12, 158–60, 172–7,
197–201
active/stative, see split-S, fluid-S
Actor 125
Addressee role 7–8
adjectives, in ergative languages 216
adpositions, used to mark syntactic
function 41–2
advancement of peripheral NP to core role
170–1
AFFECT type 7–8
affective case 121
agency, see control
Agent role 7–8, 120
agentless passive 147
agglutinative type 182–5
alternate syntactic frames 8
ambitransitive verbs 6, 18–19, 54, 140,
217–18
antipassive 13, 17–18, 28, 31, 60, 146–52,
163ff, 176, 213, 233–5
becoming an accusative construction
193–200
criteria 146
feeding an S/O pivot 13, 17, 163ff
meaning 148–9
patientless 147
when used 148–52
aspect, conditioning of split 97–102, 104–10
ATTENTION type 7–8, 121–2
avoidance speech style 18

'begin' having accusative grammar 134–7

bound pronouns, different marking from
free 94–7
see also cross-referencing

'can' having accusative grammar 134–7
causative 17–20, 30–1, 139–41
cause 139
change, see language change
citation form 10, 21, 57–66, 188
combination of types of split 104–8
complement clauses 102–4, 135–6
complex clause constructions, see
coordination, subordination
constituent order 49–52
ergative type 50–52, 77
'continue' having accusative grammar
134–7
controlled verbs 53, 71–83
controller of action 29–38, 53, 59–62,
79–83, 115ff
coordination 11–17, 33, 153ff
creoles 185
cross-referencing 42–9, 67–9, 76, 81, 95–7
cycle of change 182–6

dative subject 121–2
definiteness 91, 212
demonstratives 84–5, 90, 210
dependent-marking languages 145, 219–22
direct marking, see semantically based
marking
discourse 54, 168, 207–13, 219–23
oriented to speech participants 84
ditransitive verbs 114, 120–3
Donor role 7–8, 172

ergative case 8ff, 26, 57ff
extended, see marked nominative
first description of ergative
construction 5
first use of term 3
optional use 58–9
other functions 57

269

ergativity
  morphological 8ff, 39ff, 43ff
  syntactic 12–17, 154–6, 160–72, 175–81,
    193–7
extended ergative, *see* marked nominative
extended intransitive verbs 122–4
extended transitive verbs 120–3

'finish' having accusative grammar 134–7
first person, place on Nominal Hierarchy
    88–90
fluid-S languages 70–1, 78–83, 125–6, 211
focussing an NP 179
fronting, as a mechanism of change 188
fusional type 182–5

gender classes 10, 45, 47, 87–8, 94
get passive 28
Gift role 7–8, 120, 171–2, 199
GIVING type 7–8, 171–2, 199
Government–Binding(GB) theory 126,
    233
grammatical word 111

head-marking languages 145, 219
'hear' 116, 122
'hope' having accusative grammar 134–7

imperatives 62, 129, 131–3, 173
  typically preserve archaic patterns 189,
    200–1
imperfective aspect, conditioning
    accusative system 97–102, 104–10
Impression role 7–8, 123
indefinite, *see* definiteness
inflectional type, *see* fusional type
instrumental case 57, 195–7
instrumentive derivation 170–1
inverse marking system 90–1
isolating type 182–5, 202

labile verbs, *see* ambitransitive verbs
language change 182ff
  accusative to ergative 187–92
  ergative to accusative 193–203
Lexical Functional Grammar (LFG) 232
LIKING type 121–3
'listen to' 116, 122
locative marking of A 121
'look at' 116, 122

main vs. subordinate clause split 101–10,
    212
make 139
Manip role 7–8, 120–1
marked nominative 63–7

markedness 10–11, 56–69, 78, 85ff, 128, 188
  formal 56ff
  functional 56ff
  in cross-referencing systems 44, 67–9
Medium role 7
Message role 7–8
middle construction in Sinhalese 26–7
'might' having accusative grammar 134–7
mood, conditioning split 101–10, 133
'mother-in-law' speech style 18
'must' having accusative grammar 134–7

narrative style 220–3
'need' having accusative grammar 134–7
negation 101, 106–7, 134, 178–9
new information 208ff
Nominal Hierarchy 40, 85–97, 104–10, 148,
    151, 175, 177, 187, 201, 204, 212, 219
nominative
  as marked case 63–7
  as unmarked case 56–7, 62–3
nominative–accusative, *see* accusative
noun classes, *see* gender
noun incorporation 25, 31, 75, 140–1
number 42, 48, 91–4
-*ŋurra* suffix in Dyirbal 165–7

O, universal syntatic–semantic primitive
    6ff, 113ff
  semantic basis 120–4

P, used in place of O 6
particles, used to mark syntactic function
    41–2
parts of speech 112
passive 12, 17, 21, 27–8, 31, 133, 146–52,
    199–200, 213, 233–5
  agentless 147
  becoming ergative construction 189–91
  criteria 146
  feeding an S/A pivot 12, 17
  meaning 28, 148–9, 190
  when used 148–52
past tense, conditioning ergative system
    97–102, 104–10
Perceiver role 7–8, 123
perfective aspect, conditioning ergative
    system 97–102, 104–10
phonological word 111
pidgins 185
pivot 11ff, 33, 129–30, 143–5, 152–81,
    220–2
  basic framework 157–8
  chain 168
  S/A type 11–12, 17, 154, 158–60, 172–8,
    197–201

S/O type 12–17, 154–6, 160–72, 175–80, 193–7
pivotless languages 154–5
plural marking on verb 55
possessive marking 191
  and ergativity 219
postpositions, *see* adpositions
prepositions, *see* adpositions
presentational construction 209
primitives, syntactic-semantic, *see* S, A, O
promotion to subject 20–21
pronouns, inflections differing from those on nouns 14, 84–95, 220
prototypical marking, *see* syntactically based marking
purposive clauses 102–4, 168–71, 194–8

questions 178

Recipient role 7–8, 120, 172, 199
reciprocals 31, 147–8, 151–2
reflexives 18, 27, 31, 60, 126, 138–9, 147–8, 151–2, 185, 195, 200
Relational Grammar (RG) 127, 234–6
relative clauses 102–4, 127, 130, 159, 169–70, 175–6, 178–9, 220–2, 234
Role and Reference Grammar (RRG) 232

S is similar to A, ways in which 53–5
S is similar to O, ways in which 53–5
S, universal syntactic–semantic primitive 6ff, 75–6, 113ff
  lack of semantic basis 53, 124
S/A-type, *see* ambitransitive verbs
S/O-type, *see* ambitransitive verbs
S$_a$, subdivision of S 53, 70–83
second person, place on Nominal Hierarchy 88–90
Secondary concepts 134–7
'see' 116–17, 121–4
semantic roles 7–8
semantic types 7–8
semantically based marking 23–5, 28–38, 144–5
shifters 97
S$_o$, subdivision of S 53, 70–83
Speaker role 7–8
SPEAKING type 7–8
split conditioned by semantics of clause type (main vs. subordinate) 101–8, 212

NP 83–97, 104–10, 193, 220–2
tense–aspect–mood 97–102, 104–10
verb, *see* split-S, fluid-S
split-S languages 70–8, 82–3, 104–10, 132, 148, 211, 235
stative-active, *see* split-S, fluid-S
subject 111ff, 233–6
  dative 121–2
  definition used here 124ff
  Keenan's treatment of 127ff
  semantic criteria 112–13
  surface subject, *see* pivot
  traditional definition 111–12
subordinate vs. main clause split 52, 101–10, 192
subordination, operations of 169ff
surface subject, *see* pivot
switch-reference marking 33, 153–4
syntactic accusativity 11–12, 158–60, 172–8, 197–201
syntactic ergativity 12–17, 154–6, 160–72, 175–80, 193–7
syntactic–semantic primitives 6ff
syntactically based marking 23–8

Target role 7–8, 120–1
tense, conditioning of split 97–102, 104–110
theme, discourse 208ff
theoretical models 232–6
three-way marking, *see* tripartite marking
time, ways of viewing 97–9
topic 41, 51, 144
  discourse 208ff
  earlier use of term (now pivot) 168
transitivity 6, 18, 113–14, 122ff, 216–17
tripartite marking 39–41, 44–5
'try' having accusative grammar 134–7

unaccusative 235–6
undergoer 125
underlying structure 126, 152
unergative 235–6

voice, *see* antipassive, passive

'want' having accusative grammar 134–7
word as a linguistic unit 111
word classes, *see* parts of speech
word order, *see* constituent order
world-view 119, 214–15

Printed in Great Britain
by Amazon

81182817R00171